CANADA'S NATIONAL POLICY
1883-1900

A Study in
Canadian-American
Relations

Canada's National Policy

1883-1900

A STUDY IN CANADIAN-AMERICAN RELATIONS

ROBERT CRAIG BROWN

PRINCETON, NEW JERSEY

PRINCETON UNIVERSITY PRESS

1964

Publication of this book has been aided by
the Ford Foundation program to support
publication, through university presses, of
works in the humanities and social sciences.

Printed in the United States of America

TO MY PARENTS

ACKNOWLEDGMENTS

A GREAT MANY people have assisted me in the preparation of this book. Foremost among them has been Professor Donald G. Creighton of the University of Toronto. As teacher and friend he has been a continual source of encouragement, inspiration, and advice. Professor J. M. S. Careless, Head of the History Department at the University of Toronto, and Dean J. T. Saywell of York University have taken time they could ill afford to read and criticize the manuscript. Professor F. G. Heymann, Head of the History Department and Dr. M. G. Taylor, Principal, have offered valuable assistance since I joined the Faculty at the University of Alberta, Calgary. Miss Florence Campbell has cheerfully borne the burden of typing the final manuscript and Major C. C. J. Bond has drawn the map on the Alaska Boundary question. To these and to others unacknowledged should go whatever credit this book may have.

I am grateful to the staffs of the libraries and archives where I have had the privilege to work. Like so many scholars before me, I must express my special appreciation to Dr. W. Kaye Lamb and his colleagues at the Public Archives of Canada whose cooperation has been unbounded. I am very pleased to record my thanks to The Marquis of Lansdowne and The Marquis of Salisbury for their permission to examine and quote from the papers of the fifth Marquis of Lansdowne and the third Marquis of Salisbury and to Mr. K. W. Humphreys, Librarian, The University of Birmingham, for similar privileges with the papers of Mr. Joseph Chamberlain.

The financial burden incurred in the research for this book has been eased by the very generous assistance given to me by the Canada Council, the John W. Dafoe Foundation, and the University of Alberta Grants Committee.

My deepest gratitude must be reserved for my wife, Gail, who has helped me with the research and writing of this project from its beginnings as a doctoral dissertation to its final form.

R. C. B.

Calgary, January 1964

CONTENTS

CONTENTS

ILLUSTRATIONS

CANADA'S NATIONAL POLICY
1883-1900

A Study in
Canadian-American
Relations

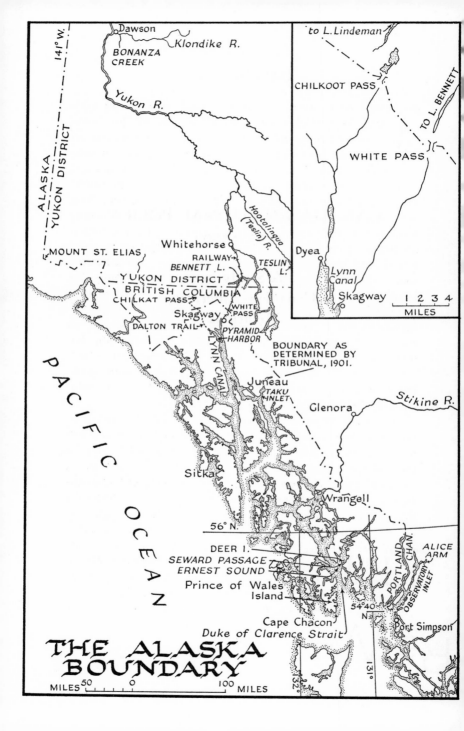

THE ALASKA BOUNDARY

Main map labels

141° W.

Dawson
Klondike R.
BONANZA CREEK

Yukon R.

ALASKA
YUKON DISTRICT

MOUNT ST. ELIAS

Whitehorse
RAILWAY
BENNETT L.
YUKON DISTRICT
BRITISH COLUMBIA
CHILKAT PASS
Hootalingua (Teslin) R.
TESLIN L.
WHITE PASS
Skagway
DALTON TRAIL
PYRAMID HARBOR

LYNN CANAL

BOUNDARY AS
DETERMINED BY
TRIBUNAL, 1901.

Juneau
TAKU INLET

Glenora

Stikine R.

PACIFIC OCEAN

Sitka

Wrangell

56° N.

DEER I.
SEWARD PASSAGE
ERNEST SOUND
Prince of Wales Island

PORTLAND CHAN.
ALICE ARM
OBSERVATORY INLET

Cape Chacon
Duke of Clarence Strait

54° 40' N.
Port Simpson

131°
132°

MILES 50   0   100 MILES

Inset map labels

to L. Lindeman

CHILKOOT PASS

TO L. BENNETT

WHITE PASS

Dyea
Lynn Canal
Skagway

1 2 3 4
MILES

Introduction

THE United States and British North America, or Canada, have shared the greatest portion of the North American continent since the American Revolution. As neighbors, they have had a common interest in the exploitation of the wealth of the continental land mass. As neighbors, they have had common problems and, to a large extent, shared a common way of life. And as neighbors, they have inevitably had their quarrels and their differences. The history of Canadian-American relations is the story of these common problems. Quite often the story has dwelt on the peaceful relationship between two states or upon their whole-hearted cooperation in facing a common problem. The "unguarded frontier" is a useful theme for study, providing as it does a contrast to the study of the relations of many other neighboring states. But it also can be a misleading theme; it can lull students of Canadian-American relations into forgetting that there have been two nations on the North American continent, and that while these nations have had common problems, more often than not they have sought dissimilar solutions to those problems.

This study treats only a small segment of the history of Canadian-American relations, the years from the abrogation of the fishery articles of the Treaty of Washington, 1871, to the collapse of the Joint High Commission of 1898-1899. It makes no pretense of even telling the whole story of Canadian-American relations in those years. Rather, it concentrates on four specific problems and upon the solutions sought by Canada in these Canadian-American disputes. The four problems to be considered are the North Atlantic fisheries dispute, the Behring Sea difficulties, the problem of Canadian-American trade relations, and the Alaska Boundary controversy.

The problem of longest standing, going back to the breakup of the First British Empire, is that of the North Atlantic

3

fisheries.[1] The Treaty of Paris, 1783, conferred upon Americans the "right" to fish on the Banks fisheries and in the Gulf of St. Lawrence, and the "liberty" to fish on the coast of Newfoundland, which remained a separate colony until 1949, "and also on the Coasts Bays & Creeks of all other of his Britannic Majesty's Dominions in America" and the "liberty" "to dry and cure Fish in any of the unsettled Bays Harbours and Creeks of Nova Scotia, Magdalen Islands, and Labrador." [2] At the conclusion of the "second war for independence," the War of 1812, no mention was made in the Treaty of Ghent of these American liberties in British North American inshore waters. The British Government claimed they were abrogated. The Americans believed them as permanent as the grant of independence. As John Quincy Adams put it, "the right or liberty to . . . exercise this trade could no more be affected or impaired by a declaration of war than the right to the territory of the nation." [3] After protracted negotiations the North Atlantic fisheries problem appeared to be settled with the signing, by the British and American Governments, of the Convention of 1818.

The first article of the Convention of 1818 gave the Americans the liberty "forever to fish" on designated portions of the coasts of Newfoundland and Labrador and to cure and dry fish along the same coasts. The Americans renounced the liberty of the same privileges along the remaining coastline of British North America. Further, American vessels were prohibited from entering the inshore waters of the remainder of British North America except "for the purpose of shelter

[1] Brief summaries of the disputes in the years before 1883 may be found in C. C. Tansill, *Canadian-American Relations, 1875-1911,* New Haven, 1943, pp. 1-13 and Goldwin Smith, *The Treaty of Washington, 1871* (Ithaca, 1941), pp. 1-7. For a broader perspective on the problem, that of "the history of an international economy," see H. A. Innis, *The Cod Fisheries,* Toronto, 1954.

[2] Cited, Tansill, *Canadian-American Relations,* pp. 2-3.

[3] Cited, *ibid.,* p. 4.

and of repairing damages therein, of purchasing wood, and of obtaining water, and for no other purpose whatever." [4]

In fact, as later events proved, the Convention of 1818 raised as many problems as it solved. And these problems were the essence of the North Atlantic fisheries dispute for nearly a century. Not the least of them was the definition of the inshore waters of British North America. Did the line between territorial waters and the open sea, for example, follow the windings of the coast, or did it pass from headland to headland at great and small bays? Until the seizure of the American fishing vessel *Washington* in 1843, ten miles from shore in the Bay of Fundy, the British Government held that all bays, large and small, were within the territorial waters of British North America. The settlement of the *Washington* case resulted in the abandonment of that claim but the problem still remained. What bays were and what bays were not part of the territorial waters? No solution was found during the period of this study. During the years of enforcement of the Treaties of Washington, 1854 and 1871, American vessels were given access to British North American inshore waters but from 1866 to 1871 and after 1883 the American, British, and Canadian Governments were all confronted with the headlands question.

Another problem was that of the commercial privileges enjoyed by American fishing vessels in the territorial waters of British North America. Between 1854 and 1866 and between 1873 and 1885 [5] American fishing vessels could buy bait, ice, and supplies, hire ship crews, and transship their catches in Canadian ports. Obviously these were valuable privileges. They made it unnecessary for the American vessels to return

---

[4] Cited, *ibid.*, p. 5.

[5] The Treaty of Washington, 1871, insofar as the fisheries articles were concerned, did not take effect until July 1873 and was in force for two years after the notice of abrogation in 1883, i.e., until July 1885.

5

to their distant home ports for supplies or to unload their catches and they gave the American masters the opportunity of hiring crews at less cost. With the abrogation of the two treaties, the Canadian Government fell back on the admittedly harsh provisions of the Convention of 1818, allowing access to inshore waters only for shelter, repairs, wood, and water. But American fishermen were more than reluctant to give up the privileges that they had enjoyed for twenty-four years between 1854 and 1885. And the fishermen were supported by the claim of the American Government that fishing vessels enjoyed the same privileges of supply and transshipment that all other American vessels enjoyed in British North American ports. On the other hand, the Canadian Government asserted that by the first article of the Convention of 1818 American fishing vessels were expressly denied these privileges. Therefore, after 1866, and again after 1885, the Canadian Government were compelled to equip and man a force of protective cruisers not only to prevent fishing by American vessels in Canadian waters but also to deny these same vessels the commercial privileges to which they had become accustomed.

The Behring Sea problem was of more recent origin. By the Treaty of 1867, the United States had become the possessor of the former Russian territory of Alaska, including the Pribilof Islands in Behring Sea. A stroke of nature dictated that the Pribilof Islands be the major breeding ground of the fur seal. Before the discovery of gold in Alaska, the exploitation of this immense source of luxurious fur provided the only sizable revenue from the territory of Alaska to the American Government. A chartered company hired servants to kill and skin the seals on the Pribilof Islands during the breeding months, May to September, and the Government received a proportion of the revenue from the sale of the furs. The American company carried out its sealing operations on land. But the habits of the fur seal also made it possible to carry on pelagic sealing, i.e., to catch and kill the seals from a vessel

6

on the high seas. This could be done as the seal herds swam to the islands at the beginning of and away from the islands at the conclusion of the breeding season. In addition, the seals often left the islands during the breeding season, swimming as far as 60 to 100 miles from land in search of food. It was therefore possible to carry on pelagic sealing of some sort at almost any time while the seals were in the vicinity of the Pribilof Islands.

In 1884 and 1885 a small number of British Columbians engaged in a commercial adventure of pelagic sealing. Apparently they quickly realized that the exploitation of the fur seal on the high seas could be a very profitable business. By 1886 a considerable fleet of pelagic sealers had been built up in British Columbia and pelagic sealing had become a large commercial enterprise. But in August of that year, under the instructions of the United States Secretary of the Treasury, Daniel Manning, American revenue cutters began to seize foreign vessels, including those of the British Columbia fleet, engaged in pelagic sealing in Behring Sea. Manning's motives were sincere; he firmly believed that pelagic sealing would quickly lead to the destruction of the seal herds. Even if that were a debatable assumption (as it was) the point still remained that the advent of serious competition by pelagic sealers in the sealing industry threatened the only extensive source of revenue from Alaska. In short, then, Manning was acting in the interests of both the chartered company, the Alaskan Commercial Company, and the United States Government.

But Manning's instructions seriously compromised his Government diplomatically. Ever since 1783 the American Government had stood firmly behind the doctrine of freedom of the seas and in the War of 1812 had engaged Great Britain in battle at least partially in defense of that doctrine. Now United States revenue cruisers were seizing British sealers on the high seas to prevent them from engaging in a legitimate enterprise. Indeed, there was a precedent for Manning's act; at the end of the eighteenth century a ukase of Czar Alexander I had virtually proclaimed the Behring Sea as a *mare clausum*. But the Russian pretension had been abandoned in treaties with the United States and Great Britain in 1824 and 1825. The seizing of British vessels reestablished in practice, though not by explicit proclamation, the claim that Behring Sea was a *mare clausum*. This implicit assertion by the United States Government was at the heart of the Behring Sea dispute. As Professor Tansill notes, it was "a little surprising to find President Cleveland engaged in a covert attack upon a principle that previous American statesmen had supported even at the cost of war." [6]

Trade questions have often disrupted amicable relations between Canada and the United States. Generally speaking, Canadians have assumed that the United States was the logical market for the surplus production of their natural products. Americans have viewed Canada as the market for their surplus of manufactured goods. During the period under review Canada sought to protect its infant but growing industrial complex and the United States erected abnormally high tariff walls against both natural and manufactured products of foreign origin.

The desire to establish a wide measure of reciprocal trade with the United States has been a persistent theme in Canadian history. The high point of success for Canadians was the signing of the Treaty of Washington of 1854 which provided an expanding market in the United States for Canadian natural products and a way out of the depression occasioned by the final collapse of the "commercial empire of the St. Lawrence." As well, the Treaty of 1854 established a precedent of tying the North Atlantic fisheries question to a measure

[6] Tansill, *Canadian-American Relations,* p. 267.

8

of reciprocity in trade. From this time, Professor Smith observes, "the fisheries became part of a larger question, that of commercial intercourse between the United States and Canada. Hereafter fishery privileges were to be balanced by market concessions." [7] This was certainly true as far as Canada was concerned. As one of the British Commissioners on the Joint High Commission of 1871, the Canadian Prime Minister, Sir John A. Macdonald, pressed for a renewal of the reciprocity privileges of the Treaty of 1854. But the Washington Treaty of 1871 provided only for free fish and a monetary payment to be determined by a commission in return for use of the inshore fisheries by United States fishermen. In 1874 the Liberal Government of Alexander Mackenzie sent George Brown to Washington to negotiate a reciprocity agreement in lieu of the monetary payment. A draft treaty providing for reciprocity in a select list of manufactured goods as well as natural products was drawn up but was not ratified by the United States Senate. Finally, the commission to determine monetary compensation met in Halifax in 1877 and awarded $5,500,000 to the Governments of Canada and Newfoundland. The "Halifax Award," as it came to be called, was considered to be little enough compensation in Canada but was greeted with intense indignation in the United States. As soon as it was possible to do so, on 26 February 1883 the United States Congress adopted a resolution directing the President to inform the British Government of the abrogation of the fishery articles of the Treaty of Washington.

Between 1883 and 1899 both Canadian political parties favored reciprocity with the United States. The difference between them was one of degree, not of kind. Conservatives,

[7] Smith, *The Treaty of Washington*, p. 3. See also on this point and with particular reference to the 1871 negotiations, D. G. Creighton, *John A. Macdonald, The Old Chieftain,* Toronto, 1955, ch. 3 and Sir Joseph Pope, *Memoirs of the Right Honourable Sir John Alexander Macdonald,* 2nd edn., Toronto, 1930, chs. xx-xxi.

mainly because of its political value, tenuously sought reciprocity in natural products. But, at the same time, they were steadfast in their pledge to protect the National Policy and Canadian industry and in their efforts to find alternative markets for Canadian natural products. Liberals, who viewed the National Policy with passionate contempt until they came to power in 1896, advocated not simply a wide measure of reciprocity embracing manufactured as well as natural products but Unrestricted Reciprocity. In their desire for office and preferment they adopted as their platform a modified version of the Commercial Union appeal that rose to prominence in the depression years following 1883. Implicitly their trade policy stressed continentalism in contrast to the national or Canadian emphasis of the Conservative policy.

Like the Behring Sea dispute, the Alaska Boundary problem arose out of the United States–Russia Treaty of 1867. As early as 1870 overtures were made toward settling the boundary between Canada and the United States. But it was, to say the least, a difficult and expensive task to undertake, particularly where the boundary left the 141st meridian and went along the narrow Alaskan panhandle. Hardly any progress had been made before the discovery of vast quantities of gold in the panhandle and the Yukon Territory. And, naturally, the gold rush made the problem both more urgent and more difficult. Uncharted territory was suddenly peopled by hordes of potentially wild and lawless miners who cared little for law and order and even less for international boundaries, defined or otherwise. Also, the whole panhandle area was potentially auriferous and delimiting the boundary might determine whether the next great strike was to be located in Canadian or American territory. Then, too, the boundary indefinitely defined in the Treaty of 1867 was dependent on the boundary provisions of the Anglo-Russian Treaty of 1825.

The appropriate clauses of the Treaty of 1825 lent themselves to various interpretations. This problem might have been easily settled were it not for the fact that their interpretation would determine whether Canada or the United States controlled the access routes into the Yukon Territory where the richest gold strikes had been made. Control of the access routes might decide the extent of law and order that would prevail in the Yukon and certainly would dictate which nation controlled the expanding Yukon trade. In essence, then, the Alaskan Boundary problem was less a question of determining the boundary itself than a question of trade and commercial rivalry.

ii

As a matter of convenience and clarity this study treats the subject topically rather than chronologically. But an examination of Canadian and British source materials reveals that the Canadian Government—and to a lesser extent the Imperial Government—did not view the North Atlantic fisheries, Behring Sea, trade, and Alaska Boundary questions as individual problems to be settled one at a time. Most obviously and most superficially this is evident in the mode of solution sought by the Canadian and British Governments in 1887-1888 and in 1898-1899: the appointment of a Joint Commission instructed to negotiate and sign a comprehensive treaty that would wipe the slate clean of Canadian-American disputes.

There is also evident in the Canadian approach to these problems one underlying principle. The National Policy adopted by the Canadian Government of Sir John A. Macdonald after the election of 1878 is usually taken to encompass a domestic policy of economic nationalism based on railway building, immigration and settlement, and protective tariffs. Even in this limited sense the National Policy affected Canadian-American relations because of the huge volume of Canadian-American trade. But the spirit of the National Policy went much deeper than railways, immigrants, and tariffs. Beneath these external manifestations was the will to build and maintain a separate Canadian nation on the North American continent. This is what Sir Leonard Tilley had in mind when he said in his budget speech in 1879 that "the time has arrived when we are to decide whether we will be simply hewers of wood and drawers of water" or will "make this a great and prosperous country, as we all desire and hope it will be." [8] This study suggests that all Canadian Governments in the period under review applied this basic assumption of the National Policy to each of these problems in Canadian-American relations.

[8] Canada, Parliament, House of Commons, *Official Report of Debates,* March 14, 1879, p. 429.

CHAPTER I
A Policy of Protection

FOR many centuries the great cod fisheries have been the center of an "international economy" and a source of both nutriment and controversy for the men and nations bordering the North Atlantic Ocean. As a result of the Anglo-American settlement following the War of 1812, British North Americans gained exclusive use of a most valuable asset for competing with their republican brethren on the bank fisheries. Save for the use of the "Treaty shores" of Newfoundland and Labrador which were of increasingly less value, the Anglo-American Convention of 1818 reserved the inshore fisheries of British North America for the exclusive use of subjects of the Crown and excluded American fishermen from resort to the harbors, bays, and creeks of British North America except for four specific purposes: shelter, repairs, and replenishment of supplies of wood and water. The reservation was important because within the inshore fisheries swam the mackerel, the bait essential to the successful exploitation of the cod fisheries. Twice in the century, during the life of the much-heralded Treaty of Washington of 1854 and again while the fishery articles of the Treaty of Washington of 1871 were in force, American fishermen had access to the British North American inshore fisheries and, for supply and transshipment of their catch, to the harbors therein. In 1883, the Americans gave notice of the abrogation of the fishery articles of the 1871 treaty. A Colonial Office official wrote in the minutes to a despatch, "some awkward questions would arise." [1]

ii

For Canadians there was no question about their right of possession of the inshore fisheries of British North America.

[1] Minute by Mercer, March 9, 1882, on Canada 4214, Despatch: CO42/773.

The very fact of the existence of the Treaty of Washington of
1854 belied any contrary opinion. Section ninety-one of the
British North America Act of 1867 had vested legislative control of the seacoast and inland fisheries in the Dominion
Parliament. "An Act respecting Fishing by Foreign Vessels"
(31 V., c. 61) was passed in 1868 formally transferring jurisdiction of such matters from the provinces to the central government. The Act, of course, implied an active Canadian
voice in the external affairs of the Empire. Hence the Act
followed closely the Imperial Act of 1819 which gave effect
to the Convention of 1818 and, observed the Governor-General, Lord Lansdowne, the Dominion was " 'in line' with the
mother country." [2] Not only did the very treaty soon to be
abrogated again recognize Canada's possession of the inshore
fisheries but also, at the Joint High Commission of 1871 from
which that treaty issued, Prime Minister John A. Macdonald
had labored diligently and successfully to secure recognition
of the fisheries as a valuable Canadian national asset.[3]

Canada's treaty rights to the inshore fisheries were admitted. But the important question in 1883 and 1884 was what
the Dominion was going to do about its rights. As soon as
the Treaty of Washington was abrogated, any entry of American fishing vessels into Canadian inshore waters would be
illegal. However, American fishermen had long been accustomed to free access to Canadian waters and harbors and continued entry seemed inevitable despite its illegality. Under
such circumstances how could the Canadian Government
protect its asset? In March 1883 the Colonial Secretary thought
there was no hurry about coming to a decision because formal
notice of abrogation would not come until July, and the

[2] Public Archives of Canada, Macdonald Papers, 86, Lansdowne to
Macdonald, May 20, 1886.
[3] See D. G. Creighton, *John A. Macdonald, The Old Chieftain,*
ch. 3; Sir Joseph Pope, *Memoirs of . . . Sir John Alexander Macdonald,*
2nd edn., Toronto, 1930, chs. xx-xxi.

treaty would then be in force for two years more. The Colonial Office would "in due course receive an expression of the views and wishes of the Dominion." [4] But two months later a despatch from Colonial Secretary Derby indicated that the Imperial Government believed that "no time should be lost" in considering what action should be taken regarding the question.[5]

It was to the building of another national asset rather than to the protection of an existing one that the Canadian Government was turning its attention, for while the treaty would still be in force for some time, the trials and tribulations of the Canadian Pacific Railway seemed to wait for no one. In addition, Macdonald told Lord Lansdowne that the Government "were really unprepared to make any suggestions" about a solution of the impending problem. The Americans were responsible for the stormy sea; American and not Canadian oil would have to be poured upon it. As Lansdowne told the British Minister in Washington, since the United States had denounced the fishery clauses, "it is for them not for us to suggest a new convention." [6] The first overture did, in fact, come from the United States. President Arthur in his December 1883 annual message to Congress suggested the creation of a commission to consider American fishery rights in Canadian waters.[7] At the end of April 1884, Charles Tupper was sent to Washington by Macdonald to test the reception of a Canadian proposal for settlement. Rather than have conflict over the fisheries or a renewal of terms that might lead to another "Halifax Award," Tupper suggested a renewal of the

[4] Derby to Lorne, March 28, 1883: CO42/776.

[5] Derby to Lorne, May 3, 1883, in Granville to Sackville West, December 1, 1883: FO115/718.

[6] Macdonald Papers, 525, Macdonald to Lansdowne, June 7, 1884; Bowood, Lansdowne Papers, Lansdowne to Sackville West, April 26, 1884.

[7] Foreign Office to Colonial Office, December 29, 1883: CO42/776.

Treaty of 1854 wherein American fishing privileges in Canadian waters were balanced by large American tariff concessions to Canadian natural products. Like the President, Secretary of State Frelinghuysen looked upon the idea with favor but also indicated that "the moment was inopportune in view of the coming Presidential election." [8]

For the moment, then, it appeared that nothing could be done. The Canadian Government, Macdonald told Lansdowne, considered the abrogation of the fishery articles deliberate and decisive. Canada had no choice but to return to the policy of protecting her inshore waters as she had done between 1866 and 1871. The Government were always ready to negotiate, particularly if such negotiation might result in "an opening of both markets and inshore fisheries to each other. Our present customs laws enable the Governor-General by proclamation to admit the articles included in the Treaty of 1854 free on the Americans passing a law or making a Treaty granting similar privileges to us." Macdonald was encouraged by the growing sentiment in the United States in favor of a lower tariff but nothing could be done until after the Presidential election. Even then great care would have to be taken. "The truth is," he wrote, "that the United States Government have so often overreached England in diplomacy that they are dissatisfied with any Treaty in which they have not gained a decided advantage." [9]

[8] Sackville West to Granville, April 28, 1884, in Foreign Office to Colonial Office, May 15, 1884: CO42/779; Lansdowne Papers, Lansdowne to Derby, May 5, 1884.

[9] Macdonald Papers, 525, Macdonald to Lansdowne, June 7, 1884. Writing to Tupper a few days later, Macdonald explained his views on the hopes for a reciprocity agreement more fully. "If Cleveland is returned, the door would be ajar, but I fear we couldn't open it wide. The U.S. won't agree to an agricultural Reciprocity Treaty like that of 1854—and we can't agree to a Zollverein. We must have our customs

16

Canada sincerely wished to avoid serious difficulty with the United States over the fisheries. With a new Democratic Administration taking office on 4 March 1885 and the Treaty coming to an end on 2 July there would hardly be time in the intervening period to affect a new and permanent arrangement. With this in mind Lansdowne was asked by his Ministers to have the Imperial Government ask the outgoing administration in Washington about the possibility of a temporary "free fishing" for "free fish" arrangement which would extend the essential features of the Treaty of 1871 from 2 July 1885, until 1 January 1886. This would not only avoid the obvious difficulty of barring American fishermen from Canadian waters in the middle of the fishing season, but would also allow time to discuss a settlement with the new administration before the 1886 fishing season.[10] Unfortunately, Frelinghuysen, after consultation with leading members of the Senate, deemed it "impracticable at this late date to carry out your suggestions"[11] and the matter had to stand over until President Cleveland took office.

Both the new President and his Secretary of State, Thomas F. Bayard, had been "much alarmed" by the "reckless action of Congress" in abrogating the fishery articles of the Treaty of Washington and earnestly hoped an amicable

duties for revenue and our manufacturers are too young and weak yet. Ten years hence they might agree that they would gain by the opening of the market of 60 millions to them on even terms, by opening our market of 5½ millions, but they would be crushed out just now." Public Archives of Canada, Tupper Papers, 5, Macdonald to Tupper, June 28, 1884. For a discussion of the fisheries protection policy of the Canadian Government, 1866-1871, see R. S. Longley, "Peter Mitchell, Guardian of the North Atlantic Fisheries, 1867-1871," *Canadian Historical Review*, xxii, 1941, pp. 389-402.

[10] Macdonald Papers, 84, Lansdowne to Macdonald, December 10 and 23, 1884; Lansdowne to Derby, December 26, 1884: CO42/778.

[11] *ibid.*, 85, Frelinghuysen to Sackville West, January 20, 1885, in Lansdowne to Macdonald, January 25, 1885.

arrangement could be made with the Canadians.[12] It was not surprising, then, that Bayard, on 12 March, favorably received a suggestion from the British Minister, Sir Lionel Sackville West, similar to that which Frelinghuysen had refused.[13] But the Canadian Government soon learned that the new Administration's hands had been tied by their predecessors. An extension of the fishery articles until 1 January 1886 could not be effected on the basis of "free fishing" for "free fish."[14] Such a proposal would, in Bayard's mind, "indispose Congress to adopt measures for the final settlement of the fisheries question." Nevertheless, a peaceful settlement was so desirable that the American Government wished to suggest that American fishermen be given the benefits of "free fishing" for the remainder of the 1885 season in return for a promise upon its part to recommend to Congress the appointment of a Commission "for the investigation of all the matters at issue." The suggestion seemed rather like a one-sided bargain to the Canadians and in itself might be difficult to explain to the Dominion Parliament and fishermen. Lansdowne and Macdonald thus wondered if Bayard would be opposed to extending the scope of the Commission to include "negotiation for the reciprocal development and extension of trade between the two countries."[15] This proposal was cordially accepted by the American Secretary of State[16] and it appeared that

[12] Allan Nevins, *Grover Cleveland, A Study in Courage,* New York, 1932, pp. 405-6. See also C. C. Tansill, *The Foreign Policy of Thomas F. Bayard, 1885-1897,* New York, 1942, chs. 6-8.

[13] Tansill, *Bayard,* p. 195.

[14] Macdonald Papers, 85, Lansdowne to Macdonald, April 27, 1885.

[15] Governor-General to Colonial Office, April 25 and 28, and May 18, 1885: CO42/780; Lansdowne Papers, Lansdowne to Sackville West, April 27, 1885. The Canadian Government would undertake, if such an arrangement were made, not to "send cruisers to protect fisheries or to interfere with American fishermen. . . ." Macdonald Papers, 85, telegram, Lansdowne to Derby, May 17, 1885.

[16] Bayard to Sackville West, June 22, 1885, in Governor-General to Colonial Office, July 9, 1885: CO42/781.

serious troubles on the North Atlantic coast had been averted.

These Canadian-American negotiations had been given a push forward by the introduction into the discussion of a "foreign" catalyst. In April 1885, Sir Ambrose Shea visited Bayard at the request of the St. Johns, Newfoundland Board of Trade. As a party to the fisheries agreement in the Treaty of Washington, the Newfoundlanders were naturally interested in the fate of their fisheries, the island's most valuable commercial asset. It was supposed by the Canadians that Shea had been given permission by the Imperial Government to effect a separate Newfoundland–United States fisheries agreement and Ottawa immediately protested.[17] The justified fear of the Canadians that such an agreement would completely undermine their bargaining position was quickly dispelled by denials of any such permission ever having been given by the Colonial Office.[18] The relieved Dominion officials later entertained Shea, who went to Ottawa from Washington to urge the Canadians to accept the Bayard proposal for a settlement.[19] In the end no serious damage had been done to the Canadian position. But the incident did cause the Prime Minister and his colleagues to reflect upon its implications and upon ways of preventing its recurrence. The very fact that Newfoundland was a separate colony hindered Canada's position in negotiations with the United States. Macdonald confided to the Governor-General that "the Dominion cannot be considered complete without Newfoundland. It has the key to our front door—and it may cause trade complications by pursuing a different policy on fishery and such questions from Canada." [20]

[17] Governor-General to Colonial Office, April 25, 1885: CO42/780.
[18] Tupper Papers, 6, Herbert to Tupper, May 13, 1885.
[19] Macdonald Papers, 526, Macdonald to Tupper, April 27, 1885.
[20] *ibid.,* Macdonald to Lansdowne, June 7, 1885. See also Macdonald to Herbert, October 8, 1885.

With a commission promised which would consider the fisheries problem in what the Canadians considered was its proper context, as a part of the more general question of the entire scope of commercial relations between Canada and the United States, and with the possibility of a settlement in the near future, the Dominion Government set about its more detailed plans for the case to be presented to the commission. The possibility of a treaty limited exclusively to fishery matters could not be discounted and if such were to be the only way to reach a settlement the Canadians would demand that not only fish and fish oil, but the oil of the whale and seal and other marine animals also be admitted duty free into the United States. This commission would have also to consider the inclusion in the treaty of the marine products of the Canadian Pacific Coast. Such a new treaty would, in addition, make imperative another arbitration similar to the Halifax meeting of 1877 which would redetermine the value of the inshore fisheries. Happily a treaty would put off the necessity of an arbitration on the potentially explosive "bays" question. Such a limited agreement would be of value, but a wider settlement would be by all odds the best. Canada desired a return to the reciprocity agreement of 1854, "with perhaps some extensions." "A treaty affecting manufactures," Macdonald told the Governor-General, "will not be entertained by the United States, nor I think by England, involving as it probably would do, a discrimination against England. . . . I am not able . . . to say whether any articles of commerce, not agricultural and not produced in England, might be included in the Treaty. I fear not." [21] As the recently retired Minister of Finance, Sir Leonard Tilley, put it, "free admission of manu-

[21] *ibid.*, 174, Lansdowne to Macdonald, August 24, 1885 and Macdonald to Lansdowne, September 5, 1885.

factures from the United States and a duty on British manufactures would be practical independence, and in the worst
form." [22] Meanwhile, in his annual message, President Cleveland urged the Congress to approve the commission. Bayard
told West that this "formed a new departure which he hoped
would be ultimately adopted." [23]

Suddenly a storm cloud appeared over Washington. On 18
January 1886, Republican Senator William P. Frye, the junior
member of the "New England trinity" of Senators Frye,
Edmunds, and Hoar, introduced a resolution stating that in
the opinion of the Senate a joint commission was unnecessary.
The motives behind the resolution were clearly mixed. Frye
suggested that the American fishermen, no longer needing
recourse to the Canadian inshore fisheries, did not desire a renewal of the provisions of the Treaty of Washington. But
Senator Edmunds probably came even closer to the real purpose of the resolution, the obstruction of executive action by
a jealous Senate. Bayard had arranged the *modus vivendi*
with Great Britain without the Senate's consent; the President's colleague had supposedly usurped the Senate's pre-
rogatives in foreign relations and Edmunds regarded this as a
"very grave question of the exertion of executive power." [24]

Canadian planning for the commission continued, but at
a more cautious pace. "We have still hope," Macdonald told
the House of Commons during the Throne Speech Debate
in February 1886. Canada's offer to extend the force of the
Treaty of Washington was "warmly reciprocated," the Presi-

[22] *ibid.*, Tilley to Macdonald, January 12, 1886.
[23] Sackville West to Salisbury, December 11, 1885, in Governor-
General to Colonial Office, December 18, 1885: CO42/781.
[24] C. C. Tansill, *Canadian-American Relations, 1875-1911,* New Haven,
1943, pp. 21-23. The changing nature of the exploitation of the fisheries
and the decreasing value of the Canadian inshore fisheries and the
decreasing value of the Canadian inshore fisheries as a source of bait
fish is explained in detail in H. A. Innis, *The Cod Fisheries,* ch. 11.

dent and Bayard had "faithfully carried out their pledge," and as yet the resolution was only the recommendation of the Committee on Foreign Relations. But, he added, "I have no hesitation in stating my opinion that that action of the committee is decisive." [25] The Prime Minister's opinion was confirmed on 13 April when the Senate heavily supported the Frye resolution by a 35-10 vote, a surprisingly large number of Democratic Senators voting in the affirmative.

What would the Canadian Government do? There had been perils in the *modus vivendi* which pointed to a commission: Macdonald remembered only too well his fears of sacrificing Canadian interests during the meetings of the Joint High Commission of 1871. And Tilley reminded him once again of the similarity of the situation. "In the present unsettled state of affairs in Europe," wrote the Lieutenant-Governor of New Brunswick, "and with the Irish difficulties at home the Imperial authorities will be most anxious to have arrangements made with reference to the fisheries and on almost any terms." [26] But these dangers paled to insignificance beside the possibilities of trouble when there was to be neither commission nor treaty. And a do-nothing policy might result in the greatest danger of all: the Canadian fishermen might take matters into their own hands. Even in the best of circumstances this had had to be considered. A year before when the *modus vivendi* was being negotiated, Bayard had demanded assurances that the American fishermen would not be molested during the 1885 season. Lansdowne's assurance was qualified: "Canadian Government . . . may not be able to prevent collisions between Canadian and American fishermen or to control individuals attempting to enforce Provincial laws against foreign intruders. Will however do everything possible to discourage such proceedings. . . ." [27] Again, it was Til-

[25] *Official Report of Debates,* February 26, 1886, p. 20.
[26] Macdonald Papers, 174, Tilley to Macdonald, January 12, 1886.
[27] *ibid.,* 85, telegram, Lansdowne to Derby, May 17, 1885.

ley who broadly hinted at the futility of inaction. "I say the fishermen of the Maritime Provinces will all want a free market for their fish in the United States, but failing that, they will not so much complain if the American fishermen *are kept out of our waters,* but here is where the difficulty will arise." [28]

The difficulty, indeed, did arise. A license system had proved ineffective in the years between 1866 and 1870. It had been abandoned in favor of a small efficient fleet of protective cruisers and this was the mode of action that would be taken again. Appropriations for fitting out cruisers were made both in 1885 and in 1886. But how strong was the legal basis for a fleet of protective cruisers? The Fisheries Protection Act of 1868 had proved to be vague in the details of enforcement just as its model, the Imperial Act of 1819, was vague. The fisheries protection force would be effective only insofar as the Fisheries Protection Act was effective. If a firm hand were to be shown to the stubborn quarrelsome Americans, and if Canadian fishermen were to be prevented from attempting to enforce their own concept of the law, it was clear that some strength would have to be put into the Act of 1868.

In May 1886, the Minister of Marine and Fisheries, George E. Foster, introduced in the House of Commons Bill No. 136 amending the Act of 1868. He explained that the Imperial Act of 1819, in line with the Convention of the previous year, forbade the entrace of foreign ships into Canadian waters except for the four purposes of shelter, repairs, and obtaining wood and water. The Canadian Act of 1868 provided penalties for fishing, preparing to fish, or having been fishing in Canadian waters. But neither Act provided penalties against entering Canadian harbors or ports for purposes other than shelter, repairs, wood, and water. The amendment contained in Bill No. 136 provided the required penalties. Macdonald

[28] *ibid.,* 174, Tilley to Macdonald, January 12, 1886.

told Lansdowne that "this legislation does not attempt to extend our rights but simply to improve our procedure by giving
the means of enforcing those rights." [29]

This was of particular importance because of the changes
that had occurred in the manner of exploiting the fisheries in
recent years. Less and less emphasis was placed by American
fishermen on fishing the inshore waters to obtain bait fish.
The unpredictable mackerel had apparently altered his swimming habits and, with the revolutionary innovation of the
purse seine net, could easily be caught beyond the three-
mile limit. In addition, larger fishing boats were being used
and competition in the industry was growing. In short, as the
American fishing industry became more commercialized and
more heavily capitalized, the commercial privileges of procur-
ing bait and supplies and of transshipment of the catch in
Canadian harbors became of ever more value to the American
fishermen. It was precisely these commercial privileges which
Bill No. 136 sought effectively to deny to the American fishermen.

An immediate protest issued from Secretary of State Bayard
against the "arbitrary, unlawful, unwarranted, and unfriendly
action on the part of the Canadian Government and its
officials" which was evident in the passing of Bill No. 136
and the issuance of Customs Circular No. 371 which implemented the essential provisions of the Act of 1868. He called
West's attention to "the wholly unwarranted proposition of
the Canadian authorities." Canada was enforcing its own
interpretation of a Convention between Great Britain and the
United States. The interpretation was calculated to "invade
and destroy the commercial rights and privileges of citizens
of the United States." [30] Doubtless the protest was expected
and the Ottawa politicians were determined not to back down.
Foster noted that "if Mr. Bayard's protests are to be heeded we

[29] *Official Report of Debates,* May 20, 1886, pp. 1421-23; Lansdowne
Papers, Macdonald to Lansdowne, May 21, 1886.
[30] Macdonald Papers, 174, Bayard to Sackville West, May 29, 1886.

shall soon have no bays, no treaty rights, and no territorial waters." [31] Sir Leonard Tilley believed that the inshore fisheries were no longer of value to the United States and that the commercial privileges in Canadian ports were "the only privilege they consider of importance." "We have rights and we have property under Treaty," he told Macdonald. "We offered to surrender these for such considerations as a joint Commission might agree upon. Then the Senate rudely refused and now they talk of unfriendly conduct on our part. 'Come into my nets says the spider to the fly.' 'No thank you' should be our reply." [32]

Bayard's criticism of Bill No. 136 and Customs Circular No. 371 was directed more at the incompetency of the Dominion Government to take such action than at the measures themselves. In a very stern note to Sackville West, the Governor-General voiced the reply that should be made to Bayard. The Bill was hardly open to objection on the grounds the Secretary of State alleged. It did not alter the terms of the Convention of 1818; rather, it merely provided a particular penalty which would be incurred by a vessel contravening the terms of the Convention. It was not the rights or liberties of either party to the Convention that were affected, simply the procedure necessary to carry out the Convention on which the Convention was itself silent. Sir Lionel should remind Bayard that the Congress on the one hand and the provincial legislatures and Imperial Parliament—and after 1867 the Dominion Parliament—on the other, had many times taken such action in regard to procedure and at no time had the provincial or Dominion legislation been seriously questioned. After all, the Imperial Parliament had delegated to Canada the power to legislate on matters affecting Canadian rights and interests; Dominion legislation received the assent of the Crown and thus became a part of the law of the Empire. Canadian intervention in matters of Canadian interest had

[31] *ibid.*, 86, Foster to Macdonald, June 24, 1886.
[32] *ibid.*, 277, Tilley to Macdonald, May 29, 1886.

been recognized again and again. Bayard might recall that "the Treaties of 1854 and 1871 so far as they related to Canadian fisheries or trade relations were made subject to ratification by the Canadian Legislature." [33]

Still, there might be some force in Bayard's protest. The competency of the Dominion Parliament was beyond question. But Lord Lansdowne did see a great danger in the American case; it might well be used to drive a wedge between the Dominion and its protective partner, the Imperial Government. On the day that Bill No. 136 received second reading Lansdowne confessed to the Prime Minister, "the more I think about your Fisheries Bill the less I like it, and the more I regret that you have determined to proceed with it." The problem was obvious. The Dominion Government was, in terms of legislation, "in line" with the Mother Country. The existing legislation, though admittedly very clumsy, had served between the Treaties of 1854 and 1871 to protect the fisheries. And a "legislative *coup de main*" would not only antagonize the Americans but also put Canada "out of line" with the Mother Country in time of crisis. Moreover, he argued, "I should like to feel that our warfare was conducted on other principles than those of the Fryes and Dingleys." [34]

Though the Bill passed quickly through the Houses of Parliament, Lansdowne's point was well taken—or at least the Colonial Office thought so. Lord Granville wired on 2 June that the Bill should be delayed or at least deferred from being brought into operation as "at present juncture [it] cannot fail to embarrass negotiations." [35] Macdonald might well

[33] *ibid.,* 174, Lansdowne to Sackville West, May 31, 1886 in Lansdowne to Macdonald, June 2, 1886. See also 86, Lansdowne to Granville, June 7, 1886, which conveys the same argument to the Imperial Government.

[34] *ibid.,* 86, Lansdowne to Macdonald, May 20 and 21, 1886.

[35] *ibid.,* telegram, Granville to Lansdowne, June 2, 1886 in Lansdowne to Macdonald, June 2, 1886.

have asked, "What negotiations?" But Lansdowne saw no other course than reservation of the Bill and Macdonald replied that such action would have to be taken solely on the Governor-General's own responsibility. A better procedure, the Prime Minister thought, would be to have the Bill passed in Canada and disallowed by Lord Granville "if he thinks fit." He noted that there could be no conviction under the act "for months . . . and long ere that Lord Granville will have plenty of time to make up his mind on the question of disallowance before the act can be enforced or any claim for redress can arise." To reserve the Bill in Canada in the face of Mr. Bayard's threat would be "humiliating"; "we will appear tamely to acquiesce." "Besides," said Macdonald with determination, "Canada will certainly pass the act next session and insist upon all its rights. Meanwhile a great irritation will arise here." [36] The colonials would yield neither to Washington's thunder nor to what they thought were the misguided counsels of officials in London.

Bill No. 136 was reserved by Lansdowne. But, shortly before his trip home the Governor-General received a note from Macdonald which again urged that Canadians must "stand upon our rights & force the U.S. into a commission or arbitration of some kind." In August Lansdowne met with Colonial Secretary Stanhope, Foreign Secretary Iddesleigh and Lord Lyons at the Foreign Office and it was agreed that the amending Act would receive the Royal assent, but only after the conclusion of the present fishing season. Macdonald concurred in this arrangement.[37] The Queen gave assent to the Act in November 1886.

The breakdown of hopes for a joint commission had left the Canadian Government with two alternatives: to stand pat

[36] *ibid.*, Macdonald to Lansdowne, June 2, 1886.
[37] *ibid.*, Lansdowne to Macdonald, September 28, 1886; 527, Macdonald to Lansdowne, July 10 and September 4, 1886; Minute by Meade on Lansdowne to Granville, July 14, 1886: CO42/785.

on the clumsy and ineffective provisions of the Act of 1868 or to move forward to a stronger assertion of their right to protect Canadian interests. They had chosen the latter course and met with protest from friend and foe alike. The American protest could not be entirely ignored because it went to the root of British complaints that the Dominion was moving faster than the Imperial authorities wished. This was neither the first nor the last occasion when such a problem would arise in Anglo-Canadian relations. But in the end the Canadian position was unassailable. If the Imperial Government had handed over to the Dominion control of certain rights of property in Canada, it was certainly the Canadian Government which had to have the ultimate decision in how those rights would be protected.

iv

The Canadian Parliament, in passing Bill No. 136, had shown its determination to protect the inshore fisheries. The Bill was intended more for long-term than immediate purposes of protection. Even if the Bill had not met with protest from the Americans and delaying doubts from the home authorities it would hardly have been possible for it to have effect during the 1886 fishing season. But while legislative protection was slow, active guardianship of Canadian inshore waters by Canadian cruisers was not; and, acting under instructions framed in accord with the Fisheries Protection Act of 1868, the Canadian force patrolled their waters throughout the 1886 season. The officers of the Canadian cruisers boarded some 700 vessels during the 1886 season and 1,362 vessels in 1887. In the two years a few vessels were seized by the Canadian authorities. "They will do good," Macdonald wrote, "it is just as well that the American Government and fishermen should know we are still on the alert." [38]

[38] Lansdowne Papers, Macdonald to Lansdowne, July 27, 1887; Innis, *The Cod Fisheries,* p. 419.

The Canadian Government attempted to ensure that the cruiser force would act with moderation rather than intemperate zeal. Officers were selected "who will avoid seizure of trespassing vessels except where the circumstances in which they are detected admit of no doubt as to the facts," Lansdowne assured the home Government.[39] As has been noted, there were problems involved in enforcement of the law, especially regarding the question of the legality of American fishermen buying bait in Canadian ports. But while the Canadian Government was attempting to remedy this difficulty by the introduction of Bill No. 136, Macdonald was fairly certain that the existing law did suggest that the purchase of bait was an illegal act. In a memorandum to Lansdowne he noted that an 1871 decision of a Vice Admiralty Court judge had considered that "buying bait was evidence of preparing to fish"[40] which was, of course, an infraction of the Act of 1868. Until the courts decided to the contrary the Canadian protective force would act as if this decision was unquestioned.

On 5 May 1886, the American fishing vessel, *David J. Adams* entered the harbor at Digby, Nova Scotia. The following day four and one-half barrels of bait and about two tons of ice were purchased by the *Adams'* crew and the owner of a fishing weir was told that the vessel was of British register. Finally, on 7 May the vessel departed from Digby and was stopped by the Canadian cruiser *Lansdowne*. The captain of the *Adams* told the boarding officer that he had been merely visiting relatives, had no fresh bait on board, and had come from the "Banks" and was bound for Maine. By entering the Nova Scotia harbor for a purpose other than for shelter, repair, wood, or water, by purchasing bait and supplies, by remaining within the harbor and failing to report to the proper

[39] Governor-General to Colonial Office, February 18, 1886: CO42/784.
[40] Macdonald Papers, 86, Macdonald to Lansdowne, March [May?] 26, 1886.

officials, the *David J. Adams* had violated the Convention of 1818, the Act of 1868, and the Customs Act of 1883.[41] The *Adams* was seized and removed to St. John, New Brunswick.

The usual protest from Bayard came rapidly to Lansdowne through the British Minister in Washington. The Secretary of State could not understand how a vessel in a "closely land-locked harbor" could be arrested for "intent of fishing." He again complained that the Canadians were acting irresponsibly to enforce an agreement to which they were not a contracting party. More important, it was clear that the question of purchasing bait had reference only to fishing beyond Canadian waters and any action to prevent such a purchase would expand the terms of the 1818 agreement "wholly beyond its purview, scope and intent." The seizure was in direct violation of the "reasonable rights and privileges of trade" of American vessels in Canadian ports.[42]

The Canadian Government denied that it was acting as an irresponsible agent or attempting to put a "special or novel interpretation" on the Convention of 1818.[43] The Governor-General did not believe there was any attempt on the part of Canada to impede the ordinary commercial intercourse between the two countries. This proposition was "altogether unsustainable" because the Convention of 1818 expressly ex-

[41] John P. Heisler, "Sir John Thompson, 1844-1894," Ph.D. Thesis, University of Toronto, 1955, pp. 144-45. The appropriate section of the Customs Act read: "The master of every vessel coming from any port or place out of Canada or coastwise, and entering any port in Canada, whether laden or in ballast, shall go without delay, when such vessel is anchored or moored, to the Customs House for the port or place of entry when he arrives and there make a report in writing to the collector or other proper officer of the arrival and voyage of such vessel. . . ." See Canada, Parliament, *Sessional Papers,* 1887, No. 16, pp. 145-46.

[42] Tansill, *Bayard,* pp. 213-14.

[43] Macdonald Papers, 175, Memorandum regarding competence of Canadian Government in relation to the seizure of the *David J. Adams,* Macdonald to Lansdowne, n.d.

cluded American fishing *vessels* from a "right to trade in Canadian ports." He hoped that the communications over the incident "may end in a reasonable and neighbourly adjustment." But, he added, "even if it be conceded that there is no use for bait except outside the three mile limit and that consequently a prohibition to obtain bait would affect not our inshore fisheries but those in the open sea which are *in hypothesi* accessible to all, it does not, I think, follow that such a prohibition would be a 'destructive expansion' of the scope of the convention." After all, he wrote, "the object of the convention and of the legislation founded upon it has been to protect British North American fishing interests generally in the same manner as the United States have sought by their system of Tariffs to protect and foster the fishing interest of their citizens." [44]

The Imperial Government stood squarely behind Canadian opinion. But Secretary of State Bayard's not totally unfriendly first inquiry was followed by harsher protests. These were undoubtedly in response to pressures within the American Government and by interested American citizens. The intemperate American Minister at London, Edward Phelps, thought the Canadians might as well have "hanged the crew" of the *Adams*. Secretary of the Navy Whitney was much in favor of sending his charges to the North Atlantic to protect American fishermen and he was ably seconded in this suggestion by George Steele, President of the American Fisheries Union. And happier than anyone else to see Bayard in such a muddle was the bellicose standard-bearer of the Republican party, James G. Blaine, with whom Canadians would become more intimately and unhappily acquainted in a short while. [45]

As American protests against Canadian seizures of American fishing vessels increased, the Imperial Authorities began to move away from their strong support of the Dominion.

[44] *ibid.*, 86, Lansdowne to Macdonald, May 18, 1886.
[45] Tansill, *Canadian-American Relations,* pp. 33 ff.

Lord Granville thought that there might be a possibility of opening negotiations with the Americans and could not "understand the position taken by [the Canadian] Government. Continued seizure of vessels must necessarily proclude [sic] friendly negotiations." Lansdowne and Macdonald agreed that the Colonial Secretary did not "fully realize the consequence of an announcement that no further seizures are to be made." Probably Granville was referring to seizures made for purchasing bait for on this point the law was not entirely clear. Here Canada could and would back down.[46] But Canada would not give in where the law was unquestionably on her side. "We cannot abandon our rights for the rest of the season," Macdonald told Lansdowne, "We have met with nothing but ingratitude and discourtesy for our doing so last year, and if the Government declined to act, our fishermen for their own protection would set the law in motion and cause the arrest of the vessels fishing or preparing to fish. . . ." Lansdowne cabled to Granville that Canada objected to an unconditional agreement to stop seizures, that further seizures for buying bait were not probable and that no seizures would be made unless there was a "clear and deliberate violation" of the law.[47]

The fate of the cause of all the furor still hung in abeyance for the case of the *David J. Adams* had not been settled. On the one hand the *Adams* seizure was regarded as a "test case,"[48] on the other the Canadian Government saw the

[46] Macdonald Papers, 86, telegram, Granville to Lansdowne, June 3, 1886, in Lansdowne to Macdonald, June 4, 1886; Public Archives of Canada, Thompson Papers, 40, telegram, Foster to Thompson, June 5, 1886 reads "Instruct N.S. captains immediately seize no vessel for buying bait."

[47] *ibid.,* Macdonald to Lansdowne, June 5, 1886; telegram, Lansdowne to Granville, June 7, 1886.

[48] *ibid.,* Lansdowne to Macdonald, June 4, 1886. See also Thompson Papers, 41, Lansdowne to Thompson, July 11, 1886; Macdonald Papers, 273, Thompson to Macdonald, July 12, 1886.

seizure of the *Adams* as a dangerous but useful diplomatic lever. The Minister of Justice, John Thompson, noted that if Canada was interested in protecting her fisheries there was "nothing to gain from expedition. The mere seizure has quite as deterrent an effect as condemnation would have, and if the decision be adverse we shall have lost the deterrent effect altogether. Everything indicates that the *Adams* is being made a test case of by Mr. Bayard. She has not been released on security." [49] Macdonald agreed. A policy of "masterly inactivity . . . to allow the law to take its ordinary course, and not to take any steps to expedite a decision" was best, he told the Governor-General.

> What we desire is to convince the American fishermen that it is for their interest to come to terms, and exclusion for a whole season from our waters and the want of bait will be a most convincing argument. On the other hand we can gain nothing by an early judgment.[50]

Lord Lansdowne reluctantly acquiesced in this decision though he could not see how it would contribute to a settlement of the dispute. But he also observed that "Sir L. West . . . tells me that at Washington the deadlock as between the President and the Senate is complete." [51] The prospects of agreement were as negligible in Washington as in Ottawa.

There was a final element in the policy of protection which the Government hoped would be of immediate value. During the Throne Speech Debate of 1886 Edward Blake chided the Prime Minister about a speech he had made while visiting London between the 1885 and 1886 parliamentary sessions. Blake criticized the inconsistency of Macdonald's position on

[49] *ibid.,* 273, Thompson to Macdonald, July 12, 1886.
[50] *ibid.,* 86, Macdonald to Lansdowne, July 26, 1886.
[51] Thompson Papers, 42, Lansdowne to Thompson, July 19, 1886. Final resolution of the *David J. Adams* case was not made until after the conclusion of the Joint High Commission of 1887-1888. See Thompson Papers, 67, W. L. Putnam to Thompson, March 16, 1888; 72, Putnam to Thompson, June 13, 1888.

Imperial defense and Macdonald forcefully rejected any inconsistency in his remarks. He said that he had always believed that "the future of the Empire of Great Britain depended upon a close and intimate alliance between the central power and the dependencies, the auxillary [sic] kingdoms." He was in favor "of having such an arrangement between the central United Kingdom and all the colonies—having an arrangement made by which the auxillary [sic] kingdom of Canada and the auxillary [sic] kingdom of Australasia should together form one great empire, and by uniting their forces, by uniting their men and money, should together be so strong as an empire that they could control the world in arms." [52]

This was, of course, long term hope and speculation. But perhaps Macdonald also was thinking of the present and vaguely hinting at his immediate plans for protecting the inshore fisheries. The final element in Canadian planning for protection was to call British armor to Canada's side. Macdonald did not deem this an unreasonable request. Indeed, he regarded it as a perfectly natural action that was in line with the defense arrangements worked out between Canada and the Mother Country in the confederation talks in London in 1865. The call had been answered in the years between the abrogation of the Treaty of 1854 and the adoption of the Treaty of 1871. Thus there was no second thought about adopting the Privy Council Report of 30 March 1886, which again requested aid. Lansdowne explained to the Colonial Secretary that Canada's small band of protective cruisers would, naturally, continue to enforce the fishery regulations. But the Canadian Government believed that their enforcement procedures would be much more impressive "if they are supported by the presence of one or more of Her Majesty's ships." [53] The real value of the presence of British ships was

[52] *Official Report of Debates,* February 26, 1886, p. 20.
[53] Enclosure in Lansdowne to Granville, March 30, 1886: CO807, North America 118, pp. 14-15.

in a show of Imperial unity. Their aid was being requested to give the Canadians a psychological advantage in their diplomatic contest with the United States.

The Imperial Government was much less willing to give aid than Canada was to request it. The central problem was one of jurisdiction over Canadian waters. The Canadians had taken a firm stand on the problem of headlands and bays, contending that the three-mile limit set forth in the Convention of 1818 should be measured in bays from a straight line drawn across the bay at the point nearest the entrance where the width did not exceed ten miles. In addition some bays including Baie de Chaleurs had been specially reserved as being within Canadian waters.[54] But Lord Kimberley, when Colonial Secretary, had stated in published despatches that the British Government could not claim any waters more than three miles from land. While the Canadian Government claimed jurisdiction over bays up to ten miles in width at the mouth, the Imperial Government was on record as claiming jurisdiction only over those bays which were less than six miles wide. There was no firmly established international law on the matter and Sir Robert Herbert put the case for the Admiralty as well as the Colonial Office in regard to the Canadian contention when he noted "there will be by no means such a firm concurrence of opinion in this country as would be desirable when a much contested principle is being upheld." [55] In fact, the Colonial Office was more worried about Canadian cruisers enforcing the Canadian view than it was about how the Admiralty would deal with the problem. Stanhope's telegram to Lansdowne of 13 August warned that "your Government should proceed with great caution in regard to Bays and Headlands question, and take no action for

[54] Philip C. Jessup, *The Law of Territorial Waters and Maritime Jurisdiction,* New York, 1927, p. 367.
[55] Minute by Herbert, August 18, 1886, on Governor-General to Colonial Office, July 14, 1886: CO42/785.

asserting British rights over any waters more than three miles from land without previously ascertaining by full communication with Her Majesty's Government, that they will be able to uphold such action." [56] Equally, the Admiralty Office was more than reluctant to send British ships to Canadian waters under such circumstances, and they were supported by the Foreign Office which regarded Canada's request as not calculated to enhance the possibility of a settlement with the United States. When no reply had been received to Lansdowne's despatch by July, the Governor-General cabled home for information and then penned another despatch urging that "the moral effect of this support was very great [after 1866], and its absence, if it is withheld under present circumstances, will be seriously felt." [57]

The support of the Admiralty was discussed by Lansdowne with Stanhope and Iddesleigh when the Governor-General went home in August. Lansdowne wrote to Macdonald that he had been "met by very determined resistance on the ground that the sudden appearance of one of H. M. ships would add to the already existing exasperation, and lessen the prospect of the negotiations now in progress leading to a satisfactory result." The Governor-General had seen no real "progress" and noted that United States Minister Phelps's professions of friendship were not accompanied by any "visible prospect of a solution." The best chance of obtaining one was by showing "a firm front" and at the present time Canada was "at an immense disadvantage by the want of support from the fleet." Stanhope had replied that the Cabinet would not "complicate matters" by giving support during the present season, but if

[56] Stanhope to Lansdowne, August 13, 1886: CO807, North America 118, p. 151.
[57] Lansdowne to Granville, Confidential, July 14, 1886: CO807, North America 118, p. 141. See also Colonial Office to Foreign Office, July 16, 1886, pp. 120-21; Macdonald Papers, 527, Macdonald to Lansdowne, July 10, 1886; 86, Lansdowne to Macdonald, July 13, 1886.

the negotiations came to nothing he suggested Canada might have Admiralty support during 1887.[58]

The Prime Minister accepted this solution to the problem, but not before he had placed on record his view of the Mother Country's obligations to Canada in time of need. Macdonald believed that there was much smoke but little fire in the United States over the fishery question. He discounted "any real exasperation" there and said that instead there was "simulated indignation among the professional politicians in Maine & along the New England Coast who are trying to catch the fishermen's vote for Blaine." But this did not alter the nature of the central question. It was not simply that the Atlantic squadron had come to Canada's aid in the past, Macdonald asserted, but that "the British Govt. is pledged to use the whole naval and military force of the Empire for us when our interests require it. . . . Canada has done nothing to forfeit her claim—her right I should rather say—to protection." He suggested that since the British Government was concerned about startling the Americans by a sudden increase in the size of the squadron, no ships need be added until the squadron went to its winter station in the West Indies, then "The fleet can return in the spring without its additional strength being noticed." [59]

As with the assent to Bill No. 136, the request for British ships to support the Canadian marine police had met with stubborn resistance on the part of the Imperial Government. During the fishing season of 1886 the Canadian cruisers alone had acted out their part of the Canadian plan. Perhaps the

[58] Macdonald Papers, 86, Lansdowne to Macdonald, August 20, 1886; Stanhope to Administrator Russell, Secret, September 5, 1886: CO807, North America 118, p. 181.

[59] ibid., 527, Macdonald to Lansdowne, September 4, 1886. Sir Lionel Sackville West also considered much of the concern of the United States over the fisheries to have been stimulated "for purely political purposes." Christ Church Library, Oxford, Salisbury Papers, Sackville West to Salisbury, January 30, 1887.

British Government with its far greater diplomatic experience had acted wisely in attempting to curb Canadian zeal. But had it really done so? The Canadians were inclined to think not. Great Britain acted on the assumption that the Americans wanted to settle the fisheries dispute. But Ottawa thought otherwise. A settlement could be bought only at the intolerable price of surrender. The incredible internal warfare between the Senate and the Executive and Blaine's politicizing at least appeared to be more important than amicable diplomacy. Under such circumstances, as Macdonald again reminded Lansdowne, "nothing can be gained by submission. Much may be gained by a calm but firm assertion of our rights and their enforcement." [60] After all, Lansdowne told Sir Henry Holland, "the intention of the Convention of 1818 was to give to British fishermen a monopoly of whatever advantages they could derive from the use of the inshore waters and fisheries of the B.N.A. coast. . . . This qualified monopoly is of immense value to us and we cannot surrender it without a reasonable equivalent. That such a monopoly is inconvenient to outsiders and out of harmony with modern ideas may be perfectly true but does not affect the validity of our rights or our claim to compensation if we are to be deprived of them." [61] If nothing else, there was consolation in knowing that, barring an improbable settlement, all three segments of the Canadian plan of enforcement of Canadian rights would be brought to bear against the Americans in the 1887 fishing season and thereafter.

v

The formulation of a plan to protect the Canadian inshore fisheries was a difficult task. The Government had to proceed against the criticism of both the United States and the Imperial Government. And there was another, and at times even

[60] *ibid.*
[61] Lansdowne Papers, Lansdowne to Holland, January 22, 1887.

38

more potent critic of Government policy, the Canadian public. Sir John Macdonald would never have admitted that the Dominion had its own "fierce democracy"—a phrase he applied freely to the politics of the Republic. He was too close to it and it can hardly be denied that deep in his heart he enjoyed too much being a part of it. Nonetheless there was a "fierce democracy" in Canada and partisan warfare in the Dominion as played out in the realm of the "fourth estate" was often more vicious than anything the most strident journals of Yankeedom could invent. The Canadian public and its spokesman, the Canadian press, had to be considered in any policy-making decisions by the Macdonald Government.

Only a few Canadians sent their opinions directly to the seat of Government. One Nova Scotia fisherman told Justice Minister John Thompson that a law prohibiting the sale of bait to American fishermen was necessary and added, "we want the Americans shown that we can live without them." Another correspondent noted that to "thoroughly protect our fisheries" would "be the best possible position for us to occupy." It would "check New England bunkem and compel them to respect treaty obligations." [62] More often the opinion of interested parties came to the Government in the form of resolutions and petitions. In New Brunswick the Charlotte County Municipal Council begged the Minister of Marine and Fisheries "to take whatever steps . . . may be necessary or practical to enforce the provisions of [the Convention of 1818] as will tend to and secure the protection of our own Canadian fishermen against the intrusion of United States fishermen into our waters. . . ." And the Halifax Chamber of Commerce resolved in favor of "a vigorous protection of our Canadian fisheries by the federal government" to prevent American fishermen "gaining any further privileges than they now enjoy

[62] Thompson Papers, 36, McGray to Thompson, March 18, 1886; 35, Purcell to Thompson, February 18, 1886.

in connexion with our fisheries." [63] Undoubtedly letters from Maritime residents and resolutions from Maritime businessmen and local officials were to be expected; they all had a vital interest in the outcome of the dispute. So too, for different reasons, did the newspapers which generally supported the Macdonald Government. No one was surprised when the *Montreal Gazette* proudly announced that "no amount of bluster will drive the Canadian Government into unequal concessions when Congress has declined to entertain a proposition for a fair, just and mutually advantageous settlement of the question." [64]

The Government, however, was concerned about the treatment it would receive from its critics. But even Liberals muted their criticism of the Government's fishery policy. There was, of course, a suitable amount of abuse heaped upon Conservative policy but it was meted out for "the insane Act of our government in throwing away a whole season of our fishing rights merely to secure a good word from the American government." Such a violently anti-Government organ as the *Halifax Morning Chronicle* observed that the only way to reach an "equitable settlement" would be by the "strict enforcement" of Canadian rights. "There is no room for any compromise at all" the editor observed, "any course other than a dignified but determined resistance . . . would be most humiliating to us." [65] The archfoe of Canadian Conservatism, the *Toronto Globe,* was moved by the seizure of the *David J. Adams* to observe that "we believe the Dominion Government should rigidly prevent all illegal proceedings of American fishermen. . . ." [66] The Conservatives probably also noted with

[63] *St. John Daily Telegraph,* January 23, 1886; *Halifax Morning Chronicle,* July 8, 1886.

[64] *Montreal Gazette,* April 17, 1886.

[65] *Halifax Morning Chronicle,* February 8 and 23, and March 8, 1886.

[66] *Toronto Globe,* May 13, 1886.

interest that approval of their decision in 1886 to take a strong stand against the Americans came from the generally detached and disinterested editors of the Canadian West. The *Manitoba Free Press* observed that the importance of the fisheries question was "too momentous to be dealt with in a perfunctory way" and warned the Imperial authorities not to "step upon Canada while too intently bent upon being friendly with the United States." And the *Edmonton Bulletin* feared that "if the principle is once admitted that because the United States wills Canada must, then the prospect of a Canadian nationality is lost and the name Canadian becomes a reproach." [67]

There seemed to be a unity of opinion throughout the Dominion as to how the Government should deal with the fisheries problem. The opposition press might, of course, complain about the details of Government action as the *Toronto Globe* criticized rather unjustly the inefficiency of the marine police force. But the editor of the *Regina Leader* appeared to speak for all Canadians when he wrote: "Let England and Canada stand to their rights and Uncle Sam will condescend to be honest." [68]

[67] *Manitoba Free Press*, May 11, 1886; *Edmonton Bulletin*, April 30, 1887.
[68] *Toronto Globe*, August 20, 1886; *Regina Leader*, June 1, 1886.

CHAPTER II
The Behring Sea Dispute

IN 1867 the Government of the United States became the proud possessor of a new empire in Alaska. "Seward's folly" was a vast, unknown, and forbidding land and most Americans viewed it with the same contempt that Voltaire had expressed regarding Canada. The "acres of snow" would, of course, become a golden paradise at the turn of the century, but for the moment only a few enterprising businessmen saw any value in Alaska. These businessmen were dealers in furs and they were attracted to one of the richest sources of the valuable fur seal. The mysterious animal swam the ocean for the better portion of the year but came to the Pribilof Islands for a few months in the spring and summer to give birth to its young and mate once again. While on the Islands, the helpless creatures could be slain with facility and their pelts gathered for sale and processing in the London fur market. With the added incentive of cheap Indian labor, here was an opportunity for American furriers not to miss.

In 1870 the Congress of the United States passed a statute limiting the catch of fur seals on the Islands to 100,000 per year. It leased the sealing privileges for twenty years to the Alaska Commercial Company of San Francisco. The Company agreed to pay the United States Treasury $55,000 per annum, a revenue tax of $2.62½ per skin and 55 cents for every gallon of oil extracted from the seals. The Company further promised to care for the welfare of the native Indians and provide them with elementary education.[1] In fact, the

---

[1] Jozo Tomasevich, *International Agreements on the Conservation of Marine Resources,* Stanford, 1943, pp. 74-75. In 1890 the new lease was awarded to the North American Commercial Company for another twenty years. The annual rent was increased to $60,000 and the revenue tax on the skins was nearly tripled to $9.62½ per skin. The new company inherited the same obligations to the natives.

Alaska Commercial Company by its lease and by Congressional default, virtually became the trustee of the new territory.

Two years later it was necessary for the American Government to make a decision concerning the legality of pelagic sealing in the waters around the Islands. In 1799 and again, with greater force, in 1821, the Imperial Russian Czar had virtually declared Behring Sea a *mare clausum*. But both the United States and Great Britain had heartily protested against this *dictum,* and had forced the Czar formally to abandon his claims in treaties in 1824 and 1825. On 25 March 1872, Secretary of the Treasury Boutwell informed Mr. T. G. Phelps that pelagic sealing could not be prevented by the United States "unless they [the sealers] made such attempts within a marine league of the shore." [2] This decision was apparently reversed in 1876 when the American sealer *San Diego* was seized by a revenue vessel twenty miles from shore, taken to San Francisco, and condemned in a United States' District Court.[3] Again, in 1881, Acting Secretary of the Treasury French declared that the killing of fur-bearing animals was prohibited by Section 1956 of the *Revised Statutes* in all waters east of the boundary set forth in the treaty of cession of 1867. "All the waters within that boundary to the western end of the Aleutian Archipelago and chain of Islands are considered as comprised within the waters of Alaska Territory." [4] Yet it is not exactly true to say that the action of 1876 and the opinion given in 1881 had overridden Secretary Boutwell's advice of 1872. Both the seizure of the *San Diego* and Acting Secretary French's letter in 1881 dealt with cases involving only United States citizens. Mr. Boutwell's letter was written in reply to an inquiry about pelagic sealing by foreigners. It was

[2] Tansill, *Canadian-American Relations,* p. 269.

[3] Tansill, *Bayard,* p. 455, n. 9.

[4] Public Archives of Canada, Bowell Papers, 5, H. F. French to A. D'Ancona, March 12, 1881, Appendix D, Privy Council Report, October 15, 1886. See also Tansill, *Bayard,* p. 455.

one thing to enforce American law on American nationals; it was quite another to attempt to enforce it upon the citizens of other states, especially when those citizens were acting outside the generally accepted marine league of territorial waters.

ii

On 24 August 1886, while Lord Lansdowne was in London urging the Canadian case for assent to Bill No. 136 and Admiralty support, the Commander-in-Chief of the Pacific Station of the Royal Navy wired to his superiors in London that three British Columbia seal schooners had been seized by the United States Revenue Cruiser *Corwin*. He observed that the sealers were in "Behring's Straits seaward 70 miles from off the land"[5] and added that British Columbia schooners had been pelagic sealing "for three years without interference although in company with *Corwin*." In a covering despatch, however, the Commander-in-Chief added some very significant facts on the apparent "about face" by the United States revenue cruisers. In 1884 one schooner had put out from Victoria for seals. The following year it was accompanied by another and both had been contacted by the *Corwin* four or five times without interference. But the successful catches of 1884 and 1885 led to the fitting out and sailing in 1886 of thirteen British Columbia schooners.[6] What had been an adventurous speculation in 1885 had blossomed into a large-scale enterprise with heavy capital investment in 1886. The hint was obvious. The United States Government could afford to let well enough alone when faced with the competition of one

[5] Commander-in-Chief, Pacific Station, Victoria to Admiralty, telegram, confidential, August 24, 1886, in Admiralty to Colonial Office, August 26, 1886: CO42/786.

[6] Commander-in-Chief, Pacific Station, Victoria to Admiralty, August 25, 1886, in Admiralty to Colonial Office, September 20, 1886: CO42/786; Lansdowne Papers, G. E. Foster to Lansdowne, December 6, 1886.

or two schooners, but a large-scale Canadian enterprise if allowed to become firmly established would seriously threaten the only significant source of revenue from Alaska and, more directly, the life of the Alaska Commercial Company.

The Commander-in-Chief was more interested in another and more fundamental problem: did the United States claim the whole of Behring Sea as its property? "The question, as I view it," he wrote, "is simply whether the Behring Sea is the 'high sea' or not. If, as I take it, Behring Sea is the 'high sea' I presume no fishing vessel can be legally interfered with." [7] This was also the point upon which the natural Canadian outcry concentrated. A Victoria correspondent wrote to Macdonald that "it seems almost preposterous claiming [Behring Sea] as American territory. If eastern lobsters don't live here Gloucester fishermen at any rate have their spawn. The three mile limit on the Atlantic and 70 mile on the Pacific is a tolerably fair rate of increase in national claims." A lead editorial in the *Halifax Morning Chronicle* was entitled "An American Outrage" and the editor of the *Victoria Daily Times* quipped: "A seal was shot last week in the river opposite Montreal. It will now be in order for the Alaska Fur Company [sic] to arrest some one, on the ground that the mammal must have wandered away from the Behring Sea." The editor of the *Toronto Globe* expressed the Queen City's indignation when he noted: "These seizures . . . afford . . . complete illustration of the American theory that 'their rights air bigger than our'n because their country's bigger.'" [8]

[7] *ibid.*

[8] Macdonald Papers, 429, J. H. Gray to Macdonald, September 1, 1886; *Halifax Morning Chronicle,* September 6, 1886; *Victoria Daily Times,* October 7, 1886; *Toronto Globe,* August 23, 1886. The highly respected international lawyer and teacher, John Bassett Moore, who was working at the State Department at the time, candidly pointed out some years later that "American diplomacy has . . . been characterized by practicality. It has sought to attain definite objects by practical methods. Even in its idealism, as in the advocacy of the exemp-

The seizure of British Columbia sealing vessels by American revenue cutters presented a very difficult problem to the Canadian Government. Seen in contrast with the North Atlantic fisheries difficulty, the Behring Sea problem clearly revealed Canada's limited field of action. In the former case the Dominion had been given control over Canadian territorial waters and in fact, if not in theory, Canada could act as a quasi-sovereign state to protect her possession. The limitations the Imperial Government sought to place on Canadian action were made not because of any questioning of the competence of the Dominion to act. Rather, they were dictated by the greater experience of the Imperial Government in the game of diplomacy. Lord Salisbury put the situation in its clearest practical light when he once described himself to Edward Phelps as the diplomatic "broker" of Canadian interests.[9] This was, of course, also true with regard to the Behring Sea problem. No action would be taken by the Imperial Government without consultation with the Government in Ottawa. Nevertheless, the "broker's" powers were much greater and his responsibility for initiating action was much larger. Where the Dominion had territorial responsibility it could initiate action; it could protect its residents. But the Behring Sea was either an American lake, as the seizures by American cutters seemed to indicate, or a part of the "high seas." In neither case could the Dominion force the initiative. As a colonial nation within the British Empire, Canada could claim no authority in its own right beyond a marine league from the coast; all extra-territorial power and responsibility was

tion of private property at sea from capture, it has shown a practical side." John Bassett Moore, *The Principles of American Diplomacy, The Collected Papers of John Bassett Moore,* New Haven, 1944, v. 4.

[9] Tansill, *Canadian-American Relations,* p. 280. Obviously, Salisbury could not really be a "broker" at all; he could not absolve himself of his responsibility for protecting Canadian interests. Nonetheless, the term "broker," used in this sense, is interesting and not altogether inappropriate.

46

vested in the Imperial Government. Nor could Canada control the schooners that sailed from Victoria, British Columbia to hunt seals. They were registered under and subject to the regulations of the Imperial Government's various Merchant Shipping Acts; they were British, not Canadian, ships. Once out of Canadian territorial waters, then, they were an Imperial responsibility.[10] Lord Salisbury had far greater freedom of decision and action in the Behring Sea dispute than in the North Atlantic fisheries conflict.

In the Canadian House of Commons, in 1888, the members of the Government fully explained their unhappy position. "Her Majesty's Government alone," Sir Charles Tupper related, "are the parties [sic] who can negotiate with respect to this question and settle the question between the United States and Great Britain." The Prime Minister contrasted the Atlantic and Pacific difficulties. The "Atlantic question pressed specially upon us here, . . . the question respecting the Behring Sea is not exclusively a Canadian question as that was. The one affected the trade along Canadian coasts . . . It was altogether a Canadian question. The other question about the Behring Sea is as much a matter of interest for all marine powers as it is for the United States, for Canada or England." It was all very confusing. And the Liberal chieftains did not hesitate to make political capital by compounding the confusion. Sir Richard Cartwright was probably right when he said that "the British Government from various courses are not by any means so well qualified to deal with those questions as the Government of Canada, and . . . we would be

[10] These legal imperfections in Canadian autonomy remained until the Imperial Conference of 1930 and the resultant passage of the "Statute of Westminster" in 1931. See the report of the 1926 Conference, in A. B. Keith, ed., *Speeches and Documents on the British Dominions, 1918-1931*, London, 1932, pp. 161-70; "The Report of the Conference on the Operation of Dominion Legislation and Merchant Shipping Legislation, 1929," *ibid.,* pp. 173-205.

better off . . . than we are now if we had to deal directly with this Administration at Washington." Many Canadians shared this view. After all, despite the lawyers, Canadian property had been seized and Canadians had been deprived of a livelihood. But satisfactory or not, George Foster's answer was decisive. In sum, said the Minister of Marine and Fisheries, it was "a large Imperial matter." [11]

Thus the hands of the Canadian Government were tied. But its vocal cords were not and remonstrances against Yankee high-handedness flooded the Canadian despatch bags to the Colonial Office. The three vessels seized were the *Onward,* the *Carolina,* and the *Thornton,* "all of them at a distance of more than sixty miles from the nearest land." [12] With the exception of the masters and the mates, the crews of the latter two vessels were shipped to San Francisco and turned adrift, destitute and penniless. The crew of the *Onward* was turned loose at Unalaska where the vessels were detained. On 30 August the master and mate of the *Thornton* were brought to trial before Judge Dawson in the District Court at Sitka. The officers of the *Corwin* testified that they had seized the vessels about sixty or seventy miles off St. George's Island for "hunting and killing seals within that part of Behring Sea which was ceded to the United States by Russia in 1867." [13]

It was rumored that Judge Dawson might be less than judiciously impartial at the trial. Sackville West reported that there was a "disposition prevalent in that neighborhood to break up all sealing enterprises not conducted by the Alaska Commercial Company. A Government officer who had been on duty in Alaska told the writer that it was practically im-

[11] *Official Report of Debates,* April 25, 1888, pp. 1014-16.

[12] Administrator Russell to Colonial Office, September 27, 1886: CO42/785.

[13] Bowell Papers, 5, Copy, Report to Council signed by Bowell, Foster, and Thompson, October 15, 1886.

possible to live or hold public employment in Alaska without keeping on good terms with that Corporation." Further, the prosecuting attorney "will have the aid of able lawyers at San Francisco paid by the Alaska Commercial Co." [14] Certainly the judge took an enlarged view of United States jurisdiction in Behring Sea. Quoting from the first article of the Treaty of 1867 he defined the limits of the cession and continued his charge to the jury by saying that "all the waters within the boundary set forth in this Treaty to the western end of the Aleutian Archipelago and Chain of Islands, are to be considered as comprised within the waters of Alaska, and all the penalties prescribed by law against the killing of fur-bearing animals, must therefore attach against any violation of law within the limit . . . described." [15] The master and mate were sentenced to thirty-days' imprisonment and fined $500 and $300 respectively. Similar penalties were shortly handed down to the masters and mates of the *Carolina* and *Onward*.

The enlarged construction placed upon the words "adjacent waters" in the first article of the Treaty of 1867 by Judge Dawson, the Canadian Government claimed, would in effect "convert a purely municipal prohibition (Section 1956) of the *Revised Statutes* into an international obligation, and . . . claim for the United States a jurisdiction which their Government have in the past not only declined themselves to assert, but which they have strenuously resisted when claimed by another Power." In October 1886, the Canadians insisted that "the conditions attaching to *maria clausa* cannot by any possi-

---

[14] Lansdowne Papers, memorandum, Sackville West to Lansdowne, September 7, 1887. "The Alaska Company is very powerful in Congress. Their annual payment for privileges conceded gives the Govt. 3½% on the purchase money ($7,500,000) paid to Russia." Sackville West to Lansdowne, November 15, 1886.

[15] Administrator Russell to Colonial Office, September 27, 1886: CO42/785.

bility be predicated of Behring Sea." The seizure of Canadian vessels "constitutes a high-handed extension of maritime jurisdiction unprecedented in the Law of Nations." [16] Unhindered by the politeness of diplomacy, the *Manitoba Free Press* observed that "it cannot be expected that the Canadian and English people will easily submit to such arrogant assumptions." [17]

iii

The first of a series of Anglo-Canadian protests was made to Bayard by West on 27 September 1886. On 12 November the British Minister had an interview with the Secretary of State about the matter. West conveyed the latest British information on the seizures by the *Corwin* but Bayard was unable to respond with the American side of the story. The latter remarked that the Canadians and British were fortunate in having information links to Victoria. Unfortunately the American western territories were not "properly organized" and communication was difficult. Bayard said he had not yet decided the exact nature of the rights Russia had ceded to the United States but it was clear that before the cession Russia had held Behring Sea to be a *mare clausum*. "Against which contention the U.S. protested," West interjected. "Yes," replied Bayard, "at that time." [18] It was evident that Bayard, lacking the information vital to any decision on the matter, would not commit himself or his Government until such information was available.

But all three Governments had to consider not only the past and present but also the future. Just three days after the interview, William Munsee of British Columbia wrote to George Foster concerning the next sealing season. The vessels

[16] Bowell Papers, 5, Copy, Report to Council, October 15, 1886.

[17] *Manitoba Free Press,* September 8, 1886.

[18] Sackville West to Salisbury, No. 250, Confidential, November 12, 1886, in Foreign Office to Colonial Office, November 26, 1886: CO42/788.

would leave Victoria in less than a month and not return until September 1887. "We are accordingly anxious to know what is being done in the case of our seized vessels, and whether or not we may look for protection against what we and even the American press is [sic] pleased to term piracy." He continued:

The industry is of too much importance to Canada to allow the Alaska Commercial Company to dictate who shall or who shall not take seals on the high or Behring's Sea. For the season of 1886 there was brought into Victoria from the Pacific Ocean and Behring's Sea, and shipped therefrom to England and the United States, 50,000 skins, valued at about 350,000 dollars. It is evident that the business is worth protection.[19]

When this request for information eventually reached West in Washington he sought out the Secretary of State and inquired if British vessels would be exposed to seizure during 1887. Bayard was more evasive than ever. He ignored the question, remarking instead on the value of the seal islands and the danger to which they were exposed by pelagic sealing.[20] By now West's exasperation was complete. But, in truth, it was matched by a feeling of total helplessness on the part of Bayard.

The Secretary of State was absolutely convinced that the seizures by the *Corwin* were wrong from the moment he first heard of them through the British protest. Writing to the President, Bayard noted that historically the United States had never claimed territorial jurisdiction anywhere beyond the accepted marine league limit. Furthermore, the United States had never assented to the right of search—much less seizure —of foreign vessels on the high seas in time of peace. "This

[19] Munsee to Foster, November 15, 1886, in Lansdowne to Stanhope, November 27, 1886: CO42/785.
[20] Sackville West to Iddesleigh, No. 274, Confidential, December 10, 1886, in Foreign Office to Colonial Office, December 28, 1886: CO42/788.

Government," he said, "is one of law, and yields the same voluntary and self-imposed submission to the rules of international regulation in the use and navigation of the high seas which it requires from other members of the family of nations." Bayard was sure of his case. Investigation by the United States Minister in St. Petersburg, George V. N. Lothrop, and the State Department's solicitor, Francis Wharton, confirmed his view. He suggested to Cleveland that prosecution of the cases be discontinued, the seized vessels be discharged and, finally, that pending a settlement no further seizures be made.[21]

Cleveland partially agreed and on 3 February West was informed that the cases had been discontinued and the vessels and imprisoned crew members had been ordered discharged. But Cleveland would not allow Bayard to commit the United States against further seizures.[22] In August West was again at Bayard's door protesting seizures made during the 1887 season. In fact, Cleveland had not been totally convinced by Bayard's high-mindedness. The Acting Attorney General, George A. Jenks, had given the President reason to think the seizures were not wholly illegal. Even in Bayard's own department Francis Wharton had changed his mind. Just before West began his new round of protests the solicitor drew up a memorandum which seemed to confirm Cleveland's doubts. Any claim to Behring Sea as a *mare clausum* was, of course, "absurd." But in a clever and logical argument Wharton developed the point that since the United States owned property in Behring Sea, it should have "sufficient police control over the waters adjacent to such property as to enable us to protect

---

[21] Tansill, *Bayard,* pp. 458-62.

[22] Tansill, *Canadian-American Relations,* p. 275; Macdonald Papers, 87, Lansdowne to Macdonald, February 4, 1887. Lansdowne told the Premier that he suspected the release order was made in order "to spoil our hand on the Atlantic coast."

it." [23] This was, indeed, a fine splitting of legal hairs and did little to help Bayard out of his predicament.

Whatever the meanderings of legal minds in Washington, the officials in Ottawa were clearly disgusted by the renewal of seizures. The revenue cruiser *Richard Rush* had impounded the *Grace, Dolphin,* and *W. P. Sayward* during the 1887 season. When the *Alfred Adams* met the same fate in September, Foster's rage was hardly concealed in the report he drafted for the Privy Council to approve and send to Downing Street. "This condition of affairs," he wrote, "is in the highest degree detrimental to the interests of Canada and should not be permitted to continue." "An important and remunerative Canadian industry has been threatened with absolute ruin." [24]

The Imperial Government, though responsible for Canadian interests, had not been greatly alarmed about the 1886 seizures. There was almost a sense of disbelief that "these illegal and in all respects apparently unjustifiable proceedings" had taken place and the Colonial Office officials rejoiced in "having a greater & more explicit grievance against the U.S. than the U.S. have against us." Sir Robert Herbert guessed that it was all part of the game of diplomacy. The vessels would be released and compensation readily given so that the United States could stand lily-white before the bar of international opinion while the shamefaced Canadians continued to hold the *David J. Adams.* As late as February 1887, when the Imperial Government had been informed of the release order, Salisbury had put aside a Canadian claim for compensation

[23] Tansill, *Bayard,* p. 467. Philip Jessup saw fit to agree with this point of view. He wrote, "the justification of the United States was based not on a denial of the three-mile limit, but upon the special conditions which made control of the fisheries further out to sea the only alternative to their destruction." Jessup, *The Law of Territorial Waters and Maritime Jurisdiction,* p. 55.

[24] Governor-General to Colonial Office, September 26, 1887: CO42/791.

until "Her Majesty's Government have had an opportunity of examining the statement as to the circumstances under which the seizures took place. . . ." And although Sackville West had protested against the seizures, he had never been instructed to protest against the United States' *right* to make the seizures. After reading the despatch which included Foster's heated Report to Council of September 1887, John Bramston finally calmly noted: "I think we may go further and ask [the Foreign Office] whether Sir L. West may not be instructed to say that H.M.G. deny the right of the U.S.A. to seize vessels 50 miles from land." [25]

iv

A strong stand on the North Atlantic fisheries had been thought necessary by the Canadian Government primarily as a measure of protection of Canadian interests. But a second motive was equally apparent to the Canadians; only by being firm could Canada, as Macdonald said, "force the U.S. into a commission or arbitration of some kind." A commission had been the objective of the Canadians from the very start of the difficulty. Yet, as Lansdowne told Stanhope, the United States Minister Edward Phelps' professions of a desire for a friendly settlement had not been matched with any specific proposals. Canadian anxiety increased when the Behring Sea dispute added another hostile element to the controversy. Bayard apparently felt the same tension and in November 1886, with the North Atlantic fishing season at an end, but with Canadian protests against the Behring Sea seizures increasing in vehemence, he finally communicated a proposal for settlement to the British Government.

The proposal was limited to the cod fisheries. The Secre-

[25] Minute by Herbert on Governor-General to Colonial Office, November 27, 1886: CO42/785; Foreign Office to Colonial Office, February 14, 1887: CO42/793; Minute by Bramston on Governor-General to Colonial Office, September 26, 1887: CO42/791.

tary of State suggested the appointment of a mixed commission to determine "the limits which shall separate the exclusive from the common right of fishing on the coasts and in the adjacent waters of the British North American Colonies in conformity with the 1st Article of the Convention of 1818." [26] Pending an agreement the British Government would instruct the Canadians to seize vessels of American fishermen only for fishing, preparing to fish, or having been fishing, i.e., in accordance only with the Fisheries Protection Act of 1868 and not including the 1886 amendment. To execute the first article of the Convention of 1818 Great Britain and the United States would each send a national vessel to patrol the Gulf of the St. Lawrence and another to patrol the south coast of Nova Scotia. The four commanders of these vessels would have the power of deciding on the legality of any seizures by Canadian cruisers. Further, American fishing vessels would have "the same commercial privileges as other vessels of the United States including the purchase of bait and other supplies." [27] And the British Government would also agree "to release all United States fishing vessels now under seizure for failing to report at custom houses when seeking shelter, repairs or supplies, and to refund all fines exacted for such failure to report."

[26] In Bayard to Phelps, November 15, 1886: CO807, North America 121, pp. 59-63. In delimiting the "boundary" the commission would use the ten-mile reference regarding bays and, further, the commission would establish the regulations to meet the prohibitory sections of Article 1 and name penalties for infractions of the regulations.

[27] ibid. Bayard was particularly emphatic on this point. In his covering letter to Phelps he wrote: "The present memorandum also contains provisions for the usual commercial facilities allowed everywhere for the promotion of legitimate trade, and nowhere more fully than in British ports and under the commercial policies of that nation. Such facilities cannot with any show of reason be denied to American fishing vessels when plying their vocations in deep-sea fishing grounds in the localities open to them equally with other nationalities. . . ."

The Colonial Office officials could hardly have been less pleased with the content of Bayard's proposal. It was, noted Sir Robert Herbert, "very discouraging as to the prospect of any settlement . . . though not so intended, perhaps, the suggestion is, in fact, insulting." "The U.S. Govt. knows thoroughly well that it is the contention of the Dominion Govt. which we have accepted and supported that the purchase of bait in Canadian ports for the purpose of fishing beyond Canadian waters is a thing absolutely outside the expressly stated permissible purposes of the Convention of 1818. And the proposal that Canada should admit all the seizures 'for failing to report' to have been wrongful, and should refund the fines, is a begging of the question which will be characterized in Canada in terms not calculated to advance a settlement." Colonial Secretary Stanhope agreed, adding that it was "a waste of time to consult Canada upon these proposals." [28]

But the Canadians had received the proposals and Herbert's dour prediction of their reaction was only too correct. With characteristic understatement the Governor-General noted that Bayard's suggestions "will require considerable modification before we can entertain them." With regard to the proposal that the seized vessels be released, and the added stipulation of a joint commission to decide on compensation resulting from the seizures, Lansdowne caustically observed, "this is the old Alabama procedure once again!" He concluded that "it is a one sided and disingenuous proposal, and decides against us all the debateable points & some which are not debateable at all!" George Foster thought the suggestion to release the seized vessels "the most 'cheeky' of all." "There is not the sparkle of a single generous sentiment in it," he fumed. On the whole, "Mr. Bayard offers nothing, settles much disputed points offhand in his own favour, and sets a machinery in motion by which he hopes to gain the remainder." Sir

[28] Minutes by Herbert and Stanhope on Foreign Office to Colonial Office, December 9, 1886: CO42/788.

John was more moderate than his Minister of Marine and Fisheries in his criticism, though no less unyielding. The first suggestion of a mixed commission was simply too loosely defined and before any such commission was appointed the headlands question would have to be thoroughly discussed. The second article of the proposal was "inadmissible" because the British Government could not determine the limitations on the Canadian right of seizure, it "cannot interfere with the Laws of Canada." [29]

Still, Macdonald did not reject the proposal out of hand as Foster or even Lansdowne seemed to do. His criticism, Lansdowne wrote, "is of a more constructive character [than mine]," and "we are ready to commit ourselves to accepting the commission when these points have been adjusted to our satisfaction." The principle of a joint commission was wholly satisfactory and Lansdowne did not see how Bayard could refuse to accept it. [30] The problem was what the commission should consider and what would be done about the fisheries until the commission had met. Regarding the latter, the Colonial Secretary had the answer. "The simplest and best solution of the present difficulties," Sir Henry Holland wrote Lansdowne, "might be found if both parties would agree to revert . . . at least for a term so as to admit of the discussion of the more extended commercial arrangements to the condition of things existing under the Treaty of Washington, the fishery being again thrown reciprocally open and fish and fish productions being again reciprocally admitted duty free." On 26 February 1887, Lansdowne cabled Holland that Canada

[29] Macdonald Papers, 86, Lansdowne to Macdonald, December 25, 1886, Foster to Macdonald, December 26, 1886; 527, Macdonald to Lansdowne, December 28, 1886. He added that "the covering letter of Mr. Bayard to Mr. Phelps is so obviously uncandid and onesided that it is almost a waste of time to dissect it."

[30] *ibid.*, 86, Lansdowne to Macdonald, December 29, 1886; 87, Lansdowne to Macdonald, January 6, 1887.

accepted the suggestion. And on 24 March Lord Salisbury suggested the same to the American Government through Henry White in London.[31] For weeks the Canadian and British Governments waited patiently for an answer.

Bayard was in the midst of his old difficulties. Phelps was his same truculent self in London, bills for retaliatory action against Canada were being aired almost daily in Congress and even the Secretary of State himself seemed to become impatient at what he regarded as Canadian obstruction to Anglo-American amiability. However, there were parties in the United States and Canada who were urging Bayard to move in the opposite direction. As shall be noted later, they were more interested in a sweeping commercial treaty than in a fisheries agreement *per se* but their efforts apparently aided in forwarding the latter arrangement. Principal among them was the President of the Canadian Club in New York City, Erastus Wiman, who suggested to Bayard the desirability of informal talks with the Canadian Government. The idea was accepted by the Secretary of State and also by the Canadian Government. In May Sir Charles Tupper traveled to Washington.[32]

The short but friendly Tupper-Bayard conversations ranged widely over the whole scope of Canadian-American relations. Both men seemed to view the fisheries dispute as but a part of a much larger commercial problem and both were anxious to have a settlement encompassing the larger problem. Shortly after Tupper's return to Ottawa an exchange of letters appeared to sweep away the animosity that had been building up for the past few years and pave the way for a settlement.

[31] *ibid.*, 87, Holland to Lansdowne, February 24, 1887, Lansdowne to Holland, February 26, 1887; Tansill, *Canadian-American Relations,* p. 53.

[32] Tansill, *Canadian-American Relations,* p. 54; Macdonald Papers, 87, Lansdowne to Macdonald, May 17, 1887. See also Sir Charles Tupper, *Recollections of Sixty Years in Canada,* London, 1914, pp. 176 ff.

Bayard shrewdly opened the correspondence by appealing to Tupper's strong nationalistic sentiment. He noted, "the gradual practical emancipation of Canada from the control of the mother country" and hinted that "awkwardness of this imperfectly developed sovereignty" which was felt most strongly by the United States might be alleviated by direct Canadian-American negotiations. "The commercial intercourse between the inhabitants of Canada and those of the United States has grown into too vast proportions to be exposed much longer to this wordy triangular duel, and more direct and responsible methods should be resorted to." The question of the day was, of course, the fisheries. Indeed, it had been the *"questio vexata"* of Canadian-American relations ever since the Convention of 1818 had been signed. Bayard seemed willing to view its solution in a broader scope which appealed immensely to the Canadians. There was, he said, "but one way" to "attain a just and permanent settlement"; "a straight forward treatment on a liberal and statesmanlike plan of the entire commercial relations of the two countries." He concluded by noting that Canada and the United States stood "at the parting of the ways," one leading to hostility, the other to lasting friendship. He was prepared to meet authorized "agents" of the British Government to prepare "for a settlement of all differences." [33]

Tupper's reply was enthusiastic. The Governor-General, he noted, "will at once bring the matter before the Secretary of State, with an expression of his hope that no time will be lost in taking steps" toward an agreement. And the Colonial Office was as pleased to see the correspondence as the Canadians

[33] Macdonald Papers, 174, Bayard to Tupper, May 31, 1887. Significantly, Bayard wrote: "I say commercial [relations] because I do not propose to include, however indirectly, or by any intendment, however partial or oblique, the political relations of Canada and the United States, nor to effect the legislative independence of either country."

had been. John Anderson guessed that Canadian manufacturers would hesitate at the phrase "entire commercial relations" and "the English manufacturers will for once be on the same side as their Colonial brethren." "But," he added, "Canada must be allowed to manage her own affairs in her own way and the removal of the 'open sore' . . . will be one enormous gain." As the Governor-General told Macdonald, "H.M's Govt. was ready to jump at the idea of a commission such as that which Mr. Bayard appears to have proposed. We shall now have an opportunity of testing his *bona fides.*" [34]

The United States Government formally accepted the proposal of a commission in August and the date for the meeting was set for the first week in November. Once again, as two years before, the work of detailed planning began. The main outline—"our inshore fisheries," Macdonald now wrote, for "the admission free of duty of some of [our] natural products in addition to free fish"—was the same as before and always would be Canada's goal. But there were other questions. Should the Pacific fisheries be included? The British Columbia Government replied in the affirmative. No mention would be made of the Hudson's Bay fisheries because "the U.S. would at once consider this as an admission that they had *some* rights there." Then, of course, there was the Behring Sea dispute; "The question is a 'burning one' and should be included." On the other hand the Canadians recognized that inclusion of the Behring Sea dispute might be dangerous. "If the Americans insist on their exclusive claims," Macdonald wrote, "it may break up the whole arrangement." [35] The Canadians

[34] *ibid.,* Tupper to Bayard, June 6, 1887; Minutes by Anderson and Herbert on Governor-General to Colonial Office, June 9, 1887: CO42/790; Macdonald Papers, 87, Lansdowne to Macdonald, July 21, 1887.

[35] Tupper Papers, 6, Nelson to Secretary of State, Canada, October 3, 1887; 8, Herbert to Tupper, August 30, 1887; Macdonald Papers, 527, Macdonald to Lansdowne, September 1 and 12, 1887.

tried desperately to get a specific mention of the dispute into the terms of reference.[36] But the effort failed, chiefly because of Salisbury's substantial agreement with Macdonald's point that it might endanger the whole commission. Besides, there was a good deal of common sense in the Colonial Office opinion that it would be much better for Canada to *insist* on the United States' giving up her claim "to exclusive control rather than make the affair a matter of negotiation and compromise." "The matter will be settled once for all," the argument ran, "if we persist in the demand for compensation for seizures." [37]

Bayard, William L. Putnam, an international lawyer, and James B. Angell, President of the University of Michigan, were the American members on the Commission. Sir Lionel Sackville West and Joseph Chamberlain were the British representatives. Tupper and Lansdowne both thought highly of the appointment of the Birmingham industrialist and politician. But Macdonald thought the British side weak; he had a "lively recollection" of the wily Americans who sat on the 1871 Joint High Commission. Moreover, he did not trust Chamberlain. "His School has never been friendly to Colonial interests & in his ambitious desire to succeed in affecting a Treaty of some kind he will be likely to concede much rather than return to England *re infecta.*" Clearly it was up to the Canadians to provide the "muscle" on the British side.

Macdonald had decided one point: "I hope that no legal man will come out from England . . . Thompson knows the legal bearings on the questions which will affect Canada . . . better than any English Counsel." [38] The Minister of Justice

---

[36] *ibid.,* 8, Tupper to Bramston, September 22, 1887, Tupper to Macdonald, September 22, 1887; Minutes on High Commissioner to Colonial Office, September 22, 1887: CO42/792.

[37] Minute on Foreign Office to Colonial Office, October 17, 1887: CO42/794.

[38] Macdonald Papers, 281, Tupper to Macdonald, September 15, 1887; 87, Lansdowne to Macdonald, August 31, 1887; 527, Macdonald to Lansdowne, September 1 and 24, and October 18, 1887.

was going South for the winter. But what of the main question? Would Macdonald be the Canadian representative as Tupper suggested? "I am very reluctant to go," he replied to the High Commissioner, "as the work may be too much for me." He did not feel strong enough to face the arduous labor of a Commissioner. In addition, the Governor-General had what he thought were better plans for his Prime Minister. It would be better, he suggested, "that you should hold yourself in reserve as there will no doubt be frequent references on the part of the Commissioners to the Canadian Government and you would very probably find that you could do more for us from your desk at Ottawa than at the table at Washington." [39] Macdonald agreed. The burden of carrying Canada's case to Washington, then, fell on the broad shoulders of Sir Charles Tupper. It was the only logical second choice. Tupper had been Macdonald's principal confidant when Macdonald was in Washington in 1871. In Canadian politics his firm and forceful speaking on the stump had earned him the title of the "Cumberland warhorse." As a diplomat he was congenial but he moved with the same resolution that had served him so well in the battles of the ballot box. "I can think of no one but [him]," said Lansdowne. "He is able and pertinacious, would speak with authority, and moreover has some claim to the vacancy from the fact that his visit to Washington was the immediate cause of the negotiations which has had this result." Tupper would go to Washington to keep Mr. Chamberlain "up to the mark." [40]

[39] ibid., 527, Macdonald to Tupper, September 12, 1887, Macdonald to Lansdowne, October 3, 1887, Lansdowne to Macdonald, August 31, 1887.
[40] ibid., Lansdowne to Macdonald, August 31, 1887.

CHAPTER III
Tupper, Chamberlain, and the Americans

NINETEENTH CENTURY diplomacy was conducted in the grand style. The successful diplomat needed to be a cultured man who could "float a treaty" on a sea of champagne and witty conversation. That Lord Elgin had such qualities largely accounted for his success in negotiating the Reciprocity Treaty of 1854. And thirty-three years later the same qualities were demanded of Tupper and Chamberlain. Handsome Joseph Chamberlain, widowed and eligible, was the absolute lion of the Washington social season of 1887-1888. A Miss Tiffany from Baltimore summed up the Capitol's impression of him when she exclaimed, "Why! I guess he is just lovely!" [1] Sir Charles Tupper and John Thompson spent their evenings at the theater with some of Washington's glamorous ladies.[2] But attention to the ladies was only part of the task of winning Washington society. The British Commissioners gave one of the most impressive and sumptuous dinners seen in years to their American counterparts. And the fourth estate was treated to a modern-day press conference replete with cigars and "bottles of various kinds with favourite labels on them" just half-an-hour after the Commissioners arrived in Washington. Lillian Russell played in "Dorothy" at the National; Mrs. Langtry starred in "As in a Looking Glass" at Albaugh's; the child prodigy, Josef Hofman, delighted his audience at the Arlington; and the beautiful young Mrs. Cleveland proved to be a smashing success as a hostess when she entertained 4,000 guests at a State recep-

---

[1] Sir Willoughby Maycock, *With Mr. Chamberlain in the United States and Canada, 1887-88*, Toronto, 1914, p. 50. An excellent description of the "social life" that accompanied the diplomacy is found in this otherwise uninformative book.

[2] See Thompson Papers, 290.

tion. But the British Commissioners received more acclaim than all the rest. During Chamberlain's last week in Washington a society editor regretfully wrote:

Never has there been such a diner out, and a giver of dinners, in this town as the gentleman who is going back in a few days to his seat in the House of Commons. To him chiefly is it attributable that the present winter has been the greatest season for dinner parties that Washington has ever known.[3]

The art of diplomacy did have its lighter moments.

ii

Despite the enjoyment of the Washington social season, the business of the Joint High Commission of 1887-1888 was a serious affair for all parties in the North Atlantic triangle. The American Commissioners had to contend with obstruction from a hostile Senate.[4] The British Commissioners were charged to heal the "open sore" in Anglo-American relations. And Tupper had to protect his country's rights and privileges from surrender without fair compensation.

For the Canadians, the key to the success or failure of the negotiations was the Birmingham politician. Tupper had been convinced in the months preceding the meeting of the Commission that he had won Chamberlain over to the Canadian point of view. But Tupper's task was to keep him in line once he landed on American soil. Tupper had strong backing from Ottawa. During the few days he stayed in New York City before going to Washington to begin his work, Chamberlain received two stern letters from the Governor-General. Lord Lansdowne urged that some settlement be made regarding the headlands controversy. To his logical mind this was of prime importance for "how," he asked, "can a give and

[3] Maycock, *With Mr. Chamberlain,* pp. 150-51.
[4] University of Birmingham Library, Chamberlain Papers, North American Diary, November 23, 1887.

take bargain be concluded unless each side knows what is its own?" But of even greater importance was the necessity for Chamberlain to stand firm on the Canadian view of the Convention of 1818. Its provisions were "an anachronism, but there they are." "Our people," he added, "will regard with great jealousy [sic] any inclination on the part of the Imperial Govt. to call in question the validity of the Convention of 1818." [5] Not only was the Canadian stand correct; it was also effective. "After trespassing fishermen became convinced that we were in earnest, they ceased to frequent our waters and the seizures fell off," wrote Lansdowne. To "climb down" now "would be bitterly resented especially in the Maritime Provinces." [6]

Chamberlain at first seemed to be encouraged by his reception in New York. He wrote to the Governor-General that "the Fishery Question *per se* is of small importance & . . . it will not be allowed to interfere seriously with good relations." But his attitude had changed considerably when he reported to Lord Salisbury a few days later. It was true that only "a few fishmongers & fishermen" really cared about the matter. But he had become disturbed by the fact that " 'it is a sop question for politicians to play with,' and each side will try to make party advantage of it." Also annoying was Bayard's "somewhat anomalous position" with the Senate. But the greatest danger came from reports about the hoped-for

[5] *ibid.*, Lansdowne to Chamberlain, November 8, 1887.

[6] *ibid.*, Lansdowne to Chamberlain, November 8 and 14, 1887. "In the Maritime Provinces the apprehension is I think very deep seated. They have had a very successful fishing season, the Americans have had a bad one, our police arrangements are working well and smoothly. 'Let us keep our own and we shall be content' is I fancy the thought uppermost in the minds of many of them. The permanent alienation of their fishery rights *or the abandonment of any of the restrictions without which those rights cease to be valuable* would scarcely be tolerated except for a compensation entirely adequate to the concession made." Lansdowne Papers, Lansdowne to Holland, October 12, 1887.

commercial negotiations. The "fish interest" was itself small but the "Protectionist feeling of the country . . . recognizes that the whole system hangs together & that the edifice is in danger if a single brick is removed." Rumors were current in New York that "Mr. Bayard has given up the idea of proposing any commercial equivalent for Canadian Rights & that he proposes only to discuss the convention suggested by Mr. Phelps for the interpretation and execution of the Treaty of 1818." This would be nothing less than a breach of faith, Chamberlain concluded, "entirely inconsistent with Mr. Bayard's letter to Sir Charles Tupper on the faith of which the Plenipotentiaries were appointed." [7]

With stern warnings from Lansdowne in his mind and fears and misgivings about the approaching negotiations, Joseph Chamberlain joined his Canadian colleagues and entrained for Washington.

iii

The introductions and pleasantries having been dispensed with, the members of the Joint High Commission settled down to work on 22 November 1887. Chamberlain's fears were immediately confirmed. He noted that the British Government had assumed the Commission would act along the lines of the Bayard-Tupper correspondence without recurring

[7] *ibid.,* Chamberlain to Lansdowne, November 10, 1887, Chamberlain to Salisbury, November 18, 1887. Replying to an earlier letter on the very same day Salisbury wrote to Chamberlain: "I am glad . . . the drift of American opinion is against purchasing fishery rights by any large tariff concessions. The embarrassement [sic] to England would be very serious if the contingency you forecasted—a commercial union —should take place. Sentiment and obvious interest, here, would be put into sharp opposition to each other & some very inconsistent & untenable compromise would probably result. But I suppose some fiscal bargain is what the Canadian Government is chiefly looking to." Salisbury to Chamberlain, November 18, 1887.

to the disputed interpretations of the Convention of 1818. In other words, the contentious convention would be swept out of the discussion on the tide of good feeling that would result from a broad commercial agreement. But Bayard was by no means convinced of this. He laid emphasis on the terms of reference agreed upon after the exchange of correspondence, and more especially on the first part of the terms which dealt with the Convention of 1818. Sir Charles Tupper angrily replied that "if the proposal of the United States had been understood to mean only a review of the Convention of 1818 it would never have been accepted." Chamberlain moderately but firmly intervened. Pressing his point home, he asked Bayard whether a renewal of the Treaty of 1854 came within the powers of the American plenipotentiaries. As far as the British were concerned the question was simply rhetorical. But they were astounded by Bayard's vague reply that if such a proposal were made the American plenipotentiaries "could then ascertain whether their Powers sufficed to enable them to deal with it." [8] What the Americans were really interested in was a reinterpretation of the Convention of 1818 which would afford to American fishing vessels the complete commercial privileges they demanded in Canadian ports. In return, the United States would offer a possibility of lowering the duties on some Canadian goods—in particular coal, lumber, fish, iron, and copper ores—by Congressional action.[9]

The possibility of lower American duties could reasonably

[8] Macdonald Papers, 178, Commission Proceedings, November 22, 1887.

[9] *ibid.*, 176, telegram, Tupper to Macdonald, November 24, 1887. Salt and wool were added to the list in the telegram, same to same, of the following day. These suggestions were made to Tupper in conversations with Speaker Carlisle of the House of Representatives. Only the vague mention of a possible lowering of duties was made in the Commission meetings.

be expected. It was a well-known fact that the Cleveland administration strongly desired a reduction in the American protective tariff. And it was common knowledge that Roger Q. Mills's bill embodying tariff reductions was going to be introduced in the next Congressional session.[10] The American stand was really quite simple and probably justified under the circumstances. The administration was pledged to tariff reform. But the Republican-controlled Senate had declared war to the death on Cleveland and all his works. A treaty which touched the pocketbook of the American Government did not stand the slightest chance of Senate approval; however, Congressional action against the protective tariff which incidentally benefitted Canadian products might weather the storm in the "cave of the winds." In fact, Bayard seemed to have no alternative which he could have put before the Commission.

But it was equally natural that the Canadians were shocked by the about-face from the Bayard-Tupper letters. The first shock was accompanied by a sense of near disbelief. "I cannot understand," Thompson wrote to Macdonald, "why they have opened battle on this line as it is the one which will be most tedious and can lead to nothing." Macdonald seemed to have expected the reversal from the very start of negotiations. "All our prognostications as to the course of the U. States Govt. are more than verified and Mr. Bayard does not come out of it in a very creditable manner." "It is a pity," he continued, in a note to Lansdowne, "that H.M. Govt wouldn't listen to our request to have the question of Commercial intercourse specially mentioned as a subject of reference in the agreement for a Conference." The Prime Minister was far from sanguine as to the results. "It will end in a bust up," he told Foster. And he warned Tupper that he should

[10] H. Wayne Morgan, "The Congressional Career of William McKinley," Ph.D. Thesis, University of California at Los Angeles, 1960, pp. 104-10.

68

"take care that if there is a final break the onus will fall on the United States and not on the British negotiators." [11]

The wrangling continued in Washington but Tupper was not as convinced as was Macdonald of an inevitable "bust up." There was yet a spark of hope in Bayard's suggestion at the first day's meeting that the British submit a proposal along the lines of the Treaty of 1854. The Americans had not rejected the idea out of hand; rather, they had in effect said "wait and see if we can consider it." With this in mind Chamberlain and his Canadian colleagues labored over two alternative proposals to put to the Americans. The first, submitted at the fourth meeting on 3 December, accepted Bayard's challenge: it proposed that in return for granting the fishery privileges in the Treaty of Washington, 1871, consideration be given to "a mutual arrangement providing for a greater freedom of commercial intercourse between the U.S. and Canada." Of course the second alternative proposal was held back on the slim hope that the Americans would return to the generous lines of the Bayard-Tupper correspondence. But Tupper wired his chief suggesting that American fishing vessels might have commercial privileges in Canadian ports by taking out a license "and paying a substantial fee therefore." The license fee would be waived if the United States made fish, fish oil, whale and seal oil from Canada and Newfoundland duty free. Finally, the United States would have to renounce the privilege of taking, drying, and curing fish on the treaty shores of Newfoundland, Labrador and the Magdalen Islands. [12]

The pessimistic Prime Minister replied that he believed

[11] Macdonald Papers, 176, Thompson to Macdonald, November 28, 1887, Macdonald to Foster, November 25, 1887; 527, Macdonald to Tupper, November 25, 1887, Macdonald to Lansdowne, November 30, 1887. See also 87, Lansdowne to Macdonald, November 30, 1887.

[12] *ibid.*, 178, Commission Proceedings, December 3, 1887; 176, telegram, Tupper to Macdonald, December 3, 1887.

"your proposition as already made will be rejected . . . & is made only for the purpose of throwing the onus of failure in coming to an arrangement on the American PPs." The prediction was true. On 7 December Bayard told the British Commissioners that after careful consideration the Americans had decided not even to bother to ask the President for authority to consider the British proposal. Their reason was quite clear. The proposal, he said, "would necessitate an adjustment of the present tariff of the United States by Congressional action, which adjustment, the American Plenipotentiaries consider to be manifestly impracticable of accomplishing through the medium of a treaty, under the circumstances now existing." Chamberlain rather irately replied that the situation was thus "very critical" and he and his colleagues, he added, might have "to consider whether they must leave at once and await the result of Congressional action on the tariff." [13]

Preliminary skirmishes were now over. The crisis in the diplomatic battle was at hand. Would the British abandon the Commission or would they submit the alternate proposal? At this point the place of decision shifted suddenly from Washington to Ottawa and, though the Commission did not end its work in Washington for another two months, in truth the fundamental decisions were made in Ottawa. For the moment the British Commissioners would neither retreat nor submit their second proposal. Rather, they adopted Lansdowne's suggestion of a tactical withdrawal. It was decided that an adjournment would give everyone "time to recover their breath and temper" and, more important, the Commis-

---

[13] *ibid.*, 527, Macdonald to Tupper, December 7, 1887; 178, Commission Proceedings, December 7, 1887. This produced a sharp reply from Lansdowne. "How Bayard can without blushing," he wrote Macdonald, "after all that took place between himself & Sir C. Tupper, state gravely that he cannot discuss commercial relations . . . passes my comprehension." 87, Lansdowne to Macdonald, December 10, 1887.

sioners would go to Ottawa "to review the situation calmly in consultation with both Imperial & Canadian Govts." [14]

Before leaving Washington, however, it was decided that Chamberlain should visit Bayard and privately mention the essential features of the second proposal.[15] On 10 December, Chamberlain read the proposal to the Secretary of State. The latter immediately rejected the idea of giving up American rights on the "treaty shores" of Newfoundland, Labrador, and the Magdalen Islands. He admitted the rights were of no value and "constituted an irritating invasion of the sovereignty of a practically independent state," but he simply could not get Congressional approval of such a plan. Still, Bayard received the whole of the proposal very favorably, and especially the license scheme. In fact, recognizing its limited nature, he wished to expand on the British suggestion. After all, the proposal left some fundamental problems unsettled. Bayard thus suggested a commission to settle the limits of territorial waters and the headlands question and to determine methods of jurisdiction and reasonable penalties for the same. The commission would be guided by the North Sea Convention of 1879 (which used the ten-mile basis for the headlands question) and certain bays such as Baie de Chaleurs would be

[14] *ibid.*, 527, Macdonald to Tupper, December 8, 1887; 178, Commission Proceedings, December 10, 1887. By now Thompson was completely discouraged. He wrote to his wife that the Commissioners were leaving Washington "nominally for a recess for Christmas—really not to return." Thompson Papers, 290, Thompson to Mrs. Thompson, December 9, 1887.

[15] There is considerable disagreement as to who made this suggestion. Tupper claimed credit for it but Chamberlain wrote to Salisbury that he and West had some difficulty in convincing Tupper that it was a wise idea. John Thompson, who lost no love for Tupper, in his letters to his wife recounts many instances where Tupper and Chamberlain each claimed responsibility for a minor diplomatic victory. See Chamberlain Papers, Chamberlain to Salisbury, December 11, 1887; Macdonald Papers, 176, Tupper to Macdonald, December 10, 1887.

agreed beforehand to be wholly within Canadian territory. Further, the United States would absolutely renounce the privilege of fishing in Canadian territorial waters. And finally, in concurrence with the British proposal, the "ordinary privileges of commercial intercourse would be extended to American fishing vessels in Canadian ports and Canadian fish, fish oil, whale and seal oil would be granted free admission into the United States." [16] Bayard cautioned Chamberlain that he could not, of course, speak for anyone other than himself about such an arrangement although he thought it favorable. Upon his suggestion Chamberlain also discussed the Bayard proposal with the President who gave his approval. The President and the Secretary of State seemed to have agreed on a workable plan. Whether the Senate would was another question. Even more important, could Chamberlain sell the proposal to Macdonald and his colleagues? As he wrote to Salisbury, "There may still be 'many a slip 'twixt the cup and the lip.'" [17]

iv

The alternative British proposal met with a mixed reception at Ottawa. Macdonald wrote to Tupper that the discussion in council "differed much," adding, "the G.G. as you know doesn't like it." But Lansdowne admitted to Macdonald that "I should be disposed to go great lengths in order to convict our opponents of unreasonableness and to carry British opinion

[16] Chamberlain Papers, Chamberlain to Salisbury, December 11, 1887. Macdonald was also concerned about the limitations of the proposal and insisted in his letters to Tupper that the inshore fisheries, territorial jurisdiction and headlands question all had to be settled. See especially Macdonald Papers, 527, Macdonald to Tupper, December 8 and 9, 1887.

[17] Macdonald Papers, 176, memoranda by Chamberlain in Tupper to Macdonald, January 25, 1888; Chamberlain Papers, Chamberlain to Salisbury, December 11, 1887.

with us." [18] Within the Council there was less inclination to be at all conciliatory. On 8 December, when the question was voted upon, only four, Langevin, White, Chapleau, and Macdonald, favored the suggestion. The remaining five, Pope, McLelan, Costigan, Bowell, and Carling, notably from the Maritime Provinces and Ontario, rejected the proposal. Macdonald hurriedly wrote Tupper that the decision rested upon himself and his two colleagues in Washington, Thompson and Foster. (The three were all Maritimers.) Their assent was given and only then, on 10 December, could Chamberlain pay his informal visit to Bayard.

With difficulty the British Commissioners had hurdled the first Ottawa opposition to their plan. During his visit to Ottawa it became evident to Chamberlain that even more effort would have to be expended to get agreement on Bayard's more comprehensive counter suggestion. Fortunately, there was no opposition from home; Salisbury was leaving the matter completely in the hands of his plenipotentiary and the Canadians. He was, in fact, quite pleased with Bayard's proposals. "From our point of view," he wrote, "they have the double merit that they take the thorn out & that they do not meddle with a larger surface than is necessary for that purpose." The British Prime Minister was not at all displeased by the lack of any large commercial arrangement. "I am rather apprehensive," he continued, "of ambitious schemes in dealing with this question. The position of England towards Canada is so unexampled—so anomalous—so eccentric—that any larger measure affecting the position of Canada may open for us wholly unexpected embarrassements [sic]." [19] A neat little treaty that removed the "open sore" of the fisheries was just the order of the day; an "ambitious" treaty might mean discrimination in Canada against English goods, dis-

[18] *ibid.*, 527, Macdonald to Tupper, December 8, 1887; 87, Lansdowne to Macdonald, December 9, 1887.

[19] Chamberlain Papers, Salisbury to Chamberlain, December 31, 1887.

rupting the Imperial relationship and leading to all sorts of unwanted questions to Salisbury in the House of Lords.

The Canadians were not so placid about their rights. They had desperately wanted an ambitious treaty, though a renewal of the Treaty of 1854, even with some extensions, would not have discriminated against British manufactures. That having been refused, many members of the Government were anxious to extract their pound of flesh in any other way possible. It was rather distressing to Chamberlain to find that he was not hailed on arrival as the great peacemaker. Rather, there was more than a little doubt and suspicion displayed towards him by the Canadians. As Macdonald had told Tupper early in December, "Chamberlain must not be in too great a hurry to get away." [20]

Chamberlain found that Macdonald and Lansdowne "both cordially approve the basis of settlement." But the other members of the Canadian Government were much more difficult to deal with. They wanted to get the best possible terms out of what they considered to be a poor bargain and they concentrated their efforts on the fee for the licenses to be issued to American fishing vessels. The British delegate was convinced that one dollar per registered ton was the highest possible fair fee. An equal amount would be sufficient penalty for purchasing supplies or transshipping without such a license. At the end of December he angrily wrote to Lansdowne that he had received a letter from Tupper "in which he says that the Council require that the licence fee shall be $1.50 per ton and that the penalty . . . shd. be $2.00 per ton. After his conversation with me at Govt. House this change of front is really a breach of faith." "I am annoyed," he continued, "that Tupper should think me a fit subject for such a bit of sharp practice." Moreover, he could not believe that Macdonald "wd. make himself a party to such a shabby transaction." "I

[20] Macdonald Papers, 527, Macdonald to Tupper, December 8, 1887.

agreed to $1 a ton," he concluded, "altho' I thought £10 wd. be ample as a maximum penalty, but what I chiefly complain of is that Tupper shd. persuade the Council to overrule our agreement the moment my back is turned." [21]

Lansdowne replied that he too was "vexed" at the disposition of Council to recede from Chamberlain's suggestion. But he went on patiently to explain to the British plenipotentiary the intricacies of parliamentary government in Canada. It was obvious that Macdonald and Tupper could not commit the whole cabinet and "at a full meeting very strong objections were raised to the $1 fee and . . . the malcontents pressed hard for $2; the discussion ended by 'splitting the difference' and asking for $1.50." He added that Tupper had "stood up loyally" for Chamberlain's proposal "so . . . you may dismiss from your mind the idea that he has played fast and loose with you." Still the problem remained. "A very low license fee without limitations as to time might in fact act as an inducement to the U.S. *not* to put fish on the free list and to be content with the cheap privileges which they would enjoy by license," Lansdowne told Lord Salisbury.[22]

The Prime Minister and the Governor-General agreed that it was foolish to jeopardize the whole negotiation for $5,000.[23] Still there were two other considerations with which Mac-

[21] Chamberlain Papers, Chamberlain to Salisbury, December 22, 1887, Chamberlain to Lansdowne, December 31, 1887.

[22] *ibid.*, Lansdowne to Chamberlain, January 3, 1888; Salisbury Papers, Lansdowne to Salisbury, January 15, 1888.

[23] This would be approximately the amount of additional revenue that would accrue to the Canadian Government from a license fee of $1.50 per ton rather than $1.00 per ton. There is no evidence to suggest that Bayard and Chamberlain had discussed any fee for the fishing vessels. On the contrary, the $1.00 per ton was what Chamberlain himself felt a sufficient fee and hence the only point at stake in this rather foolish dispute was Chamberlain's own judgment about a problem of which he was totally uninformed until he had been appointed to the Commission.

donald and Tupper were concerned, considerations which Chamberlain as a skilled politician should have recognized. First, a principle and a valuable national asset were being bargained for a price which would have to appear just to all Canadians. The second was what was politically possible for a government that drew heavy support from the provinces directly affected by any settlement. Thus, wrote Lansdowne, Macdonald

> is evidently uneasy as to the manner in which the proposal will be regarded in the Maritime Provinces. I remember telling you that most of the fishermen would ask for nothing better than the failure of the conference and the retention of the advantage which they now enjoy under a strict monopoly of the inshore fisheries. The introduction of the license system would be regarded by them as an encroachment on that monopoly and it will be difficult to induce them to look at the matter from the broader point of view of Imperial interest.

The Governor-General assured Chamberlain that he would see the Ministers involved and "press them very hard . . . to clear this detail out of the way." [24]

Tupper and Chamberlain returned to Washington but the matter was not settled immediately. Strangely enough the two leading "malcontents" were Thompson and Foster who had been in Washington from the start of the negotiations. Behind them they carried, as Lansdowne wrote Chamberlain, a "party . . . stronger in the Cabinet than I had imagined." Thompson's complaint was soundly based on the lack

[24] Chamberlain Papers, Lansdowne to Chamberlain, January 3, 1888. Chamberlain apparently profited little from this lecture on Canadian politics and government. He replied that he was pleased that Tupper had not "crossed" him but "it is difficult," he added, "for an outsider to believe that 2 such men as Sir John Macdonald and Sir Charles would have serious difficulty in securing the assent of the rest of their cabinet to an arrangement freely accepted by themselves."

of definition of time in the proposal itself. He was quite prepared to accept the one dollar fee "but thought that steps should be taken to prevent our being saddled with a ton fee for all time or for a long period of years in the event of our failing to get free fish either by Treaty or by the voluntary action of Congress." In other words, a low fee was a concession which should be given only for such a period of time as would allow the United States to abolish the duties on Canadian fish and for no longer. It was a reasonable objection and Lansdowne did not "anticipate much difficulty from him." "Foster was much stiffer." "He was full of the advantages of the status quo and admitted frankly that he disliked the idea of licences." Even at $1.50 per ton the yield would only be about $33,000 and this "was ridiculously out of proportion to the value of the concession of commercial privileges, & the House of Commons and fishermen would never stand it." But Lansdowne pressed the Minister of Marine and Fisheries "and he ended by telling me that altho' he felt very strongly on the subject he would not risk the failure of the negotiations." [25]

When the Commission meetings resumed on 9 January the British plenipotentiaries submitted their proposal (substantially the Chamberlain-Bayard informal agreement) to the Commission. But no mention was made of a license fee. Rather, free licenses would be given to American fishing vesels allowing them commercial privileges in Canadian ports in return for the free entry of Canadian fish into United States markets. Chamberlain explained this rather shrewd plan in a letter to Salisbury. Mention of the license fee might jeopardize the Treaty in the Senate. The treaty, then, would only include the exchange of commercial privileges for free fish with the other necessary clauses dealing with territorial

[25] *ibid.,* Lansdowne to Chamberlain, January 4, 1888. See also Macdonald Papers, 88, Lansdowne to Macdonald, January 4, 1888; 527, Macdonald to Tupper, January 5, 1888.

jurisdiction and headlands arbitration. But, should the Treaty be delayed, or rejected, the Commissioners would also initial an executive agreement which would provide a temporary solution to the fishery problem that "would not necessarily require the sanction of Congress." The *modus vivendi* would bind the Governments of the North Atlantic triangle "for a limited period . . . to accept as a solution the system of licences to be issued by the Canadian Govt. on payment; and that such licences should confer the privileges of obtaining bait, ice, and supplies—and of transshipping catch." [26] The arrangement admirably met the complaints of both Foster and Thompson.

This, in fact, was the general outline of the agreement eventually reached by the Commission. There was, of course, much heated discussion in the meetings before the settlement was made. The first reply by the Americans to the British proposal included a demand that the Canadians also allow American fishermen to fish the Canadian inshore waters. Tupper and Chamberlain nearly exploded with anger, for the Americans had consistently noted in the discussions that they no longer desired this privilege. Bayard and his colleagues rather sheepishly withdrew the tattered remains of their suggestion for reconsideration.[27] Finally on 23 January the British proposal was accepted as the "general line" of a treaty and *modus vivendi* and serious work began on the detailed wording of the Treaty.[28]

[26] Macdonald Papers, 176, Tupper to Macdonald, January 10, 1888; 178, Commission Proceedings, January 9, 1888; Chamberlain Papers, Chamberlain to Salisbury, January 12, 1888.

[27] Macdonald Papers, 178, Commission Proceedings, January 18 and 21, 1888. John Thompson was led to remark to his wife that "Yankee politicians are the lowest race of thieves in existence." Thompson Papers, 290, Thompson to Mrs. Thompson, January 16, 1888.

[28] Macdonald Papers, 178, Commission Proceedings, January 23, 1888 and following.

On 16 January the Governor-General wrote to Chamberlain expressing his pleasure that the latter had "been able to establish a modus vivendi with *us*." "You need not apprehend any trouble on our side upon points of detail." But unfortunately, Anglo-Canadian difficulties did arise once again when the Canadians stubbornly adhered to their rights during the final exhausting days of negotiation. The dispute was reminiscent of the difficulties Macdonald faced in the negotiations of 1871. Chamberlain believed—upon faulty and hasty advice given by his Foreign Office adviser, Mr. Bergne—that the Canadians could not demand licenses for the privilege of transshipping the catches from American fishing vessels in Canadian ports. Rather, he was inclined to think that such transshipments were already permitted under the general transshipment of goods article, Article XXIX, of the Treaty of Washington, 1871. He further believed that if the Canadians insisted on their fallacious demand that licenses were necessary, the Americans would then denounce Article XXIX and all transshipment privileges to both countries would be lost.[29]

John Thompson, who thought of Bergne as "not a lawyer at all but a factotum merely for Chamberlain," was convinced that the plain wording of Article I of the Convention of 1818 proved the British plenipotentiary to be wrong. In fact, Chamberlain's "notions . . . were silly in the extreme" and a rather heated debate took place between Chamberlain and Tupper and Thompson. After the exchange Chamberlain wired home for an opinion on the point. Salisbury's telegraphed reply could not have been more straightforward: Article XXIX did not apply to transshipment of catch. "The U.S. fishing boats are entitled to enter these ports for shelter, repairing damages, purchasing wood and obtaining water, and for no other pur-

[29] Chamberlain Papers, Lansdowne to Chamberlain, January 16, 1888; Macdonald Papers, 176, telegram, Tupper to Macdonald, January 22, 1888.

poses whatever." [30] Thompson gleefully told his wife, "Chamberlain got a bad settling yesterday . . . he thought to get an opinion which would shut me up but he got shut up himself." [31]

As the meeting moved into its final days of negotiations the last round of dinners and teas seemed to calm the irritated nerves of the Commissioners. Only John Thompson remained heartily discouraged by the long months of weary labor. "I hope to leave Washington soon—and forever," he wrote to Macdonald. But Tupper's reaction was more characteristic of that of the other five negotiators. "I need not enumerate the great advantages this Treaty will give us," he told the Canadian Prime Minister. "I hope it may be ratified by the Senate but even should that be delayed much will have been gained by our having come to an agreement. When I think of the great difficulties we have had to encounter I cannot but congratulate myself upon a result that I believe will be most beneficial to Canada." [32] At last, on 15 February 1888 Tupper wired that the Treaty had been signed at seven in the evening. Canadian fishermen would have the same commercial privileges in American ports that American fishermen had in Canadian ports. The Treaty itself would be permanent—the territorial jursdiction and headlands problems would finally be settled forever. Only the contingent clause regarding the exchange of commercial privileges for free fish was not perma-

[30] Chamberlain Papers, Salisbury to Chamberlain, January 24, 1888.

[31] Thompson Papers, 290, Thompson to Mrs. Thompson, January 25, 1888. The intensity of the negotiations and the frayed personal relationships that resulted are clearly revealed in the following passage from the same letter. "The best part of the incident yesterday I forgot. T [upper] explained it to the company at dinner thus: That *he* and C. had differed as to the point and that the English Law Officers had sustained *his* opinion! We should be humble in the presence of such gifts!"

[32] Macdonald Papers, 176, Thompson to Macdonald, February 11, 1888; 177, Tupper to Macdonald, February 10, 1888.

nent and would come to an end if the American Government ever adopted a retaliatory policy of commercial noninter-course. The *modus vivendi,* finally, was also agreed upon on the terms the British had suggested and it would be valid for two years.

Neither side had received all that it desired. This had been expected. The Canadians had wanted a broad commer-cial agreement, in effect, a renewal of the Treaty of 1854. But the declining importance of the Canadian inshore fisheries to American fishermen, regardless of the other difficulties of making a treaty affecting the American tariff, made the Cana-dian desire an impossible one. Still, a renunciation by the Americans of their privileges to fish the inshore waters was a major concession and was, perhaps, as valuable as a renewal of the Treaty of 1854 might have been. Once the hope for an "ambitious" treaty had gone, a successful settlement was so much the closer to accomplishment. All parties, Canadian, British, and American, were agreed on the necessity of de-limiting the Canadian inshore waters and establishing without question an agreement as to what bays on the Canadian coast were exclusively within those waters. Everyone also agreed that the provisions of the first article of the Convention of 1818 were outmoded and nearly inhuman—as Lansdowne had put it: "an anachronism." The Treaty of 1888 did away with the "anachronism" by providing, in Sir Charles Tupper's words, "right of purchasing supplies only such as humanity would compel us to grant" in return for the free admission of Canadian fishery products into the American market. Joseph Chamberlain gave the best summary of the Treaty of 1888 in a single sentence to Lord Salisbury. "In fact it secures the recognition of all the essential rights of the Canadians while at the same time it binds them not to construe these rights in a spirit of hostility and exasperation." [33]

[33] *ibid.,* 177, Tupper to Macdonald, February 13, 1888; Chamberlain Papers, Chamberlain to Salisbury, February 16, 1888.

V

Sir Charles Tupper opened the debate on the Fisheries Treaty in the House of Commons on 10 April 1888 with a detailed explanation of the clauses of the treaty. He was especially forceful in his elaboration of the benefits which would accrue to the Dominion through the United States' renunciation of its privilege to fish the Canadian inshore waters. With the recent innovations in the fishing industry, particularly the purse seine net, unlimited and uncontrolled access to the inshore fisheries might have rapidly destroyed their value as a national asset. That possibility had now been prevented. Tupper explained how urgently he and his fellow commissioners had pressed for a broad commercial agreement and how their effort had failed.[34] John Thompson covered much of the same terrain and told why he supported the treaty. It was not, he said, because the United States had made all the concessions and Canada had made none. Rather, it was obvious that each side had had to make concessions and that they had been "fair and liberal concessions" in each case. Still, there were even greater reasons for making the treaty and supporting it. If one considered Canada's position in the power structure of the North Atlantic, "we were bound to do it, in the interests of harmony between the two countries, and it was our duty to do it in view of our relation to the Empire of which we form a part." [35]

Liberal criticism of the Treaty was markedly moderate. There appeared to be two reasons for the Liberal chieftains not assuming their full war party regalia. The main Liberal assault for the session on the bulwarks of Canadian conservatism had already been made in the famous reciprocity debate of 1888. Of equal importance was the very obvious fact best put by the indignant and independently minded Peter

[34] *Official Report of the Debates,* April 10, 1888, pp. 712-19.
[35] *ibid.,* p. 744.

Mitchell. "Of course this Treaty will pass," the former Minister of Marine and Fisheries shouted, "there is no doubt about that." [36] The Tory army was just too strong to be defeated. And it was perhaps because of this that the debate soon moved to wider considerations.

An obvious point of attack seemed to be the apparent inconsistency in Government policy when one looked at the bold plan of 1886 and compared it with the conciliatory Treaty of 1888. Davies of Prince Edward Island spoke of Tupper's preparedness "with a light heart to go into war a year ago" and noted how the Macdonald Government "retrace their steps and adopt a policy antagonistic to the policy they pursued a year ago." The whole Treaty was "a record of surrender on our part." [37] Jones of Halifax thought the Treaty was "a sacrifice to conciliate the Americans," a sacrifice made necessary because the policy of the Canadian Government could have led only to retaliation by the Americans or to the present "sacrifice to peace." [38] George Foster did not quite see the problem in that way. He took the position that had so long been taken by Macdonald himself: that a strong stand was the only way to make a settlement possible. "I believe," Foster told the House of Commons, "that both the holding out of the offer of a proposition respecting the fisheries in 1885-86, and the prudent, strict enforcement of the rights of Canada in those years . . . contributed towards the negotiations for the commission . . . [and] the settlement which has resulted therefrom." "So much then," he retorted, "for the fickleness and inconsistency of the policy." [39]

But the Liberals did not stop here. If the Treaty was a "sacrifice," a "surrender," then there was yet another step in the argument to bring it to a conclusion. The former Tory,

[36] *ibid.*, April 13, 1888, p. 853.
[37] *ibid.*, April 10, 1888, pp. 735-36.
[38] *ibid.*, April 13, 1888, p. 824.
[39] *ibid.*, p. 855.

Sir Richard Cartwright, completed the Liberal attack. Canada's position *vis à vis* the United States was unique, he contended, "entirely out of all ordinary categories." Canada had "the right to deal with the United States as we have the right to deal with no other nation." "Those of us who were not blind and deaf to the whole situation," he concluded, "saw that this was the case the moment the first Treaty of Washington was concluded, and . . . we must make, from this time forth, the best bargain we can with the United States, and . . . we must do it alone." [40] The argument was potent and would recur again when the Behring Sea dispute was discussed; but it was not potent enough. Cartwright's proposal was politically enticing because if accomplished it would be a clear-cut political and constitutional recognition of Canada's growth in stature. But Sir John Macdonald was not concerned with such fine distinctions of international stature; to him it was rather more a question of power and survival. There was a large amount of truth in his reply, enough to carry the day in the debate and, indeed, for many years thereafter. "In effect," said the pragmatic Prime Minister, "Canada has made her own treaties of late years, and will in future make her own treaties." "And she will have this advantage," he continued, "that when those treaties require to be enforced, she will have not only the moral, but the material support of the mother country at her back." [41]

On 17 April 1888, a week after its second reading, the bill giving approval of the Treaty was passed. In summing up the Liberal argument the day before, the Opposition leader, Wilfrid Laurier, in large measure seconded Macdonald's reply to Cartwright. The Liberals did not vigorously oppose the Treaty, he said, because the consequences of its rejection might be too calamitous to contemplate. "The greatest calamity which could befall the civilized world would be an armed collision

[40] *ibid.,* April 16, 1888, pp. 888-89.
[41] *ibid.,* p. 891.

between the two greatest branches of the Anglo-Saxon race
. . . it would be almost as criminal and as guilty as a civil
war." "The policy of the Opposition," he said, "is simply this:
that, while asserting that the treaty is a surrender of most
valuable rights that belong to Canada, still, it is the duty of
Canadians to adopt this treaty, because it will put an end to a
most dangerous state of things." [42]

The fourth estate adopted attitudes similar to those upheld
by the Parliamentary combatants regarding the Treaty. Independent opinion varied with its source. *The Week,* the highly
reputable Toronto magazine, suggested that though the
Treaty would be accepted by Canadians, its conclusion nonetheless revealed once again the necessity for independent
treaty-making power being acquired by Canada. Peter Mitchell's "independent" *Montreal Herald* condemned the Treaty
with a violence that evidenced more of Mitchell's personal
animosity than anything else. "By piecemeal," the *Herald*
cried, "rights, possessions and interests of Canada are abandoned to the United States, and so, we presume, it will remain as long as Sir John remains in power, until there remains
but nature and geographical position." [43]

On the very same day, 22 February 1888, the friendly
Montreal Gazette happily noted that the Treaty confirmed
the Canadian definition of Canadian rights, provided for
reciprocity in an "important industrial product" (fish), and
most satisfactorily removed "a cause of dissatisfaction with
our nearest neighbor." But the *Halifax Morning Chronicle*
continued to wage war against the Government. "The whole
matter may be summed up in a nutshell," wrote the editor
with gross distortion of the facts. "In 1854 we got for our
fisheries an ample treaty of reciprocity. In 1871 we got free
fish and $5,500,000. In 1888 we got—*nothing."* More moderate
Liberal opinion was voiced in the *St. John Daily Telegraph*

[42] *ibid.,* p. 893.
[43] *The Week,* March 3, 1888; *Montreal Herald,* February 22, 1888.

which admitted "no great admiration" for the Treaty but contended that if it had to be rejected, then let it be rejected by the Americans. Then they would have no complaints if Canada reverted to a strict enforcement of its treaty rights. And even if the Treaty did not contain all that had been hoped for, the same paper probably best expressed the view of most Canadians when it said: "There is much in it which will receive the approbation of persons of moderate views in Canada." [44]

vi

In the United States Secretary of State Bayard had made elaborate preparations to put pressure on the Senate to force its approval of the Treaty. But the Treaty was reported out of the Republican-dominated Foreign Relations Committee with an adverse majority report and on 21 August 1888, it was rejected 30-27. There were undoubtedly many reasons for the failure of the Treaty. Senator Henry M. Teller of Colorado, for example, through strongly protectionist eyes viewed the Treaty as being concluded "not for the purpose of making a treaty on the fishery question, but a reciprocity treaty." [45] Senator John Sherman, who was financially involved with S. J. Ritchie in mineral lands in the Sudbury region and who cast an annexationist eye toward Canada, said in the Senate a month after its rejection that the Treaty would only have increased irritation between the two countries. Since the goal of the United States was to enhance friendly relations with Canada the "one-sided" Treaty had to be rejected. [46] These opinions may have been of some weight, especially Teller's,

[44] *Montreal Gazette,* February 22, 1888; *Halifax Morning Chronicle,* February 23, 1888; *St. John Daily Telegraph,* February 23 and 27, 1888.

[45] "The Fisheries Treaty, Speech of Hon. Henry M. Teller . . . in the Senate . . . July 21, 1888," p. 21.

[46] "Relations with Canada–Annexation, Speech of Hon. John Sherman . . . in the Senate . . . September 18, 1888."

THE FISH-WIFE FIGHT RENEWED

as the major concern of the session was the "Great Tariff Debate of 1888." But in the last analysis one reason superseded all others: a Republican Senate could not forego the pleasure of tying a knot in the British lion's tail in an election year. "The Republican Senators saw from the first that the only way to defeat it was to make it a political issue," Sackville West reported to Lord Salisbury.[47]

With such high stakes, if such were to be the rules of this political game, two could play it as easily as one. In 1887 Cleveland had reluctantly accepted a Congressional resolution providing for commercial retaliation which would have affected only Canadian fishermen and would have benefitted only New England interests. Now that the Senate had precipitately rejected the Administration bid for Anglo-American amity, Cleveland quickly sent to the Senate a request full of Democratic thunder. The astounded Senators were caught short by their own tactics. Cleveland judged that if retaliation were the prevalent mood in the "cave of the winds" then he would ask for broad powers that would "benefit the national rather than regional interests." In effect, he asked for the discretionary power to establish virtual commercial nonintercourse between Canada and the United States. Professor Nevins points out that Cleveland never intended to use such power and that the request was designed solely to embarrass the Republicans by using the rules they had established to effect their logical conclusion.[48] This thesis is generally valid but there was apparently more to it than Nevins has suggested.

Sir Lionel Sackville West reported to Salisbury a few days after Cleveland's bid to the Senate that the bill giving the President his retaliatory powers was introduced in the House by Representative Wilson. Wilson, "who appears to have been in the President's confidence, has been solicitor for some years for one of the North Western & Chicago Trunk lines, which in connection with the Vanderbilt lines have suffered great

[47] Salisbury Papers, Sackville West to Salisbury, August 20, 1888.
[48] Nevins, *Cleveland*, pp. 410 ff.

loss of trade and traffic thru' the building of the Duluth, South Shore and Atlantic road, the Minneapolis, Sault Ste. Marie and Atlantic, and other short lines which are carrying grain and other produce to the seaboard by a partial transportation through Canada." [49] West summed up the effect of the retaliatory powers if they were given:

The President of the Canadian Pacific Railway is reported to have said that the non-intercourse policy of the United States would damage American railroad interests between two or three dollars, where it would injure Canadian interests one. All the Michigan roads would be heavily damaged, and the New England Lines [Hoar, Edmunds and Frye were New England Republican Senators] depending upon Canadian lines for an outlet would likewise suffer. The same is true of the lines centering at Niagara and roads like the Wabash. The balance to all this damage would be found only in the advantage which would accrue to the New York Central, the Pennsylvania, and the Baltimore and Ohio lines.[50]

In short, embarrassing the Senate was a small price to pay for reelection—especially if the support of the major eastern trunk lines could be gained by so doing. That the Senate meekly shelved Representative Wilson's bill takes no interest away from this little episode in the politics of the age of the spoilsmen.

Meanwhile the *modus vivendi* agreed to by the members of the Joint High Commission had been in force for some months previous to the rejection of the Treaty by the American Senate. In May 1888 Lord Lansdowne had informed Colonial Secretary Knutsford that the continued operation of the *modus vivendi* might depend on the Senate's action on the Treaty. But the fisheries protection fleet acted under liberal instructions framed in accord with the temporary arrange-

[49] Sackville West to Salisbury, August 26, 1888, in Foreign Office to Colonial Office, September 10, 1888: CO42/799.

[50] *ibid.,* Sackville West to Salisbury, August 27, 1888.

ment throughout the 1888 fishing season. In October Lord Stanley, who had succeeded Lansdowne as Governor-General, informed Macdonald that West believed the Senators were desirous that Canada reject the *modus vivendi* so that they might strike some retaliatory blow against the Dominion. But Tupper reassured the worried Colonial Office officials that the *modus vivendi* remained in force.[51] Macdonald decided to take a wait and see attitude. He rightly believed that no action should be taken which would reopen the North Atlantic Fisheries question until the attitude of the new Harrison Administration was known. Finally, ten days after the inauguration of the Republican President, Macdonald informed the Governor-General that the Canadian Government had agreed "to a continuance of the modus." He said that in light of "absence of unfriendly expression in Harrison's inaugural message, and the expressed desire of Congress, or rather of the House of Representatives, for extended trade relations, we think it will have a favourable and conciliatory effect in the U. States." [52] As long as there was any prospect of bettering general trade relations with the Republic, once the Canadian rights in the North Atlantic fisheries had been recognized and a workable *modus vivendi* had been agreed upon, the Dominion Government was determined not to reopen a bitter dispute with the Americans. Canadian rights had been affirmed and were recognized in both the rejected Treaty and in the *modus vivendi*. On this basis the North Atlantic Fisheries question remained in a quiet state of suspended animation from August 1888 until it was reconsidered by the Joint High Commission of 1898-1899. In the meantime, the Canadian Government turned its attention to the unsettled Behring Sea dispute.

[51] Lansdowne to Knutsford, June 1, 1888: CO42/796; Macdonald Papers, 89, Stanley to Macdonald, October 3, 1888; Tupper to Colonial Office, October 11, 1888: CO42/797.
[52] Macdonald Papers, 89, Macdonald to Stanley, March 14, 1888.

CHAPTER IV

An International Dispute Disrupts Imperial Amity

THE Behring Sea dispute could be seen simply as the threat which British Columbia pelagic sealing interests posed to the Alaska Commercial Company or, after 1891, to the North American Commercial Company. In this sense it was just another of the numerous battles of commercial interests that dominate the history of North America in the latter part of the nineteenth century. But it was much more than a battle of commercial rivals. The company which held the monopolistic lease to sealing rights on the Pribilof Islands was but an agent of the United States Government. And the United States Government, in attempting to protect the monopoly for itself and its agent, imposed restrictions on pelagic sealing in the Behring Sea which were contradictory to the commonly accepted precepts of international amity. As the victims of harsh American jurisdiction in Behring Sea, the British Columbia sealers sought redress through the Canadian and Imperial Governments. The Ottawa Government could do little to further a settlement of this problem. It might advise the Imperial Government of its opinions about the dispute; it might caution against a hasty settlement that would prejudice Canadian interests; it might even display a justified loss of temper at the inactivity of the Imperial Government. But the crucial decisions about how and when the problem would be solved were made in London and Washington, not Ottawa. This was all the more disturbing because, as Lord Stanley reminded Lord Salisbury, "Canada is just at the stage when she cannot walk alone, & yet rather resents being led." [1] Because of this, the story of the Behring Sea dispute reveals as much about the difficulties of the Imperial relationship as it

[1] Salisbury Papers, Stanley to Salisbury, October 11, 1891.

does about the problems created for Canada by the sharing of a continent with a vastly more powerful neighbor.

ii

Sir Charles Tupper, as Canadian High Commissioner in London, had labored in vain in September and October 1887 to get a specific mention of the Behring Sea dispute in the terms of reference of the Joint High Commission of 1887-1888. The British Commissioners were empowered to deal with the problem in Washington and mention of it was made at the early meetings of the Commission. Chamberlain referred to the matter again at the informal talks he had with Bayard during the December crisis and the latter impressed Chamberlain with his hope for a settlement "voluntarily" without "any appearance of pressure." But it was obvious that the seal fisheries question would not be discussed over the conference table at Washington. Bayard wanted it handled through the regular channels of diplomatic exchange. And here Sir John Macdonald agreed. Chamberlain told Salisbury that the Canadian Prime Minister did not wish to hinder a settlement of the North Atlantic fisheries problem by mixing it up with the Behring Sea troubles. "He anticipates a voluntary settlement . . . by the American Govt. & fears that the insertion of terms in any treaty wd. further prejudice its chances of success in the Senate." [2]

Bayard did move rapidly toward a "voluntary" settlement. While the Joint High Commission was still meeting, on 7 February 1888, he sent a proposal to Edward Phelps, the United States Minister in London, noting that all the evidence pointed to the conclusion that pelagic sealing would eventuate in the complete destruction of the seal fisheries. "The only way of obviating this lamentable result," he con-

[2] Chamberlain Papers, Salisbury to Chamberlain, November 28, 1887, Chamberlain to Salisbury, December 22, 1887 and January 13, 1888.

tinued, would be to establish a closed zone "north of 50° of north latitude, and between 160° of longitude west and 170° of longitude east from Greenwich, during the period intervening between 13 April and 1st November." Any lesser measures, such as a smaller closed zone around the islands, would be ineffectual. And the destruction of the fishery would be as important in London as in Washington. Most of the seal skins were sent to London for processing, Bayard wrote, and "it is stated that at least 10,000 people in that city find profitable employment in this work."[3]

Lord Salisbury greeted this proposal with no little pleasure. It seemed to be an easy and obvious way out of a very difficult situation. He expressed to Phelps "the entire readiness of H.M. Govt. to join in an agreement with Russia & the U.S. to establish a close time for seal fishing north of some latitude to be fixed."[4] In a conversation with Lord Stanley a few months later Salisbury put great stress on "the importance of removing by amicable negotiation, a cause of friction between ourselves and the U.S. with respect to which public opinion at home & indeed in Europe, could hardly sustain us in adopting an extreme view of our rights."[5] Lord Knutsford, Secretary of State for the Colonies, agreed with his Cabinet colleague. "I am inclined to view the proposal of the U.S. Govt. with favor," he noted. "The proposed regulations will benefit all countries who send seal fishing vessels to Behring Sea; and our legal position can be guarded by some kind of protest or reservation." In so deciding he ignored the advice of his subordinates. John Anderson, Sir Robert Herbert and Baron de Worms all agreed that there was no "equity in the proposal." "As long the United States do not surrender their

[3] Bayard to Phelps, February 7, 1888, in Foreign Office to Colonial Office, March 3, 1888: CO42/798.
[4] Salisbury to Sackville West, February 22, 1888: CO42/798.
[5] Macdonald Papers, 89, Stanley to Macdonald, July 5, 1888.

claim to Behring Sea, they are asking all other powers to join them in protecting the monopoly which they claim." [6]

This was certainly true. But more important was the point made by the Governor-General of Canada. "You will observe," Lansdowne told Macdonald, "that the proposed close time renders it unlawful to kill seals only when they are 'at sea,' this means that the Alaska Company may nevertheless have its customary battles on the Pribilof Islands." [7] In short, the Bayard proposal firmly entrenched in an international agreement the best of possible solutions for the United States, leaving the Alaska Commercial Company unhindered in its activity and prohibiting Canadian pelagic sealing for the entire season in Behring Sea. Salisbury's response to this objection was difficult to understand. For some reason he had originally suggested to the Canadians that the close time apply to all waters north of the forty-seventh parallel between America and Russia. Now he reverted to Bayard's original suggestion of a close time north of the fiftieth parallel, which, of course, was still far south of Behring Sea. He further urged Knutsford to warn the Canadians that "if the objections of the Canadian Government should lead to a discontinuance of the negotiations the result might be that the United States Government would deal with Behring Sea, as they have hitherto done, as part of the territory of the United States." But, as Lansdowne candidly said to Macdonald, "Ld. Knutsford has missed the point of our objection." [8]

In June, Lansdowne, who had just been succeeded by Lord Stanley as Governor-General, paid a visit to Salisbury and Knutsford in London. "I think I rather opened their eyes

[6] Minutes by Knutsford, Anderson, Herbert, and de Worms on Foreign Office to Colonial Office, March 3, 1888: CO42/798.

[7] Macdonald Papers, 88, Lansdowne to Macdonald, April 21, 1888; Lansdowne to Knutsford, April 9, 1888: CO42/796.

[8] Foreign Office to Colonial Office, April 28, 1888: CO42/798; Macdonald Papers, 88, Lansdowne to Macdonald, May 10, 1888.

upon one or two points," he wrote to Macdonald. "I don't think they realized how completely the U.S. proposal would annihilate the seal fishing industry of all but the Alaska Fur [sic] Company." [9] Two months later, after carefully reading and approving ("I agree with every word of it") [10] a testy Privy Council Report by Foster on the subject, Stanley sent the paper in a despatch to the Colonial office. Foster quickly wrote off Bayard's proposal as "an unjust and unnecessary interference with, or rather prohibition of, rights so long enjoyed to a lawful and remunerative occupation on the high seas." [11] Canada was not obstructing negotiations to prevent a settlement. Rather, as Lansdowne had written home early in April, "a one sided restriction such as that which appeared to be suggested in your telegram, could not be suddenly and arbitrarily enforced by my Government upon the fishermen of this country." Canada was more than willing to enter into "a reasonable agreement for protecting the fur bearing seals of the Pacific Coast from extinction." [12] After all, protection of the seals from extinction was as important to the Canadian as it was to the American sealers.

The Colonial Office officials agreed that "it will be necessary for the U.S.A. to make some modified proposal if these negotiations are to have any useful result," [13] and Salisbury reluctantly presented the Canadian objections to Phelps. The American Minister hedged about altering the proposal and belligerently advised Bayard to take "firm action" to "show Canada that she cannot outrage us with impunity." [14] Happily,

[9] Macdonald Papers, 88, Lansdowne to Macdonald, June 17, 1888.

[10] *ibid.*, 89, Stanley to Macdonald, July 14, 1888.

[11] Privy Council Report 1236G, in Stanley to Knutsford, August 2, 1888: CO42/796.

[12] Lansdowne to Knutsford, April 9, 1888: CO42/796.

[13] Colonial Office Minute on Stanley to Knutsford, August 2, 1888: CO42/796.

[14] Phelps to Bayard, September 12, 1888, cited, Tansill, *Canadian-American Relations*, p. 290.

Bayard ignored this advice and the Behring Sea dispute was momentarily shelved during the 1888 Presidential campaign. In fact, Macdonald had long suspected this would be the result. It was obvious that in an election year the only arrangement the Secretary of State could have made would have been one-sided. Bayard probably would have been greatly surprised had the Canadians accepted his offer. And it is reasonable to suggest that Macdonald was right when he wrote to Stanley that "Mr. Bayard desires to play with the subject and postpone a settlement. . . . Cleveland dare not give the least evidence of concession just now as it would at once be used as a cry against him at the polls. He will listen to reason after his re-election." [15]

Even so, the laborious negotiations of 1888 were beneficial to Canada. With negotiations in progress Bayard did give vague but, as the event proved, effective assurance that Canadian sealers would not be molested during the 1888 pelagic sealing season. But what was given with one hand seemed to be taken away very quickly with the other. Against Bayard's judgment the Cleveland Administration and the outgoing 50th Congress fired a parting shot at the Canadians. In February 1889, Poindexter Dunn, Chairman of the House Committee on Merchant Marine and Fisheries, reported to the House of Representatives a bill which provided for better protection of the Alaska salmon fisheries. One section of the bill amended section 1956 of the *Revised Statutes* so that it extended, in explicit legislation to "all the waters of Behring Sea" within the boundaries set forth in the Treaty of 1867. The section further provided that the President each year issue a proclamation warning against entering the said waters for any purpose violating section 1956, which, of course, prohibited pelagic sealing. In debate, Mr. Dingley frankly stated his opinion that "the State Department has steadily maintained

[15] Macdonald Papers, 528, Macdonald to Stanley, July 17, 1888.

the position that Behring Sea is a closed sea." This obviously
was not true though it had seemed to Canadians at times to
be very nearly so. But when Cleveland put his signature to
the Dunn Bill, in Professor Tansill's words, "the President
abandoned the principle of the freedom of the seas, and gave
to the British Government the opportunity to stand as a
leader in the fight for a free sea." [16] For Lord Salisbury this
was a rather dubious gift from the Democrats vacating Washington. It was just the sort of present that the new Secretary
of State, James G. Blaine, could use most effectively. And
with the Canadians in a cantankerous mood the prospects did
not seem all bright.

iii

President Cleveland's signature on the Dunn Bill gave the
United States Government just the peg it needed on which
to hang its contention that American revenue cruisers had a
legal right to exclude pelagic sealers from Behring Sea. The
Harrison Administration wasted no time in acting on this
contention. Less than three weeks after his inaugural the new
President issued the proclamation called for in the Act. The
British *Chargé d'Affairs* in Washington wired to Salisbury
that "This proclamation virtually declares that the Behring
Sea is a *mare clausum.*" [17]

Lord Salisbury was not so sure of the intent of the proclamation. He informed Knutsford that "the interpretation thus
put by Mr. Edwardes upon the Act and Proclamation is not
the only one which the words . . . will bear, and . . . taken
strictly they do no more than assert the rights of the United
States in their territorial waters." This was precisely the point.
But did Lord Salisbury and President Harrison agree on the
extent of "their territorial waters"? The Foreign Secretary

[16] Tansill, *Canadian-American Relations,* p. 295.
[17] Edwardes to Salisbury, in Foreign Office to Colonial Office, March
25, 1889: CO42/802.

97

tried his best to believe they did. He reminded Knutsford that a majority of the Senators, in debating the bill, had shown great reluctance to put in the bill any phrase which could be taken as an expression of extension of jurisdiction in the Behring Sea. Knutsford agreed that "a mare clausum is a different question." By siding with Salisbury on a dubious legal distinction and ignoring the whole history of the dispute he again contradicted his subordinates. John Anderson thought it was "impossible to understand how the F.O. can imagine that it [the proclamation] does nothing more than assert the U.S. dominion in its territorial waters. . . . What they really intend to do is to assert & maintain their absurd claim as long as they can, and the sooner we let them know that we cannot assent to it the better." Sir Robert Herbert prudently advised that "we cannot very well attack the F.O. again officially on this point . . . but," he added, "it seems like the ostrich hiding its head in a bush to let this matter drift on and Canadian fishermen start for the seal fishery with a chance of being told later on that we had acquiesced by our silence in the view of the U.S. Govt." [18]

In Canada Harrison's proclamation was greeted with anger and frustration. Mr. Prior, M.P. from British Columbia, precipitated a heated debate in the House of Commons by reading a telegram from Washington which stated that the captain of the revenue cruiser *Thetis* had special instructions to be "very vigilant in . . . capturing any foreign, as well as American, vessels found in the Behring waters." [19] Sir John Macdonald tried once again to explain Canada's awkward position but his sympathies clearly rested more firmly with the complainers than with the conciliators as he referred angrily to the "iniquitous attempt of the United States Government to claim Behr-

[18] Minutes by Knutsford, Herbert, and Anderson on Foreign Office to Colonial Office, April 11, 1889: CO42/802.

[19] *Official Report of Debates,* April 26, 1889, p. 1576.

ing Sea as a *mare clausum.*" [20] "If the British Government are not able to protect our fishermen in the Behring Sea or wherever else they may fish, carrying the British flag," Louis Davies bluntly concluded, "it is well that the Canadian public should know it." [21] The *Globe* assailed "the apparently shallow pretence that Great Britain will stand by Canada's rights against any American aggression" and the *Halifax Morning Chronicle* sneered at the "half-hearted remonstrance and snail footed diplomacy." [22] All the criticism added up to the same thing: Canadians were resolved that the intolerable situation could not continue.

Nowhere was this more plain than in the report drafted by the Minister of Marine and Fisheries, Charles Hibbert Tupper, approved by Council and sent to London on 12 June. The reason for the despatch was to remind the British Government again of its dilatory way of pressing the claims for compensation made by the owners of seized British vessels. But Tupper and apparently the whole Canadian Government were more than a little sensitive to the criticism which flew about their heads. Not satisfied to treat only the immediate problem, Tupper started by saying that "so far back as the month of September 1886, the Canadian Government first called attention to the Imperial Authorities" about the unwarranted action of the United States. After "constant inquiry" there was "practically no result other than the virtual and continual exclusion of Canadian sealers from those open waters." Tupper stressed the "great damage" that was "not only sustained, but is now being suffered by British subjects." "Under these circumstances," he wrote, "it is not surprising that the public mind in Canada has become excited if not alarmed by even the appearance of delay." He concluded by telling the Im-

[20] *ibid.*, pp. 1579-80.
[21] *ibid.*, pp. 1577-78.
[22] *Toronto Globe,* April 18, 1889; *Halifax Morning Chronicle,* August 28, 1889.

perial authorities that "some of the leading Representatives in the Canadian Parliament have already been induced to express the opinion that the British Government would not actively protect the rights of British subjects resident in Canada" and he hoped action would be taken to quell this sentiment.[23]

Tupper's hope was dashed even before it was known in London. In April, while the discussion was taking place on the President's proclamation, Salisbury told Knutsford that Sir Julian Pauncefote had been appointed as the new British Minister in Washington and that nothing would be done "until he has had time to examine into the question on the spot." Pauncefote received high marks of approval from former Governor-General Lansdowne and Macdonald predicted in Parliament that his appointment would bring a change for the better.[24] But as John Anderson read Tupper's report he remembered that "the F.O. told us that Sir J. Pauncefote was to take the matter up as soon as he got to Washington, but if he did so they have carefully kept it to themselves." [25] Now, in June, Pauncefote was on his way home and more delay would ensue. He wrote to Stanley that "the policy of the Home Government . . . is at present not to move in the two great questions (Behring sea & the Fisheries) but to await a movement on the other side." [26]

Movement there was of the worst possible kind for Anglo-

[23] Stanley to Knutsford, June 12, 1889: CO42/800.

[24] Foreign Office to Colonial Office, April 18, 1889: CO42/802; Macdonald Papers, 88, Lansdowne to Macdonald, June 23, 1889; *Official Report of Debates,* April 26, 1889, p. 1580.

[25] Minute by Anderson on Stanley to Knutsford, June 12, 1889: CO42/800.

[26] Macdonald Papers, 528, Macdonald to Stanley, June 21, 1889. See also Salisbury Papers, Pauncefote to Salisbury, July 12, 1889. Macdonald was far from pleased. He agreed that the fisheries question "might rest a while . . . but it is otherwise with respect to the Behring Sea Question." Its present standing "paralizes [sic] our seal fishery."

Canadian and Canadian-American relations. On 2 August Sir Charles Tupper questioned the Colonial Office about reports that the American cruiser *Rush* had seized the British sealer *Black Diamond*.[27] Twenty days later Lord Salisbury asked Mr. Edwardes in Washington to see if he could get any confirmation of the seizure. He then instructed Edwardes to ask the United States Government to issue "stringent instructions" to prevent further seizures, basing his request on the "clear assurances from Mr. Bayard that no further interference . . . should take place pending the general discussion of questions at issue." He concluded by saying that Pauncefote "will be prepared to discuss the whole question in the autumn."[28] Despite the right or wrong of his case, Blaine was obviously negotiating from a much stronger position than his adversary and skillfully parried Salisbury's thrust with a reply that the seizure rumor was "probably authentic." He appeared to be delighted to hear that Pauncefote would be ready to negotiate in the autumn and expressed "the earnest desire of the President to come to a friendly agreement." But he ignored the request regarding instructions and when pressed on the point indignantly replied that "a categorical response to the request . . . would have been, and still is impracticable, unjust to the U.S. Govt., and misleading to H.M. Govt."[29]

[27] High Commissioner to Colonial Office, August 2, 1889: CO42/801. Anderson self-righteously noted in his minute: "We warned the F.O. that his wd. happen when the President's Proclamation was issued but they pretended to know better and this is a beautiful commentary on their ingenious belief in American good intentions."

[28] Salisbury to Edwardes, Nos. 15 and 16, August 22, 1889, in Foreign Office to Colonial Office, August 22, 1889: CO42/802. Salisbury's position was very weak. Bayard's assurance had been wiped away by Cleveland's signature of the Dunn Bill and in Herbert's phrase, the Foreign Secretary had remained "ostrich like."

[29] Edwardes to Salisbury, in Foreign Office to Colonial Office, September 20, 1889. See also Foreign Office to Colonial Office, August 28, 1889: CO42/802.

Meanwhile, Sir Charles Tupper had suggested that the only way to fight fire was with fire. He had concluded his inquiry to the Colonial Office by saying, "The time is most opportune for sending a British ship of war into Behring Sea with instructions to prevent any further seizure of British vessels in the open waters. I feel sure that if this course be adopted the result will be the promotion of a peaceful settlement of the question." [30] While Tupper was not alone in advocating belligerency, Macdonald felt that such action would be a very "serious step" and the Governor-General argued that "the proposal to send a ship of war to Behring Sea . . . is not one which the Dominion Government should undertake the responsibility of making." [31]

This did not mean that the Canadian Government would wait to see if the British Government would, as the *Toronto Globe* phrased it, "again humbly eat the leek." [32] Lord Stanley informed the Colonial Office that

A sense of irritation is growing up in the public mind not only against the Government of the United States but against the Imperial Government which may at any moment result in serious trouble, and there is reason to apprehend that if the supposed inaction of the Home Government continues the Sealers may be driven to armed resistance in defence of what they believe to be their lawful calling, and it would be difficult if not impossible for the Dominion Government to prevent such a state of affairs. . . . Up to the present time there has been every disposition on the part of the Canadian people to rely on the maintenance by the Imperial Government of the inter-

[30] Public Archives of Canada, C. H. Tupper Papers, M106, Sir C. Tupper to Knutsford, August 2, 1889.

[31] Macdonald Papers, 529, Macdonald to Stanley, August 3, 1889; 32, Stanley to Macdonald, August 4, 1889; 529, Macdonald to Tupper, August 7, 1889.

[32] *Toronto Globe,* August 1, 1889.

national rights which the Foreign Office is charged with the duty of protecting; and if the question of the free navigation of the North Pacific . . . were fully maintained I do not think that any reasonable measures which could be proposed for the protection of the so-called seal fishery would meet with a refusal here provided that they were not as in a former case entirely one-sided.[33]

The despatch was shot through with the tone of a last warning. Apparently it had some effect upon the Imperial Government although Canada was kept strictly uninformed of the fact that Pauncefote was finally negotiating with Blaine. In utter frustration Charles Hibbert Tupper wrote to his father that "the delay in Behring Sea matters is doing terrible harm to the British connection, but it must be enjoyed hugely by those of our United States neighbours who wish us to enter the Union some day in desperation!"[34]

At last, on 23 November 1889, Knutsford informed Stanley that close time negotiations were going to be resumed in Washington. The British Government desired beforehand an admission from Blaine that the United States did not claim Behring Sea as a *mare clausum* and an assurance that no further seizures of Canadian vessels would be made in Behring Sea. Since Russia would also be included in the negotiations it would not be possible to discuss compensation at the general meetings. It would be desirable for Pauncefote to be "assisted . . . by an officer or officers of the Canadian Government."[35] Macdonald was not pleased with the news. He told Tupper that the proposal was "vague and unsatisfactory. . . . It is quite evident that Blaine's whole aim is to mix up the two questions of mare clausum & the preservation of seals." It was not at all clear that the British would refuse

[33] Stanley to Knutsford, August 8, 1889: CO42/800.

[34] C. H. Tupper Papers, 17, C. H. Tupper to Sir C. Tupper, November 8, 1889.

[35] Macdonald Papers, 32, Knutsford to Stanley, November 23, 1889.

to negotiate on a close time if Blaine refused to repudiate the claim to a *mare clausum*. The Canadians believed that there was good evidence that there was no danger of extermination of the seals; however, if the Imperial Government deemed it wise to renew negotiations for a close time Canada would comply with the wish. But certain conditions were essential if negotiations were to begin again. The Canadians "shall be directly represented on British Commission" as they had been in 1871 and 1888 and any agreement must be subject to Canadian approval. And Russia must be excluded from any negotiations relating to compensation and seizures. One thing above all else was necessary: "the *mare clausum* claim shall first be abandoned and any American legislation apparently supporting that contention repealed or amended." [36]

The Colonial Office's reply was disappointing. Russia would not interfere with talks on the seizures but Pauncefote had assured Salisbury that the United States "have never asserted *mare clausum* . . . and will make no disclaimer but . . . the question will be disposed of by international agreement for a close time." Macdonald was right; the close time was, in fact, the glove to the *mare clausum* hand of American authority over Behring Sea and Salisbury as much as admitted it. Furthermore, there would be no Commission but simply a "diplomatic conference" at which a "Canadian assistant would advise British Minister"; Blaine would not agree to a Canadian representative *per se*.[37] The Prime Minister failed to see how the Imperial authorities could be so completely hoodwinked by Blaine. The very facts of the dispute revealed that no matter what the Yankees said they had erected huge "no trespassing" signs all around Behring Sea and Canada still expected Great Britain either to see they were taken down or to leave the conference table. It was clear that further protests to

[36] *ibid.*, 529, Macdonald to Tupper, December 7, 1889; 32, Stanley to Knutsford, December 6, 1889.

[37] *ibid.*, 32, Knutsford to Stanley, December 11, 1889.

Lord Salisbury were futile.[38] But it was equally clear that
Charles Hibbert Tupper began his new year in Washington as
Sir Julian Pauncefote's "assistant" with the greatest of mis-
givings about his mission.

iv

Charles Hibbert Tupper was not the type of man who
makes an ideal diplomat. His merits were many; he was unquestionably one of the ablest of Macdonald's later Cabinet
colleagues. He did his work with a thoroughness and depth
of understanding that few other Ministers could equal. Above
all, he was the most "Canadian" of all the Canadian Ministers;
his state papers almost glowed with the righteousness of the
Dominion's cause. But this passionate conviction had its drawbacks; Macdonald once referred to it as "bumptiousness."
Perhaps it could be attributed to his having to live in his
father's shadow. He had all the argumentative power yet
lacked the charm and finesse of Sir Charles. Pauncefote already knew the sting of Charles Hibbert's pen and quickly
learned the sharpness of his tongue. "Blaine . . . would not
see Tupper any more," he reported to Salisbury on 18 March,
and has "asked me to continue the negotiation alone." [39] By
the time Tupper left Washington he was definitely *persona
non grata*. Yet it would be wrong to attribute this wholly to
the younger Tupper's character. Rather, the clash of personal-
ities was but a surface manifestation of a much deeper conflict of opinion between Sir Julian and Tupper as to what was
a just and reasonable solution to the Behring Sea problem.

Tupper arrived in Washington on 26 February 1890, and
reported to Macdonald that Pauncefote was satisfied Blaine
had "practically abandoned" the *mare clausum* claim, but
could not publicly acknowledge it at the moment because of

[38] *ibid.*, Stanley to Knutsford, December 13, 1889. Draft in Macdonald's hand.

[39] Salisbury Papers, Pauncefote to Salisbury, March 18, 1890.

political pressure. Though the Canadian view of how the problem should be solved was being ignored, the situation did appear hopeful. Blaine wished to have negotiations regarding damages proceed simultaneously with the talks on the close time. The very next day, however, the prospect of some settlement seemed to diminish as the result of a stormy interview between Blaine, Pauncefote, and Tupper. Blaine, "showing more excitement than I had expected," began by quoting Canadian statistics which he said proved pelagic sealing was destructive to the seal herd. Tupper countered with American statistics showing pelagic sealing was not hurting the seal herd and concluded by alluding to the *mare clausum* claim. At that point former President Cleveland's chickens came home to roost. "I have never claimed the sea was a *mare clausum*," said the Secretary of State, but "I have never abandoned that claim which my predecessor set up." He went on to express a desire "for the sake of peace" to have a close time and arbitrate the damages question but threatened that time was running out and if an agreement was not quickly reached "the Proclamation would issue and more arrests would follow." [40]

All this was probably to be expected. Pauncefote noted that "while Blaine talks 'big words' all may come well" and Stanley concurred that "these are only preliminary skirmishes." [41] More disturbing was the constant flow of reports from Tupper regarding the British Minister. "Outside of the question of *mare clausum* we have no advocate in Sir Julian," he wrote. "He is in no humour to fight for the Canadian case with any degree of hope, and seems to cling to the idea that we must give up a large area around the islands forever." "He is a gentleman but seems to me over anxious to settle all disputes

[40] C. H. Tupper Papers, M106, Tupper to Macdonald, February 26, 1890; Macdonald Papers, 30, Tupper to Macdonald, February 27, 1890.

[41] Macdonald Papers, 30, Tupper to Macdonald, February 28, 1890, Stanley to Macdonald, March 4, 1890.

no matter how—simply to settle them!" [42] In the past, of course, there had been the effective counter pressure of appeal to the Home Government. But now even this was impossible. "We must not expect any help from outside," Stanley told Macdonald. "Lord Salisbury has always taken a strong line in favour of fishery protection." [43]

This was the heart of the problem. The Canadians were not convinced that pelagic sealing was destroying the seal herd. It is true that in 1898 Sir Wilfrid Laurier would admit that pelagic sealing was detrimental, but as late as 1896 the Colonial Office, which generally supported the Canadian view, could assert that "as far as we can make out there is no fear of the early extermination of the seals & if it be true that there has been great mortality among the pups it is not due to pelagic sealing." [44] Furthermore, the Canadians asked, if the Americans claimed that pelagic sealing was harmful, must they not also admit that indiscriminate slaughter on the islands by the North American Commercial Company also threatened the seals with extinction? [45] Even Pauncefote admitted that Tupper's argument against a close season was "very able and exhaustive." [46] On the other hand, Lord Salisbury was equally convinced that there was "no doubt that shooting seals during the breeding season must exterminate the species" and he saw no reason to overexert himself in support of the Canadian argument or "the cheap chauvinism of

[42] *ibid.,* Tupper to Macdonald, March 3 and 7, 1890; Thompson Papers, 103, Tupper to Thompson, March 13, 1890.

[43] *ibid.,* Stanley to Macdonald, March 7, 1890.

[44] Salisbury Papers, Chamberlain to Salisbury, April 3, 1896.

[45] On this point see the excellent article by C. S. Campbell, "The Anglo-American Crisis in the Behring Sea, 1890-1891," *Mississippi Valley Historical Review,* XLVIII, December 1961, pp. 393-414. Both the Elliott report prepared for the U.S. Government in 1890 and the report of the British investigators in 1892 declared unequivocally that land sealing was destroying the herd as much as pelagic sealing.

[46] Salisbury Papers, Pauncefote to Salisbury, March 17, 1890.

their Government." His subordinates in Washington agreed. Pauncefote believed that "a close season is necessary, and should be established as soon as possible" and Cecil Spring Rice advocated "a close season with or without the assent of the U.S. Govt. and at once." [47] These sharply divergent opinions made it extremely difficult for the Foreign Office and the Canadian Government to reach any common understanding on the Behring Sea dispute. Holding the view that he did of pelagic sealing, Lord Salisbury naturally viewed the establishment of a close season as the essential achievement in any negotiations with the United States. Conversely, the Canadian argument buttressed their opinion that a renunciation of the practical *mare clausum* and compensation for the seized sealing vessels was the most important point to be won from the American Government.

Canada, then, would have to battle alone. Stanley, with Macdonald's "entire assent & concurrence" wrote Pauncefote "very frankly what our feeling is here." He admitted that the British Minister was in a tight spot; Blaine was a tough diplomatist with his country thoroughly behind him. Moreover, Salisbury's apparent declaration of agreement to the Bayard close time proposal of February 1888 was far from helpful. Still, it was Canada that was suffering and it was Canada which might be "forced to believe that our interests here are not considered of any importance to the Home Government." Stanley reported that on a recent trip to Victoria he "was not without a feeling of humiliation" when asked by loyal citizens if the Imperial Government "really were going to protect them or no."

Of course, there were only two simple questions involved in the dispute: was Behring Sea legally a *mare clausum* and

[47] *ibid.*, Salisbury to Knutsford, July 29, 1888, Pauncefote to Salisbury, March 17, 1890; Chamberlain Papers, Spring Rice to Chamberlain, April 21, 1891.

what was a reasonable close time that would afford some protection to the seal herd. But, he added,

> I know that you are pressed by the Home Government to conclude a Treaty and to settle the question, but I do not think I do my late colleagues much injustice in saying they know nothing and care less about details. We on our part think details are the very essence of the question. . . . we do not object to the area over which the close season is to extend, and we do not object to a close season, but we do object to the duration of such close season being regulated exclusively under information given only by interested and hostile parties or their paid agents.

Stanley concluded by suggesting a possible settlement of the question. The seal fishery might be regulated over an area already agreed upon at Washington. Because the United States contended that pelagic sealing threatened the herd with extinction and Canada believed the contrary, the obvious thing to do was establish a commission of experts to study the problem for two years and settle *ad referendum* the details as to the duration of a close time and the necessary regulations to enforce it. In the meantime a *modus vivendi* might be established under which limited sealing might occur or "we might adopt the extreme course of an international arrangement that no seals whatever [either on land or sea] should be taken within the period named." The enforcement of all regulations would be carried out "by the cruisers of the various nations interested." [48]

The negotiations in Washington continued on their slow and laborious course. Tupper drew up a draft convention with some minor modifications of Stanley's proposal. Pauncefote had drawn a similar document and when the two were com-

[48] Macdonald Papers, 32, Stanley to Pauncefote, March 12, 1890. Tupper wrote to Stanley that "your letter will greatly stiffen Sir Julian's back." C. H. Tupper Papers, M106, Tupper to Stanley, March 14, 1890.

pared Tupper reported to Macdonald that the British Minister was "much disappointed" with the Canadian draft. A new draft by Pauncefote "follows the lines of ours generally," Tupper wrote, "but leans more to the side of concession, and provides that in the event of the disagreement of our governments, on receipt of the report of experts, for a reference to an independent Government." Hardly any suggestion could have been more objectionable to a Canadian nationalist of Tupper's stripe. If the Canadian contention was confirmed by a scientific inquiry, and simply because the Americans still disagreed, to "put us at the mercy of a foreign government . . . would be humiliating." "It is in my opinion most unfortunate," Tupper ranted regarding Pauncefote,

> that he has conducted negotiations in such a way that Mr. Blaine has been able to learn all that he personally was willing to do. The consequence is that he fights now for his own reputation and standing before Mr. Blaine . . . having informally told Mr. Blaine of his intended & very handsome concessions, he dare not retreat.

> It may be out of place for me to say it, but I cannot refrain from urging that in future negotiations with the United States no British Minister at Washington should act for us.[49]

Finally, on 29 April, the British Minister submitted the Anglo-Canadian proposal to Secretary Blaine with a covering letter. While the mixed commission of experts was meeting, Pauncefote proposed that *all* sealing, both on the islands

[49] *ibid.,* 31, Tupper to Macdonald, April 10 and 11, 1890. Pauncefote applied to the Home Government for assistance. The Colonial Office urged an immediate reply from Canada to Pauncefote's draft. Stanley's answer, directly to Pauncefote, read, in part: "No wish here unduly to hamper your action but concession to United States if carried too far would produce most serious consequences in Dominion. Minister of Marine represents unanimous feeling of his Government but I am sure he will do his best to assist you." 32, Colonial Office to Stanley, April 11, 1890, Stanley to Pauncefote, April 11, 1890.

and at sea, be stopped during the seals' "migratory periods," the months of May, June, October, November, and December, and that at all times sealing vessels would be prohibited from approaching within a ten-mile radius of the breeding islands. The commission itself would inquire into the necessity of properly enforced regulation on the islands and at sea and into the extent and necessity of a close season both on the islands and at sea.[50]

The Canadian and British Governments then waited for Blaine's answer. On 10 May the Secretary of State informed Pauncefote that he would send him a letter in a few days on the proposal. Meanwhile, Blaine considered "the proposal was a satisfactory basis for a settlement, but he added that some important changes must be made before the United States Government would accept it. Mr. Blaine, however, declined to point out what these changes are likely to be." A few days later the "changes" were made known through reports in the American press that Harrison's cabinet had rejected the draft proposal and again ordered the revenue cruisers to seize pelagic sealing vessels in Behring Sea. Stanley could not be sure but what "it may be bulldozing on the part of the U.S." "But I fear we may be in for some trouble," he concluded.[51] The reason for this change of face by the American Government was the pressure put upon Blaine and Harrison by the North American Commercial Company. Among the important stockholders in the company were D. O. Mills and S. B. Elkins. Mills was the father-in-law of Whitelaw Reid, editor of the New York *Tribune,* an influential figure in the Republican party and soon to be Harrison's running mate in the 1892 campaign. Elkins had been Blaine's financial adviser and friend for years and was soon to be Harrison's Secretary of

[50] C. H. Tupper Papers, M106, Pauncefote to Blaine, April, 1890; Tansill, *Canadian-American Relations,* p. 310.

[51] C. H. Tupper Papers, M106, Tupper to Macdonald, May 11, 1890; Macdonald Papers, 32, Stanley to Macdonald, May 23, 1890.

War. Pauncefote learned from a secret source that Elkins "looks after the 'Washington end'" of the North American Commercial Company affairs and possessed "an influence with the present administration . . . that no other one person can in the least degree approach." Before taking out the lease for land sealing, the company "took all possible pains to assure themselves that there would be no marine sealing permitted in Behring Sea."[52] But the Tupper-Pauncefote draft convention went much too far by applying the close season to the company as well as the pelagic sealers, a stipulation Tupper had insisted be included in Pauncefote's draft.

Harrison's orders to the revenue cruisers raised the possibility of renewed seizures of British sealing vessels. The British Government had decided in March that "we cannot tolerate a renewal of the captures." Salisbury told Pauncefote that "from the judgment I can form of the state of opinion here, . . . we shall not be allowed, even if we were inclined, to permit the United States cruisers to treat Behring Sea as if it were their private property." Accordingly, four British warships were alerted to protect British sealers in Behring Sea. The Canadians would have been heartened by the news that the Foreign Secretary had finally abandoned his apparently compromising attitude to the United States. But, unfortunately, they were not informed. Salisbury rationalized, perhaps correctly, that "unless they allow it to be known, such information is useless to them; and if they allow it to be known, it will be repeated in every newspaper throughout the Union, and will almost drive Blaine into an aggressive policy." Besides, he had "another and personal reason" for not informing Canada, he told Knutsford when the latter asked if Sir Charles Tupper might see him. "I am so penetrated with a sense of what seems to me the unreasonable atti-

[52] Salisbury Papers, Pauncefote to Salisbury, June 27 and May 23, 1890; Campbell, "The Anglo-American Crisis in the Behring Sea, 1890-1891," pp. 396-98, 405-8.

tude of the Colonies, and their injustice to the Mother Country, that in conversation with a Colonist on public affairs I find it very difficult to prevent these sentiments from peeping out." [53]

Blaine's official reason for not accepting the draft convention gave no hint of the pressure put on the United States Government by the North American Commercial Company. Indeed, the extraordinary length to which Blaine reached to attempt to justify his position revealed that his diplomatic position had been seriously compromised. He did indicate his displeasure with the provision for pelagic sealing during July, August, and September "when the areas around the breeding places are most crowded with seals." And the ten-mile limit "would give the maurauders . . . the opportunity . . . for stealing silently upon the islands and slaughtering the seals." But the onus of the letter was on two points, the duplicity of Lord Salisbury and his subservience to "one of Her Majesty's provinces." Blaine carefully extracted from Phelps's letter to Bayard in 1888 evidence to prove that Salisbury had committed himself verbally to both Phelps and the Russian Ambassador at London to Bayard's close season proposal and then gone back on his word because of the "desire of the Canadian Government." Again, in 1890, Blaine said, "our negotiations . . . were suddenly broken off . . . by the interposition of Canada." "In diplomatic intercourse between Great Britain and the United States," Blaine sarcastically wrote, "be it said to the honor of both governments, a verbal assurance from a minister has always been equal to his written pledge." [54]

[53] Salisbury Papers, Salisbury to Pauncefote, March 28, 1890, Salisbury to Knutsford, June 26, 1890; Campbell, *op. cit.,* p. 401.

[54] United States, *Papers Relating to the Foreign Relations of the United States, 1890-1891,* Washington, 1891, Blaine to Pauncefote, May 29, 1890, pp. 425-29. See also A. T. Volwiler, ed., *The Correspondence Between Benjamin Harrison and James G. Blaine, 1882-1893,* Philadelphia, 1940, pp. 101-14.

Meanwhile, at Pauncefote's suggestion, Charles Hibbert Tupper had left Washington for Ottawa, his work having been completed when the British Minister's proposal had been sent to Blaine. But he left an impression on both Blaine and Pauncefote by his zealous insistence on what Canadians considered to be the essential points in the Behring Sea dispute. So, at least, seemed to be the opinion of Charles F. Benjamin, a Washington lawyer close to the diplomatic circles there. *"Entre nous,"* he confided to Goldwin Smith, "the Minister is in a somewhat troubled and despondent state of mind. Blaine and he started off well, but the former is feeble, dilatory and pottering, and no longer has his son to supply his own needs and defects, and Sir Julian, under Canadian pressure, has been led to so contract his original view of a regulated fishery as to get into a deadlock." [55]

v

It was quite apparent that the resolute stand against Blaine's unreasonableness taken by Canada was greeted with hearty approval by the Canadian public. A Halifax correspondent told Colonel Denison of Toronto that the United States could not "persevere" much longer "in their preposterous claim regarding the Behring Sea question." "It is well," he noted, "that the U States should realize that Canada is going to have a voice in shaping the course of events on this continent—that she is not a mere crown Colony as they have imagined all along." Charles Mair told Denison of the reaction in Winnipeg "when the news came that England had told Uncle Sam to stand off in the Behring Sea." "It was really inspiring to hear people speak. Every man felt the gravity of his position and the position of the North West but there was but one unanimous voice—'we will fight!'" And the editor of a small Ontario newspaper wrote to Macdonald that "Behring

[55] Mann Library, Cornell University, Goldwin Smith Papers, C. F. Benjamin to Goldwin Smith, May 28, 1890.

Sea reflects credit on you—so the boys here think. That abrupt closing for Canada's consideration is good." [56] For the moment it even appeared that the British and Canadian Governments were as one on the question. Sir John Thompson reported from London that Knutsford "was much elated at the fact that H.M. Government had taken such a firm stand, and at the fact that the U.S. Government appeared to be staggered by it. He fully appreciates the bluster and mendacity of the Americans." [57]

Canada's position was not one of obstruction of the Anglo-American negotiations which eventually resulted in the Paris arbitration tribunal.[58] Indeed, the Tupper-Pauncefote proposal well summed up the case for a reasonable settlement. Both sides were interested in the preservation of a useful industry. But was it reasonable that pelagic sealing should be denied to Canadians while land sealing by Americans went on unhindered? The contention of the United States that it had an extraordinary right to protect its property was questionable. Even more debatable was the assumption that the United States had property rights in the seal herd. Was it not more reasonable to suggest that sealing be stopped during certain months both on land and at sea pending scientific investigation by a mixed commission of experts? And yet with every passing year the solution of the problem seemed more difficult because the two governments primarily interested increased their stakes in the industry. When the new lease was issued to the North American Commercial Company in 1890-1891 the United States Government received about

[56] Public Archives of Canada, Denison Papers, 4, C. O'Brien to Denison, July 31, 1890, Mair to Denison, August 8, 1890; Macdonald Papers, 487, Sam Hughes to Macdonald, July 27, 1890.

[57] Macdonald Papers, 274, Thompson to Macdonald, July 25, 1890.

[58] A detailed analysis of the negotiations is well related in Tansill, *Canadian-American Relations,* chs. 11-12, and Campbell, *op. cit.,* and it seems unnecessary to repeat it here.

three times more revenue from each seal skin than it had from the Alaska Commercial Company. In Canada what had started in 1884 as an adventure of exploitation by one vessel had expanded to the point where, in 1892, it was reported that more than fifty vessels were clearing Victoria for Behring Sea and another ten had sailed around "the Horn" from Canadian Atlantic ports.[59] Obviously both governments, for political and economic reasons, had a deep interest in the sealing industry. But that interest rested on the assumption that the seal herd would continue to survive. Thus, while the interest in exploitation deepened, so too did the interest in preservation, and hence in a settlement of the problem.

Lord Salisbury was acutely aware—perhaps too much so—of this dilemma. He chose to ignore the insulting character of Blaine's despatch and proposed to submit the problem to arbitration on 2 August 1890. Blaine's counterproposal, which John Anderson labeled "a red herring across the scent" and which Tupper justly considered entirely one-sided, was not submitted until late December 1890. Finally, on 15 June 1891 Pauncefote and Blaine reached agreement on a *modus vivendi* that would prohibit sealing until May 1892. The United States Government was allowed to kill 7,500 seals for the subsistence and care of the natives and the British Government, with a view to preparing to submit the question to arbitration, was allowed to send "suitable persons" to the seal islands to make inquiries into the sealing industry.[60] The agreement did not pass without vigorous protest from the

[59] Stanley to Knutsford, April 22, 1892: CO42/811.

[60] Foreign Office to Colonial Office, January 3, 1891: CO42/808; Stanley to Knutsford, January 22 and June 26, 1891: CO42/806. Dr. G. M. Dawson of Canada and Sir George Baden-Powell, M.P., were sent to the Pribilof Islands. Their report, which recommended a close time on both land and sea, may be found in *Behring Sea Arbitration. Report of the Behring Sea Commission,* and *Report of British Commissioners of June 21, 1892.* London, Her Majesty's Stationery Office, 1893.

Canadian Government which had given its consent on condition that the general arbitration agreement be signed either beforehand or simultaneously, a condition not met.[61]

Since the failure of the Tupper-Pauncefote proposal, however, Lord Salisbury had kept the negotiations with the United States carefully under his control. The Canadian Government was consulted and its views were considered. But the Foreign Secretary made the crucial decisions as to how the problem would be settled.[62] Eventually, on 18 December 1891, Pauncefote wired his superior that an agreement had been reached with Blaine on the terms of an arbitration treaty. Simultaneously it was agreed that each "Government shall appoint two Commissioners to investigate . . . all the facts having relation to seal life in Behring Sea, and the measures necessary for its proper protection and preservation." The reports of these investigations would be submitted to the arbitration tribunal.[63]

There was little response, favorable or otherwise, in Canada to the news that agreement had been reached. Canadians generally were much more interested in the fate of the Manitoba Schools Question or reciprocity negotiations taking place in Washington early in 1892 than they were in the now tiresome Behring Sea dispute. A passing question by Laurier summed up Parliament's interest in the problem. The Government simply informed the Imperial authorities that it did "not ob-

[61] Macdonald Papers, 32, Stanley to Macdonald, May 24, 1891; Thompson Papers, 130, Privy Council Report by C. H. Tupper, June 1891.

[62] "The Cabinet decided—and very rightly if I may say so—that the negotiations with the United States must be conducted by you alone." Salisbury Papers, Knutsford to Salisbury, June 26, 1890.

[63] Pauncefote to Salisbury, in Foreign Office to Colonial Office, December 19, 1891: CO42/809; Public Archives of Canada, Abbott Papers, Privy Council Report 981H, n.d. On the British side Dawson and Baden-Powell had already made their investigation and completed their report. See CO42/807 and CO42/809.

ject to proposed arrangements." With a bit more enthusiasm the *Montreal Gazette* commented that "Canada, like other civilized communities, would welcome a supreme international tribunal . . . for the hearing and deciding of all points of dispute between one nation and another." [64]

The tribunal did not meet until February 1893. But the intervening year was not simply wasted time. The arbitration treaty was approved by the Senate in March 1892. The Canadian Government spent the early months of 1892 in a contentious squabble with the Imperial authorities over the merits of renewing the *modus vivendi* until October 1893.[65] But of greater importance was the determination of the membership of the British side of the tribunal. As early as November 1891, the Foreign Office was pressing the American Government to accept a Canadian as one of the British arbitrators. The only real difficulty was that the best Canadian jurist, Sir John Thompson, was one of the leading members of the Canadian Government and, as everyone suspected, would soon assume the mantle of its leadership. All doubt was apparently dispelled, however, when Senator Morgan was selected as one of the American arbitrators. When asked about the possibility of a "committed" arbitrator, Lord Salisbury dismissed any worry with the comment that "as pleasing Canada is the whole object of all we have been doing, I could not at the very end of the transaction seriously trouble her." [66]

The problem of further Canadian representation was not so easily resolved. The Imperial authorities planned to appoint both the counsel and the agent and ask for a Canadian assist-

[64] Stanley to Knutsford, January 8, 1892: CO42/811; *Montreal Gazette,* February 12, 1892.

[65] The *modus vivendi* was renewed. See numerous communications on the subject between February and June, 1892 in CO42/811.

[66] Salisbury to Pauncefote, in Foreign Office to Colonial Office, December 2, 1891: CO42/809; Foreign Office to Colonial Office, attached to Stanley to Knutsford, April 25, 1892: CO42/811.

ant to the latter. But the Ottawa Government wanted a Canadian agent and also a Canadian co-counsel, the latter wholly at Canadian expense. Mr. C. Robinson was appointed to the latter post without difficulty. Because "Canada is most concerned" the British Government also accepted a Canadian agent and even went on to suggest Charles Hibbert Tupper. But, ever mindful of his wordy duels with Salisbury, the suggestion was not made without some misgivings. "He is of course thoroughly conversant with the question and able to perform the duties," Lord Knutsford told Stanley. But, he warned, "you will know best how far he is otherwise qualified, whether he is sufficiently conciliatory, and likely to command a certain influence with the Tribunal and the opposite party." Stanley persisted in Tupper's appointment, replying that "he possesses many qualifications. He would be duly cautioned as to his manner which is sometimes brusque." Knutsford accepted the assurance gracefully but betrayed lingering doubts in concluding that "we must hope that the influence of the British arbitrators and counsel will soften any possible asperities." [67]

As spring lapsed into summer Tupper left Ottawa for London to oversee and assist in drawing up the British case to be placed before the tribunal. His frequent letters to Prime Minister Abbott reveal that he worked diligently but without total satisfaction in his task. Having complete command of the subject, he was distressed by the more haphazard approach to the problem in London. Considerable work had been done, he told Abbott, "but no system has been adopted in connection with the preparation of the case." Not less distressing were the "impending elections" which further disrupted work on the Behring Sea problem. "I have no one to assist me in drafting," he complained on 7 July, "except Dawson. . . . Of course I have great aid from Maxwell and Anderson, in

[67] Stanley to Knutsford, May 21 and 27, 1892, Knutsford to Stanley, May 24 and 30, 1892: CO42/811.

the Foreign and Colonial Offices, so far as hunting up such papers as I require; but Cross has been in Liverpool—the Attorney General away—and Baden Powell has just turned up and caused further delay on Dawson's part by beginning *his* own draft on question 5." [68] Generally, however, Tupper found himself in congenial surroundings. He was "delighted" with Attorney General Webster, "with his executive ability and easy manner." And John Anderson of the Colonial Office "is very keen for us." The effort of the long and sometimes difficult summer had been worthwhile; a strong British case had been prepared to present to the arbitration tribunal.[69]

vi

The Behring Sea Arbitration Tribunal met in Paris from February to August 1893. Five key questions, all dealing with the assumptions upon which the United States based its practical *mare clausum* claim over Behring Sea, were to be answered by the arbitrators:

1. What exclusive jurisdiction in the Sea, now known as the Behring Sea, and what exclusive rights in the Seal Fisheries therein, did Russia assert and exercise prior and up to the time of the cession of Alaska to the United States?

2. How far were these claims of jurisdiction as to the seal fisheries recognized and conceded by Great Britain?

3. Was the body of water, now known as the Behring Sea, included in the phrase "Pacific Ocean," as used in the Treaty of 1825 between Great Britain and Russia; and what rights, if any, in the Behring Sea, were held and exclusively exercised by Russia after said Treaty?

4. Did not all the rights of Russia as to jurisdiction, and as to the seal fisheries in Behring Sea east of the water

[68] Abbott Papers, 4, C. H. Tupper to Abbott, June 16, 1892; Thompson Papers, 158, C. H. Tupper to Thompson, July 7, 1892.

[69] Abbott Papers, C. H. Tupper to Abbott, June 16 and 17, 1892.

boundary, in the treaty between the United States and Russia of the 30th March 1867, pass unimpaired to the United States under that treaty?

5. Has the United States any right, and, if so, what right of protection or property in the fur seals frequenting the islands of the United States in Behring Sea when such seals are found outside the ordinary three mile limit? [70]

One thing further had to be considered by the tribunal. If, in answering the first five questions regarding the "exclusive jurisdiction of the United States," the subject were left in such a position that the tribunal thought "the concurrence of Great Britain is necessary to the establishment of Regulations for the proper protection and preservation of the fur seal," then the arbitrators were to recommend regulations to be applied outside the jurisdictional limit and the extent of waters covered by the regulations. The tribunal would be guided in this task by the report of the mixed commission of experts.

The submission of the arguments to the tribunal and the wait for its decision was, of course, a long and grueling experience.[71] As Charles Hibbert Tupper told Bowell in June, "it has been a continual worry." Earlier, Sir John Thompson had told Bowell that "so far, everything looks well, excepting as to the question of Regulations, and on this subject it is impossible to say what the result will be." In July, again, Tupper's secretary, Joseph Pope, recorded in his diary that "things are not looking very bright for our side" but a few days later added that "the foreign arbitrators are with us in all questions of right which is highly satisfactory." Finally, on 11 August,

[70] *Papers Relating to the Foreign Relations of the United States, 1891*, p. 605.

[71] Summaries of the meeting of the tribunal may be found in Professor Tansill's two works: *Canadian-American Relations*, pp. 330-37 and *Bayard*, pp. 507-11. An unsatisfactory and, where pertinent, partisan account is found in the memoirs of Tupper's private secretary, Sir Joseph Pope. See Maurice Pope, ed., *Public Servant, The Memoirs of Sir Joseph Pope*, Toronto, 1960, pp. 86-102.

he noted that the tribunal "show a disposition to squeeze us in the matter of regulations." [72]

When the award was delivered four days later, Pope's summary was substantially correct. On question four it was decided that Russian rights did pass unimpaired to the United States in the Treaty of 1867 but the other four questions were decided in Great Britain's favor climaxing with the judgment on question five that the United States "has not any right of protection or property in the fur seals . . . when such seals are found outside the ordinary three mile limit." [73] The regulations determined by the tribunal, however, were a different matter for the Canadians. Much against Thompson's wishes, his fellow arbitrators established a closed zone of sixty miles around the seal islands and prohibited all pelagic sealing from the first of May until the end of July.[74] Though Pope later admitted that "the expectation of trouble proved worse than the reality," at the moment it seemed that the regulations "would effectively cripple if not entirely destroy the industry of pelagic sealing." As Sir Richard Cartwright commented, "Canada gets the shells and the United States gets the oyster." [75]

Canadian opinion regarding the arbitration award was mixed. The *Edmonton Bulletin* laid stress upon the virtues of

[72] C. H. Tupper Papers, M107, Tupper to Bowell, June 20, 1893; Thompson Papers, 261, Thompson to Bowell, May 10, 1893; Public Archives of Canada, Pope Papers, Diary entries of July 18 and 27 and August 11, 1893.

[73] A summary of the award may be found in Tansill, *Bayard,* p. 510, n. 74. The full text is in *Papers Relating to the Foreign Relations of the United States, 1894,* Appendix 1, pp. 109-16.

[74] This, of course, gave ample time for the cow seals to enter Behring Sea and give birth to their young on the islands and was, in fact, a fair preservative measure for the herd without damaging the pelagic sealing interest.

[75] Pope, *Public Servant,* p. 100; Public Archives of Canada, Pope Papers, Diary entry of August 11, 1893; *Official Report of Debates,* March 3, 1894, p. 67.

a settlement by arbitration, more particularly on the fact that "England has not come off second but first best." The newly established *Queen's Quarterly* was pleased that "the Republic will have to pay damages for Mr. Blaine's piratical policy while his preposterous assumptions have been laughed at by the civilized world." Always contentious, the *Halifax Morning Chronicle* belabored the British Government for an Imperial, rather than a Canadian settlement, and was not overjoyed "that Great Britain had scored a moral and the United States a material victory." But *The Week* countered by contending that the decision and the regulations made a fair settlement for both sides.[76]

One matter remained to be settled, the question of damages. Quite fairly, when Blaine and Pauncefote signed the agreement to submit the Behring Sea dispute to arbitration, they admitted that they "found themselves unable to agree" on the damage claims. Obviously, no equitable settlement could be made until the various questions of right had been answered by the tribunal. In the autumn of 1893 negotiations began again between the new Gladstone and Cleveland administrations. These long-drawn-out talks included another trip to Washington for Sir Charles Hibbert Tupper in August 1894[77] and the offer by Secretary of State Gresham of $425,000 to settle all claims against the United States. The offer was accepted by the British Government but rejected by the Senate. Eventually, on 16 June 1898, after the sum had been determined by a mixed commission, the United States paid $473,151.26 to settle the question of damages.[78]

On balance there is no question but that a fair settlement

[76] *Edmonton Bulletin,* August 23, 1893; *Queen's Quarterly,* 1, p. 250; *Halifax Morning Chronicle,* August 17 and 18, 1893; *The Week,* August 25, 1893.

[77] Thompson Papers, 218, Tupper to Thompson, August 19, 1894; 219, Aberdeen to Thompson, August 24, 1894.

[78] *Papers Relating to the Foreign Relations of the United States, 1898,* Day to Pauncefote, June 15, 1898, p. 371.

was reached in 1893. The question of right was determined wholly, and justly, to British advantage. A measure of protection to the herd was afforded by the close time and the closed zone around the islands. But the regulations far from hindered pelagic sealing as the Canadians had feared. Indeed, in 1894, when pelagic sealing was resumed, a record catch of 61,838 skins was taken by the sealing vessels, most of which were Canadian.[79] The most unfortunate aspect of the dispute was that a settlement was so long delayed. Doubtless the bursts of temper on both sides and the adamant stand taken by President Cleveland and perpetuated by Secretary of State Blaine did little to further the cause of Anglo-American amity. But it is equally clear that Lord Salisbury, despite Canadian protest, did his very best to keep the problem submerged beneath the growing tide of Anglo-American understanding.[80] Nor did Canada suffer unduly from the dispute. Except for the 1891-1893 seasons the pelagic sealing industry continued and, in fact, greatly increased its activities. It is true that a continuing and, at times, serious quarrel between the Canadian and Imperial Governments was one result of the Behring Sea trouble. But the quarrel brought home to Canadians the realization that in external as well as domestic affairs there were sometimes sharp distinctions between national and Imperial interests. Doubtless the editor of the *Canadian Manufacturer and Industrial World* had this in mind when he proudly proclaimed at the height of the crisis: "Canada has rights in this matter, and . . . those rights must and shall be protected and defended." [81]

[79] Tomasevich, *International Agreements on the Conservation of Marine Resources*, p. 86.

[80] For further evidence on this point see L. M. Gelber, *The Rise of Anglo-American Friendship*, London, 1938; J. L. Garvin, *The Life of Joseph Chamberlain*, v. 3, London, 1934, *passim;* F. R. Dulles, *America's Rise to World Power*, New York, 1954, *passim.*

[81] *Canadian Manufacturer and Industrial World*, August 15, 1890.

CHAPTER V

The Rise of Continentalism

BOTH the North Atlantic and Behring Sea disputes were
played out in Canada against a backdrop of domestic
economic difficulties. Undoubtedly some of the frustration and disappointment apparent in Canada's position on
these problems was a reflection of the letdown from the high
hopes of economic independence that had been a part of the
spirit of Confederation. The historians of the Royal Commission on Dominion–Provincial Relations concluded their survey of the first thirty years of Confederation with the judgment that "the period was one of trial, discouragements, and
even failure." [1] At no time during the period was the failure
more apparent nor more roundly discussed than during the
second half of the 1880's. The inception of the "National
Policy" tariff in 1879 and the construction of the Canadian
Pacific Railway together with a general world economic up-
swing from 1879 to 1883 gave the Dominion the appearance
of boom times. When prosperity gave way to renewed depression the brief uplift after the years of trial during the
Mackenzie period made the depression all the worse and
caused many Canadians to ponder their future. Perhaps the
most conclusive index to hard times was the population statistics. In the decade 1881-1891 the population of the Dominion
increased by 1.5 million people but two-thirds of this increase
was lost to emigration,[2] largely to what appeared to be the
greener fields of the United States.

Neither the depression nor the response to it was uniform
throughout the Dominion. British Columbia experienced depression during the 1870's and early 1880's but rode on a wave

[1] *Report of the Royal Commission on Dominion-Provincial Relations*,
Ottawa, 1954, Book 1, p. 65.
[2] *ibid.*, pp. 53, 62.

of prosperity during the late 1880's and early 1890's.[3] In Manitoba distress at the fall of the price of wheat and the collapse of a land boom based on false optimism in 1883 combined with sharp criticism of the Canadian Pacific Railway to give birth to the abortive Farmers' Union movement. But within a few months the movement's call for a stoppage of immigration, and the presence of at least one secessionist in its ranks, killed the protest and the province spent the next decade consolidating the gains of the past. This did not mean that all complaints were silenced in Manitoba. Rather, it was evident that the necessary reforms would be taken within the framework of the Dominion and not by appeal to the neighboring Republic.[4] The Maritime Provinces appeared to be in a state of perpetual depression but during the decade the fishing industry maintained stability and even expanded with the successful exploitation of the lobster fishery. Nova Scotia released its frustrations by reelecting the Fielding Government in 1886 on a secessionist platform but returned to the Conservative fold in the Federal Election of the following year.[5] And in Quebec serious financial difficulties existed but were overshadowed by a renewal of Anglo-French strife over the execution of Louis Riel and the passage of the Jesuit Estates Act. Like British Columbia, Ontario seemed to have no financial problems of great magnitude. But the Ontarians played a leading part in the "revolt of the provinces" and the meeting of the Interprovincial Conference dispelled any notions that the grand scheme of 1867, economic and political, had been

[3] M. A. Ormsby, *British Columbia: A History*, Toronto, 1958, chs. 10-11.

[4] W. L. Morton, *Manitoba, A History*, Toronto, 1957, chs. 9-11. See also D. F. Warner, *The Idea of Continental Union*, Lexington, 1960, pp. 163-75; Denison Papers, 3, Mair to Denison, June 20, 1884.

[5] *Report of the Royal Commission on Dominion-Provincial Relations*, p. 53; Warner, *The Idea of Continental Union*, pp. 196-97; E. P. Dean, "How Canada Has Voted, 1867-1945," *Canadian Historical Review*, xxx, 1949, pp. 227-48.

rounded out by 1887. Quite the contrary. The rise of the appeal for Commercial Union challenged the very concept of Confederation itself.

ii

The idea of a Commercial Union with the United States was not new. Making the North American continent an economic unit had been much more the direct concern of the Montreal merchants in 1849 than political unity. And, of course, economic cooperation between the two North American nations was and is a continuing feature of Canadian history. The real question was one of degree—how far should cooperation go? The various Macdonald Governments persistently advocated reciprocity in natural products. The Mackenzie Government committed itself to extending the free list to certain manufactured goods. Either of these measures of economic cooperation would undoubtedly have been approved by a large proportion of the Canadian electorate. But during the 1880's a larger degree of cooperation, in fact, economic integration of the two countries, became the subject of conversation and consideration in both Canada and the United States.[6] All Canadians wanted reciprocity with the United States in some form. But were Canadians willing to accept Commercial Union? That, in fact, was the key question in Canadian-American relations for some years in the latter part of the nineteenth century.

What was the essence of the proposed Commercial Union? A concise answer was provided by a Canadian advocate, Thomas Shaw, secretary of the Farmers' Institute at Hamilton, in a pamphlet entitled "A Farmer's View of Commercial Union." "Commercial Union between Canada and the United States," Shaw wrote,

[6] A summary of the rise of American sentiment for Commercial Union may be found in Tansill, *Canadian-American Relations*, pp. 381-97.

implies a free interchange of all products of both countries of whatsoever nature, whether of the waters, the soil, the sea and the mine. It would involve (1) an assimilation of tariff rates against all other countries; (2) of internal revenue taxes; and (3) very probably an arrangement for pooling receipts and customs, and distributing the same. It would be followed by the discontinuance of the services of a strong force of customs house officials on both sides of the boundary line of nearly 4,000 miles between the two countries, which is maintained at a cost to Canada of at least half a million dollars annually.[7]

John Charlton, lumberman and Liberal M.P. from southwestern Ontario, attempted to clarify any doubts about the pooling and distribution of customs receipts in a speech to the House of Commons in 1888. Under a Commercial Union agreement, he said, the powers would "throw that whole revenue into one common fund, after taking out the cost of collection, either upon the basis of a *per capita* division or upon such other division or upon such other basis as may be mutually agreed upon by the contracting parties.[8]

There was much to be said for Commercial Union. Canada was experiencing serious economic difficulty and the answer to its problems, said Erastus Wiman, a Canadian financier living in New York City, was to abolish the protective tariff wall between the two countries. The advocates of Commercial Union could also appeal to higher sentiments. All good social Darwinists agreed with Wiman that "the world moves as the Anglo-Saxon civilization progresses." "A new hope would open its portals of promise . . . for all mankind" if the "great schism" in Anglo-Saxon unity created by the American Revolution could be healed. The way was clear. "Anglo-Saxon unity on the ground of unrestricted trade" would be

[7] Commercial Union Club of Toronto, *Handbook of Commercial Union,* Toronto, 1888, p. 54.

[8] *Official Report of Debates,* March 16, 1888, p. 228.

forwarded "enormously" by the adoption of Commercial Union.[9] Again, nature could always be appealed to for proof in the Commercial Union argument. The Maritimes, Ontario, Manitoba, and British Columbia, each by the dictates of nature, traded with the corresponding productive region in the neighboring republic. Nova Scotia's Attorney General, J. W. Longley, wrote that "Sir John Macdonald and the Canadian Parliament have decreed that the people of Manitoba shall sell their wheat in Montreal or Toronto, and trade with Ontario and Quebec. God and Nature have decreed that they shall sell their wheat in and trade with St. Paul, Minneapolis and other contiguous western cities." [10] S. J. Ritchie, sometime president of the Ontario Central Railway, owner of large mineral holdings in the Sudbury region, American capitalist and one of the most persistent lobbyists for Commercial Union, put it more succinctly in a letter to Goldwin Smith. "What God and nature hath joined together, let not politicians keep asunder." [11]

But there were also some rather obvious objections to Commercial Union. The scheme masqueraded under the guise of free trade and, generally speaking, most Canadian sympathizers were free traders. Longley regarded "absolute Free Trade as a better solution of our difficulties" than Commercial Union but believed the former "not to be a practical question at the present moment." Goldwin Smith consoled himself with the thought that "the largest measure of Free Trade ever passed was the American Constitution, which forbade a customs line to be erected between States. This it is—not the protective tariff on the seaboard—that has been the source of American prosperity." [12] Of course, an extension of the economic aspects

[9] *Handbook of Commercial Union*, pp. 35-40.
[10] *ibid.*, p. 113.
[11] Goldwin Smith Papers, Ritchie to Smith, February 9, 1888.
[12] *Handbook of Commercial Union*, p. 111; Goldwin Smith, *Canada and the Canadian Question*, Toronto, 1892, p. 230.

of the sacred document would bring the same happy results to the rest of the continent. Yet was it not peculiar that free traders in Canada were supporting a policy which was most strongly advocated by ardent protectionists in the United States? Free trade was simple heresy to the four politicians, Senators Payne and Sherman and Representatives Hitt and Butterworth, who were most prominently connected with Commercial Union in Congress. The Philadelphia financier, Wharton Barker, who urged Commercial Union as the road to settlement of the fisheries question, was a publisher of the protectionist weekly, the *American*.[13] Secretary of State Bayard examined the scheme closely and wrote that "the support of this plan is very marked from high protective sources, . . . and Blaine's fugleman Hitt, of Illinois, has been very prominent in favoring a Commercial Union with Canada."[14] In the United States, then, Commercial Unionists frankly admitted that theirs was a protectionist, not a free trade scheme. In May 1887, Benjamin Butterworth told the Canadian Club of New York City that "as against the old world, both Americans and Canadians may invoke the protective system; but as between Canadians and Americans it has no proper place."[15] If nothing else was clear the most undiscerning eye should have seen that "assimilation of tariffs" simply meant retention of the American "Chinese Wall" and added bricks on the Canadian structure.

[13] Public Archives of Ontario, Campbell Papers, Barker to Campbell, June 14, 1886; Allen Johnson, ed., *Dictionary of American Biography*, New York, 1928, v. 1, pp. 606-7. In 1887 Barker wrote, "Protectionists perceive that if the two countries agree with each other for the common maintenance of the protective system the stability of that policy in each must be all the more assured." Wharton Barker, "Memorandum . . . to Hon Justin S. Morill, Chairman Finance Committee United States Senate," Philadelphia, 1887, p. 18.

[14] Cited, Tansill, *Canadian-American Relations*, p. 396.

[15] B. Butterworth, "Commercial Union between Canada and the United States . . . ," New York, 1887, p. 4.

There was potentially an even more serious objection to Commercial Union. Would the United States grant economic union without political union? Apparently a few American advocates thought so. "Canadians are satisfied with their form of government. There is not desire on this side to change it, nor yet to have them adopt any phase of our own," Butterworth told the New York Canadian Club.[16] Yet when he introduced his resolution to Congress on 13 December 1888 it frankly invited the President to open negotiations "looking to the assimilation & unity of the people of the Dominion of Canada & the United States under one Government." British Chargé d'Affairs Herbert told Salisbury that "Canada is given to understand that political union is the wages of Commercial Union, & that she cannot expect to enjoy unrestricted privileges of trade with the U.S. without severing the political ties that connect her with Great Britain, & that on any other terms Commercial Union is not to be considered a practical question." [17]

This did not mean that Congress was unanimous in its desire to see the Dominion become a part of the Republic. In fact, in March 1889, when a sharp debate occurred in the Senate over the appointment of a Select Committee on Relations with Canada the discussion turned from commercial relations to annexation. Senators Hoar (Massachusetts), Cullom (Illinois), Sherman (Ohio), and Blair (New Hampshire) voiced guarded or outright approval of political union. But Senators Edmunds (Vermont), Hale (Maine), Morrill (Vermont), and Butler (South Carolina) protested strongly against

16 *ibid.*, p. 30.
17 Herbert to Salisbury in Foreign Office to Colonial Office, January 8, 1889: CO42/802. See also Senator Hale's resolution of January 16, 1888 which Bayard described as "an unheard of attempt to dismember the dominions of a friendly power" in Foreign Office to Colonial Office, February 2, 1888: CO42/798.

union and even against the appointment of the committee.[18] In the House of Representatives Commercial Union appeared to fare even worse than in the Senate. Robert Hitt told Goldwin Smith that "Czar" Reed, Speaker of the House, "is a strict partisan, and . . . for various reasons, some personal, does not care to aid in the slightest degree in empowering the State Department to shape reciprocity treaties, [he] has the control and direction of business in the House, and I have little expectation of being able hereafter, as I have not been able heretofore, to get him to permit the Canada resolution from the Committee on Foreign Affairs . . . to be taken up and considered by the House." [19] It is true that under the then-existing House rules, Reed did have nearly dictatorial control of the subjects for debate. It is also true that both Houses of Congress waged incessant war on the Executive Department over the control of commercial treaties. But it should be added that if Commerical Union had the exaggerated amount of public appeal in the United States that many Canadians thought existed, neither Reed nor anyone else could have stopped debate on the measure. In short, Commercial Union, despite its vociferous supporters, was not and would not be an important political question in the United States.

In Canada the shadow of annexation behind Commercial Union was sometimes a difficult burden for the advocates to bear. Longley gave an evasive reply to a direct question about annexation from Goldwin Smith: "I know of no rule in political life which compels a public man to declare every hour in the day what he is aiming at. Is it not quite sufficient that he should be continent of his own thought? I am satisfied that the avowal of annexation might injure a man not only as a candidate in his constituency but his usefulness generally

[18] Edwardes to Salisbury in Foreign Office to Colonial Office, March 28, 1889: CO42/802.
[19] Goldwin Smith Papers, Hitt to Smith, June 30, 1890.

as a public man in Canada. Under these circumstances I am pursuing what I conceive to be the most judicious course." Goldwin Smith occasionally pooh-poohed the annexation bugbear of Commercial Union. "Commercial Union need produce no more effect on political relations than the railway union and the partial monetary union which have already taken place," he told the Nineteenth Century Club in New York early in 1890. But for Smith it never really mattered. He always believed that the days of the artificially created Dominion were numbered. As his biographer put it, "his hopes for Canadian nationalism were dimmer than his hopes for the union of Canada and the United States, which he liked to describe as the reunion of the English-speaking peoples of the continent." [20]

Neither Smith's nor Longley's particular view on annexation was typical of the argument advanced to Canadians interested in Commercial Union. More to the point was the opinion expressed in a letter from Erastus Wiman to Valancey Fuller of the Farmers' Institute. "All that annexation would bring in its material advantages," Wiman wrote, "Commercial Union brings; all that the closer political alliance would accomplish in benefits to Canada is accomplished by complete reciprocity." [21] Commercial Unionists seemed to argue that political overtones did not matter, that Canada's interest, and particularly Canada's material interest, was the only important consideration. Speaking for the "manufacturing interests" in favor of the project, J. Dryden said, "Our first duty

[20] *ibid.*, Longley to Smith, September 11, 1890. Longley told a meeting in Boston on 28 December 1887 that he was "both a commercial Unionist and an annexationist." Tansill, *Canadian-American Relations*, p. 401; Goldwin Smith, *The Political Relations of Canada to Great Britain and the United States*, Toronto, 1890, p. 24; E. Wallace, *Goldwin Smith, Victorian Liberal*, Toronto, 1957, p. 242.

[21] Wiman to V. Fuller, May 10 [?], 1887, in *Commercial Union Pamphlets*, collected and bound by the University of Toronto Library, n.d.

133

is to ourselves. Self-preservation is nature's first law." John Charlton recorded in his autobiography that "this arrangement . . . would work smoothly and without friction; would afford complete reciprocity, would be mutually advantageous and I could devise no other arrangment that would meet so fully all these requirements." And while Commercial Union would be advantageous to the United States and Canada it would also benefit the Imperial Power. W. R. Lockhart Gordon, a Canadian sympathizer, pointed out that "by improving the prosperity and increasing the wealth of the country we are strengthening the whole of the British Empire. We are keeping our young men in Canada who otherwise will leave." [22]

iii

When William McDougall said that Commercial Union spread across Canada "as spontaneously as the light of the morning" [23] he set a pattern for exaggeration of the movement in Canada. Both the extent of its appeal and the spontaneity might well be questioned. It is true that the five Premiers who attended the Interprovincial Conference adopted a resolution in favor of "unrestricted reciprocity." But the Premiers were concerned with "better terms" from the federal government and "provincial rights" rather than the trade problems of the Dominion and the resolution was clearly an after-thought resulting from a speech on the subject by Erastus Wiman.[24] In general the appeal of the movement was quite limited and its spontaneity was carefully contrived by its leaders.

[22] *Handbook of Commercial Union*, pp. 106, 186; University of Toronto Library, Charlton Papers, MS autobiography, p. 165.

[23] Cited, W. R. Graham, "Sir Richard Cartwright and the Liberal Party," Ph.D. Thesis, University of Toronto, 1950, p. 154.

[24] "Minutes of the Proceedings of the Interprovincial Conference held at the City of Quebec, from the 20th to the 28th October 1887, inclusively."

In Nova Scotia the *Halifax Morning Chronicle* kept up a constant din for Commercial Union but Longley complained that "nearly every person believes in reciprocity with the United States and but few persons seem to care enough about the subject to take any active measures to bring it about. . . . I have had large and attentive audiences, but I have seen no healthy political agitation follow my remarks." Doubts about the movement in Quebec arose from the fact that its chief Canadian proponent saw in it a means to accomplish the assimilation of French Canada proposed by Lord Durham nearly half a century before. "French Canada may be ultimately absorbed in the English-speaking population of a vast continent," Goldwin Smith hopefully wrote, but "the forces of Canada alone are not sufficient to assimilate the French element." As late as March 1890 Wiman wrote to a friend in Winnipeg that "up to this time we have not had much communication from the far west." And from British Columbia D'Alton McCarthy learned that "Commercial Union is not thought of—Annexation treated with contempt." In short, the appeal of Commercial Union was centered in Ontario and, more particularly, within the region which had been the seedbed of radical agrarian political sentiment in an earlier day, the Western Ontario peninsula.[25]

During the depression of the late 1880's the farmers of the peninsula momentarily responded to the Commercial Union proposal. The movement was advanced by some formal organization. Two groups, the Farmers' Institutes, which sprang up at about the same time as the rise of Commercial Union sentiment, and a few Commercial Union Clubs, called attention to economic continentalism. The first, given active encouragement by Wiman and Smith, was centered on Toronto

[25] Goldwin Smith Papers, Longley to Smith, May 14, 1889; Denison Papers, 4, Copy, Wiman to Dwight, March 17, 1890; Public Archives of Canada, McCarthy Papers, Crease to McCarthy, December 13, 1888; Smith, *Canada and the Canadian Question,* pp. 234, 275.

and spread across the province. Valancey Fuller was president of the central organization and Thomas Shaw was secretary. At the first meeting a resolution was adopted urging the removal of all trade barriers between Canada and the United States. In May 1887 a circular was sent to the local organizations urging the adoption of Commercial Union resolutions.[26] Apparently the pressure on the local institutes was considerable and the issue of Commercial Union was confusing to the Ontario farmers. At local meetings speakers used such diverse terminology as extended commercial relations, unrestricted free trade, a large measure of reciprocity, and Commercial Union to describe their proposals. Only occasionally were the farmers offered opposition speeches and serious debate of the proposal seldom occurred. At meetings of the central institute in the spring of 1888 attempts by the executive officers to adopt a Commercial Union resolution were stoutly resisted by many farmers who feared that meddling with a political problem of that sort would kill the Institute in the way that politics had killed the Grange. Hereafter, writes one student of the subject, "the Farmers' Institutes more and more confined themselves to business of a strictly agricultural nature."[27] It is even more interesting to note that at the first meeting of the central organization an alternative to Commercial Union found expression in the second resolution; a resolution that perhaps presaged the attitude of the Patrons of Industry a decade later on the trade question. Failing the abolition of the tariff barrier with the United States the Institute urged the Dominion to ask the British Government for a preferential tariff favoring Canadian foodstuffs.[28] Apparently the farmers of Ontario were not willing to put all their eggs

[26] A copy of the Circular is in *Commercial Union Handbook*, p. 168.

[27] I. A. Hodson, "Commercial Union, Unrestricted Reciprocity and the Background to the Election of 1891," M.A. Thesis, University of Western Ontario, 1952, pp. 98, 100.

[28] *ibid.*, p. 91.

in the basket woven for them by Wiman, Smith, Fuller, and Shaw.

The Commercial Union Clubs did not fare much better than the Farmers' Institutes in arousing popular sentiment for the movement. The constitution of the Toronto club cited its object as improving trade relations and developing the industries of Canada. Again the confusion within the movement was apparent when "unrestricted reciprocity of trade" was named the means toward that goal. On the other hand "it invites the cooperation of persons of whatever political party, who are favourable to Commercial Union." In May 1890, the success of the club was indicated in a letter from Goldwin Smith to John Charlton. "The absence of response to the call of the C.U. Club for pecuniary aid was undoubtedly disappointing," Smith wrote, "especially on the part of those who had themselves a large interest in the success of the movement." [29]

Two individuals stand out as leaders of the movement, the Canadian in New York, Erastus Wiman, and the Englishman in Toronto, Goldwin Smith. Wiman was a cousin of the old Clear Grit, William McDougall, and worked for him on the *North American.* He went to the *Globe* with McDougall and became its commercial editor. In 1860 he gained control of the Ontario branch of the Dun Mercantile Agency, moved on to Montreal and then to New York City where he eventually became a full partner in the organization. He maintained business interests in Canada principally as president of the Great North Western Telegraph Company. The adoption of Commercial Union would have benefited at least two other Wiman enterprises. In 1887 he was a member of an international syndicate seeking to control the known iron ore resources of Canada. Along with Senator Payne of Ohio, S. J. Ritchie, James MacLaren of Ottawa, A. B. Boardmen and

[29] *Handbook of Commercial Union,* p. 296; Goldwin Smith Papers, Smith to Charlton, May 9 [?], 1890.

others in New York City, Wiman realized that the abolition of mineral duties in the United States and duties on iron products in Canada would greatly forward the plans of the syndicate. Again, he had a personal interest in abolishing the transportation competition of the Canadian Pacific Railway with eastern American trunk lines and in the integration of the whole North American transport system. He owned extensive transport and dock facilities on Staten Island and these would profit if the trade of the middle and north west, stolen away by differential rates on the Canadian Pacific, could be restored to the eastern American railways.[30]

Wiman was a tireless worker for Commercial Union, seizing every opportunity to expound his favorite doctrine on the platform, in print, or before Congressional Committees. He traveled extensively in Ontario bringing the word to the Canadian nationalist heathen and eventually, in 1890, spoke in Montreal. Perhaps his most lasting contribution to amicable trade and business relations between the United States and Canada was the founding of the Canadian Club in New York City. The Canadian Club historian records that as first president Wiman was "an earnest advocate of improving friendly relations between Canada and the United States, and . . . he lavishly entertained many eminent men of both countries."[31] When the issue was before the people of Canada in 1891, Wiman did his best to arouse enthusiasm for the movement in the United States. He had a letter sent to influential persons

[30] Hodson, Commercial Union, pp. 32-41, 86.

[31] I am indebted to Mr. H. A. Anderson, past president and historian of the Canadian Club of New York for this bit of information from the Club's quarterly, *The Maple Leaf,* Spring, 1956, p. 2. Mr. Anderson informed me that the present Club is a reorganization (1903) on a much more elaborate basis of the original Club started by Wiman in 1885. The original Club apparently had sporadic dinner meetings as occasion demanded and it would probably be fair to say it was used largely to promote Commercial Union. Unfortunately, there are no records of the original Canadian Club.

throughout the Republic giving information about Canadian trade and "the last election." "The whole question to be decided," he wrote, "is what hereafter shall be the relations of the two people that together hold this continent in common." "Shall these relations be commercially hostile, restrictive, and mutually dangerous and hurtful; or shall they, on the other hand, be of the most intimate and friendly character, immediately adjusting, by an Unrestricted Reciprocity, all differences, and mutually contributing to each other's enormous advantage?" Wiman went on to urge "some action . . . by the Congress of the United States, expressive of the almost universal desire of the commercial community for Enlarged Markets . . ." and enclosed a blank to be signed by the reader and sent to his Senator or Congressman expressing approval of Commercial Union.[32]

Wiman led the group of Commercial Unionists who made the somewhat labored distinction between economic and political union. Unquestionably he would not have opposed the full measure of integration but he seemed to be totally absorbed in the trade question. After the 1891 election he hopefully wrote to Laurier that "five years ago we could not get this people to agree to Reciprocity, because they thought Annexation was the next best thing. Today nine out of every ten business men would vote for Unrestricted Reciprocity." In February 1890, he wrote to E. W. Thomson of the *Toronto Globe* that it was necessary to "undo the impression that Farrer, Glen and others have endeavoured to convey—that if Canada did not get Commercial Union Annexation will follow." Speaking of his plan to speak in Montreal Wiman said he wanted "especially to show the progress of the question and the gradual elimination of the Annexation element on both sides of the Line, reiterating the conviction that it now stands

[32] New York Public Library, Misc. Collection, Erastus Wiman, Wiman to ——, February 19, 1891 (printed).

on a trade basis of its own merit, and aside from political or fanciful considerations." [33]

This problem never bothered Canada's most distinguished advocate of Commercial Union, Goldwin Smith. Anti-imperial and Anglo-Saxon in his heart of hearts, Smith believed that the Dominion was simply an abortive political and military contrivance to maintain British Imperialism in North America and that eventually and inevitably Canada would become a State or a number of States in the Union.[34] Throughout his life he promoted this course, using whatever argument seemed most appropriate at any particular time. In the late 1880's that argument was Commercial Union. S. J. Ritchie called Smith "one of the Daniels," "a gallant master and leader"[35] of the movement. Smith founded the first Commercial Union Club in Canada and was a power behind consideration of the question by the Farmers' Institute as well as a frequent speaker on the Institute circuit. He served as middleman and interpreter between Commercial Unionists in Canada and the United States. Unlike Wiman and many other Commercial Unionists, Smith had nothing to gain materially from the plan. He championed the cause on principle, because he thought it would benefit the people of Canada. As befitted his career, his leadership was primarily academic in character and his greatest effort was devoted to putting the stamp of scholarly approval on the movement. The result was his lengthy and well-known argument for continentalism in *Canada and the Canadian Question,* perhaps the most thorough and devastating attack on Confederation that has ever been penned. The

[33] Public Archives of Canada, Laurier Papers, 5, Wiman to Laurier, March 6, 1891; Denison Papers, 4, Copy, Wiman to Thomson, February 12, 1890.

[34] For Smith's ideas see E. Wallace, *Goldwin Smith, Victorian Liberal.* On anti-imperialism see R. C. Brown, "Goldwin Smith and Anti-Imperialism," *Canadian Historical Review,* XLIII, 1962, pp. 93-105.

[35] Goldwin Smith Papers, Ritchie to Smith, February 8, 1888.

"fruits of confederation" were all bitter. Newfoundland had thwarted and would forever thwart all attempts at absorption. Manitoba and the Northwest would be peopled by immigrants. The "cohesion and stability of Confederation" would be shattered. The Intercolonial and Canadian Pacific Railways were simply political and military abortions with no commercial value whatever, rendered largely useless by arctic weather and, what was even worse, competing against rather than cooperating with each other. Of course, interprovincial trade was against the dictates of all reasonable men and God and Nature. The real object of the National Policy was "to capture the manufacturer's vote and his contributions to the election fund of the party in power."[36]

Special scorn was heaped upon Quebec. It was an "uncommercial" backward province, "a non-conductor between the more commercial members of the Confederation." Only corruption served as a bond with English Canada and the portent of the future was seen in the way all the rest of Canada was dancing Quebec's tune regarding the Jesuit Estates Act and the Manitoba Schools legislation. Obviously, French domination was too great a price to pay for union. And there was no use hiding behind happy phrases about dual culture and a uniquely blended nationality.[37]

Let those who prophesy to us smooth things take stock of the facts. When one community differs from another in race, language, religion, character, spirit, social structure, aspirations, occupying also a territory apart, it is a separate nation, and is morally certain to pursue a different course, let it designate itself as it may.

The last and most bitter fruit of Confederation was the Election of 1891, said Smith. The whole election had been a fraud. It had been called to cover up the McGreevy scandal. It had been won by the Conservative's use of stolen documents and

[36] Smith, *Canada and the Canadian Question,* p. 228.
[37] *ibid.,* pp. 228, 237.

false accusations of treason. "To divide a community on such a line for a party purpose, and incite one-half of the citizens to treat the other half as public enemies, thus kindling among them the passions of civil war, is in itself the highest treason." But even out of so much evil could come good. The Liberals had nearly won on their platform of Unrestricted Reciprocity. "The Liberal Party . . . has come out of the struggle a continental party, with a continental policy, and resting at bottom on the forces of its own continent. It will probably, at the cost of a temporary increase of weakness, slough off its reactionary element, and its next step is likely to be from Unrestricted Reciprocity to Commercial Union." [38]

iv

The Commercial Union movement had many internal difficulties and was plagued by continual confusion about its terms and its objectives. Its appeal was largely limited to the empire province in Canada's heartland. Even there the Farmers' Institute quickly turned to less political questions and the Commercial Union Clubs suffered from lack of financial support. But this did not mean that Canadians turned a deaf ear to the siren song of continentalism or that the idea was not fully discussed in the Canadian press. The Conservative party Government and its National Policy were seriously embarrassed by the depression of the late 1880's and Commercial Union appeared to be a logical alternative to Conservative policy.

As might have been expected, newspapers which were generally critical of government policy could not resist the temptation to further embarrass the government by "booming" continentalism. The *Manitoba Free Press* reflected the farmers' discontent with a tariff drawn in the interests of eastern manufacturers and with the Canadian Pacific Railway monopoly in the province by declaring that free trade with the United

[38] *ibid.*, pp. 262, 265.

States was "both natural and desirable." The *Halifax Morning Chronicle* agreed that the protective tariff was "a false and pernicious policy" and in 1886 paraded the double banner of "repeal and reciprocity . . . they *stand* or *fall* together; reciprocity means prosperity to all parts of this province as in days of old. We can only get it through *repeal,* which will give us power to make our own trade relations." After the repeal movement succeeded in electing the Fielding Government only to find that it preferred Confederation to isolation or annexation, the paper abruptly switched to a blatant cry for Commercial Union. Across the Bay of Fundy the *St. John Daily Telegraph* announced its approval of "complete reciprocity." And all of these newspapers seemed to take their cues from the leader of the opposition pack, the *Globe.* Toronto readers were graced on New Year's Day 1886, with an annual policy statement headed by "Unrestricted Commercial Reciprocity with the kindred people of the United States." In June the paper declared that Canada's destiny "is not to be kept in pantalets to all eternity . . . she cannot go on much longer dissociated from the commerce of the continent." [39]

Rebuttal came from the Conservative-minded *Montreal Gazette* which expressed its grief that Canadians were being led down the garden path by "a self-seeking notoriety hunter," the "charlatan" Wiman. No true Canadian would "leap into the lap of the United States" and "give away the right to direct our own affairs." With approval the *Gazette* cited the warning of *Le Pionnier* of Sherbrooke that to the people of Quebec Commercial Union meant annexation, absorption, and the extinction of French Canadian rights and privileges. Far away in British Columbia both Victoria papers rejected continentalism. The *Daily Times* was convinced it "would relieve the American Manufacturer [but] would ruin the Ca-

[39] *Manitoba Free Press,* January 26, 1886; *Halifax Morning Chronicle,* January 22 and June 3, 1886; *St. John Daily Telegraph,* May 10, 1887; *Toronto Globe,* January 1 and June 12, 1886.

nadian." The *Weekly Colonist* stood firmly behind the National Policy and suggested that the only possible alternative was Imperial Federation which merited the attention of "every loyalist." And from the territories came a strong appeal to national pride. "Those who belittle Canada," noted the editor of the *Edmonton Bulletin* in an attack on Commercial Union, "because it is not equal to the United States in population or wealth would cut down the twig because it is not a tree." [40]

The editors of the *Canadian Manufacturer and Industrial World* expressed their opinion on Commercial Union when they learned that an "annexation picnic" was to be held at Dufferin Lake on Dominion Day 1887. They suggested that the picnickers be entertained by "the great and only original troupe of International Itineraries and Political Acrobats" who would perform a "side-splitting Farce" entitled: [41]

HEADS I WIN, TAILS YOU LOSE

CAST

Tweedledum (a speculator)	Rastus Stateniland
Tweedledee (an *honorable* politician)	Benny Butterprier
The Professor (a professional theorist of uncertain conviction)	P. Lucre Smeath
Buttons ⎰ two gentlemen engaged in ⎱ Tassels ⎱ commerce ⎰	Henry W. Drygoods E. York Everytime
Miss Canada	
Miss Ontario	
Miss Quebec, etc., etc.	
Camp Followers, Henchmen, Sycophants, etc., etc.	

[40] *Montreal Gazette,* October 10, 1886, May 31, August 9 and 29, 1887; *Victoria Daily Times,* December 30, 1885; *Victoria British Weekly Colonist,* March 19 and August 27, 1886; *Edmonton Bulletin,* September 3, 1887. This sentiment is echoed by the *Regina Leader,* December 27, 1887. See also R. C. Brown, "Canadian Nationalism in Western Newspapers," *Alberta Historical Review,* 10, 1962, pp. 1-7.

[41] *Canadian Manufacturer and Industrial World,* July 1, 1887.

ORCHESTRA

Act I.   Overture, "Yankee Doodle"

Act II. "The Pirate King"

Act III. "The Traitor's Hand is on Thy Throat, Ontario, Ontario"

Act IV. "Not for Joe," followed by the National Anthem

The journal did not confine its comments on Commercial Union to playful joshing. For manufacturers who owed their existence to the National Policy, and for their spokesman, Commercial Union was a very serious matter, perhaps a matter of commercial life and death. This, of course, was expected. More interesting, however, were the comments of the self-proclaimed "nationalist" Toronto journal, *The Week*, which purported to speak for serious-thinking nonpartisan Canadian opinion. "When discussing Commercial Union the American Press are delightfully innocent of any thought of Annexation," the paper commented in May 1887. But thinking Canadians were wiser; they saw the dreaded ghost lurking in Mr. Wiman's shadow. Overstating its case, *The Week* warned: "sink a shaft from an unsuspected direction, and Annexation is found everywhere at the bottom of American policy." "We do not think," the editors wrote a few months later, "Canada should lightly imperil her separate national existence by forming a commercial co-partnership with a Power so much greater in every material aspect to herself that in the nature of things political union will probably follow. We believe we discern abundant promise of Canada's growing into a nation with a strong individuality, and of a vigorous, healthy type." "We say wait awhile," they concluded, "let us see if we cannot walk alone." At least for this segment of Canadian opinion there could be no thought of compromising political separateness on the North American continent for economic gain. Indeed, in twenty years Canada had come a long way "with the qualities that self-help are developing" and a detour from the road to political maturity now would be disastrous.[42]

The effort to "boom" Commercial Union made a great impression on the lords of Canada's fourth estate. The gains and losses to Canada accruing from a continental trade policy were hotly argued in the press from the Atlantic to the Pacific. In retrospect it is clear that the newspaper debate gave an impression of greater support for the movement than it ever possessed. But at the time it was much more difficult to discern the extent of the appeal of continentalism on the Canadian mind. Lord Lansdowne, an acute observer of the Canadian scene feared that "the question is one which will sooner or later force itself to the front." With its obvious consequences for the Imperial relationship he noted that it "will not be by any means an easy one to deal with." [43] With this in mind, on 31 October 1887, he prepared a long, important and "extremely confidential" despatch on Commercial Union.

The movement, Lansdowne said, was of "recent origin," it had not been an issue in the recent general election "and even at the present time it has not to any considerable extent been discussed by prominent public men." It was, however, being advocated "with great ability and persistency" by men like Smith, Wiman, and Butterworth and "both the leading journals of Toronto (the *Globe* and the *Mail*) have declared themselves in favour of the new policy." The reasons why the politicians of Canada had not identified themselves with the movement were quite clear. The Conservative party "depends largely for support upon the manufacturers whose industries . . . are kept alive by the high protective tariff adopted in 1878 [sic] for the express purpose of artificially stimulating them." Adoption of Commercial Union would be "fatal" to the manufacturers. Still, "the Conservatives . . . have nothing to gain by prematurely declaring themselves against a movement

[42] *The Week,* May 5 and October 13, 1887.
[43] Lansdowne Papers, Lansdowne to Holland, October 29, 1887.

which is apparently regarded with some favour by the farmers and which may rapidly hereafter find a wide measure of acceptance amongst them."

The Liberals were "in a position of somewhat similar embarrassment." During the general election Edward Blake had committed his party, if elected, to abstain from "a sudden or violent interference with the fiscal policy of his predecessors." Moreover, the Province of Quebec "would not be likely to offer much encouragement to a measure which might have its outcome in the establishment of more intimate political relations between Canada and the United States. The people of Lower Canada are well aware that their annexation . . . might involve if not their own effacement as a distinct political community at all events the sacrifice of many of the privileges civil and religious assured to them under the British connection." To date the statements of the new Liberal leader, Wilfrid Laurier, justified the conclusion that Quebec would "probably be adverse to any change pointing in this direction." Within the last few days, however, Sir Richard Cartwright had spoken for the Ontario Liberals in favor of Commercial Union and it was improbable that the subject would "remain outside the area of ordinary political controversy" much longer.

As for himself, the Governor-General noted that "in its strictly commercial aspect . . . there appears to be no room for doubt that Commercial Union would be greatly to the advantage of the people of the Dominion or at all events to that of a large majority of it." The "natural channels" of trade were north-south, i.e. between the Maritimes and New England, and not east-west. "Reciprocal commerce between them would be more to their convenience and advantage than a system which has for its object to compel the people of Nova Scotia and New Brunswick—the bulk of whose products in spite of the high tariff find a market in the United States—to purchase commodities in Montreal and Quebec." Of course, it was "idle to deny" that most of the protected manufacturers would be destroyed "root and branch." "There seems however no reason why the more vigorous of them where the natural conditions are favourable to their existence should not survive and prosper even after the withdrawal of . . . protection."

But Lansdowne was troubled about the "political aspect" of the question. "The centre of political activity," he told Holland,

> in regard to all commercial questions affecting the North American Continent would inevitably be at Washington: Congress would be the arbiter of the Commercial destinies of the Dominion and the Canadian Parliament would find itself comparatively impotent to affect any changes which it might desire in the interests of its own Country.
>
> That such a change would tend towards the estrangement of Canada from the Mother Country and towards an approximation political as well as commercial between Canada and the American Republic is hardly doubtful.

Lansdowne concluded by reminding the Colonial Secretary that Canada could not afford free trade with the whole world. If there was to be free trade at all for Canada, it would have to be with the United States, "the community with which she already does more business than with any other." Despite the fact that Commercial Union would mean discrimination against the mother country, Great Britain was "so deeply committed to a free trade policy" that it was his opinion that the Imperial Government could only deny Canada "the advantages of free trade with the United States" on "purely selfish grounds" should it be desired by the Ottawa Government.[44]

When Joseph Chamberlain arrived in New York on his way to the Joint High Commission, he found a letter from Lansdowne waiting for him. The Governor-General gave the

[44] Macdonald Papers, 44, Copy, Lansdowne to Holland, October 31, 1887. Minutes to the despatch are found in CO42/791. The despatch was printed and is found in CO807, North America 131.

British Commissioner a summary of his despatch to Holland and added that Commercial Union was "gaining strength." The Conservatives had hedged the question because of the "dry nursed manufacturers"; the Liberals, because of Blake's "pledge" on the question of protection which "left his followers virtually without any policy at all." Cartwright's speech at Ingersoll made it certain that "the idea may 'take' and become the popular cry all over the country." Chamberlain had stated before leaving England that "if Canada determines to ask for Comml. Union she will have to get it." "The political results are inevitable," Lansdowne said, "altho I am not sure that annexation would follow commercial union so rapidly as some people suppose." In any case, the fundamental point was that if Canada wanted Commercial Union, "we can hardly refuse." [45]

Chamberlain replied that he did not see how the development of the idea of Commercial Union could be prevented if it were favored in the United States. "In fact if I was a Canadian I would certainly adopt the policy as the best for the Dominion," he said, adding, however, that "at the same time it is desirable that the Canadians should themselves appreciate the full consequences of their action." It was on the "Imperial aspect" that Chamberlain laid emphasis, repeating the warning he had made in England before leaving for the Joint High Commission. Yes, Great Britain probably would have to yield Commercial Union if it were desired. On the other hand, he told Lansdowne:

The nominal supremacy of the mother country involves us in heavy responsibilities and undoubtedly tends to make the Dominion more still in its relations with other Countries than it would be if it were entirely left to its own resources.

I do not believe that our manufacturers and the British

[45] Chamberlain Papers, Lansdowne to Chamberlain, November 8, 1887.

people generally will continue to accept the obligations of the position for long, after the establishment of preferential intercourse with the U.S. & I should myself be ready frankly to tell the Canadians that they may have Commercial Union whenever they like but that they must be prepared to assume their political independence at the same time. Possibly our Govt. would shrink from such a declaration, but the result will be the same in any case after a longer or shorter interval.[46]

The British Commissioner had held this opinion for some time. In mid-September he had written to Goldwin Smith that the adoption of Commercial Union by Canada meant political union with the United States and the end of the British connection. And there appeared to be total agreement in London on the grave implications of Commercial Union. Sir Robert Herbert, on reading Lansdowne's secret despatch, noted that having yielded "a sulky consent to this commercial union Great Britain would no doubt intimate pretty clearly that a Dominion which had so differentially treated it must not look for the same amount of defence against foreigners as it now claims: must, in fact, look to the United States for everything." In short, as far as the Imperial authorities were concerned, Commercial Union would shatter the Imperial connection.[47]

Lansdowne replied to Chamberlain that the time was not ripe for a declaration from the British Government. "The Canadians are themselves well aware of the ultimate consequences." It was true that some people were arguing that Commercial Union would strengthen rather than weaken the Empire by removing a cause of friction with the United States "but the country as a whole knows what it is about and

[46] *ibid.*, Chamberlain to Lansdowne, November 10, 1887.
[47] Goldwin Smith Papers, Chamberlain to Smith, September 13, 1887; Minute by Herbert on Lansdowne to Holland, October 31, 1887; CO42/791.

an attempt to enlighten it might be regarded as a threat and do more harm than good." Even if an offer were made the Canadians should have to make the decision to accept or reject it. If they were going to grow to maturity, if they were going to show the responsibility they talked so much about, then they had to make up their own minds. As it was, "their representatives would under such cirs. be only too well pleased if they were able to shew that we had shut the door in their face." [48]

In any case Chamberlain stood fast to his opinion. Erastus Wiman gloomily told E. W. Thomson of the *Globe,* "my conclusion . . . is that he is not at all in favour of Commercial Union and that he is not open to conviction in any way—He looks at it purely and solely from an English manufacturer's point of view." The British Commissioner happily reported to Lord Salisbury that the Ottawa Government "entirely shared" his view of Commercial Union. It was clear that if the offer were made the Macdonald Government would refuse. "The utmost that Canada requires or desires is that natural products . . . shd. be reciprocally admitted free into the U.S. & the Dominion." [49]

The Canadian Government had no knowledge of Lansdowne's despatch, which appeared on balance to favor Commercial Union. They probably would have remained in innocence had not it been included in the dossier given to the British members of the Joint High Commission. Tupper discovered it when he returned to Washington after the Christmas recess. He was very upset. With "equal surprise and regret" he sent it to Macdonald, urging the Prime Minister to see Lansdowne. If the Governor-General retained his view and it was adopted by the Imperial Government "no one can

[48] Chamberlain Papers, Lansdowne to Chamberlain, November 14, 1887.

[49] Denison Papers, 4, Copy, Wiman to Thomson, n.d., 1887; Chamberlain Papers, Chamberlain to Salisbury, November 11, 1887.

predict the result to Canada." [50] On seeing the despatch Macdonald had "some regret but was not surprised." The Prime Minister explained to his colleague that the Governor-General "is a free trader to the bone, and all such men are deaf and blind to any other considerations but the blind teachings of abstract political economy." Furthermore, Tupper should remember that the despatch was confidentially sent by an Imperial Officer "with which we here have no concern & which indeed we had better not know. . . . We can afford to be perfectly indifferent as to what the private opinions of GG's may be." Besides, wrote the Prime Minister, "the logic of events has deprived it of much of its force. It is now comparatively harmless." Macdonald remembered that before leaving Canada Chamberlain had spoken to the Toronto Board of Trade on Commercial Union [51] and that Sir David Macpherson reported that the speech had shattered the sentiment for the movement. He noted that the by-elections all went against Commercial Union, that "the Globe had abandoned it in despair," and prominent Liberals like Alexander Mackenzie and James Young opposed it. Watchful waiting had been the Prime Minister's guide and he had been proven correct. "C U is a dead duck," he concluded, "and I think Lord L sees now that my policy, as announced to him last spring of allowing the cry of C U to blaze, crackle & go out with a stink, without giving it undue importance was a wise one." [52]

v

Commercial Union provided Canadians with an extreme proposal for extending trade on the north-south axis. Imperial Federation provided Canadians with an extreme proposal for extending trade on the east-west axis. When the Imperial

[50] Macdonald Papers, 176, Tupper to Macdonald, January 11, 1888.
[51] The text of the speech is reproduced in Maycock, *With Mr. Chamberlain*, pp. 101-12.
[52] Macdonald Papers, 250, Macpherson to Macdonald, December 31, 1887; 527, Macdonald to Tupper, January 15, 1888.

Federation League was organized in the mother country in 1884 no mention of furthering Imperial trade was made in the objects of the movement. This was hardly surprising in a country where the writings of Cobden and Bright were second in sanctity only to the Gospels. Rather, the emphasis appeared to be on "permanent Unity of the Empire" and an "organized defence of common rights." With appropriate fuss and flurry a League in Canada was organized in Montreal in May 1885 and three branches at Ingersoll, Halifax, and Peterborough were organized in the next two years. However, the League singularly failed to strike a loyal Imperial response in most Canadians.

The project was too vague; it had too many dangerous implications for the many Canadians who were concerned with the less visionary problems of Canadian nationalism. Speaking to the National Club in Toronto on 23 May 1887, the Governor-General said: "I have never seen any scheme . . . worthy to be called a scheme of Imperial Confederation which would have been likely to work in practice for six months." George Stephen told Sir Charles Tupper in 1884 that "we out here will have enough to do if we take good care of the Empire *here* without attempting to extend our efforts to the management of affairs in England or in other outlying parts of the Empire." Oddly enough, on the same day the Prime Minister also wrote to Tupper that he did not "believe that a practical scheme can ever be worked out for a *legislative* confederation of the Empire." Macdonald, of course, always adhered to this line of thought. Imperial Federation, like Commercial Union, carried with it the threat of legislative absorption by a larger power; it would diminish, not enhance, Canadian stature. Of course, Imperial cooperation was not only desirable but necessary. But how to cooperate? Macdonald's answer was consistent. "The great subjects of common defence and preferential trade can be arrived by *treaty* arrangements." [53] In short, Imperial Federation would create more problems than it would solve; it left too many questions unanswered, it proposed no single, concrete idea that would "take" with the Canadian people.

Erastus Wiman and Goldwin Smith forced some Canadians to look to the League with renewed interest. Sir Leonard Tilley told the Prime Minister early in 1887 that a branch of the League had been formed in St. John. "I have encouraged this," he said, "as there has been an effort made in certain quarters to propagate annexation sentiments and it was necessary to counteract this by bringing out the latent loyal sentiments of our people." The poet, Charles G. D. Roberts, wrote to a friend that "I am supporting the movement now, down here, quietly, being turned from my *Independence* line by the necessity for all loyal Canadians to unite against the Annexationists. Imp. Fed. will satisfy me!" Another Canadian poet, Charles Mair, showed Colonel Denison the other side of the coin. From Prince Albert he wrote that "there is not an annexationist in the place, and therefore nothing to organize against." Denison, himself, made clear the impact of Commercial Union on the Imperial Federation movement. Some years later he wrote that "it was not until the Commercial Union movement alarmed the people and proved the necessity for prompt action that the cause of Imperial Federation became a strong and effective influence upon the public opinion of Canada." [54]

The new sense of urgency in the League was reflected in March 1888, in the formation of a Toronto branch and an

[53] Governor-General to Colonial Office, June 2, 1887: CO42/790; Tupper Papers, 5, Stephen to Tupper, August 13, 1884, Macdonald to Tupper, August 13, 1884; Macdonald Papers, 529, Macdonald to Rev. C. H. Mackin, April 4, 1890, italics mine.

[54] Macdonald Papers, 277, Tilley to Macdonald, February 11, 1889; Denison Papers, 4, Roberts to Denison, May 7, 1888, Mair to Denison, January 8, 1889; G. T. Denison, *The Struggle for Imperial Unity*, London, 1909, p. 97.

amendment to its constitution calling for an Imperial preference in both natural and manufactured products. Toward the
end of April the League's president, D'Alton McCarthy introduced a motion in the House of Commons for an Imperial
preference with the significant qualification of "due regard
being had to the policy adopted in 1879 for the purpose of
fostering the various interests and industries of the Dominion,
and to the financial necessities of the Dominion." McCarthy
made it clear that he considered the National Policy a success. Imperial preference should supplement, not substitute
for, the National Policy. Its chief benefit would be to the
farmers as the National Policy's chief benefit was to the in-
dustrialists. It would restore to the farmers the markets "lost
in consequence of the enormous competition on the other
side of the line." "Manufacturers," he said, "must to a certain
extent be protected, and to a certain extent they must surrender in favour of the great farming population the extreme
protection they possess at this moment." [55] No one, least of
all McCarthy, hoped to have this novel approach to Canada's
trade problem adopted immediately and after some discussion
the matter was dropped.

Still, it was a strong argument and a good one. The great
difficulty was that the Canadian League was at odds with the
home organization. "Are we to stand still whilst the Greater
question is held in abeyance at its fountainhead?" asked
Charles Mair. "The work is to be done in England," William
Kirby wrote Denison. *"There* they must learn that the Empire
is to be preserved only on the basis of mutual tariff advantages." The point was, as Denison discovered when he went
to Great Britain in 1890 to urge approval of the Canadian
suggestion, the English League could not support a scheme
of Imperial preference. Both political parties were committed
to free trade with the world. Popular support for the League
would vanish if the League declared itself in favor of a prefer-

[55] *Official Report of Debates,* April 30, 1888, pp. 1069, 1073.

ential tariff.[56] Imperial sentiment was one thing. The price of bread, as Joseph Chamberlain would discover a decade later, was quite another.

While it is true that the Imperial Federationists received far less support in Great Britain than the Commericial Unionists received in the United States, it would be wrong to conclude that this alone made it impossible for the Imperial Federation League to be an effective counterbalance to Commercial Union. Of perhaps even greater importance were the internal difficulties of the Canadian organization. Not the least of these troubles was that some of the League adherents continued to talk about almost everything but Imperial preference. Had they taken McCarthy's cue and concentrated on Imperial preference, then a clear issue between east-west or north-south orientation of Canadian trade would have been joined. But many, instead, continued to argue with F. B. Crofton about the visionary prospects of a larger Canadian voice in Imperial diplomacy and the reduction of the "chance of our being involved in a European complication" that would result from Imperial Federation.[57]

Colonel Denison usually made a point of neither arguing for Imperial Federation nor against Commercial Union. The latter was simply an "insidious scheme," a "movement designed by traitors." His concept of the former was generally confined to its being designed to "demolish . . . that nefarious scheme." Significantly, any positive benefits were given second place when he spoke. In fact, the subtleties of argument were singularly foreign to his militaristic mind. He rightly said that he had "fired" his "first public shot against Commercial Union" when he spoke briefly at the Toronto Board

[56] Denison Papers, 4, Mair to Denison, December 19, 1888, Kirby to Denison, October 1, 1889; Denison, *Struggle for Imperial Unity,* ch. 15. See also detailed study by G. R. MacLean, "The Imperial Federation Movement in Canada, 1884-1902," Ph.D. Thesis, Duke University, 1958, especially pp. 88-106.

[57] F. B. Crofton, "For Closer Union," *The Week,* October 23, 1884.

of Trade dinner for Joseph Chamberlain in December 1887. At the annual general meeting in Toronto in March 1888, Denison combatted Commercial Union by cataloguing the sins of Yankee expansion in Florida, Louisiana, Texas, Alaska, California, Mexico, and Maine and then saw fit to comment on the American Revolution, the War of 1812, the Civil War, and the Fenian Raids. Years later, Denison recalled that "Sir Oliver Mowat . . . once spoke to me, advising me not to be so violent in my language. My reply was that if the matter became dangerous I would resign my Police Magistracy one day, and he would find me leading a mob the next." [58]

Naturally, there were others who felt the threat of Commercial Union as deeply as Denison. William Kirby commented on the Colonel's speech at the Board of Trade dinner: "It was a good & timely reminder to all concerned, that some *big fighting* would have to be done before Canada could be severed from the Empire—and that the Militia of the Dominion were the men who would have the most to say about it." On the other hand, Kirby realized that threats of war did not make up for sound argument against Commercial Union. Something positive was needed. As he said, "Nations, like individuals, are saved by HOPE, not by despair." "To me Imperial Federation must be put before the people of this country as a material question, as What is to be gained by it?" "Cannot we take a lesson from our enemies?" he asked. [59]

A much more serious difficulty for the Imperial Federation League in Canada was the leading part its president played in the renewed religious and cultural strife that swept across Canada in the late 1880's. D'Alton McCarthy had led the fight against the Jesuit Estates Act and was the principal spokesman of the Equal Rights Association. [60] By December 1890,

[58] Denison, *Struggle for Imperial Unity,* pp. 88, 92, 126.

[59] Denison Papers, 4, Kirby to Denison, January 2, 1888, September 13, 1889; 5, Kirby to Denison, September 17, 1891.

[60] See F. Landon, "D'Alton McCarthy and the Politics of the Later Eighties," *Canadian Historical Association Annual Report,* 1932, pp. 43-50.

CANADA'S DON QUIXOTE

some of the leading figures in the Imperial Federation League were finding McCarthy's presidency a liability. Under Sanford Fleming's guidance, the Ottawa branch had sent out a questionnaire on Imperial Federation. Fleming wrote to Principal Grant of Queen's University that the replies were numerous but that they all came from the outlying Provinces. The heartland of the Dominion was silent and Fleming thought he knew why. Grant frankly stated to McCarthy that "[Fleming] thinks that the agitation of which you are the leader prevents any French Canadian from considering the subject & that it has an influence in the same way even in Ontario; & therefore while fully recognizing your services to the League, he considers that it would be in the general interest to secure for a time another President." Fleming had told Grant: "The opinion held by all the best friends of the League, and I have seen quite a number from all the Provinces, is that Mr. McCarthy would promote the prospects of the League in Canada by retiring from its Presidency for a time." [61]

On 6 January 1891, Principal Grant again wrote to McCarthy. He had received a reply to his first letter and was pleased that McCarthy had privately consented to give up the presidency of the Imperial Federation League: [62]

in my opinion you have never proved yourself a truer friend of the Cause of Union than at present, when you privately intimate your willingness to retire from the Presidency, & I will tell you why. The President should be as little of a party man as possible, as we must for a time include all parties. Your great fitness for the post when you were called to it was due to the fact that everyone knew that you were not an aggressive party man. . . . But within the last two years you have become the recognized head of what I believe will grow into the

[61] McCarthy Papers, Grant to McCarthy, n.d. [December 1890 or January 1891].
[62] *ibid.,* Grant to McCarthy, January 6, 1891.

159

strongest party in Canada. That of course connects you with antagonisms which the Cause of Union should not be necessarily identified with, & I therefore think that you show a right appreciation of the circumstances by offering to retire.

Naturally, this correspondence was not known to the public. But the public did know of McCarthy's stand on the Jesuit Estates Act, the French language question in the Northwest Territories, and the Manitoba Schools Question. Obviously, it was very confusing. Was Imperial Federation just another front for the extreme Protestantism of the Equal Rights Association? Did Imperial Federation mean a political union of the Empire, an economic union of the Empire, a defensive union of the Empire, or did it mean all three of these things? Or was it simply a platform for Colonel Denison to stand on to vent his fanatical hatred of the United States? Even if it could be assumed that Imperial Federation was, in fact, a proposition for Imperial preference as an alternative to Commercial Union, the puzzling fact remained that the English League refused to countenance a preferential trade scheme and even broke up on this very point in 1891. Having few satisfactory answers to these questions, Imperial Federation did not provide an effective counter proposal to Commercial Union. Perhaps the acute sense of frustration felt by some of the League members was best summed up in these anonymous lines found in the McCarthy papers:

> The words "Imperial Federation"
> Convey their own self-condemnation.
> Their mildest screed (I underscore it)
> Is: EMPIRE—AN IDEAL FOR IT.
> The tangled phrase, as I respin it,
> Yields: O, A MERE FAD—PERIL IN IT.
> Lastly, the League receives its ban,
> In: I DIE ERE IT FORM A PLAN.

CHAPTER VI
Response of the Parties

COMMERCIAL UNION presented a direct challenge to the Canadian National Policy, particularly to the protective tariff and the validity of the assumption that an east-west trade axis could be created on the foundation of the Canadian Pacific Railway. Indirectly, but as Goldwin Smith revealed, no less potently, it questioned the political basis of Confederation itself. At face value it was an economic question. But Commercial Union was an economic question that could be solved only by political means. And its deeper logic, the assumption on the part of most Commercial Unionists that economic union would be a prelude to annexation, was entirely political. It was not surprising that the political parties in the Dominion had to respond to the challenge.

The Liberal party was especially interested. The party's prospects in 1887 were dim, indeed. In February they had lost their third successive battle against wise old Sir John Macdonald and his National Policy. With an unwitting foretaste of future Liberal policy, the party leader, Edward Blake, in a vain effort to win the general election, had granted all the assumptions upon which the National Policy rested and pleaded only for reform of the existing system. Having lost, the Liberals were virtually stripped of any policy attractive to Canadian voters and shortly they lost their leader.[1] The new chief was the gifted young French Canadian orator, Wilfrid Laurier. But many regarded his appointment as only temporary and it was quite obvious that Ontario Liberalism was not entirely reconciled to his leadership. With no "old leader," with no "old policy," Canadian Liberals were anxiously looking for an attractive lure to cast before the Canadian electorate.

[1] See M. A. Banks, "The Change in the Liberal Party Leadership, 1887," *Canadian Historical Review*, XXXVIII, 1957, pp. 109-28.

At first glance Commercial Union did not appear to be promising. An early pronouncement by James Young, M.P., publisher of the *Galt Reformer* and an influential Ontario Liberal, was definitely opposed to Commercial Union. In a letter to the *Globe* in March 1887, Young flatly denied any worth in either Commercial Union or Imperial Federation. The "ULTIMATE AIM OF BRITISH AMERICA," he said, was the firm establishment of a "Canadian nationality." Neither proposal could be accepted by "any patriotic citizen." "My protest against a Zollverein is, that it is UTTERLY ANTI-CANADIAN, and subversive of the idea of an independent national future." [2] And in his first public address at Somerset after assuming the mantle of leadership, Laurier said on 2 August that "for my part I am not ready to declare that commercial union is an acceptable idea." Indeed, Laurier was not basically concerned with the trade question. His emphasis at Somerset was on what was for him always a more important point: "to be Canadian." "That was the object of Confederation in the intention of its authors; the aim and end of Confederation was to bring the different races closer together, to soften the asperities of their mutual relations and to connect the scattered groups of British subjects." Still, Laurier did not repudiate Commercial Union. He qualified his apparent repudiation by adding that Commercial Union should not be adopted "at the present moment." In short, it was too early to decide one way or the other what the party would do. [3]

A month before, Laurier had discovered that James Young's opposition to Commercial Union was not the authoritative word of Ontario Liberalism on the trade question. Sir Rich-

[2] *Toronto Globe,* May 28, 1887.

[3] Graham, "Sir Richard Cartwright and the Liberal Party," p. 160; O. D. Skelton, *Life and Letters of Sir Wilfrid Laurier,* New York, 1922, v. 1, p. 355. See also H. B. Neatby, "Laurier and a Liberal Quebec, A Study in Political Management," Ph.D. Thesis, University of Toronto, 1956, pp. 76-81.

ard Cartwright, the unquestioned leader of the Ontario group, wrote that "matters have been moving fast in Ontario in the last two weeks." He said that it was impossible to rise on a rural platform without pronouncing on Commercial Union. "We may as well face the Music," he added. It was a simple matter of political life and death. "I am doubtful if we can fight any constituency without speaking plainly on this subject." The new leader responded quickly. Within a few days the Liberal Members of Parliament were reading a party circular about "a new question . . . upon which it will be incumbent for the reform party to at once take some action; I mean Commercial Union with the United States." Laurier was quite sure that the party favored closer commercial relations with the United States "and indeed there can be no sounder liberal principle than freedom of trade, wherever freedom of trade is obtainable." With this cavalier treatment of the "question of principle," which Laurier appears to have considered already settled, he moved on to say: "The chief point . . . is whether, if commercial union is to be made an article of our programme, it would be advisable to do so at once, or to wait for some future occasion." Urgency was the keynote of the circular. The Liberals had to face a number of by-elections and, though he did not say as much, it was apparent that Laurier was aware that Liberalism was without a platform. He pleaded for a full treatment of the subject itself, and also the views of members "as to the duty of the party with regard to it and as to the tactics to be followed." [4]

The former leader, Edward Blake, was one of the first to respond. It was apparent that he had some grave doubts about the advisability of making Commercial Union the chief item in the Liberal program. "It wd. take so long to put down my views on paper here . . . that I shrink from the task. But I

[4] Laurier Papers, 2, Cartwright to Laurier, July 8, 1887, Laurier to Liberal Members of Parliament, July 11, 1887.

will take it up later," he said. "It would however be very much better if we could talk it out." Meanwhile Cartwright had decided not to raise the issue in the South Renfrew by-election. Apparently for the first time he discovered that "there is a serious difficulty." "We have not as yet any authoritative declaration of the willingness of the U.S. authorities to treat with us and we can not therefore do more than speak very generally on the subject." [5]

Just six days after his Somerset speech Laurier had received enough replies to feel safe in flatly declaring to Cartwright, "I am afraid that we are doomed to defeat following defeat unless we come out & square in favour of commercial union. There is no doubt, there can be no doubt, that the feeling throughout the whole country is one of ever growing dissatisfaction at the present condition of things. Unless we meet the evil squarely & present the most adequate remedy, the average elector will vote for whoever comes out with subsidies & public works." A correspondent from Assinaboia had written that "unrestricted intercourse with the great nation to the south of us . . . could not fail to be of incalculable benefit to the whole country." Significantly, he added, "if the Conservative party is allowed to take this policy in hand . . . the chances are that it will keep that party in power at least as long as the N.P. has." An Essex County Liberal told Laurier that he was much in favor of adopting Commercial Union; it was the only way to stop a budding sympathy for annexation. [6]

[5] *ibid.,* 737, Blake to Laurier, July 18, 1887, Cartwright to Laurier, July 26, 1887. See also F. H. Underhill, "Edward Blake, The Liberal Party, and Unrestricted Reciprocity," *Canadian Historical Association Annual Report,* 1939, pp. 133-41; F. H. Underhill, "Laurier and Blake, 1882-1891," *Canadian Historical Review,* xx, 1939, pp. 392-408; W. R. Graham, "Sir Richard Cartwright, Wilfrid Laurier, and Liberal Party Trade Policy, 1887," *Canadian Historical Review,* xxxiii, 1952, pp. 1-18.

[6] Public Archives of Ontario, Cartwright Papers, Laurier to Cartwright, August 8, 1887; Laurier Papers, 737, F. Kennedy to Laurier,

On 12 October Cartwright explained his "individual" view to an audience at Ingersoll, Ontario. As far as he was concerned, if the Americans were willing "to deal with us on equitable terms" regarding trade, "scarcely any sacrifice is too severe to secure them." Cartwright was definitely opposed to annexation, to the loss of Canadian political independence, "but I cannot shut my eyes to the facts. We have greatly misused our advantages, we have been foolish in our expenditures, we have not means of satisfying the just demands of large portions of the Dominion, except through such an arrangement as commercial union." [7] *The Week,* though usually opposed to Commercial Union, on 20 October hailed Cartwright's speech and predicted that if the Liberals took up Commercial Union it would return them to power.

Despite all the favorable replies to the circular, Cartwright acted quite independently; Laurier and the remainder of the party kept their peace. And it was apparent that some of his senior Liberal colleagues in Ontario did not share Cartwright's views. James Edgar praised Laurier's "wise words at Somerset on Coml. Union" and noted that Cartwright's "trial balloon" "pleases some but annoys others." Young considered "the Com. Union agitation one of the stupidest mistakes ever made by any section of our party" and Alexander Mackenzie believed the scheme was "impracticable." "We complain of protection and propose to bind ourselves to a more extreme system," he wrote. "We are to raise a barrier against English trade and so commence a down grade political life. My feelings

---

July 15, 1887; 2, J. Brille to Laurier, August 2, 1887. It is perhaps worth noting that Professor Warner is quite wrong in saying that only Cartwright and Charlton gave strong favorable responses to Laurier's circular. Warner, *The Idea of Continental Union,* p. 188, n. 66. A survey of the appropriate volumes of the Laurier Papers shows quite the opposite.

[7] Laurier Papers, 2, Cartwright to Laurier, August 13, 1887; Graham, "Sir Richard Cartwright and the Liberal Party," p. 165.

revolt at the proposal." [8] These doubts were echoed by correspondents from other Provinces. "Notre prospérité matérielle augmenterait: je le crois," noted a Quebec member. "Mais devons-nous nous livrier ainsi entre les mains des Etats et abdiquer nos pouvoirs. . . . Un Traité de réciprocité serait incontestablement avantageus aus Etats & à nous. Mair frère Jonathan veut tous au rien." Louis Davies, one of Laurier's most trusted advisers, cautioned that much depended on what action would be taken on reciprocity by the Joint High Commission. Canadians would only accept Commercial Union in desperation and if "Tupper succeeds in getting partial reciprocity the Com. Union agitation will collapse like a pierced wind bag." [9]

These, then, were the criticisms which Laurier had to balance with the unquestioning approval of adopting Commercial Union that came from the party's lesser figures. Certainly the points were well taken; Young's nationalism, Mackenzie's truth about protectionism in Commercial Union, and Davies' warning about the Conservatives stealing Liberal thunder by getting reciprocity in Washington, all had their point and deserved serious consideration. But how to reconcile these with the fervent urging of the Ontario leader Cartwright to adopt Commercial Union? Probably without Laurier's prior knowledge, the doubting James Edgar seemed to provide the answer. Late in November, in three open letters to Wiman printed in the Globe, the Toronto Liberal attempted to meet the most serious objection to Commercial Union, that it would deprive Canada of her separate identity at first fiscally and then politically. Edgar proposed, in sum, a commercial union of the North American continent that would leave control

[8] Laurier Papers, 2, Edgar to Laurier, August 18 and October 14, 1887; 737, Young to Laurier, November 19, 1887; Cartwright Papers, Mackenzie to Cartwright, September 27, 1887.

[9] Laurier Papers, 2, Amyot to Laurier, August 5, 1887; 737, Davies to Laurier, November 26, 1887.

of the tariffs against the outside world in the hands of the respective governments rather than turning them over to a joint control subservient to the American Congress. He further urged that the scheme, which he called Unrestricted Reciprocity, be worked out over a period of years rather than at one quick decision, thus preventing a sudden unbalance of existing trade patterns and allowing, instead, for their gradual readjustment.[10] A few days after he had written his letters to Wiman, Edgar told Laurier, "I believe it will be found that Unrestricted Reciprocity as distinguished from Commercial Union with uniform tariffs, will be as far as we can go as a party, unless events march very fast." Davies was mollified by this suggestion. Personally, reciprocity in natural products "would give us ¾ths of what we want. . . . George Brown's treaty . . . would give us all we want . . . ," he thought. If it were necessary to go further to get either of these, then Unrestricted Reciprocity would be the answer. Commercial Union just went too far. Even if, under Commercial Union, a uniform tariff against the rest of the world would apparently be fixed by a joint tariff commission, it was obvious that Congress would never surrender its control over the tariff and the commission would, in reality, be subservient to Congress. Practically, Canada would completely surrender the fiscal responsibility for which she had labored so long. "That would be a pretty hard proposition for a Canadian statesman to present to a constituency. . . . The entire difficulty is however surmounted by our retaining our respective tariffs . . . and retaining our customs houses along the frontier to prevent the [free] admission of foreign imported goods."[11]

Of course, there still were objections. *The Week*, having praised Cartwright's Ingersoll speech, now turned back to its original stand and criticized Edgar's compromise proposal.

[10] *Toronto Globe,* November 15, 22 and 29, 1887.
[11] Laurier Papers, 737, Edgar to Laurier, November 30, 1887, Davies to Laurier, November 26, 1887.

Unrestricted Reciprocity, it said, was just as objectionable as Commercial Union. Abolition of the tariff wall on the south would obviously mean an even higher wall than the National Policy had built on the east and the west and heavy discrimination against British goods. That "might be expected from a hostile State, but would certainly not be borne from a colony." [12] Nevertheless it was quite clear that the Liberals would go ahead and adopt Edgar's proposed compromise. It still might be dangerous; as Davies warned, "The great question . . . comes up, what will our neighbours do?" But that Laurier would have to worry about later. For the moment the only important point had been put by Cartwright: "We will at least have the satisfaction of a plain tangible issue to battle for." This had been true in the early autumn and it continued to be so throughout the remaining months of 1887. Cartwright wrote in October that "looking at it from a purely tactical standpoint what alternative policy have the objectors to offer? You and I know well that we cannot go through another session in the fashion we did the last with half our men seeking by any and every miserable pretext to shirk a vote on the very simplest and plainest questions." In January he added that there was no longer "any choice left. We *must* make a new departure and there is nothing which will fill the bill half so well as 'unrestricted reciprocity.' " Of course, he said, "The U.S. may refuse to treat altogether on any such basis," but "this is not likely and anyway as we can hardly hope to carry our point you need not bother about it now." [13] The time was propitious for a "new departure." The *St. John*

[12] *The Week,* November 24, 1887.

[13] Laurier Papers, 737, Davies to Laurier, November 26, 1887, Cartwright to Laurier, January 2, 1888; 2, Cartwright to Laurier, August 3 and October 29, 1887. The Commercial Unionists were not entirely pleased. William Dymond Gregory later wrote: "Those of us who had taken an active part in support of Commercial Union were rather disgusted with the attitude of the Liberals." Douglas Library, Queen's University, Gregory Papers, MS autobiography, p. 99.

Daily Telegraph commented on 2 January 1888 that "among Canadian journals advocating freer trade relations with the United States unrestricted reciprocity is now receiving much more favor than commercial union." The idea had taken. In a slightly modified form the Liberal Party had cast its lot for continentalism.

ii

The Conservative party leadership was well aware of the dangers economic distress provided for the party in power. Rightly or wrongly government parties were always blamed for bad times and the discontent revealed itself in adverse majorities at the polls. Gloomily Macdonald commented on the Nova Scotia election of 1886. "Fielding has defeated the Conservatives on the Secession Cry—horse, foot and artillery. Never was there such a rout." The Prime Minister's mood was clearly indicated in a letter to a friend when he said "the present is a grave crisis in the political history of Canada." [14] And it seemed as if one crisis was just over when another began. The Liberals were defeated for the third straight time in February 1887, but late in the spring both Wiman and Butterworth invaded the Dominion, joined forces with Goldwin Smith, and the trio began the battle of Commercial Union against the National Policy.

From the first Macdonald had considered Commercial Union a dangerous policy. In May 1887, he told a New York City correspondent that it was not "in the present interest of Canada." Canadian manufacturers had "too little capital," they were "yet in their infancy and struggling for existence," and could not "compete with the enormous amount of capital and skill generated by your protective system." But Macdonald was not ready to condemn the movement too quickly. The Prime Minister was too good a politician to do that; he would

[14] Tupper Papers, 6, Macdonald to Tupper, June 21, 1886; Macdonald Papers, 527, Macdonald to Patterson, November 2, 1886.

A PARADOX, A PARADOX, A MOST AMUSING PARADOX!

U.S. Senator Sherman (*angrily*)—I'm against Commercial Union
tooth and nail, because it would head off Annexation!

Mr. Canadian "Patriot" Boodle (*emphatically*)—I'm against it heart
and soul, because it would bring about Annexation!

wait and let events take their course. Some of his advisers, however, professed to see further dangers in the movement than the obvious threat to the manufacturers. Sir Leonard Tilley, who had played so large a part in the creation of the National Policy, warned Macdonald that Commercial Union would undermine not only his handiwork but the nation itself. Wiman's movement was so insidiously attractive that it was "the most dangerous organization to our national and British connection that has been made during the last fifty years." Under the guise of benevolent friendship, Tilley believed Commercial Union to be *"veiled treason* and the booming of United States interests, as against Canadian and Imperial." This rather extreme opinion was shared by the Minister of Customs, Mackenzie Bowell, who flatly asserted that Goldwin Smith was "endeavouring to indoctrinate seditious sentiments in the minds of the people." [15]

The problem, however, was not to deprecate Commercial Union or Unrestricted Reciprocity, but to counter the argument for continentalism. Ostensibly this would be a relatively simple task for the rejoinder was implicit in Conservative policy. It was found in the worn out assertion that Canadians no longer would be "hewers of wood and drawers of water" for their neighbors. It was found in the 1879 tariff which established the standing offer for reciprocity with the United States in natural products. Indeed, the Conservatives could even argue with some justice that their policy in 1879 was simply a continuation and an elaboration on the fundamental economic tenets of Confederation laid down at the Confederate Council of Trade in 1865. Then it had been decided that while reciprocity with the United States was desirable it was not absolutely essential to the economic development of British North America. The establishment of the National

[15] Macdonald Papers, 527, Macdonald to Ellison, May 5, 1887; 277, Tilley to Macdonald, June 22, 1887; Bowell Papers, 90, Bowell to Aikens, September 5, 1889.

Policy meant the same thing. Of course, the electors had been told that reciprocity in tariffs would eventually bring reciprocity in trade. But everyone recognized that the National Policy tariff was a frank assertion of a determination on the part of Canadians to remain a separate economic as well as a separate political entity on the North American continent.

Furthermore, the National Policy claimed to look outward from the North American continent, to favor participation in the commerce of the world rather than withdrawal into a self-contained continentalism. The first task, then, was to break the chains holding Canada to her more powerful neighbor. The tariff helped by giving more favorable import rates to commodities imported directly to Canadian ports rather than through the "middleman" United States ports. More important was the direct and protective encouragement given to the steadily growing Canadian industrial complex. And most important of all was the railway; the Canadian Pacific would bind the country together and would give access at either end to the commerce of the world. On all counts dependence on the Republic would be appeciably lessened.

The Conservatives had two other points in their favor. The first was the fact that they were the party in power and despite the pressure of discontent that came from hard times, this remained a very large advantage. The second was that Conservative policy had been implemented; Liberal policy remained an untested theory. The National Policy was a fact and the Conservatives believed its results were not unimpressive. The completion of the Canadian Pacific Railway was a tremendous accomplishment. To that could be added a 51.8 per cent increase in the number of industrial establishments between the years 1881 and 1891, a 114 per cent increase in the amount of manufacturing capital, a 44.4 per cent increase in the number of industrial employees and a 53.5 per cent increase in the gross value of manufactured products. Further, Canadian exports and imports had increased from a total value of $1,094 million in the five-year period 1874-1879 to $1,236 million in the years 1880-1885 and even remained steady at $1,235 million in the depression years 1886-1891.[16]

Nor did the Conservatives intend to rest on their oars as they waged verbal war with Commercial Union. "Finality and introspection do not 'enthuse,'" George Stephen told Macdonald. By 1886 the internal phase of the National Policy was firmly established and it was time for the "Party of *Progress*" to turn to the development of foreign trade and commerce.[17] After the 1887 election it was rumored that Sir Charles Tupper would not return to London as High Commissioner but would remain at Ottawa and head a new Department of Trade and Commerce.[18] Tupper did return to London and the new department had to wait for brighter days for its birth. But in London the High Commissioner worked diligently for an Imperial subsidy for a line of steamers from Vancouver to China and Japan.[19] Through the Imperial Foreign Office, inquiries were sent to British Consular posts in Europe about the possibilities of opening new channels of Canadian trade.[20]

[16] O. J. McDiarmid, *Commercial Policy in the Canadian Economy,* Cambridge, 1946, pp. 181-85.

[17] Macdonald Papers, 270, Stephen to Macdonald, May 24, 1886.

[18] Thompson Papers, 290, Thompson to Mrs. Thompson, June 27, 1887; Lansdowne Papers, Macdonald to Lansdowne, July 11, 1887.

[19] Tupper Papers, 8, Tupper to Goschen, July 28 and August 11, 1887, Goschen to Tupper, August 8, 1887. See also Campbell Papers, Campbell to Macdonald, April 23, 1887, Campbell to Young, May 5, 1887.

[20] See, for example, Foreign Office to Colonial Office, March 28, 1887: CO42/791. This was a group of replies from Bucharest, Stuttgart, Rome, Stockholm, and Constantinople to the Canadian inquiry. It closely followed another group from other British Consular Posts in Europe. John Anderson commented on the result of the inquiry and added to his minute a reflection of his own on the problems of the extension of Canadian trade: "Except in the case of Portugal these Rpts are not very helpful as to the possibility of an extension of Canadian trade. Countries like Canada which do their best to prevent imports cannot expect to be able to do much of an export trade."

In 1889 George Foster introduced three resolutions in the House of Commons that clearly revealed the plans of the Macdonald Government. The resolutions called for subsidies for steamship lines between Canada and Australia, Canada and the Orient, and Canada and Great Britain and France. Foster explained that the steamship services would be "distinctly Canadian." The proposals were "a sequence of the policy of Canada and the development of Canada during the series of past years." The development of the Canadian Pacific Railway "has had in it a larger idea, and has looked out to a wider reach than simply the benefit which would incur in Canada itself," he explained. "It was not meant and never supposed that this line should simply begin at Halifax or St. John and end at Vancouver or New Westminster." [21]

"Our course is plain," wrote Sir John Macdonald, "the N.P. [is] to be maintained in its entirety." "Development of our industries in every direction—Extension either directly or by subsidy of our means of transport by land and water—utter rejection of Commercial Union, Unrestricted Reciprocity with the U.S., Goldwin Smith, Wiman—Extension of commerce with all the world, U. States included. And a preferential system of Trade with the Mother Country & her Colonies when the time comes." After all, asked Mackenzie Bowell, "if we have proved to the Americans and to the world that we have been able to live and prosper, to accomplish the most gigantic enterprises and progress (as statistics will show) at a greater ratio comparatively than any other country, since the abrogation of the Reciprocity Treaty of 1854, why in the name of common sense should we go on our knees to the Yankees and say we are prepared to forego the policy which

[21] *Official Report of Debates,* April 18, 1889, p. 1870. See also W. T. Delworth, "Canada's Commercial Relations with Great Britain and Europe, 1878-1895," M.A. Thesis, University of Toronto, 1956, for the theory and practice of the National Policy.

has done so much for us, in order to obtain what at best is a problematic advantage?" [22] It was a good question; one that needed to be asked. And it clearly revealed the advantage fact had over theory. In short, the Conservative party had a substantial store of verbal ammunition that could be used in the argument against Commercial Union.

iii

On 14 March 1888 Sir Richard Cartwright rose from his seat in the House of Commons and proudly announced the new Liberal trade policy. His resolution proclaimed the desirability of having "the largest possible freedom of commercial intercourse . . . between the Dominion of Canada and the United States" in "all articles manufactured in, or the natural products of either of the said countries" and urged the Government to take "steps at an early date to ascertain on what terms and conditions arrangements can be effected with the United States for the purpose of securing full and unrestricted reciprocity of trade therewith." "Beyond all question," Cartwright asserted, if the Liberal policy were adopted, "very important changes would . . . take place in the mode of administering our public and commercial affairs." He appealed to his colleagues' reasonableness, to their ability to see what marvelous benefits would come from allowing trade to flow in its "natural" channels. Did someone dare accuse him of disloyalty? He admitted he had no respect "for 35 per cent tariff protection loyalty or for 35 per cent tariff protection loyalists." But he was a true loyalist. His policy would keep Canada Canadian and would do even more. The Mother Country stood isolated and friendless in the world. Unrestricted Reciprocity would reunite the English race, wipe out Canadian-

[22] Macdonald Papers, 528, Macdonald to John Sim—— [?], June 7, 1888; Bowell Papers, 90, Bowell to Ostrom, October 12, 1889.

American difficulties, and give Great Britain a trusted friend and powerful ally on the other side of the Atlantic.[23]

An able reply came from the Government benches the following day. George Foster alluded briefly to the danger to Canadian economic and political separateness on the North American continent and then went on to attack Cartwright's reasoning. It seemed to Foster that a "natural market" was one complementary to the Canadian market, not one where the same goods Canada produced were produced in even greater abundance. Further, Cartwright's case was speculative, the National Policy had already been proved. Certainly the Government wanted to extend its trade with the United States: it always had and would continue to have that desire. But not at the price of Unrestricted Reciprocity. This was clear in Foster's amendment which noted the Government's desire of "extending trade relations with the United States," but only "in so far as they do not conflict with the policy of fostering the various industries and interests of the Dominion which was adopted in 1879." [24]

On and on, for three weeks with scarcely an interruption, the respective merits of Commercial Union and Unrestricted Reciprocity echoed through the House of Commons. Gradually the debate narrowed to one point, what Mr. Davin said was the "real issue": "Shall we take a step that will land Canada into the United States and make this country part and parcel of it?" [25] Tactically this was an unfortunate turn in the argument. Foster's ground had been solid, a forthright

[23] Canada, Parliament, House of Commons, *Debates on Reciprocity and the Fisheries Treaty, March 14-May 3, 1888,* University of Toronto Library, March 14, 1888, pp. 160-76. It should be noted that the pagination in this supplementary volume is different from that in the original *Official Report of Debates* where the resolution is found on p. 144. All citations on this debate are from the supplementary volume henceforth referred to as *Debates on Reciprocity*.

[24] *ibid.,* March 15, 1888, p. 210.

[25] *ibid.,* March 16, 1888, p. 251.

attack on Unrestricted Reciprocity. As long as the argument was limited to the economic merits and faults of Unrestricted Reciprocity, the Liberal Opposition was forced to reply in kind. But Davin raised a more fundamental and a more contentious issue, the problem of political loyalty. Undoubtedly this was the "real issue," Canada's economic survival was inextricably tied to her political survival on the North American continent. And clearly Davin believed, as did so many others, that Unrestricted Reciprocity threatened both Canada's economic and political self-expression, that economic union was but the prelude to political union with the United States. But the Liberals chose to interpret his remarks otherwise. They preferred to cloud the issue by interpreting Davin's remarks as an appeal to loyalty to the Empire rather than loyalty to the Canadian nation and its economic policy. It was true that the two concepts were tied to each other. Canadian nationalism was to a very large degree expressed as "British Empire nationalism." Canada in the late nineteenth century was still too much a part of and too dependent upon the British Empire to have a completely separate mode of expression. As Joseph Chamberlain had acutely observed a few weeks before the debate took place, in Canada "patriotism & loyalty to the British connection are identical." [26] The Liberals chose to treat loyalty to the Empire in superficial terms by suggesting that loyalty to the Empire was synonymous with common rather than separate economic policies within the Empire. On this ground there might be some question as to who was the greater friend of the Mother Country, the Liberals or the Conservatives. During the Mackenzie regime British imports were taxed at 16 per cent, during the National Policy years at 19.4 per cent. Similarly, duties on American imports had been raised from 9.5 per cent to 14.9 per cent after 1879. Nevertheless, British imports were being taxed 4.5 per cent more

[26] Chamberlain Papers, Chamberlain to Collins, January 22, 1888.

177

than American imports under the National Policy. And since 1880 trade with the United States had risen from 43 to 47 per cent of the total Canadian trade while the British share had declined from 51 to 49 per cent.[27] In this sense there was just enough sting in Cartwright's phrase about "35 per cent protection loyalty" to put the Government benches on the defensive. On the surface the Liberals had been more "loyal" than the Conservatives to the economic policy of the Mother Country.

Then the Liberals reversed their argument and appealed to Canadian national sentiment. The National Policy was not, Laurier charged, the means of advancing but rather of retarding Canada's economic and political advancement. The Conservative economic policy had been defended as consistent with loyalty to the Empire as well as to Canada. The preservation of that policy, the Conservatives said, would preserve both the Imperial tie and the separate Canadian identity in North America. "To pretend," Laurier replied, "that our colonial allegiance demands from us that we should be deterred from the spirit of enterprise is not loyalty, but is mere flunkeyism." "This is not a question of sentiment. This is a question of duty, and, if you put it in this light, that I have to choose between the duty I owe to England, and the duty I owe to my native land, I stand by my native land." [28] The argument had passed from reasoned debate to emotional pleading. In the end it made no difference. Cartwright's resolution was swamped in a heavy party vote favoring the Government. But continentalism was not dead. "Time is with us," Laurier told the House of Commons, "the cause is true and it will prevail." [29] The Liberal Party had taken a stand and they were going to stick by it. Oliver Mowat, the Liberal Premier of Ontario, wrote to Laurier: "your course . . . has been all that

[27] McDiarmid, *Commercial Policy in the Canadian Economy,* p. 166.
[28] *Debates on Reciprocity,* April 5, 1888, pp. 595-96.
[29] *ibid.,* April 5, 1888, p. 598.

could be desired; and . . . perseverance in it will be the best policy." [30]

iv

The defeat of Cartwright's motion was expected. But the discussion of the loyalty question had touched the Liberals as deeply as the Conservatives and they began to reassess the position they had so hastily taken in the past few months. Perhaps there was some merit in the Conservative charge of disloyalty, perhaps Canadian Liberalism had gone too far. This thought was obviously bothering Louis Davies. "I don't advocate the policy because I believe it to be the best possible one for us," he told Laurier, "but simply because I believe it to be the best possible *attainable* one. I would prefer Geo. Brown's treaty of 1874 & would even be satisfied with the old treaty of '54." [31]

Then there was the matter of Edward Blake. His imposing shadow loomed over the formation of Liberal policy. Laurier and Cartwright knew that Blake strongly disapproved of the new departure. He saw many fallacies in Unrestricted Reciprocity but was concentrating his attack on the loss of revenue that would result from the scheme if it were accomplished. His intensely logical mind was pointing out how general all this Unrestricted Reciprocity talk was, how little planning there was in the proposal. With some heat Cartwright wrote Laurier that "our proposal 'in natura rerum' involves a great experiment and some financial disturbance. No one can say how much revenue may be involved nor how soon this increased wealth of the people (which we assume as an assured consequence) will show itself in augmenting revenue in other quarters. All we can say positively is that no additional burthen will be imposed in any case though there may be considerable alterations in the *mode* of collecting the

[30] Laurier Papers, 2, Mowat to Laurier, n.d. [June or July 1888].
[31] *ibid.*, 737, Davies to Laurier, November 8, 1888.

required amount. The plain fact is (though perhaps Blake does not realize it) that as a political organisation we simply had no alternative. We had to adopt this project or to go to pieces." There was another point in Blake's argument; Unrestricted Reciprocity was really only Commercial Union under another name and that if they had been honest, the Liberals would have taken their stand on the latter. For this Cartwright had, apparently, no answer. "It is enough that we formally declared for Unrestricted Reciprocity and have made it our battle cry. . . . We cannot afford to change front on such an issue in a few months." [32]

Still, the second thoughts on the wisdom of their adoption of Unrestricted Reciprocity were enough to force some alterations in Liberal strategy. Unrestricted Reciprocity was deliberately downgraded in Liberal discussions during the 1889 Parliamentary Session. Laurier confined himself to platitudes like "the great reform of the extension of our trade with the great and powerful nation to the south of us" in the Throne Speech debate. It was true that the Liberal leader did move for "unrestricted freedom in the trade relations of the two countries" late in February, but the resolution combined extension of trade with continuance of the *modus vivendi* regarding the North Atlantic fisheries. The motion was defeated 108 to 65 on the day it was presented. For a few days a sporadic debate ensued on a motion by Cartwright for Unrestricted Reciprocity but it too was defeated on 19 March by a sound 121 to 77 vote. [33] These efforts were cautious prodding, not an all-out assault on the National Policy fortress.

In fact, when the Liberal chieftains had planned their spring campaign a few months before, there had been scarcely a mention of Unrestricted Reciprocity. In November Cart-

[32] *ibid.*, 2, Cartwright to Laurier, September 17, 1888; 737, Cartwright to Laurier, September 22, 1888.
[33] *Official Report of Debates,* February 1, 1889, p. 8, February 26, 1889, pp. 328-423, March 19, 1889, p. 739.

wright had told Laurier the Liberals might attack on two fronts. The first was to berate the Government for the American Senate's rejection of the fishery treaty. "The other is to move that Canada should have power to negotiate commercial treaties at any rate with the U.S., in fact to revive the old motion we made some years ago on that subject.[34] This *may* bring us face to face with the question of independence though we can pass it if we please. This . . . motion has the advantage of breaking new ground—may compel some of our opponents to vote with us and will relieve us from even the appearance of seeming to lay too much stress on the friendship of the U.S." Such a motion seemed to meet admirably the suppressed but not eliminated worries Liberals had about their policy. It would make "a useful separate plank in our platform." Better yet, it would "appeal to Canadian patriotic feeling in the abstract." And best of all, "Blake (if he likes) can support this powerfully which is more perhaps than we can depend on his doing with any other." [35] On 18 February, with appropriate gusto, Cartwright moved that "Canada be granted the power of negotiating commercial treaties with foreign states." The effort fell flat. Only Foster rose to reply from the Government side and after a short speech by Davies the motion was defeated 94 to 66.[36]

In May 1889, E. W. Thomson of the *Globe* wrote to Laurier that the paper was "endeavouring to make Unrestricted Reciprocity *the* subject of discussion again in Ontario." Liberal trade policy had suffered throughout the session because of the heated debate over the Jesuit Estates Act. It was now time "to 'boom' the question steadily all summer." Apparently the effort had some effect. Willison wrote in July that "the farmers

[34] This is a reference to Blake's Commercial Treaties Resolution of 1882. See *Official Report of Debates,* April 21, 1882, p. 1075ff.

[35] Laurier Papers, 2, Cartwright to Laurier, November 28, 1888.

[36] *Official Report of Debates,* February 18, 1888, pp. 172-93.

will hear nothing but reciprocity." [37] All the same, appearances might be deceiving. Sir John A. Macdonald noted about the same time: "the Commercial Union cry is pretty nearly dead and the new version of it, unrestricted reciprocity, is also *in extremis.*" In contrast to what the Prime Minister thought to be the fortunes of the Unrestricted Reciprocity campaign were the signs of improvement in Canadian trade. It appeared that the financial crisis was coming to an end. The Dominion's annual exports increased by $5 million between 1886 and 1888 and total annual trade jumped from $189 million to $201 million.[38] Clearly caution would once again be the Opposition watchword in planning for the 1890 session. "As to the general line," Cartwright wrote to Laurier, "I advise strongly making this what one may call a 'farmers' session, i.e. devoting ourselves in a long hot debate on the budget or earlier . . . to pointing out the effects of the tariff and of the general extravagance of Govt. in depressing the agricultural section, in increasing the exodus, depreciating value of farms and loading them up with mortgages etc. Make this our 'piece de resistance.'" [39] Again in 1890 there was no major debate in the House of Commons on Unrestricted Reciprocity.

All of these factors combined to give the outward appearance that the Liberals had curiously dropped the main plank in their revised platform. But another problem created even greater difficulty for the Liberals; Benjamin Butterworth's peaceful annexation resolution of 13 December 1888 in the House of Representatives caused the party acute embarrassment. James Edgar hurriedly wrote to Laurier that "Butterworth has, for the present, rendered it necessary for us to

[37] Laurier Papers, 3, Thomson to Laurier, May 12, 1889, Willison to Laurier, July 16, 1889.
[38] Public Archives of Ontario, Kirby Papers, Macdonald to Kirby, July 8, 1889; Canada, Department of Agriculture, *The Statistical Yearbook of Canada,* Ottawa, 1901, pp. 195-96.
[39] Laurier Papers, 3, Cartwright to Laurier, December 6, 1889.

adopt some other policy than Unrestd. Recipty." Within days Laurier had sent another circular letter to the Liberal members. The switch from Unrestricted Reciprocity to annexation, he noted, had "caused alarm among some of our friends." Personally, he felt the Butterworth resolution "is much to be regretted" but he saw "no cause to abandon our position." "No one ever could expect that we could carry our programme without a hard and protracted struggle and without many deceptions," he explained. "We must be prepared for such disappointments and prepared also to meet them without flinching from our purpose." [40]

As usual James Young of Galt could not accept Laurier's view and saw Unrestricted Reciprocity as placing "our Party out of harmony with the national aspirations . . . of the great majority of the Canadian people." But Young stood virtually alone. Everyone agreed with the leader's suggestion that the main resolution in the 1889 session should be on commercial treaties. But they also agreed that to drop Unrestricted Reciprocity as the Liberal trade policy would be "suicidal." If the policy were abandoned in the face of the Butterworth resolution it would seem "to admit that the erratic talk of a few Yankee statesmen expresses the true aim, and natural result, of our movement." Rather, suggested George Casey, "there is all the more reason why we should stand firmly to our contention that international free trade will rather tend to prevent than to hasten political union." "Surely," wrote Davies, "we are not a parcel of children solemnly to adopt as the chief plank in our platform an important policy such as Unrestricted Reciprocity & then drop it because some of those we hoped were acting with us on the other side choose to adopt a most damaging course for us." [41]

[40] ibid., 2, Edgar to Laurier, December 16, 1888; Public Archives of Ontario, Blake Papers, Laurier to Blake and others, December 24, 1888.
[41] Laurier Papers, 737, Young to Laurier, January 23, 1889, Casey to Laurier, December 31, 1888, Davies to Laurier, January 10, 1889.

No, the Liberals were not going to be frightened off their course by bumptious talk from the renegade Congressman Butterworth. But his resolution did point up in the sharpest form another of the difficulties of their policy. As far as the Liberals were concerned, a continental trade policy demanded continental cooperation. "We will, I have not the faintest doubt, *win,*" Davies told Laurier, "if we can get such assurances as we hope for from the Repub. leaders." "The truth is," Cartwright concluded, "we ought to be in steady communication with certain of their [the United States] leaders and we are very much handicapped because we are not." [42]

Some unofficial efforts had already been made in this direction. Charlton was in Washington when Butterworth introduced his resolution and he sharply rebuked the Ohio Congressman, telling him it would only hinder the cause.[43] It is doubtful that Laurier instructed Charlton to go to Washington as a Liberal emissary. Charlton owned large timber holdings in Ontario and processing plants in Tonawanda, New York and he made numerous trips yearly to the United States. Through his intimate contacts with members of Congress he usually spent more of his time lobbying for free lumber entry into the United States than he did advocating a more general scheme of continental free trade. And when he did appear to speak for the Canadian Liberals he often did so without their knowledge or advice.

In any case, the Liberals knew that they had to establish fairly close contact with some of the more important people in Washington. An effort was made even before the introduction of the Butterworth resolution. The November 1888 elections had put the traditionally protectionist Republican party in power. It was obvious that what support there was in the United States for Unrestricted Reciprocity came from the

[42] *ibid.,* 3, Cartwright to Laurier, December 29, 1889.
[43] Charlton Papers, Diary, December 10 and 13, 1888.

G.O.P. And it was equally obvious that the key man in the new administration was James G. Blaine, the Secretary of State. Cartwright wrote to Laurier that Blaine was the man to contact. "Whoever gets his attention first may have a great deal to do with shaping his policy and he will shape the policy of the U.S." He cautiously added, "I need hardly add that this must remain *absolutely between you, Davies and myself."* Davies agreed that "good, possibly great good would come out of a frank interchange of sentiment between some of us & some of the Republican leaders." [44] In January Davies took the initiative by writing directly to Blaine, asking for a confidential interview to explain the Liberal's trade policy. He assured Blaine that "the Liberal Party desires to cultivate the most friendly & cordial relations with the people of the U.S." [45] and asked whether it was possible for Canada to treat with the United States "on any other terms than those of Commercial Union." Shortly after the letter was written Davies had an interview with Blaine. He explained that Canadians could not accept Commercial Union "because it would place the control of the Canadian tariff practically in the hands of the United States." Unrestricted Reciprocity, however, "left the control of the tariffs in the hands of the respective countries." Blaine raised objections to some particular items such as wool and sugar and it was agreed that these might still be scheduled and not made part of a reciprocity arrangement. The Secretary of State asked what difficulties Canada would encounter by discriminating against the mother country in such an arrangement. Davies replied that "we were prepared to stand by our scheme and take our chance of Great Britain insisting on that objection." Finally, Davies mentioned "the difficulty we would have owing to the loss of revenue, and that possibly it might be necessary in any ar-

[44] Laurier Papers, 737, Cartwright to Laurier, November 9, 1888, Davies to Laurier, November 17, 1888.
[45] *ibid.,* draft letter, Davies to Blaine, January 4, 1889.

rangement come to to provide for it coming into force gradually. This also seemed to him feasible." [46]

Late in 1889 a chance was afforded for close Liberal cooperation with American Commercial Unionists. Robert Hitt had prepared a resolution advocating a Commercial Union between the United States and Canada and was planning to introduce it in the House of Representatives. Erastus Wiman procured a copy of Hitt's proposed resolution. On 3 December he wrote to Laurier and told him that he had been corresponding with Cartwright about amending the resolution to make it "more acceptable to our friends in Canada and help matters along very much." On 17 December Wiman told Laurier that Cartwright had sent him an amended resolution which Wiman thought Hitt would accept "with some slight amendments." Hitt's original resolution called upon the President to appoint a commission to meet with a similar Canadian commission to prepare a plan for "commercial union" involving "the assimilation of the import duties and internal revenue taxes of the two countries, and an equitable division of receipts." Cartwright's amended version suggested a commission to study the "commercial arrangements" of the two countries with a view to "extending trade relations between Canada and the United States, and to ascertain on what terms complete freedom of intercourse . . . can be best secured." Obviously, Cartwright's amended resolution was much less definite than Hitt's original and reflected the doubts about Commercial Union which were evident even to the most ardent Liberal continentalist. As it was, Hitt introduced his original motion. Wiman did tell Laurier that the House Committee would report out Cartwright's amended draft,[47] but the damage had already been done.

Once again the Americans had compromised their Canadian

[46] Blake Papers, Davies to Laurier, April 13, 1892.
[47] Laurier Papers, 3, Wiman to Laurier, December 3, 17 and 24, 1889; 4, Copy of Hitt Resolution and Cartwright's amendment, #1182-1184.

allies. It was apparent that this kind of cooperation simply was not enough. Cartwright wrote to Laurier that he was disposed to go to the United States to see some of the Americans and he suggested that "Davies who has already seen him would do well to interview Blaine again." Wiman had already suggested that both Cartwright and Laurier come to New York and then go to Washington with him. This appeared to be necessary because Messrs. Farrer and Bunting of the *Toronto Mail* had seen Blaine and were trying to convince the Secretary of State that Canadian sentiment had gone beyond Commercial Union and now favored outright annexation.[48]

Neither Laurier nor Davies went to the United States but in mid-February, under Wiman's auspices, Sir Richard Cartwright made a "capital speech" at a New York Board of Trade and Transportation banquet. The next day Cartwright and Wiman went to Washington where Cartwright met Butterworth, Sherman, Senator Morgan, ex-speaker Carlisle and others. Wiman reported that they

were together from half past six to one in the morning, the whole time being taken up with an exchange of opinions, and a cross-examination by Sir Richard as to the closest details, and a practical conclusion by all present that of all things to be desired was the encouragement by Congress of the Liberal Party in Canada. The day following, being Sunday, we were invited to Mr. Hitt's house where, by arrangement, Mr. Blaine met us and . . . Sir Richard and Mr. Blaine spent two hours together, alone. What transpired I had no right to know, but as I left, Mr. Blaine put his hand on my shoulder and thanked me heartily for having arranged an interview with so in-

[48] *ibid.*, Cartwright to Laurier, December 29, 1889, Wiman to Laurier, December 3 and 17, 1889; 4, Wiman to Laurier, January 2, 1890; Denison Papers, 4, Copy, Wiman to Thomson, January 5 [?], 1890.

telligent a man, and from whom he derived so much information, and urged me again to bring him into contact with such men, especially mentioning Mr. Laurier, whose acquaintance he desired to make. Sir Richard was greatly pleased with the interview. He also had an hour alone with Senator Sherman, and the result of the whole visit to Washington was one exceedingly gratifying. Since that time I have had two communications from Mr. Blaine asking me for information and literature.[49]

Subjected to pressures within the Liberal party against Unrestricted Reciprocity, principally from the former leader Edward Blake, Laurier and his colleagues carefully put their public pleas for continentalism into the background from 1888 to 1890. Precipitate mouthing of annexation sentiment by some supposed economic continentalists in the United States had added to Liberal troubles. Hence it was necessary for the Liberals to seek cooperation in the United States. On two counts their program was worthless without that cooperation. First, it was obvious that Unrestricted Reciprocity was only as good as the Americans wished it to be; there had to be a willing party to the bargain on each side of the border. Of greater immediate importance, however, was the fact that there would not even be a willing party in Canada unless American enthusiasm was kept within strictly economic terms. Thus, between 1888 and 1890 the Liberals placed themselves in the anomalous position of publicly withholding their wares in Canada while privately selling them in the United States.

v

Events in the United States were rapidly moving to a conclusion that would unintentionally be a great boon to the Liberal cause. In the Republic, as in the Dominion, the tariff was a subject of immense importance in the politics of the

[49] Denison Papers, 4, Copy, Wiman to Dwight, March 17, 1890.

latter part of the nineteenth century. And though it seems un-believable to present-day observers, many Americans in the late 1880's were deeply concerned because their high protective tariff was working too well. Serious-minded students of political affairs were worried about the enormous revenue surpluses that were pouring into the United States Treasury. In 1888 Roger Q. Mills, the free trade Texas Democrat, sought to cure this abnormality with an orthodox remedy, a tariff with greatly reduced import duties on foreign goods including a complete free schedule on raw materials. The storm of pro-test that has been labeled the Great Tariff Debate of 1888 forced all other matters, including the Joint High Commis-sion's North Atlantic Fisheries Treaty, into the background. The Mills Bill was torn to pieces and killed by the protection-ist Republican Senate.

Protectionism appeared to receive further vindication from the election in November 1888. For the first time since 1872 the Republicans gained control of both Houses of Congress as well as the Presidency. But the Republicans were just as concerned about the revenue surpluses as the Democrats had been and they vowed to rid the country of this plague of money with their own brand of tariff reform. This was clearly evident in President Harrison's first message to Congress in December 1889. The tariff, he said, was unjust and needed revision. Not only was it yielding too much revenue but it also was full of inequality, benefiting only the manufacturers and giving no aid to the farmers. Harrison recommended that "the inequalities of the law should be adjusted, but the pro-tective principle should be maintained and fairly applied to the products of our farms as well as of our shops." [50] After all, the protective principle was working well, why abandon it? The inequality could easily be done away with by extending

[50] Cited, H. U. Faulkner, *Politics, Reform and Expansion, 1890-1900,* New York, 1959, p. 106.

protection to the farm. Of course, the economic orthodoxy objected that this would only raise further the hated Treasury surpluses. But American protectionists had perfected their argument to too great a subtlety to be stopped by this objection. They shrewdly replied with the undebatable fact that if the duties were raised high enough all importation of foreign goods would be stopped and there would be no customs revenue at all.

William McKinley was a devout believer of the doctrine that tariff protection was the great benefactor of American industry by providing high wages for laborers and keeping the home market free for American products. As a Congressman McKinley made himself the Republican expert on tariff matters and was rewarded for his industry by being asked to draw up the tariff plank in the 1888 platform. His pleasant personality and his tariff expertise made him a popular figure in the House of Representatives and a strong candidate for the speakership in the newly elected House in 1889. But popularity fell the victim to power politics and the quiet machinations of Maine's illustrious Representative Thomas B. Reed. As the leading defeated candidate for the speakership, McKinley was appointed chairman of the Ways and Means Committee by the "Czar" and along with Joseph Cannon, chairman of the Appropriations Committee, Reed and McKinley ruled the House of Representatives with mailed fists. The "Czar," McKinley, and Cannon were the three key members of the Rules Committee and they had absolute control of what legislation would and what would not reach the floor for debate.[51]

McKinley's committee was "one of the strongest ever to sit in Congress."[52] The other Republican members were Joseph E. McKenna, Sereno E. Payne, Robert M. LaFollette, and Nelson Dingley, who would soon make his own distinc-

---

[51] M. Leech, *In the Days of McKinley*, New York, 1959, p. 44.
[52] Faulkner, *Politics, Reform and Expansion*, p. 106.

tive contribution to American protectionism. The Democrats were represented by ex-speaker Carlisle and Roger Q. Mills. Within a few days of Harrison's message the Ways and Means Committee began extensive hearings on a new tariff bill. The testimony went on for months and every conceivable interest was given its say. John Charlton saw McKinley and told him that the Canadian Government would remove its export duty on logs if the American import duty on sawn lumber were reduced to $1.50 per thousand feet.[53] S. J. Ritchie labored diligently in the cause of Commercial Union and his own pocketbook. During March and April 1890, he traveled between Ottawa and Washington in an attempt to get some measure of natural products reciprocity in return for a subsidy for his Central Ontario Railway. Sir John Macdonald was willing to play only half of Ritchie's game; he used Ritchie in the futile attempt at reciprocity but refused to concede the railway subsidy.[54] Ritchie also got Charles Hibbert Tupper an interview with McKinley when the former was in Washington discussing the Behring Sea difficulty with Pauncefote and Blaine.

Macdonald had authorized Tupper to tell McKinley that the export duty on logs would be abolished if the American import duty on Canadian lumber was reduced to one dollar per thousand feet. Tupper found McKinley "most agreeable" and not opposed to a fair trade arrangement between Canada and the United States. McKinley told Tupper that "he considered . . . Commercial Union utterly chimerical and went on to observe that he could not see with such a scheme how we could raise our revenue or be permitted to remain a part

[53] C. H. Tupper Papers, M106, C. H. Tupper to Macdonald, May 14, 1890.
[54] Macdonald Papers, 45, Ritchie to Macdonald, March 12 and 15, April 21 and July 30, 1890; 530, Macdonald to Ritchie, July 30, 1890; 31, C. H. Tupper to Macdonald, May 11, 1890.

of the British Empire." [55] Regarding the lumber offer by
Macdonald, McKinley intimated that nothing could be done
with his Bill in the House, where it was already being de-
bated, but that some consideration might be given to the offer
when the Bill reached the Senate. He added, however, that
in his opinion "trade arrangements with foreign countries
must be with the State Department and he again mentioned
that his Bill was a domestic Bill and not a foreign Bill." That
McKinley was firm in his belief that his measure should not
be cluttered up with any amendments touching foreign trade
was clearly shown in his strenuous opposition to Secretary of
State Blaine's pseudo-reciprocity amendment when it was inserted by the Senate.[56]

The McKinley Bill was reported to the House on 16 April

[55] C. H. Tupper Papers, M106, Macdonald to C. H. Tupper, May 12,
1890, Tupper to Macdonald, May 14, 1890. There is not the slightest
reason to doubt that McKinley was opposed to Commercial Union.
Ritchie told Macdonald that McKinley had no connection with the
Commercial Unionists and some years later told Laurier that "McKinley was himself opposed to it, as he has ever since been and continues
to be. . . ." Macdonald Papers, 45, Ritchie to Macdonald, April 21,
1890; Laurier Papers, 61, Ritchie to Laurier, January 3, 1898.

[56] The Blaine amendment was truly backhanded reciprocity. While
the new tariff was being discussed Blaine was chairing the first Pan-
American Conference. Enamored with the idea of furthering friendship
with Latin America, Blaine desired the power to negotiate reciprocity
agreements by executive action. The trouble was that even under the
new tariff better than eighty per cent of Latin American imports were
admitted free. The only way to get reciprocal trade agreements, then,
was to give the President power to *impose* duties on Latin American
imports if the American Government considered that the duties on
American goods in Latin American countries were subject to excessive
import duties. It was this power which was given in the Senate amendment. As Professor Faulkner says, "it was reciprocity of a curious
type. . . . It was a threat to raise tariffs in this country if other countries did not lower theirs." *Politics, Reform and Expansion*, p. 108. See
also Leech, *In the Days of McKinley*, pp. 44-47, and Morgan, "The
Congressional Career of William McKinley," pp. 168-77.

1890. True to the curious Republic philosophy of raising import rates to reduce revenue, it was entitled "an act to reduce the revenue." One of the chief features of the Bill, and one subsequently copied in the National Policy tariff in Canada, was the abolition of duties on raw sugar coupled with a bounty system to protect domestically grown sugar. To protect the refiners, the duties were retained on foreign refined sugar. Naturally, this provision was viewed as removing an "inequality" in the tariff intended to reduce the cost of a mass consumption item. While this was probably true, the duty on foreign refined sugar and the bounty system left no doubt that the chief benefit remained with the American sugar interests. While the sugar schedule might gain some votes for the Republicans there were other items in the tariff that might gain even more. And these items were of particular interest to Canadians. The Republicans desperately needed support from the agrarian west which was rapidly turning away from the traditional parties toward the Populist revolt. Half of the Republican bid was in the compromise Sherman Silver Purchase Act. The other half was in the first complete schedule of duties on farm products ever found in an American tariff. Wheat, hay, barley, eggs, and other items were now placed on the duty list in fulfillment of the promise to erase the tariff "inequality" that had been made by President Harrison.[57]

The claim has often been made that the McKinley Tariff was expressly designed to coerce Canada into Commercial Union and eventually annexation. McKinley himself frankly stated that his object was to cut off the entry of Canadian agricultural products into the United States. But all the evidence suggests that there is little foundation for the larger claim. McKinley, after all, told Tupper of his low view of the Commercial Union movement, and ardent Commercial Unionist S. J. Ritchie told Macdonald (and later Laurier) that

[57] See Morgan, "The Congressional Career of William McKinley," pp. 147, 184.

McKinley was opposed to Commercial Union. Subsequent events in his career certainly proved him to be a most reluctant expansionist in the first decade of American Imperialism. McKinley was not very interested in Canada in 1890 nor were many of his colleagues. They had come to power for the first time in many years in both Houses of Congress and the White House and they were determined to stay there. To do that they had to retain their traditional support in the industrial east and put an end to the revolt in the former Republican stronghold in middle America. The G.O.P. had been founded on a coalition of the agrarian west and the industrial east and had seen its great days under that tradition. That coalition had to be maintained if Republicanism was to retain power in the 1890's. Surely this was the underlying assumption in Harrison's remarks in December 1889. And this, plus a rock-bound belief in protectionism, was the motivation behind the agricultural duties in the McKinley tariff.

Nonetheless, the McKinley tariff would seriously affect Canadian trade when it came into operation in October. In September 1890, Macdonald told a Halifax audience that the real aim of the McKinley tariff was "to starve Canada into annexation." [58] A few days later the Prime Minister told Tupper that the tariff had been passed "with the avowed object of forcing Canada to give the United States a preference over England in her market." He sincerely regarded the whole affair as part of a great Canadian-American plot aiming at eventually sweeping the Dominion out of existence. "The McKinley Bill so strongly hits our agricultural classes that the disloyal opposition is working on them in concert with Wiman and other American filibusters to promote unrestricted reciprocity with the United States, giving the preference, in our markets to the Americans." [59] And it was true that the Liberals were making the most of their unwitting

[58] Creighton, *John A. Macdonald*, v. 2, p. 546.
[59] Macdonald Papers, 532, Macdonald to Tupper, September 26, 1890.

194

gift from McKinley, preaching blue ruin and claiming that only they could save Canada from destruction. Unrestricted Reciprocity, which had quietly slumbered in Liberal minds for two years was once again put before the Canadian public as the only alternative to annexation.

vi

There was no doubt about the effect the McKinley tariff would have upon Canada. The closing of the American market would seriously hurt the farmers of the Dominion. The substantial Canadian-American trade in barley, eggs, and animals, as well as other agricultural products, would come to an end. Faced with the closing of the American market and an already glutted domestic market, the farmers would seek relief from their distress at almost any cost. W. T. R. Preston, the general secretary of the Ontario Reform Association, wrote to Laurier in November 1890 that "there is no longer the slightest doubt about an extended movement being under way among the agricultural population on the question of greater trade relations with the United States." Naturally, the Liberals were making the best of the situation. "The meetings that have been held by Sir Richard and Charlton," Preston reported, "have given an impetus to an undercurrent that was moving previously." [60]

In their more sanguine moments the Conservatives remembered their faith in the ability of the National Policy to withstand economic aggression from the Republic. "I do not look upon [the McKinley Tariff] with so much fear as many of our friends do," Bowell told a friend. The Government was pursuing a "vigorous policy" of finding other markets for Canadian agricultural produce. "From what I can learn," Bowell concluded, "I do not believe the ravings of Wiman, Charlton, and Cartwright will do much towards poisoning

[60] Laurier Papers, 4, Preston to Laurier, November 10, 1890.

the minds of thinking people." And despite his publicly expressed fears, apparently even the Prime Minister privately thought the Dominion would meet the threat. "I quite agree with you," George Stephen wrote in reply to a letter from Macdonald, "that the effect upon Canada of the McKinley Tariff will not be half as serious as is generally supposed both in Canada and the U.S." Canada had weathered the storm caused by the abrogation of the Reciprocity Treaty in 1866 and weathered it without any National Policy. "If she survived that blow at her independence," Stephen continued, "she will easily overcome the drawbacks and disadvantages arising out of this last increase of duties on her barley, eggs, horses, &c. &c." In November, too, there was a hopeful omen from south of the border. McKinley's bid for western support had backfired. In the mid-term Congressional elections the Republicans had suffered heavy defeat, McKinley himself being one of the many decisively beaten candidates for reelection. "Let us hope for the best!" Macdonald told Stephen. "The rising of the people of the U.S. against the McKinley bill is most wonderful." Certainly the Canadian "unrestricted reciprocity folk are going to enter upon a crusade." But that had been expected for many months and the Conservative strategy was simple. "We must countermine when they begin to mine," Macdonald told a friend. All things considered, the Conservatives seemed in their better moments ready and willing to meet the challenge posed by the McKinley tariff.[61]

Besides, in the autumn of 1890 it seemed that the Americans were raising an even more serious attack on another front, and, unhappily, with the anxious help of a supposed ally of the Dominion. Newfoundland, with the support of the Imperial Government, was negotiating a separate trade agree-

[61] Bowell Papers, 90, Bowell to Aikens, November 10, 1890; Macdonald Papers, 272, Stephen to Macdonald, October 11, 1890; 530, Macdonald to Stephen, November 10, 1890; 529, Macdonald to Blaine, January 6, 1890.

ment with the United States. The agreement would allow American fishing vessels to purchase bait and touch and trade in Newfoundland ports. In return, the products of the Newfoundland fisheries would be allowed free entry into American markets. Obviously this was of major importance to the Newfoundlanders. Their principal export products came from the fisheries; indeed, the island's economy depended on the prosperity of the fishing industry. That prosperity would be ensured by a free market in the United States for Newfoundland fish and fish products. In fact, the Newfoundland Government was so anxious to secure this prize that it further conceded that a number of American manufactured products would be given free entry into Newfoundland and that the island's duty on American natural products would remain fixed at a specific low rate.[62] On the other hand, if the agreement were to come into effect, it would totally undermine the *modus vivendi* regarding the North Atlantic fisheries which had been drawn up by the Joint High Commission of 1887-1888. Under the *modus vivendi* Canada and Newfoundland jointly issued licenses to American fishing vessels allowing them commercial privileges and the liberty of purchasing bait in Canadian or Newfoundland ports. The proposed arrangement would make it unnecessary for American fishing vessels to call at Canadian ports and would destroy the joint license system. Of even greater importance to Canadian fishermen, however, was the fact that the agreement would undoubtedly deprive them of a market for their fish. Obviously, American buyers would rather purchase duty-free Newfoundland fish than Canadian fish on which a one and one-half cent per pound duty was levied. As far as Canadians were concerned, Secretary of State James G. Blaine and the Newfoundland representative in Washington, Robert Bond, were enacting an elaborate plan

[62] *ibid.*, 9, Privy Council Report 446H, 1891.

to squeeze Canadian fish out of the American market at the same time McKinley was closing the market to Canadian agricultural products. Equally the Newfoundland market for Canadian natural and manufactured products was being closed as it opened to similar American products. Commercially, Canada was being isolated on the North American continent. Apparently James G. Blaine was quietly effecting a policy of economic blockade against Canada.

It all began innocently enough, in February 1890, when the Dominion Government consulted the Newfoundland Government about continuing the fisheries *modus vivendi* for the year 1890. The island Government replied that the question was being studied. But it further urged the Governor, Sir Terence O'Brien, to inform the Imperial Government that "the interests of this Colony are not identical with those of the Dominion of Canada" and that Newfoundland desired to open negotiations with the United States "for a distinct arrangement with reference to this Colony as regards the fishery question and trade relations." [63] While the Macdonald Government patiently awaited a more conclusive reply to their inquiry, the Imperial authorities considered this request for separate Newfoundland negotiations with the United States. In April Knutsford told O'Brien that a decision on the request would have to be held over until the Newfoundland Premier, Sir William Whiteway, came to London. Whiteway arrived in London in July and convinced the Imperial officials that separate negotiations with the United States were feasible and in September the Newfoundland Colonial Secretary, Robert Bond, went to Washington to begin his talks with Blaine. By the end of October a draft convention had been drawn by Pauncefote which seemed to meet the approval of both Blaine and Bond. In sum, the draft called for the

[63] *ibid.*, Copy, Newfoundland Minute of Council, February 27, 1890, enclosure in O'Brien to Knutsford, February 28, 1890.

exchange of free importation of Newfoundland products of the sea for the right of American fishing vessels to purchase bait and to touch and trade in Newfoundland waters. On 17 October Pauncefote wired to Salisbury that progress was being made toward a separate Newfoundland–United States fisheries agreement. He added that "before negotiations go further I would suggest that the Government of Canada might be informed, as they might wish to negotiate on the same lines as regards the Provinces of New Brunswick and Nova Scotia." [64] This message was passed on to Governor-General Stanley and to High Commissioner Tupper in London.

Macdonald, however, had learned of Bond's negotiations in Washington through the American press and before Pauncefote's message had been relayed to Ottawa, he had cabled Tupper to enter a protest to the Imperial Government. Tupper had followed Macdonald's instructions on 21 October so that Pauncefote's message to Salisbury was no surprise to him when he received it two days later. On the 27th Macdonald cabled Tupper that the Canadian Government could "scarcely believe Newfoundland has received authority from Imperial Government to make a separate arrangement respecting fisheries. The relations of all the North American Provinces to the United States and to the Empire would be affected." He told Tupper to point out to the Imperial authorities "how

[64] *ibid.,* Copies, Knutsford to O'Brien, April 12, 1890, Whiteway to Colonial Office, July 12, 1890, Whiteway to Colonial Office, September 9, 1890, Pauncefote to Salisbury, October 17, 1890 in Knutsford to Stanley, October 22, 1890. The Newfoundland plea for separate negotiations met with Knutsford's approval. He wrote to Salisbury that "I hope you will assent to the Newfoundlanders being allowed to make separate & independent Treaty as to fishery with the U. States. . . . I do not see that Canada has any ground for interfering in such a question. It is quite certain she would not allow Newfoundland to interfere or object to any arrangement which she [Canada] might make with the U. States." Salisbury Papers, Knutsford to Salisbury, August 24, 1890.

disastrous from a national point of view it would be for a separate colony to effect an arrangement with the United States more favourable than would be given to the Confederated Provinces. Our difficulties under the new American tariff are sufficiently great now." On the 30th of October Lord Stanley asked Knutsford for information concerning the powers given to Bond and told the Colonial Secretary that Canada wished to have the opportunity of being included in any arrangement between Bond and Blaine.[65]

By late November the Imperial Government had decided that the Newfoundland negotiations should be delayed so that Canadian negotiations with the United States might proceed concurrently, or, as Lord Salisbury vaguely put it, "until Canada is satisfied." On 13 December the Canadian Government proposed a formal joint commission be appointed to consider, *inter alia,* a reciprocity treaty, a renewal of the fishery treaty of 1888, protection of mackerel and other fisheries, and a settlement of the Alaska boundary problem.[66] In other words, the Canadians wished to use the opportunity afforded by the Bond-Blaine negotiations for the purpose of settling every existing Canadian-American problem of magnitude save the Behring Sea dispute. Meanwhile, in Washington, in a series of private conversations of which Pauncefote was unaware, Bond and Blaine had materially altered their fisheries agreement so that it included fixed low Newfoundland duties on American natural products and free entry of a specified list of American manufactured products in return for the free entry of Newfoundland products of the mine into the United States.

Secretary of State Blaine told Pauncefote on 22 December

[65] Thompson Papers, 115, Tupper to Macdonald, October 25, 1890, Macdonald to Tupper, October 27, 1890; Stanley to Knutsford, October 30, 1890: CO42/803.

[66] Salisbury Papers, Knutsford to Salisbury, December 27, 1890; Stanley to Knutsford, December 13, 1890: CO42/803.

that it would be "utterly idle to attempt to secure the appointment of a formal commission to consider any arrangements for reciprocal trade between the United States and the Dominion." Having suffered severe reverses in the November election, Blaine apparently thought it would be politically impossible for the Republican Administration to agree to any such plan. On the other hand, he was willing to have a "full but private conference" with the Canadians to discuss outstanding issues. "If an agreement is reached all is well," Blaine told Pauncefote. "If not, no official mention is to be made of the effort. Above all things it is important to avoid all public reference to the matter. This the President insists upon." [67]

By mid-December the separate Newfoundland–United States negotiations, the objection to them by Canada, and the Canadian attempt to extend these negotiations into a full scale discussion of most of the problems between British North America and the United States had lost any sense of separate identity. They had become an integral part of the politics of the Dominion. Macdonald's Government had been elected in February 1887 and could easily wait another year before again going to the people. But was delay the wisest course? The Liberals were rapidly gaining strength as a result of the imposition of the McKinley tariff. To wait another year, during which the full effect of the McKinley tariff would be felt, might be of even greater benefit to Laurier and his colleagues. In addition, a separate Newfoundland–United States fisheries and trade agreement would further discredit the Canadian Government. But now, by persistent pressure on the Imperial authorities, the Macdonald Government had managed to secure a reluctant assent from Blaine to private talks on reciprocity. If the Conservatives could counter the Liberal cry for Unrestricted Reciprocity with their own claim

[67] Cited, Tansill, *Canadian-American Relations,* p. 427.

to be negotiating with the United States, then perhaps the time for the appeal to the people was the present.

Rumors of Canadian-American trade negotiations circulated throughout the Dominion as the year 1891 commenced. On 14 January the *Toronto Mail* announced that the Imperial Government had urged an extensive trade agreement between the United States and Canada. Two days later the *Toronto Empire,* the paper which had been called into existence by the Conservatives to meet the Liberal threat of Unrestricted Reciprocity in 1888, printed the misleading information that trade negotiations were, in fact, going on with the United States at the request of the American government. It is important to note that this information was put before the public in a series of newspaper exchanges. Despite the admittedly close connection between the *Toronto Empire* and the Government in Ottawa, there is no evidence which suggests that the Government or any of its members inspired the *Empire*'s despatch regarding trade negotiations. It is also true that it was not until a week later that Macdonald and his colleagues were aware of the fact that Secretary of State Blaine considered not only the trade talks but also the existence of the trade talks with the United States as private information. "You will observe," Macdonald wrote to Thompson somewhat later, "that we had no intimation that the private & informal meeting had to be kept secret until January when we applied for leave to publish our minute in Council proposing a formal Conference. We knew that the Conference proposed by Blaine was to be unofficial & in that sense private, but had no idea that the fact of the meeting was to be kept private." [68]

Nevertheless, the newspaper exchange between the *Mail* and the *Empire* had leaked out information about the trade talks in a seriously distorted context. Blaine's note of 22 December to Pauncefote had been the first indication that had

[68] Thompson Papers, 127, Macdonald to Thompson, April 27, 1891.

been given by the United States that it would even privately discuss trade relations with Canada. And Blaine's note had been in reply to requests initiated in London at the insistence of the Canadian Government. On 30 October Stanley had requested that Canada be included in any arrangement made between Newfoundland and the United States. On 13 December the Canadian Government had proposed a joint commission to settle Canadian-American differences. Pauncefote's inquiry to Blaine as to the acceptability of the Canadian proposal was what had prompted the Secretary of State's reply of 22 December. To claim, as the *Toronto Empire* did, that the American Government had taken the initiative and had requested negotiations with the Canadians, whether formal or private, was a simple misstatement of fact.

On 21 January 1891 Lord Stanley wired to Knutsford that Macdonald had requested to dissolve Parliament, thinking that "a new Parliament would be better able to deal with the reciprocity question." Under these "special circumstances" Stanley requested permission to publish the Canadian proposal of 13 December "stating authoritatively that it was agreed to on both sides that any treaty of reciprocity of commerce between Canada and the United States would, of course, be so framed as not to place imports from the United Kingdom at a disadvantage, and that Canada would retain control of her own tariff." Knutsford replied that permission was granted provided that no mention be made of Blaine because "Her Majesty's Government cannot commit the United States to any expression of opinion" and, further, that the words "agreed to on both sides" were taken to refer to the Imperial and the Dominion Governments. On 24 January Stanley asked that the Imperial Government ascertain "whether Mr. Blaine would object to its being known that the United States Government were willing to discuss the question of reciprocity fully, though informally . . . your permission would not serve any good purpose here . . . without any intimation of the general attitude of the United States Government." He added that the dissolution "is suspended for the moment. It is most important, therefore, that Mr. Blaine's assent should be obtained to publication as proposed." [69] Salisbury wired Pauncefote to see if the British Ambassador could obtain Blaine's assent to the Canadian request. Blaine did not reply to Pauncefote's note until 31 January when he gave the curt answer that "I see no reason for changing the conclusion we reached in our confidential talk of 22nd. ultimo." In other words, Pauncefote told Salisbury, "Mr. Blaine . . . considers as confidential his reply to the Canadian bases." Officially then, Blaine refused to acknowledge that there had been any discussion between Pauncefote and himself regarding Canadian trade relations and the Canadian Government was forced to publish their proposal of 13 December under the conditions laid down by Knutsford in his reply to Stanley's request of 21 January.[70]

This was a serious blow in itself. The high card held by the Macdonald Government to be played against Laurier's forces in the election campaign was the ability to say that the Government was carrying on trade discussions with the United States. But an even greater blow fell on 29 January while the Canadian Government was seeking permission to give to the public its version of the Blaine-Pauncefote talk of 22 December. The principals to the incident were Blaine, Edward Farrer, an editorial writer for the *Toronto Globe,* and Charles S. Baker, Member of the House of Representatives for Rochester, New York. One of Farrer's friends, W. D. Gregory, recorded the incident in his autobiography some years later:

[69] Stanley to Knutsford, January 21 and 24, 1891, Knutsford to Stanley, January 23, 1891: CO807, North America 143, pp. 85, 89.

[70] Foreign Office to Colonial Office, February 2, 1891: Stanley to Knutsford, February 3, 1891: CO807, North America 143, pp. 96-98.

Sir John Macdonald was an avowed believer in reciprocity with the United States. He knew the hold it had on the people of Ontario and he had witnessed the great benefits of the reciprocity treaty [1854-1866] with the United States. . . . He stated that his Government were carrying on negotiations with the United States to obtain reciprocity. At the instigation of Farrer, a letter was written to Mr. Blaine, the Secretary of State, by an American Congressman, [Baker] inquiring as to whether negotiations with Canada were going on. Mr. Blaine replied that they were not. Farrer, I have no doubt, acted at the suggestion of Sir Richard Cartwright or, at any rate, the Liberal leaders.[71]

Blaine's letter to Baker read:

I authorize you to contradict the rumours you refer to. There are no negotiations whatever on foot for a reciprocity treaty with Canada, and you may be assured no such scheme for reciprocity with the Dominion confined to natural products will be entertained by this Government. We know nothing of Sir Charles Tupper's coming to Washington.[72]

Blaine's letter was naturally widely published throughout the Dominion. Macdonald's forces could now neither officially give their side of the story nor even successfully keep before the Canadian people unofficial rumors that negotiations were in progress. Who would believe the rumors when they had Blaine's explicit denial right before their eyes? Apparently the efforts of the Liberal party to cultivate the friendship of the Secretary of State had paid off in large dividends.

But there was no stopping at this point. The decision had been made to go to the people and the Conservatives would press on in spite of Blaine and Farrer. "We have burned our

[71] Gregory Papers, MS autobiography, p. 99.
[72] Official Report of Debates, May 4, 1891, p. 83.

boats and must now fight for our lives," Macdonald told a friend. There were, ostensibly, two issues in the election of 1891: trade relations with the United States and loyalty to Dominion, Crown, and Empire. The Prime Minister guessed that the election would be "the last great fight on trade questions." On the other hand, as early as July 1889, he told William Kirby that "the only way to fight is by bringing the loyalty question to the front." And, in the final analysis, there was but one issue, loyalty. Unrestricted Reciprocity was but Commercial Union very thinly disguised and Commercial Union would undoubtedly be a stepping stone to annexation, the Conservatives argued. Macdonald told another friend that "the great contest that is now going on . . . will determine whether Canada is to remain British or become part of the United States. I can assure you, we are in great danger." [73]

If there seemed to be any doubt about what the issue was, it vanished when Macdonald spoke in Toronto on 17 February 1891. He read portions of what was purported to be a pamphlet written by Farrer of the *Globe*. How Macdonald acquired the portion of Farrer's pamphlet remains a mystery. There are, however, indications that it came into his hands through a one-time friend who had close connections with both Canadian Liberals and American Commercial Unionists. In 1889 William McDougall, probably in an effort to regain favor with Macdonald and his colleagues, wrote to Sir Charles Tupper and offered to turn over to him information regarding Unrestricted Reciprocity and Commercial Union. At the crucial moment, McDougall's offer was apparently taken up with reward to the Conservatives and promised (though unfulfilled) reward to McDougall. Tupper told of the incident in a letter to Sir John Abbott in 1892. "I have been awaiting the reconstruction of the Cabinet," Tupper wrote,

[73] Macdonald Papers, 530, Macdonald to Galt, February 3, 1891, Macdonald to Baird, January 31, 1891, Macdonald to Callum, February 12, 1891; Kirby Papers, Macdonald to Kirby, July 8, 1889.

to bring before you a pledge that I gave to the Hon. W. McDougall with the authority of the late Premier that he should be made a Senator.

When Sir J. A. Macdonald and I were both apprehensive of the result of the general election we decided that it was very important that the attack he made on Farrer and his associates should be backed up and confirmed by the papers that Mr. McDougall had confidentially placed in my hands. Sir John then authorized me to assure Mr. McDougall that he would shortly be made a Senator and I gave him Sir John's assurance to that effect. Mr. McDougall is one of the fathers of confederation & did all he could, in the face of great difficulty, to support us at a most important crisis, the last general election. I sincerely hope you will take an early opportunity of redressing the pledge given to him.[74]

McDougall did not get his senatorship but Macdonald did get Farrer's pamphlet and put it to good use.

The pamphlet had been written on the fishery question. As Farrer himself confirmed in a letter to the *Globe* the day following Macdonald's speech, an "American friend asked me to give him my own views of the case so far as it related to the refusal of commercial privileges in Canadian ports to American vessels, and to put myself in his place, as it were, and say what line I should take if I were an American. The pamphlet was written at odd times under those circumstances." The line Farrer would take if he were an American provided Macdonald with his choicest revelation. Farrer had recommended an imposition of a tonnage tax on all Nova Scotia vessels laden with fish entering American waters, or the suspension of the bonding privilege on Canadian goods traveling through the United States, or cutting the connection of the Canadian Pacific Railway with American territory at

[74] Tupper Papers, 9, McDougall to Tupper, May 11, 1889; Abbott Papers, 3, Tupper to Abbott, February 22, 1892.

Sault Ste. Marie. "It would be better still to oblige Britain to withdraw her countenance and support from the Canadian contention as she did in 1871," Farrer continued. "That would secure the end desired without leaving the United States open to the charge of being animated by hatred of Canada, on which Sir John Macdonald trades. Whatever course the United States may see fit to adopt, it is plain that Sir John's disappearance from the stage is to be the signal for a movement toward annexation." [75] Farrer, naturally, disclaimed that the pamphlet had any connection with the Liberal party; his position at the *Globe* did not mean that he could not "privately" write what he pleased. Further, he denied that it was written for any other purpose than the private use of "an American friend of mine, not in politics." [76] But these were subtle distinctions which would be dismissed by the Canadian electorate. Farrer was a known annexationist and his position at the *Globe* did, at least outwardly, implicate the Liberals. Many Canadians agreed with Macdonald's verdict that "there is a deliberate conspiracy, in which some of the members of the opposition are more or less compromised; I say that there is a deliberate conspiracy, by force, by fraud, or by both, to force Canada into the American union." [77]

Annexationist or not, the Liberal trade policy nevertheless commanded heavy support. J. D. Cameron wrote to Edward Blake from Winnipeg that "the people of this province are . . . practically unanimous in favor of free trade with the United States." George Foster who was campaigning in the

[75] *Toronto Empire*, February 18, 1891. See also Stanley to Knutsford, February 19, 1890: CO42/806; CO807, North America 151; Thompson Papers, 275, memoranda, North Atlantic Fisheries which contains a typed copy of the proof sheets of the Farrer Pamphlet.

[76] *Toronto Globe*, February 18, 1891. W. D. Gregory, who knew Farrer well, in his autobiography referred to the pamphlet as "a report Farrer was making I believe for the use of the United States Senate."

[77] *Toronto Empire*, February 18, 1891.

Maritimes told Macdonald that he was "a little anxious about the 'Free Trade' cry with the farmers. It takes, and the disadvantages are concealed as much as possible." In Ontario, Mackenzie Bowell reported, "There is no hiding the fact that the free trade idea, with the United States, has a much stronger hold upon the farmers mind than I could have believed, particularly along the frontier counties." [78]

"So you have gone and done it," Sir Leonard Tilley wrote Macdonald, adding that "matters look well in New. Bk." But Tilley, like many other Canadians, could not help wondering if the activities of the Liberals in the United States would not have even more direct results than Blaine's letter to Congressman Baker. "The result all over should be satisfactory," the former Finance Minister judged, "unless Wiman and his associates send in a big pile of money." Naturally the Conservatives suspected that Americans were financing the Liberal campaign. The suspicion was not without foundation. It is quite impossible to say how much money was sent into Canada by interested Americans or to say who those Americans were. But J. W. Longley, the Nova Scotia Attorney General, arranged for American financing of the Liberal campaign. In September 1890, Longley wrote to Laurier from New York that he was "having a delightful visit with Mr. Wiman." "I think I shall be able to get the little arrangement I was hinting at when I saw you last in working order," he added. In February while the election campaign was at its height, Longley told Laurier, "I have *some* means from the States, but not enough." [79]

[78] Laurier Papers, 5, Cameron to Blake, February 4, 1891 in Blake to Laurier, February 7, 1891; Macdonald Papers, 215, Foster to Macdonald, February 28, 1891; 190, Bowell to Macdonald, February 17, 1891.
[79] Macdonald Papers, 277, Tilley to Macdonald, February 21, 1891; Laurier Papers, 4, Longley to Laurier, September 2, 1890; 5, Longley to Laurier, February 10, 1891.

When the battle was over it appeared as if the Macdonald Government had withstood fairly well the assault of Blaine's letter, Wiman's money, and the promises of Canadian Liberalism. In 1887 Macdonald and his colleagues garnered a majority of 35 seats in the House of Commons; in 1891 they had a majority of 31 seats. But these figures were somewhat deceptive. In Quebec the Conservative party won only a minority of seats (30 out of 65) for the first time since Confederation. A number of reasons could be given for the reverse in Quebec. Mercier's alliance with Laurier Liberalism in the campaign, the rumors of the McGreevey scandal, the lack of cooperation between Langevin and Chapleau in the Macdonald cabinet, the appeal of Unrestricted Reciprocity, or the attraction of a French Canadian leader of the Liberal party; any one of these things or any combination of them could have influenced the Quebec vote. The point was that Macdonald had lost his hold on Quebec. This was not without significance. "French Canada was Conservative long before it became Liberal," E. P. Dean wrote in 1949. "Until 1887, it proportionally returned far more Conservative members than Ontario and it was regarded as much the surer province. During the thirty years from 1857, when the historic Liberal-Conservative alliance was first tested at the polls, until 1887, Quebec only once returned a Liberal majority." [80]

In English Canada there was less question about issues. From Victoria to Winnipeg to Toronto to Halifax the fourth estate conceded that there was but one issue, the trade question. Except for Prince Edward Island, the Conservatives held majorities of seats in every English Canadian province. Naturally, in the final analysis, this was all important because it was in the House of Commons that the decision would be made on any trade question with the United States. Again, however, the Conservative majority did not tell the whole story. Thirty-one seats was a safe, if not entirely comfortable,

[80] E. P. Dean, "How Canada Has Voted: 1867 to 1945," *Canadian Historical Review*, xxx, 1949, p. 232.

majority. But thirty-one seats did not accurately reflect the sentiment of the Canadian people. It was, perhaps, significant, that the popular vote in the Dominion was much more evenly divided. In fact, the Conservatives had captured only 51.1 per cent of the popular vote. And in Ontario it was quite clear that Unrestricted Reciprocity had a wide appeal. There the Conservatives won 48 of the 92 seats but only earned 48.9 per cent of the popular vote. The following table gives some evidence of the margin of Macdonald's victory.[81]

PERCENTAGE

	POPULAR VOTE		SEATS WON	
	Government	*Opposition*	*Government*	*Opposition*
Ontario	48.9	51.1	48	44
Quebec	51.0	49.0	30	35
Nova Scotia	54.5	45.5	16	5
New Brunswick	56.0	44.0	13	3
P.E.I.	48.8	51.2	2	4
Manitoba	53.5	46.5	4	1
N.W.T.	65.4	34.6	4	0
British Columbia	73.1	26.9	6	0
Canada	51.1	48.9	123	92

The election of 1891 was the "last great fight" in a general election on the question of trade relations with the United States in the nineteenth century. When it was over, when all the skulduggery that had taken place on both sides was finished, it did appear to be a vindication of the "old leader" and the "old policy," a vindication of the National Policy, of a separate Canadian entity on the North American continent, and a rebuke of the idea of continentalism. But the margin of victory was narrow and the "old leader," recognizing it, prepared to kill continentalism as it had not been killed by the Canadian electorate.

[81] The percentage calculations are based on election statistics compiled by George Johnson, the Dominion Statistician, in 1891. A copy may be found in Bowell Papers, 9.

CHAPTER VII

Problems of Consolidation and Expansion of Trade

THE Conservatives won a close victory in the general election of 1891. It was clear that a majority, slim though it was, of the Canadian electorate had rejected continentalism. But to reject continentalism as it was offered by the Liberals did not necessarily mean an acceptance of the Conservative party's National Policy. There were many people like Edward Blake and Alexander Mackenzie who repudiated Unrestricted Reciprocity but also damned the National Policy. This was sensed by the wise old Conservative leader, Sir John Macdonald. A vote against Unrestricted Reciprocity might have been a "loyalty" vote but that did not mean it was a National Policy vote. Macdonald realized that to revive confidence in the National Policy, the National Policy must advance and expand. The tariff and the railway were, by 1891, old accomplishments whose glitter had been tarnished by years of depression. Since 1885 the achievements of the National Policy had been singularly few and it was time to move ahead once again. It was time for Canadian Conservatism to consolidate and expand its policy of economic nationalism.

ii

For Canadian Conservatism the Imperial tie had assumed immense importance. In the election of 1891 it seemed even more important than the assertion of Canadian self-preservation as an effective counterweight to the pull toward the Republic. In large measure this had always been true. It was implicit in the three-year drive toward Confederation and was explicit in the debates on Confederation and in the British North America Act. But of late years the Governments of Sir John Macdonald had shown more and more interest in self-assertion, in an economic nationalism with obvious political ends called the National Policy. Yet, as had been suggested by the debate on Cartwright's resolution in 1888, in the moment of crisis, economic and political facts in the garb of Canadian national identity were covered over by the protective emotional wraps of the Imperial connection.

Shortly after the election Macdonald gave some indication of the severity of the battle and the element that had tipped the balance toward victory in a letter to Sir George Stephen. "The effect of the McKinley tariff is so disastrous," he wrote, "that if our election had been postponed until another harvest we would have been swept out of existence. As it was, I was surprised and grieved to find the hold unrestricted reciprocity had got of our farmers. . . . I have, of course, pointed out that U.R. meant annexation, and the movements of Cartwright, Farrer & Wiman enabled us to raise the loyalty cry, which had considerable effect." Macdonald told an English friend that "our farmers were as much taken with Free Trade with the U. States . . . as your agricultural labourers were with 'three acres and a cow.' This cry would have I think submerged us if the disloyal intrigues of the opposition leaders in Washington had not [influenced?] our loyalists. We worked the 'Loyalty' cry for all it was worth and it carried the country. . . . But we are not safe yet." [1]

"We are not safe yet." Surely that was the point. The election had narrowly been won and, as shall be seen, the subsequent informal trade talks between Tupper and Blaine had ended with no concrete results. As Sir Alexander Galt, an old friend, told Macdonald, "some very decided action is imposed upon you." Macdonald agreed. The Blaine-Tupper conversations, he wrote in reply, "turned out just to suit us. We shall throw over all discussions until 1892 & meanwhile push trade

[1] Macdonald Papers, 534, Macdonald to Stephen, March 31, 1891, Macdonald to Smith, April 8, 1891.

matters in England." [2] Macdonald's thinking was clear. Sentimentalism for the Imperial tie had won the election. With the Mother Country looming so large in the Canadian mind, now was the time to strike for practical results. By "pushing trade matters in England," emotionalism could be put to work for the benefit of both the Imperial relationship and the National Policy. After all, he had been thinking of this for some years. In 1888 he had written, "our course is plain, the N. P. is to be maintained in its entirety . . . And a preferential system of trade with the Mother Country & her Colonies when the time comes." The time had come. It was true that there was a large element of uncertainty in forwarding Anglo-Canadian trade. Just as the Liberal plan of Unrestricted Reciprocity required willing partners in both Canada and the United States, so too, the Conservative plan for an Imperial preferential tariff needed strong support in the United Kingdom as well as in Canada. Macdonald thought the plan had a chance of success with a Conservative Government in London. But an election was pending in the United Kingdom and Macdonald admitted that "nothing effectual can be done until after Lord Salisbury goes to the country." "If he wins," he wrote, "which Heaven grant! some Imperial policy can be framed and carried out." [3]

While Macdonald waited for the coming British election, preparation for the assault against free trade's hold on the British mind began in Canada. The Prime Minister turned to Galt as he had done so many times before when he needed someone to draft a superb state paper that would argue his case. In early April 1891, Galt labored over a draft address to be presented to the Queen by the Canadian Parliament begging the implementation of a system of Imperial preferential trade. In a few days he sent it to Macdonald and on 13 April

[2] Abbott Papers, 1, Galt to Macdonald, April 10, 1891, Macdonald to Galt, April 11, 1891.
[3] Macdonald Papers, 534, Macdonald to Smith, April 8, 1891.

214

the Prime Minister telegraphed in reply that it was a "first rate state paper." [4]

The address urged the Queen "to cause to be submitted to the Parliament of the United Kingdom such remedial measures as have become necessary to protect and encourage the commercial interests of the Empire, in their relations to Foreign Nations." Galt noted that the approaching termination of existing British commercial treaties made it a "fitting time" to consider not only their past effects, but also "the serious consequences that may arise from their renewal without material attention to alteration." In particular Galt singled out the Belgian and Zollverein treaties of 1862 and 1865 which compelled the Colonies to admit the products of foreign countries into the Colonies upon the same terms as imports from the Mother Country and which "debarred [the Colonies] from shewing that favor to their fellow countrymen and fellow subjects, which undoubtedly in many cases would be their desire." He noted that Canada considered Article XV of the Belgian treaty and Article VII of the Zollverein treaty "an infringement of the rights conferred upon the Parliament of Canada, by the Act of Confederation, which gave full power to establish such Tariff regulations, as might be judged in the best interests of the Dominion." If the most-favored-nation clause were renewed, it was "calculated to lead to serious complications and embarrassements [sic] in such an Empire, as that under the rule of Your Majesty, wherein the self-governing Colonies all now recognized as possessing the right to define their respective fiscal relations to all Foreign nations—to the Mother Country—and to each other." [5]

[4] Abbott Papers, 1, Macdonald to Galt, April 13, 1891.
[5] *ibid.*, draft address to the Queen from the Senate and the House of Commons of Canada. Mackenzie Bowell explained the restrictions of these treaties in detail to the delegates to the Colonial Conference in 1894. He noted that "restrictions do exist in certain treaties entered into between England and Foreign powers which bind all the colonies

It was thus imperative, in the interests of the Colonies and the Mother Country alike, that the restrictive most-favored-nation clauses be done away with so that the Imperial Government might have a free hand in negotiating commercial treaties. While the United Kingdom had maintained a policy of free importation for many years, other nations had moved progressively toward "protective and discriminating duties" which were "distinctly opposed to the interests of the United Kingdom and each of and all of its Possessions" and the Imperial Parliament should have the "power of dealing with every . . . case as it may occur." It was clear that the time had come to initiate an Imperial policy that "will neutralize the selfish isolation apparently desired by Foreign Nations and introduce the nearest approach to free trade within Your Majesty's wide-spread Dominions, which varying circum-

---

to terms and conditions respecting most-favoured nation treatment; that, in 1862, between Great Britain and Belgium, contains the following clause:—

" 'IX. Articles the produce or manufacture of Belgium shall not be subject in the British colonies to other or higher duties than those which are or may be imposed upon similar articles of British origin.'

"And in the treaty of commerce between Great Britain, Prussia and the Zollverein signed in the English and German language, at Berlin, May 30, 1865, clause VII provides:—

" 'The stipulation of the preceding Articles I. to VI. shall also be applied to the colonies and foreign possessions of Her Britannic Majesty. In those colonies and possessions the produce of the states of the Zollverein shall not be subject to any higher or other import duties than the produce of the United Kingdom of Great Britain and Ireland, or of any other country, of the like kind; nor shall the exportation from those colonies or possessions to the Zollverein be subject to any higher or other duties than the exportation to the United Kingdom of Great Britain and Ireland.'

"It will be seen that these provisions make each British Colony a party to what is known as the 'most-favoured nation clause,' whether such provisions are in their interest generally or not." M. Ollivier, ed. *The Colonial and Imperial Conferences from 1887 to 1937*, Ottawa, 1954, v. I, p. 84.

stances will admit." Recent events in North America made the demand for a change in Imperial trade policy especially important. The McKinley Tariff was "avowedly hostile to the commerce of the United Kingdom, and exceptionally so towards Canada." In addition, the political effects in Canada were "fraught with danger to the maintenance of the connection with Your Majesty's Empire." If the Imperial Government would impose import duties on United States natural and manufactured products, both countries would benefit. Canada would reciprocate by a one-third reduction in the Canadian duties on all British imports and extend this preferential treatment "to any of the Colonies giving similar advantage to Canada in their markets."

This then was the proposal for turning the sentiment that had won the election of 1891 for the Conservatives into practical results. It was distinctly Canadian. While incidental benefit might come to the United Kingdom from imposing duties on foreign goods, the gain was at least questionable. On the other hand, an Imperial system of preference would free Canada from the fetters of both McKinleyism and the Belgian and German treaties. Moreover, it would give Canada a preferred market for all her natural produce in Great Britain and, as D'Alton McCarthy had argued, it would compliment rather than undermine the National Policy.

Galt pressed Macdonald to move quickly with the address. He was convinced that it would do most good before rather than after the next British election. "After the election," he argued, "whether Salisbury or Gladstone wins, neither will want to raise the trade question and to affront the Cobdenites, while your independent action, before the election, will probably have such an influence on public opinion in England as to make one or other of the great leaders adopt it—*possibly both*." But Macdonald still believed that "no action on the part of Canada would be of any value until after the next

General Elections." Besides, as far as the Prime Minister was concerned, there was an even more practical reason for hesitation. The plan of attack had been made and Galt had provided the necessary argument, but, Macdonald told him, "I don't think it would be well to introduce the resolutions at the beginning of the Session. The House is new and a good many M.P.'s have not sufficiently defined their position. I must get them in working order before talking politics to them." [6]

Ultimately little result came from this ambitious plan. The Prime Minister passed from the Canadian scene shortly after the main lines of the project had been formulated. And the confusion and lack of direction within the Government party after his death probably had much to do with the watering down of the appeal for an Imperial preferential tariff. Galt heartily urged the new Prime Minister, Sir John Abbott, to push the address in the Canadian Parliament. "The time is propitious," he said. The United States had announced in the boldest possible terms its intention to remain flagrantly protectionist. Indications were many that France was going to travel in the same direction and the Galt-Macdonald proposal of "a bold policy of fostering British industry may not be an unlikely card for the English Ministry to play at the coming General Election." [7]

Indeed, in September 1891, an address was adopted by the Canadian Senate and House of Commons. But it was a sadly pale imitation of the original. It mentioned many of Galt's arguments about the rising tide of protectionism, the renegotiation of British commercial treaties being an appropriate time to take a new look at the policy of free trade, and it even cas-

[6] *ibid.*, Galt to Macdonald, May 22, 1891, Macdonald to Galt, April 16, 1891; Public Archives of Canada, Galt Papers, 4, Macdonald to Galt, May 14, 1891.

[7] Galt Papers, 4, Galt to Abbott, July 23, 1891.

ually mentioned the great productive capacity of the Dominion and its possible role as the bread basket of the United Kingdom. But the address called only for the denunciation of Article XV of the Belgian treaty and Article VII of the German treaty. There was not even an allusion to the establishment of an Imperial preferential tariff system—much less any pledge that the Dominion would reduce its duties on British goods as an incentive to move toward an Imperial preference.[8] In short, the tight-fisted Dominion politicians were simply begging redress from a grievance. They were asking the Imperial Government to take an action which would be plainly harmful to British interests and offering nothing in the way of compensation.

This was patiently and politely intimated in Lord Knutsford's despatch to Governor-General Stanley of 2 April 1892, which stated that the Imperial Government could not comply with the Canadian request.[9] It was a pitiful commentary on Dominion politics. Probably the Canadian Government had refrained from offering a reduction in the duties on British imports and from suggesting a system of Imperial preference because of its fear of adverse reaction from the Canadian manufacturers. In any case a bold and constructive plan of give and take which might have benefited both Canada and the Mother Country had been scrapped. In its place had been substituted a petty plea for redress from a colonial grievance. Perhaps it was fair to say that the National Policy which had been proclaimed as a means of encouraging Canadian commerce with the world had been converted by its advocates into a policy of self-interest and economic isolation, a miniature imitation of McKinleyism on the northern half of the North American continent.

[8] Abbott Papers, 1, Copy, Address on the Belgian and Zollverein treaties, #000050-52.

[9] Thompson Papers, 152, Knutsford to Stanley, April 2, 1892, in Memorandum on Commercial Treaties, April 1892.

iii

Though the Dominion Government showed little interest in the establishment of a system of Imperial preference in trade immediately after Macdonald's death, it would be wrong to assume that Canadian officials were not concerned about Canadian trade. And there was some reason to believe that the best trade policy was to maintain the status quo. The trade statistics revealed that the volume of total trade increased by $14 million between 1889 and 1890, remained steady at $218 million in 1891, and then jumped to $241 million in 1892. Exports rose from $89 million in 1889 to $96 million in 1890, $98 million in 1891, and $113 million in 1892. Significantly the United Kingdom was buying 55.31 per cent of Canada's exports in 1892 in contrast to 41.74 per cent in 1889. In contrast, the United States bought 49.23 per cent of Canadian exports in 1889 but only 35.21 in 1892.[10] The fact was, as Mackenzie Bowell happily told his Senatorial colleagues in January 1893, "The McKinley Bill, instead of destroying the trade of this country, has only diverted it from the United States to England. . . . Our neighbours are cutting off their own noses to spite us."[11]

The McKinley tariff hit especially hard at the products of the Canadian farm. American imports of Canadian agricultural products dropped from $9 million to $4.5 million between 1889 and 1892 and animals and produce exports to the United States dropped from $7 million to about $4 million. But exports of agricultural products to Great Britain rose from $3.5 million to $15 million and animal and produce exports increased from $16 million to $24 million between 1889 and 1892. Among the most startling shifts in trade from

[10] Canada, Department of Agriculture, *The Statistical Yearbook of Canada, 1900,* Ottawa, 1901, pp. 195-96, 259, 284.

[11] Canada, Parliament, *Debates of the Senate of the Dominion of Canada,* January 31, 1893, p. 28.

a north-south to a west-east axis were two products all Canadians guessed would be most seriously affected by the McKinley tariff, barley and eggs. British purchases of Canadian barley jumped from $750 in 1889 to $1,975,485 in 1892. Eighteen dollars worth of Canadian eggs found a market in Great Britain in 1889. In 1892, $592,218 worth of Canadian eggs crossed the Atlantic to the United Kingdom.[12] The figures were impressive. Bowell was, in large part, correct; Great Britain had replaced the United States as the market for Canada's agricultural exports. This being so, there was, perhaps, no need to strike out for a policy of Imperial preference. Canadian products were being sold in the Mother Country in ever increasing amounts without it.

The McKinley tariff, again, did not even have such disastrous effects on Canadian-United States trade as had been predicted. The aggregate trade between the Dominion and the Republic fluctuated between $92 million and $94 million per year for each year between 1889 and 1892 and rose to $102 million in 1893.[13] Even in the crucial matter of Canadian exports the decline as a result of the McKinley tariff was less than might have been expected. The United States purchased $36 million of Canadian exports in 1889 and $31.5 million in 1892. In short, trade statistics reveal two all-important facts about the effect of the McKinley tariff on Canada. First, the market for Canadian agricultural produce in the United States was being replaced by a market in the United Kingdom. Second, the export of Canadian goods to the other corners of the North Atlantic triangle rose steadily throughout the years under discussion. And, interestingly enough, this occurred without undue governmental inspiration (such as the Macdonald-Galt plan) in either Canada or Great Britain and in

[12] Canada, Parliament, *Sessional Papers,* 1893, No. 2e, pp. ix-xix.
[13] Canada, Department of Agriculture, *The Statistical Yearbook of Canada, 1900,* p. 198.

spite of the increasingly protective measures taken in the United States.

While the Canadian Government might congratulate itself about this pleasing phenomena it nevertheless kept in mind that the National Policy was geared to other aspects of Canadian trade than simply those of the North Atlantic triangle. Ever since the early 1880's sporadic efforts had been made to encourage trade with other countries. Chiefly, the burden rested with the first two High Commissioners in London, Galt and Tupper, who had labored without result to get trade treaties with France and Spain. Sir Charles Tupper did manage to get a limited treaty with France in 1893. Also, in 1885, the Canadian Parliament voted $10,000 for establishing "commercial agencies" in foreign countries. In 1887 Sir John Macdonald had introduced a bill for the establishment of a department of trade and commerce and the bill passed with a provision that the department would be established by proclamation.

A persistent source of attraction of the possibilities of expanding Canadian trade was the British West Indies, a traditional market for Canadian goods that had declined with the passing of the sailing ship and the increasing productive power of the United States. In 1886 the Canadian Government had sent J. T. Wylde to the Indies to explore the possibilities of expanding Canadian trade. In 1890, perhaps as a reaction against the impending McKinley tariff, the West Indian market became sufficiently alluring that the Finance Minister, George E. Foster, was sent off on another voyage of exploration. Foster proposed that in return for Canadian tariff concessions on West Indian raw sugar and fruits, the West Indian islands give Canada differential rates on a large number of natural products and some manufactured products. He found the prospects rather bright. Of course, there were difficulties such as the loss of revenue which would be incurred by the islands and competition with the United

States. But, he wrote encouragingly to Bowell from Antigua, "the steamer on which I am a passenger is filled with just the products which Canada can & should send to these islands. I find too a very warm & friendly feeling towards Canada—not lessened by the McKinley Bill."[14] The trade between Canada and the West Indies was small, infinitesimal in comparison with that with either Great Britain or the United States. It rose only from $1.8 million to $3.4 million between 1887 and 1892. But this trade on the fringe of the National Policy was important; every dollar counted and though no actual agreements were drawn by Foster, at least Canadians knew that a market—and potentially a large market—for Canadian goods existed in the British possessions to the south of the United States.

The difficulty with this approach to the expansion of Canadian trade and commerce was its disorganization. Foster's mission, for example, smacked of a hasty spur of the moment dash to a distant part of the world to find a market that would replace the rapidly closing one in the United States. Of the $10,000 appropriated in 1885, $901 were spent on "commercial agencies." The act creating the department of trade and commerce in 1887 was not put into effect. Tupper divided his time between promoting Canadian trade in Antwerp, Paris, Madrid, and London and promoting the fortunes of the Conservative party in Halifax, Montreal, Toronto, and Windsor. It was clear that if the announced intentions of the National Policy advocates were going to have substantial results in finding new markets for Canadian trade some more centralized direction was needed.

Finally, in 1891, the work began in earnest. On 14 September, while discussing the estimates of his department, Foster told the House of Commons that he was continuing the appropriation for commercial agencies. "Commencing with a

[14] Canada, Parliament, *Sessional Papers,* 1893, No. 2e, pp. ix-xix; Bowell Papers, 8, Foster to Bowell, November 17, 1890.

few countries," he said, it was his intention "to establish a kind of commercial agency, not on a large scale at all, but to make the beginning of a kind of stationary agent, who could report the state of markets, the requirements of the markets, the prices of goods and the like of that, and these being sent to the department could be published for the benefit of the commercial public. . . . I intend this year to bring before Council a plan, not at all ambitious or large, for the establishment of commercial agents in several of the more important points of the West Indies, and in other points in countries, especially those with which we might be able to establish trade." [15] On 21 November the Privy Council approved a request from Foster that "he be authorized to establish such a system of Commercial Agencies as he may deem most suitable." And in March 1892, six men, Edgar Tripp, G. Eustace Burke, Edwin McLeod, H. Ogilvie Bennett, S. L. Horsford, and Darnley C. Da Costa, were appointed as commercial agents at a salary of $250 a year at various points in the West Indies and British Guiana. With this step formally taken, the beginnings of an organized effort to expand Canadian trade was made. By the end of 1892, partly as a matter of convenience in the reorganization of the cabinet made necessary by Sir John Thompson's elevation to the Premiership, and certainly as an indication of the increasing concern of the Government about Canadian trade, the Act of 1887 was proclaimed and Mackenzie Bowell became the first Minister of Trade and Commerce.[16]

Bowell was confined to his desk in Ottawa during the better part of 1893 because he served as Acting Prime Minister while Thompson went to Paris for the Behring Sea arbitration. But toward the end of the year he left Ottawa on a mission similar to Foster's in 1890. This time the Minister looked

[15] *Official Report of Debates,* September 14, 1891, p. 5429.
[16] P.C. 2795, November 21, 1891; P.C. 488, March 3, 1892; P.C. 3052, December 3, 1892.

for trade prospects out of Canada's western doorway. Since 1886 the Canadian Pacific Railway had carried on an extensive trade in tea between Vancouver and Japan and the Orient. But in 1893 the Huddart Line, partially subsidized by the Canadian Government, began regular steamship communication between Canada and Australasia. Canadian-Australasian trade was dismally slight and, in fact, decreasing year by year. In 1889 the total trade was $888,610; in 1893 it had dropped to $501,419. Even more important, while Australasian imports remained fairly steady, Canadian exports were rapidly decreasing. If the Government were going to secure a return on its 25,000 pound subsidy, the trade had to be bolstered.[17]

Bowell was not entirely optimistic about his trip to Australasia. Realistically, he wrote to a friend, "I confess I do not anticipate any great immediate results from our visit to Australia. The parties with whom we have been estranged so long, can scarcely be brought into a close relationship at a moment's notice. However, we have heavily subsidized a line of steamers for that route, [and] we must do what we can to make it a success." On the way to Australasia Bowell and Sandford Fleming, long an advocate (as was Bowell) of direct cable communication between Canada and Australasia, stopped in Hawaii to seek an island to be used as an intermediate landing point for the Pacific cable. For Bowell, the duties of his newly acquired portfolio assumed prime importance but he was forced to report to Thompson that "at present there is little or no hope of any trade arrangements with the Hawaiian group of islands, the Government being in a transitory state—undecided whether to return to a monarchy or establish a permanent Republic." Bowell was more encouraged by the time he had had some conversations with Sir George Dibbs in Sydney, New South Wales. "In respect of trade matters," Bowell told Thompson, "there is a general

[17] Aberdeen to Ripon, May 25, 1894: CO42/823.

feeling among all classes—as you will observe from the news-papers I have sent you—in favor of closer and more liberal relations between Australia and Canada." Dibbs had urged him to make some specific trade proposals but Bowell had replied that "my mission was more particularly to seek in-formation as to the articles in which we might trade re-ciprocally." The information was quite favorable.[18]

I pointed out . . . that their hard woods might be ex-changed for our soft woods. I may say that their streets here are paved with a certain kind of hard wood which seems to wear exceedingly well and to show but little injury after being subjected to very heavy traffic for years. This wood seems to be as hard as iron and to be about as endurable. This we might take while they could take our soft woods. I also pointed out that as we ad-mitted their wool free of duty they should give us free fish. I have no doubt, also that we could take some of their tropical, or semi-tropical fruits, providing they would accept some articles of our manufacture. From what little observations I have been able to make, I am also of the opinion that a trade might be worked up in Australian wines, which would take the place of the light European wines now brought into Canada. . . .

When Bowell returned to Canada he reported that "the great possibilities of that country were a revelation to me." He wrote to Sir Leonard Tilley that "on the whole I had the satisfaction of knowing that an interest has been created in Australia in favor of closer trade connection with Canada which did not exist before. In fact, they declared it a new experience to see what they called 'a live Canadian' among them." With much satisfaction he observed that "the leading men were intensely British. This strong Imperial sentiment

[18] Bowell Papers, 95, Bowell to Aitkins, September 5, 1893; Thompson Papers, 186, Bowell to Thompson, September 24, 1893; 187, Bowell to Thompson, October 12, 1893.

had something to do with the desire shown by their states-men for closer trade relations with us." Certainly the trip had been worth while, if only to demonstrate that the Canadian Government was seriously interested in increasing trade with other seemingly logical markets within the Empire.[19]

Another result of the trip was a further step in the develop-ment of the Department of Trade and Commerce. The Min-ister had been able to see only parts of the Australian conti-nent and had not visited New Zealand. Moreover, his stay was only of short duration and largely confined to talks with Government officials. In truth, Bowell was just laying the groundwork for a more serious effort of promoting Canadian trade with Australasia. "I hope ere long to send out a live man to take up his residence there as a Commercial Agent," Bowell wrote in April 1894. "A good live agent, having the interest of Canada at heart, would be the man to set the meat canners right as to methods of packing and quality. . . . It is a trade that cannot be worked up in a day, but with a little persever-ance it might be made profitable." By August, Bowell had picked his "live man," Mr. J. S. Larke. "For such a position, and having regard to the high cost of living in that country, his salary should not be less than $4,000 per annum," Bowell told the Prime Minister. "It would be little enough to enable him to live and keep up the dignity of his position." In fact, Larke's appointment was not as a "commercial agent" in the sense that Foster had used the term in 1891. Tripp and the other "commercial agents" were residents of the West Indies or British Guiana, usually businessmen closely connected with the export-import trade. They were paid the trifling sum of $250 per year to do the tasks which Foster had outlined in addition to their regular business activities. Larke's case was quite different. He was the first Canadian to be sent by the Department of Trade and Commerce to a foreign country

[19] *ibid.*, Bowell to Aitkins, December 3, 1893; 96, Bowell to Tilley, February 1, 1894.

for the sole purpose of reporting on and promoting Canadian trade in that country. In truth, J. S. Larke was Canada's first trade commissioner.[20]

Another important outgrowth of Bowell's Australasian visit was the convening of the Colonial Conference of 1894 in Ottawa. In part this was an expression of the new sense of the reality of the Imperial connection between Canada and the Australasian colonies. But more important, the Conference had to discuss very practical difficulties in the way of developing intercolonial trade. In a letter to Sir Charles Tupper on 6 November 1893, Bowell explained that while each Australasian colony had the power to discriminate in its trade relations with any other Australasian colony, none of them could levy any discriminating duties against foreign countries. Thus Canada, for example, could not acquire a favored position in the tariff of any Australasian colony because any favor given to Canada would have to be given to all nations. As Bowell said, "it is evident, therefore, that better trade relations between Canada and Australia cannot be established until that clause in their constitutions has been repealed and power given to permit reciprocal arrangements." Further, it was clear that Canada had colonial allies who desired as strongly as herself that the restrictive clauses of the Belgian and Zollverein treaties be denounced in the interest of promoting Imperial trade. Finally, of course, there was the matter of the Pacific cable which Bowell considered directly linked with the trade treaties in developing Canadian-Australasian trade. "Personally," he wrote, "I am convinced that one [the cable] is essential to the success of the other [trade]." [21]

In his address of greeting to the Conference on 28 June

[20] *ibid.*, Bowell to Buchanan, April 18, 1894; Thompson Papers, 217, Bowell to Thompson, August 6, 1894; 270, Thompson to Bowell, August 9, 1894.

[21] Thompson Papers, 214, Bowell to Tupper, November 6, 1893, enclosure in Tupper to Thompson, July 6, 1894.

1894, Sir John Thompson was pleased to note that "the business for which the delegates are assembled on this occasion is not necessarily connected with our relations with foreign countries—not necessarily connected with considerations of peace or war—but is immediately concerned in all those questions which relate to the increase of commerce, the cultivation of the arts of peace and the promotion of civilization and prosperity generally throughout the colonies of the Empire." He warned the delegates that they had gathered for many sessions of hard bargaining. "While there is ample field for patriotism and loyalty," he said, "methods of business have to be followed. Matters connected with trade, tariffs, with steamboats, and with telegraphs, will require the most practical as well as the most patriotic deliberations of the gentlemen who are assembled to-day." [22]

The discussions on trade matters resulted in resolutions begging the removal of the restrictions of the Belgian and Zollverein treaties, expressing favor for an Imperial preferential trade scheme, and, until that might be accomplished, calling for intercolonial preferential trade agreements. Mackenzie Bowell enumerated the principles underlying the discussions in a Privy Council report dated 24 August 1894:

(a) That all existing treaties between Great Britain and any foreign power, which prevent self-governing dependencies of the Empire from entering into more favoured trade relations with Great Britain and each other, should be abrogated.

(b) That Customs arrangements between Great Britain and her Colonies, should be such as to give a preference to the Mother Country in the markets of the Colonies; and to the Colonies in the markets of Great Britain.

(c) That the stability of the Empire can best be secured by the adoption of a policy which would lead to the cul-

[22] Ollivier, *The Colonial and Imperial Conferences,* p. 79.

tivation and extension of a mutual and profitable interchange of products.

(d) That this could best be accomplished by a Customs arrangement between Great Britain and her Colonies by which advantages would be secured in the markets of either not granted to foreign powers.

(e) That until the Mother Country is prepared to enter into such an arrangement all impediments in the way of the Colonies adopting reciprocal arrangements with each other should be repealed.

(f) That the South African Customs Union be included within the scope of any such trade arrangements.[23]

Lord Jersey came to the Ottawa Conference as a representative of the Imperial Government. His role was that of adviser and observer rather than delegate and he had no power to commit the Imperial Government to any of the plans proposed by the Colonial delegates. Some months after he had submitted his report to the British Government the Board of Trade commented at length on the proposals of the Colonial Conference. The Board of Trade made it clear from the outset that the adoption of a system of Imperial preference was most unlikely. It was pleased to observe that many of the Ottawa delegates recognized that "a free trade policy must almost certainly be maintained by Great Britain as a manufacturing country, dependent on other countries for raw materials and food, and it was even urged that any other policy, by preventing this Country from manufacturing as cheaply

[23] P.C. 2562, August 24, 1894. The resolution regarding the Pacific Cable urged the rapid development of plans for completing the scheme on a cooperative basis between Great Britain, Canada, and the Australasian Colonies. The Canadians, probably because of severe financial difficulties in 1894, rapidly drew away from any major expenditures regarding the cable, much to the distress of Sir Charles Tupper. See Thompson Papers, 214, Tupper to Thompson, July 6, 1894; 270, Thompson to Tupper, August 4, 1894; 208, Foster to Thompson, May 5, 1894; Bowell Papers, 97, Bowell to Wallace, October 17, 1894.

as she otherwise could, would be likely to injure the Colonies themselves." The Board also noted its "apprehension . . . that commercial difficulties are likely to arise in the Mother Country whenever differential duties against goods produced in Great Britain are imposed in any of the Colonies under an inter-Colonial arrangement." It appeared, then, that as a practical matter neither of the stated objectives of the Ottawa Conference, Imperial preference or intercolonial preference, was thought possible of implementation by the Board of Trade.

But as a matter of principle, the Board of Trade's letter struck a different, almost contradictory note. While it was "decidedly of opinion that the Colonies, in their own interests, ought to abstain from intercolonial arrangements," they nevertheless took note of the strong contrary opinion in the Colonies and believed that the power to levy discriminating duties against foreign nations ought to be given to the Australasian colonies as it had long since been granted to Canada. With regard to the resolution calling for the removal of the restrictions in the Belgian and Zollverein treaties, the Board of Trade believed that "the restrictions in the Treaties in question fetter that liberty of action in its own internal affairs which every Government should possess, . . . trade between different parts of the Empire is obviously an internal affair in which no foreign Government should have anything to say." It was therefore recommended that "the resolution of the Ottawa Conference on this head should not be put aside indefinitely."

As Bowell's enumeration of the principles governing the Ottawa Conference clearly revealed, a system of Imperial preferential trade was the chief objective of the Colonial Conference of 1894 and the Belgian and Zollverein treaties were the main obstacles to the rapid accomplishment of that end. Bowell and his colleagues would have been pleased by the Board of Trade's recommendation but they probably would have been puzzled by the strange dichotomy between principle and practice in the letter. And as far as the Colonial Office was concerned, the Board of Trade had made a meaningless distinction. Minuting the Board of Trade letter, John Anderson rather caustically gave a final comment of the attitude of the Imperial Government toward the principal desire of the delegates at Ottawa. "The pious opinion of the Board of Trade as to recovering our freedom of action in connexion with the German & Belgian treaties," he said, "is interesting & may be useful hereafter, but in that matter we are bound to follow the F.O. and though 'freedom is a noble thing,' it is not of very much practical importance to us to be free to do what we have no desire or intention of doing." [24]

iv

During the last years of Conservative rule in the nineteenth century the effort to find diverse markets for Canadian exports was of immense importance. So too was the attempt to strengthen the east-west or Imperial trade axis by abolishing the restrictive clauses of the Belgian and Zollverein treaties. For Canada either or both would lessen her dependence on trade with the United States. But this did not mean that Canadians ignored the problem of improving Canadian-American trade relations. The Ottawa politicians continued to express faith in their belief in the freest possible trade patterns with the United States compatible with Canadian interests. Indeed, just five days after the election of 1891 Lord Stanley inquired of Macdonald, "what are we going to do about the Washington negotiations?" Stanley was "anxious to say that we are doing something so as to justify the NFland delay & to keep faith with the C.O." At first the Prime Minister had thought he should go to Washington but he was ill. "The M. of Fisheries [Charles Hibbert Tupper],"

[24] Board of Trade to Colonial Office, April 30, 1895: CO42/832.

Stanley cautioned, "is not a *persona grata* at Washington." Thompson or Sir Charles Tupper seemed to be the alternative choices of persons capable of dealing with Blaine. By the end of the month it was decided that Tupper would go to Washington and make a preliminary reconnaissance of the situation.[25]

Probably no one in Ottawa had very high hopes that Tupper's mission would be successful. Mackenzie Bowell wrote to Sir Leonard Tilley that he did not "believe the Americans will consent to any scheme of Reciprocity which does not involve the total surrender of our right to control our tariff. The assistance given Blaine by the unpatriotic opposition will lead him to refuse any fair measure of reciprocity." Tupper arrived in Washington on Wednesday, 1 April, and had a long interview with Blaine, in the company of Pauncefote, the next morning. No substantial problems were discussed, the main portion of the interview being taken up by Tupper's telling Blaine how loyal to the Northern cause he had been as Premier of Nova Scotia at the time of the Chesapeake affair, how many thousand Canadian troops there had been in the G.A.R., and how emphatically a recent article by himself in the *North American Review* proved that Canada was "warmly in favour of the most friendly relations with the United States." Blaine bowed to Tupper's blandishments and consented to a conference on the following Monday. Tupper immediately left Washington after wiring to Foster and Thompson to join him in Ottawa for a return journey over the week end. But suddenly, on Sunday, Blaine informed Pauncefote that President Harrison was not ready to talk over trade matters with Canada. "The President, owing to pressure of other questions desires to postpone the conference until October." Tupper and his colleagues, of course, were en route to Washington and could not be stopped. Blaine, Pauncefote, and

25 Macdonald Papers, 90, Stanley to Macdonald, March 10, 1891.

the Canadians were all clearly embarrassed by Harrison's upsetting intervention but Blaine saw the Canadians on Monday morning and the date for the conference was fixed as 12 October.[26]

The Canadians approached the October meeting with caution. "The original intention . . . was understood to be, in effect, the consideration of the preliminary question whether negotiations could be entered upon with advantage, and we would gladly have the discussion limited to that point for the moment," Abbott wrote in September 1891. "If it should be concluded that there are grounds upon which negotiations for extended trade relations could rest we should endeavour to fix a later day on which those negotiations could take place. If on the other hand, it appears that no basis for negotiations can be found, of course there will be an end to the whole matter." When, therefore, the Canadians learned a few days before the appointed meeting date that the Americans again wanted to postpone the conference, they may have sensed some exasperation, but no significant amount of either surprise or disappointment.[27]

As happened in April, so again the postponement was chiefly the President's doing. Harrison, more than a little attracted by the idea of annexing Canada, knew full well what the Canadians wanted in the way of a trade arrangement and was not anxious to effect an agreement that would forestall political union. As he said to Blaine, "I do not myself see how they can make us a proposition that would be acceptable." Blaine, too, was decidedly adverse to a limited reciprocity arrangement but was somewhat more anxious to meet the Canadians. His attitude was governed by a curious

[26] Bowell Papers, 90, Bowell to Tilley, April 3, 1891; Thompson Papers, 126, memorandum of Sir Charles Tupper's visit to Washington written by Tupper, telegrams, Pauncefote to Stanley, April 5 and 6, 1891.
[27] Tupper Papers, 10, Abbott to Tupper, September 19, 1891.

mixture of practical Republican politics and the correctness of his position and his word as Secretary of State. Politically, he told the President, another postponement would be "considered a dodge, if not a cheat, and it will injure us with our own people." On the other hand, Blaine was quick to point out his opposition to the reciprocity in natural products which the Canadians clearly desired. "It would be considered a betrayal of the Agricultural interests," he wrote. "The fact is we do not want any intercourse with Canada, except through the medium of a tariff, and she will find that she had a hard row to hoe and will ultimately I believe seek admission to the Union." In short, the politics of the Republican party demanded that the Canadians be met and sent home emptyhanded.[28]

Blaine did finally meet the Canadian representatives, Thompson and Foster, in 1892. Regarding trade, Foster proposed a renewal of the Treaty of 1854 "with such modifications and extensions as the changed conditions might make necessary." The Canadians were willing to extend reciprocity beyond the limits of natural products, perhaps even willing to accept something like George Brown's draft treaty of 1874. "As to trade relations," Abbott wired to Thompson on 10 February, "perhaps our strongest position would be to propose a reciprocity not limited entirely to natural products nor embracing without distinction all such products, in other words to propose a reciprocity not universal, but extending over such subjects, whether natural products or manufactures, as could be agreed upon." [29]

Blaine replied to Foster that "a treaty, based on natural products alone, could not be discussed, as it would lack the

[28] Volwiler, *The Correspondence Between Benjamin Harrison and James G. Blaine,* Harrison to Blaine, September 26, 1891, p. 195, Blaine to Harrison, September 23, 1891, pp. 193-94.

[29] Abbott Papers, 3, draft, Abbott to Thompson in reply to Thompson to Abbott, February 10, 1892.

essential element of an arrangement for reciprocity, as far as the United States is concerned. If a proposition could be made 'for taking down the bars,' it would be quite another question." The Secretary of State went on to explain that "American manufactures must be included" and Canada had to be willing to discriminate against the products of other nations, particularly Great Britain. "We should expect to have the Canadians to compete with in manufacturing, but no one else." When Foster inquired of the details of this discrimination Blaine replied that the arrangement "could, in his opinion, only be done by making the tariff uniform for both countries, and equalizing the Canadian tariff with that of the United States." "Mr. Blaine . . . said he could easily understand why Canada was reluctant to enter into a treaty of unlimited reciprocity, but that it was clear in his mind that no other arrangement would suit the United States, and that it must be accompanied by discrimination in favour of the United States, especially against Great Britain, who was their great competitor, and that it must likewise be accompanied by the adoption of a uniform tariff for the United States and Canada equal to that of the United States." [30]

While "no other arrangement would suit the United States," it was equally clear that Blaine's proposition would not suit Canada, or at least not the Canadian Government, and Foster and Thompson returned to Ottawa empty-handed. The Minister of Finance explained the results of the conference to the

[30] Thompson Papers, 254, letterbook, memorandum by Thompson, pp. 431½-89. This memo is reprinted in Canada, Parliament, *Sessional Papers,* 1892, No. 52. Note that, as the words, "uniform tariff . . . equal to that of the United States" reveal, Blaine was actually talking about Commercial Union rather than "unlimited reciprocity" as Edgar had suggested with a system of autonomous tariffs against the outside world. This goes a long way to prove Blake's contention in the West Durham letter that as far as Americans were concerned there was only one workable scheme and that scheme was "to take down the bars" and adopt Commercial Union.

House of Commons in his annual budget speech of 22 March.[31]

> so long as the present party and the present policy is maintained in the United States, in one branch or the other of the Legislature or in the Executive, we cannot hope for any treaty with the United States, except on these lines, viz., a treaty which will take in both natural products and manufactured goods; a treaty unlimited in its scope, of which the basis is a preferential treatment in our market with discrimination especially against Great Britain and against other countries; a treaty that must be accompanied by a uniform tariff, and this tariff equal with that of the United States of America. . . . I regret that no *modus* can be found by which profitable trade relations could be established between these two countries without our being called upon to sacrifice too much of Canadian interests and too much of Canadian nationality.

It was a matter worth regretting. Canadian interests would have benefited from a more limited reciprocity agreement with the United States than that which Blaine demanded. Equally, however, as Abbott wired Thompson, "Blaine's stand as to discrimination as condition of reciprocity not bad for us." In some respects it was even better than a treaty would have been. A treaty, any treaty, would have met with fierce opposition from the Liberals. But now the Conservatives had just the thing to spike the Liberals' guns. They had it from Blaine himself that Edgar's Unrestricted Reciprocity compromise, having as its chief point autonomous Canadian and American tariffs, was totally unacceptable to the United States. The Yankees would take Commercial Union or nothing. There was good reason for Mackenzie Bowell to crow happily to E. W. Rathburn that "we succeeded admirably in our mode of conducting the negotiations. . . . We were qui-

[31] *Official Report of Debates,* March 22, 1892, p. 332.

etly asked 'to take down the bars,' as Blaine termed it, between Canada and the United States, and erect a still higher tariff wall against England and the rest of the world. Our answer was that the question required some consideration. When we met the next day the question of reciprocity on those terms was dropped like a hot potato." [32]

This was the last time the Canadian Conservatives sent an official mission to Washington to seek more favorable treatment in the American tariff. In November 1892, Grover Cleveland was reelected President on a platform built around tariff reform. For a while it seemed to some Canadians that the millennium had come. "Cleveland's success is a great fact," Principal Grant of Queen's University cheerily told a friend. "It means the 'N.P.' in its present form is doomed." In the first issue of the *Queen's Quarterly* Grant wrote that "Cleveland will leave a deeper mark on American public life than any of his predecessors in this century, Lincoln alone excepted." *The Week* added that "the great American nation has changed front and taken up its line of march towards freer trade and a higher civilization. . . . We rejoice that it is another great Anglo-Saxon people which is falling into line with Great Britain in this great crusade. Where these lead the van all others must sooner or later fall into the ranks or be left hopelessly behind in the progress of the world." Government officials were not so optimistic. "I have very little confidence in the outlook for a radical change of policy on the part of the statesmen who direct the affairs of the neighbouring Republic," Mackenzie Bowell wrote. "They seem, at the present moment, to have but one ruling idea, and that is that Canada is ripe for annexation and ready to drop into the arms of the United States. In view of this, the instinct of self-

[32] Abbott Papers, 3, Abbott to Thompson, February 12, 1892; Bowell Papers, 92, Bowell to Rathburn, March 29, 1892.

preservation suggests the pursuing of an independent policy on the part of the British American dependencies." [33]

While Sir John Thompson was in Paris for the Behring Sea Arbitration Tribunal, he discussed by letter with Sir Charles Tupper in London the advisability of making another Canadian pilgrimage to Washington. This was immediately discounted but the Canadians did think that it might be of benefit to let the Americans know that Canada would reciprocate in legislation any tariff reductions on Canadian products entering the United States. The latter plan had the advantage of being compatible with the wishes of the Cleveland Administration. Bayard, who had recently assumed the ambassadorship at the Court of St. James's, informed Tupper that the Cleveland Administration was firmly convinced of the "necessity of dealing with fiscal matters by legislation in preference to Treaties." [34] In the end the Canadians decided to adopt a wait-and-see attitude. The logic of their position was inescapable. They had been humiliated time and again by their persistent efforts to convince Americans that reciprocity was feasible. Moreover, Cleveland had decided to tackle the Silver Question before tariff reform; he was meeting serious opposition and there was no guarantee that any substantial tariff reform would be carried out. In addition,

[33] Public Archives of Canada, Grant Papers, 8, Grant to Hopkins, November 9, 1892; *Queen's Quarterly,* July 1893, p. 74; *The Week,* November 18, 1892; Bowell Papers, 93, Bowell to Whiteway, January 3, 1893. See also Bowell to Aitkins, February 4, 1893; 94, Bowell to Tilley, March 23, 1893.

[34] Trade and Commerce, File 671, Tupper to Thompson, August 15, 1893. See also Thompson Papers, 261, Thompson to Bowell, May 2 and 12, 1893, Thompson to Tupper, August 11, 1893; 181, Tupper to Thompson, May 9 and 11, 1893; Tupper Papers, 10, Bayard to Tupper, July 11, 1893; High Commissioner to Colonial Office, May 9, 1893: CO42/818; Stanley to Ripon, June 17, 1893 (two despatches): CO42/816.

the increasingly independent attitude of the Canadians was reflected in the final crushing argument against another appeal of any sort to the United States. "The changes which they propose to make by way of tariff reduction will be made, of course, in the interest of their own country," Thompson told Tupper, "but if we seek to negotiate for concessions now we shall be expected to pay a price for much of that which we shall, no doubt, eventually secure without compensation." As the Minister of Trade and Commerce said, "it would be singularly unfortunate if we were to just now approach the American Government, seeking anything like better terms, as in all probability their craze for tariff reform will meet, to a great extent, that for which we could ask. . . . I . . . advise strongly that no action be taken." [35]

The wait-and-see attitude did not mean that Canada would be totally without a voice in Washington once Congress came to consider the Wilson Bill. No elaborate mission was sent and little was done through official channels. But, to a certain extent the Canadian Government lobbied the Wilson Bill like any other interest likely to be affected by tariff reform. Sir Julian Pauncefote attempted, through the State Department, to have a clause giving free entry to Canadian fish inserted in the Bill. Senator Drummond of Montreal and Senator Sanford of Hamilton both went to Washington hoping to charm American Senators into concessions to Canada. The latter was so persistent in his efforts that he reported innocently to Thompson that "I . . . feel so much at home on the floor of the Senate, that I am referred to as one of our Senators from the State of Canada." [36]

[35] Thompson Papers, 261, Thompson to Tupper, May 2, 1893; 181, Bowell to Thompson, May 16, 1893.

[36] P.C. 141J, March 28, 1894; P.C. 218J, May 8, 1894; Thompson Papers, 197, Drummond to Thompson, January 21, 1894; 198, Sanford to Thompson, January 26, 894; 201, Sanford to Thompson, February 23 and 25, 1894; 202, Sanford to Thompson, March 1, 3 and 8, 1894.

These efforts were without any appreciable measure of success. But so too, for that matter, were those, in the larger framework, of Cleveland and Wilson for tariff reform. When the Wilson Bill emerged from the vicious and lengthy battle in the Senate as the Wilson-Gorman tariff, if was an entirely different document burdened with 408 amendments. And when it finally became law—without the President's signature and with a total of over 600 amendments—there was little to distinguish it from the McKinley tariff. The rates under the Wilson-Gorman tariff were 41 per cent on dutiable goods and 21 per cent on all goods, and under the McKinley tariff they had been 49 per cent on dutiable goods and 22 per cent on all goods. Perhaps the Canadians would have gained some concessions by adopting a more active policy, by once again traveling the well-beaten path to the south. But the evidence all seems to point to the opposite conclusion. Bayard had said the Administration would not discuss concessions in the form of a treaty. And if the American electorate, which had apparently voiced a demand for tariff reform, could not obtain its demand in legislation, it seems unlikely that one or two Canadian Ministers on an official mission to Washington could have done more.

CHAPTER VIII
The Rejection of Continentalism

NEITHER the Conservatives nor the Liberals were pleased with their performance in the 1891 general election. The Conservatives began immediately to turn their emphasis on loyalty in the election campaign to ends commensurate with the National Policy. Meanwhile the Liberal party looked for the reason for its defeat. From every quarter Laurier heard from his lieutenants that Macdonald's wizardry in raising the loyalty cry was the reason. "The changes were rung upon it in every way," complained John Ellis. "I have not a doubt that our policy of Unrestricted Reciprocity when it came to be analysed and all its difficulties brought to the surface alarmed some timid people both in our ranks and in the ranks of those who do not take an active part in political contests," wrote Longley. These opinions from the Maritimes were matched by a similar assessment from Western Ontario. David Mills warned that "the people are in financial distress & they want pecuniary relief and not revolution," adding that in future Unrestricted Reciprocity should be "minimized." Even so committed a continentalist as Cartwright worriedly asked Laurier "what are the views of the doubtfuls on the subject of unrestricted reciprocity? Can we muster a full vote on this?" [1]

But such doubts did not mean that the Liberals were ready to drop their trade policy. Rather it was time to consider how the Canadian people, worked into a heat of loyalty sentiment by the election, would react to the idea of discrimination against Great Britain in trade matters. Naturally, any treaty that even approached Unrestricted Reciprocity—much less

[1] Laurier Papers, 5, Ellis to Laurier, March 7, 1891, Longley to Laurier, March 10, 1891, Mills to Laurier, March 18, 1891, Cartwright to Laurier, March 16, 1891.

Commercial Union—would involve a substantial amount of discrimination against British goods. There was no question of Laurier's opinion. "The policy of this country must be based not upon sentiment but upon business principles," he told the House of Commons. "It is absurd to suppose that, situated as we are, the interest of Canada will always be identical with the interest of Great Britain. Some day must come when these interests will clash, and . . . for my part, whenever it comes to that, and, however much I must regret the necessity, I will stand by my native land." John Willison, editor of the *Globe,* agreed. "Everybody who thinks at all," he wrote, "knows that we must discriminate and we ought to be educating opinion to the justice and necessity of discrimination." The process of "education" in the details of Unrestricted Reciprocity would go on. For the moment nothing more could be done.[2]

Apparently Laurier had considered taking the drastic step of going to Washington to attempt to undermine Tupper's exploration of the possibility of Canadian-American trade talks. It was clear that if the Conservatives could arrange a limited reciprocity agreement with the United States the Liberal trade policy would be worthless. And the fear of this probably led Laurier to consider making such a move. He sounded Willison out and was reminded of the political danger of the trip. "Besides," Willison added, "all that can be done there is being done." "The Globe correspondent at Washington can be relied upon for knowledge of the situation regarding reciprocity. He is a professional journalist of great experience in close touch with all classes of politicians." [3]

If Laurier could not go to Washington himself, the continual postponements of trade talks by Blaine and Harrison gave ample opportunity for his party colleagues to visit the

[2] *Official Report of Debates,* May 1, 1891, pp. 27, 29; Laurier Papers, 5, Willison to Laurier, March 26, 1891.

[3] Laurier Papers, 5, Willison to Laurier, March 26 and April 9, 1891.

American capital. J. D. Edgar reported in November after an interview with Harrison that "there seems to be no possible chance of rec[iprocity] except on our lines—to include manufactures & to discriminate in favour of the U.S. On those lines I believe even this administration will make a treaty and any attempt by the Tories will result in utter failure." The news was encouraging. But it really said much more about what the Americans would not do for the Conservatives than what they would do for the Liberals. There was, in fact, some doubt in the United States about Liberal trade policy. Edward Farrer reported from Washington that "the men here are disposed to think that the Liberals have not gone quite far enough—that they have not differentiated their position with sufficient clearness and boldness. . . . They are particularly anxious that Liberals should show that they are not afraid of discriminating against Britain." Laurier, fortunately, had accepted an invitation to speak at a dinner in Boston on 17 November. Edgar, Cartwright (who had just returned from New York City), Goldwin Smith and Farrer all urged that he plainly say the Liberals had no qualms about discrimination against the Mother Country. He followed their advice to the letter.[4]

In the spring of 1892, while Thompson and Foster were meeting with Blaine, Laurier learned that Goldwin Smith was in Washington advising that the Americans insist that reciprocity could be had only on the basis of political union and intimating that the Liberals would not object to this. He hastily summoned John Charlton and asked him to go there "as the envoy of the Liberal party" to counteract Smith's influence. Charlton recorded in his diary:

> Goldwin Smith has been advising a declaration on the part of the United States that if we want reciprocity we must take it in connection with Political Union and

[4] *ibid.*, Edgar to Laurier, November 9, 1891, Farrer to Laurier, October 24, 1891.

we want to prevent that. Reciprocity is what we want, the declaration for Political Union would create a ferment, fire the tory heart, and solidify prejudices. We want free Commercial intercourse, Commercial Union in fact, and the Political Union question may be left to take care of itself. The future will settle it and all we are called upon now to do is to secure a policy that will give material prosperity to Canada.[5]

The missions of Charlton and others were clear indications that the Liberals were not ready to abandon their trade policy. They did point out, however, the apprehensions of the Liberals that the Conservative Government might possibly effect a trade agreement with the United States. It was probably with some sense of relief that Laurier and his friends learned of the failure of Thompson and Foster to come to terms with Blaine in 1892. More important, however, was the fact that the Liberals concluded from this failure that their policy, and only their policy, would find a willing ear in Washington. This, of course, was useful in itself. But this information also could be used for other desired ends, not the least of which was to point out to Edward Blake the error of his ways and induce him to return to the fold.

Blake was a major problem for the Liberals—perhaps their greatest and certainly their most embarrassing problem. Shortly before the 1891 election Blake had decided not to contest his seat in West Durham and had given John Willison for publication a copy of a letter to his constituents explaining the reasons for his withdrawal from Canadian politics. Blake's long and argumentative West Durham letter brought to a boil the long-simmering dispute between himself and his party over trade policy. He still favored "a moderate revenue tariff approximating to free trade with all the world" but admitted that the scheme was not practicable at the time. But much

[5] Charlton Papers, Diary, March 16, 1892.

more important was his severe castigation of Unrestricted Reciprocity which, he argued, would only be possible under the Commercial Union scheme. The latter inevitably meant "practical control . . . by the States." Furthermore, the Liberals were deceiving the Canadian people by discussing their trade policy in a vacuum when, in fact, it was "intimately connected with, and cannot properly be divorced from, the question of our political future." Indeed, "absolute free trade with the States, best described as commercial union, may or ought to come only as an incident, or at any rate as a well-understood precursor of political union, for which, indeed, we should be able to make better terms before than after the surrender of our commercial independence." "To put forward opinions we do not hold," Blake concluded, "or ignore difficulties we cannot solve, or deny or conceal the tendencies and results of policies we undertake to propound, would be dishonest and unworthy." [6]

To publish the West Durham letter before the general election would be, as Willison told Blake, "absolute disaster to the Liberals; and whether justly or not they would hold you responsible and feel that after their long and enthusiastic service under your leadership they deserved better at your hands." "You should never publish such a document," Laurier pleaded, "why should you sever from your friends, & why should you strike at them such a blow at such a moment?" With great reluctance Blake agreed to withhold publication until after the election. The West Durham letter was published in the *Globe* the next day, 6 March 1891. [7]

Conservative cheer matched Liberal grief when the West Durham letter came to light. "Blake's pronunciamento will do great good," chortled Sir David Macpherson to Macdonald.

---

[6] *Toronto Globe,* March 6, 1891.

[7] Blake Papers, Willison to Blake, February 12, 1891; Laurier to Blake, February 2, 1891, Cited, F. H. Underhill, "Laurier and Blake, 1882-1891," *Canadian Historical Rievew,* xx, 1939, p. 406.

And some months later Mackenzie Bowell rejoiced over the use the Tories had made of Blake's letter in recent by-elections: "we expected to carry one or two Ridings, but our success has been beyond our most sanguine expectations." "With respect to the great E.B.'s letter," Davies complained to Laurier, "I think it a very powerful one & calculated to do us great harm." This was true. The problem was how the Liberals could extricate themselves from their predicament. Laurier apparently believed that the only way for the party to save face was to induce Blake back into the fold—in short, to force Blake explicitly or implicitly to admit that he was mistaken in his judgment on the party's trade policy.[8]

A tentative and unsuccessful attempt was made by Laurier in August 1891. Then in February 1892, the dispute with Blake reached a state of urgency. There were rumors that he was going to run in the East York by-election. Cartwright best expressed the fears of the Liberals: "Touching Blake it is necessary to have a clear understanding. . . . I do not fear him as an open foe but I do dread him as a secret one in our camp." Fortunately for the Liberals, Blake took the initiative. Following Foster's résumé in the House of Commons of the trade talks with Blaine, he believed an excellent opportunity had arisen for the Liberals to revise their policy and recede from the dangerous tenets of Unrestricted Reciprocity. How, he asked David Mills, could the Liberal "men of mystery"

[8] Macdonald Papers, 250, Macpherson to Macdonald, March 7, 1891; Bowell Papers, 92, Bowell to Wood, March 3, 1892; Laurier Papers, 5, Davies to Laurier, March 29, 1891. Mackenzie Bowell listed in the Senate thirteen seats the Conservatives had held with increased majorities in by-elections in 1892 and thirteen seats (Lennox, East Bruce, North Victoria, Soulanges, Vaudreuil, South Perth, Montmorency, East Hastings, South Ontario, East Simcoe, West Huron, Monck, West Northumberland) captured by the Conservatives from the Liberals. By 1893 the Conservative majority in the House of Commons had been increased to 70. *Debates of the Senate of the Dominion of Canada,* January 31, 1893, pp. 25-26.

continue any longer to advocate Unrestricted Reciprocity when Foster had told Parliament that Blaine would accept Commercial Union and nothing less? Mills retorted that the Liberals regarded Foster's summary as "a thoroughly dishonest statement," but left the way open for discussion when he gave Blake what must have seemed a singularly novel definition of Liberal trade policy. "Unrestricted Reciprocity with me," he wrote, "means a large measure of reciprocity—negotiations not confined to natural products—not restricted to any particular articles of commerce. I believe that with Blaine you can have a treaty which will embrace a large list of scheduled articles leaving many things still subjects of taxation." [9]

Of course, in the end neither Laurier nor Blake would recede and the attempt to get Blake back into the party failed. But one point did emerge from the discussions between Blake, Mills, and Laurier which sheds considerable light on the Liberals' conception of Unrestricted Reciprocity. It was clear that Laurier had given little thought to the economic implications of his party's policy. In the same letter he told Blake that "I would be ready tomorrow to go the length of Commercial Union" and that "you are pressing the point too far when you understand that Unrestricted Reciprocity meant a treaty including absolute interchange of all products of the two countries, without any exception at all." In fact, economic considerations and long-range political implications had been, at best, of secondary interest in formulating or maintaining the Liberals' policy. Rather, the primary concern had been to find some way to differentiate between Liberal and Conservative desires for reciprocity with the United States. The Liberal approach was, in this sense, extremely naïve: the Conservatives wanted reciprocity in natural prod-

[9] Laurier Papers, 6, Cartwright to Laurier, February 11, 1892; Blake Papers, Blake to Mills, March 23, 1892, Mills to Blake, March 24 and 29, 1892.

ucts (limited reciprocity), the Liberals wanted a broader agreement (Unrestricted Reciprocity). Blake replied to Laurier's argument that if the party did not mean Unrestricted Reciprocity when it advocated Unrestricted Reciprocity, then the time had come to abandon ambiguous terminology and speak out plainly for what the party desired. But Laurier remained adamant.[10]

ii

Among the forces tending to push the Liberal party away from continentalism following the 1891 election was a shift in the position held by the pseudo-allies of the party, the Commercial Unionists in Canada and the United States. The election of 1891 and the publication of the West Durham letter were death blows to the Commercial Union movement in Canada. Blake's destruction of the argument that Commercial Union would prevent annexation left the followers of the movement with no choice but to move on to outright advocacy of political union. And political union sentiment seemed to be growing on both sides of the border. Another of Laurier's emissaries in Washington, Thomas P. Gorman, reported that "I found that on making the acquaintance of prominent men almost the invariable question was 'what do your people think of annexation?' " [11]

In Canada Laurier learned from William D. Gregory that the political union movement, with Goldwin Smith at its head, was gaining ground. "Mr. Smith is of opinion," wrote Gregory, "that the present movement for political union has come to stay and that in the western and frontier counties of Ontario at any rate it will probably be an important factor in future political contests. He thinks that if an acknowledged

[10] Blake Papers, Laurier to Blake, April 29, 1892, Blake to Laurier, April 23, 1892.

[11] Laurier Papers, 5, Gorman to Laurier, October 15, 1891. See Warner, *The Idea of Continental Union*, ch. 7.

leader were to head the movement here it would acquire great impetus." Smith himself reported in the summer of 1892 on a "Political Union Conference" in Toronto and noted that men from the western Ontario peninsula were anxious for "the commencement of a crusade." The plan was "to capture the Ontario legislature and get it to declare for them."[12]

Enough talk of political union was taking place to arouse the fears of Oliver Mowat, the Liberal Premier of Ontario. "The Globe is creating an annexation party out of members of the Reform party," he complained to Laurier. "I find that at meetings in rural parts, even in my own constituency, the Globe is being cited to old Reformers as going for annexation, and that this is bearing fruit amongst them." In December of 1891 Mowat urged that "one thing to be done if you can see your way to it would be a very distinct declaration, so clear and emphatic that there could be no cavil as to its meaning, against political union as a price too great to pay for unrestricted reciprocity." Mowat sensed that his party was drifting toward acceptance of political as well as economic union with the United States. "If that is to be the policy of the Dominion Liberal party," he threatened, "I cease to be a member of it." The threat was of immense importance. Mowat was the most prominent Canadian Liberal in a position of power. With Blake already at odds with the party, the defection of Mowat would be an incalculable disaster for Canadian

[12] Laurier Papers, Gregory to Laurier, October 24, 1891; 6, Smith to Laurier, June 1 and July 10, 1892. The available evidence suggests that interest in political union in Canada reached its peak in the last months of 1892 and that there was a slight resurgence in June of 1893. The conclusion is based on the letters received by the secretary of the Continental Union Association which survive expressing an interest in political union. Thomas White, the secretary, received 19 letters in October 1892, 26 in November, 18 in December, 4 in January 1893, and 14 in June. In the period 1892-1893 less than half a dozen letters were received from outside the Province of Ontario. Gregory Papers, 1892-1893.

Liberalism. Laurier had no choice but to bide his time and hope that political union sentiment would gradually fade away.[13]

But if the Liberals were indecisive, the political unionists were not. They were convinced that statehood was a much more honorable position than colonial status. Further, they now argued, just as the Conservatives and Blake had argued, that Commercial Union had to go hand in hand with political union. Once the Liberals had lost the election of 1891 there no longer was any point in advocating half-way measures. William Dymond Gregory explained:

> The transformation of supporters of Commercial Union into supporters of political union was not unnatural and there was a good deal of feeling in favor of political union expressed before the election of 1891, but Goldwin Smith said that nothing should be done in this direction until the election was over as a movement of this kind might injure the Liberal chances. There was, I think, a feeling that commercial union would not accomplish what we hoped, for the great difficulty was that commercial union would have to be effected by treaty or concurred legislation. How then could manufacturers build up their enterprises here, if by a stroke of a pen 13/14 of continental customers might be taken away? . . . This was an unanswerable argument. . . . When the Liberals were defeated in 1891, the movement for continental union which had been discussed before, took definite form. No pressure, however, was brought by Goldwin Smith himself to induce anyone to take part in this movement. It was wholly voluntary. . . . I regarded it . . . as putting Canada in a much more honorable position than it occupied as a colony. To be part of a great North American union with equal rights with all other members of

13 *ibid.,* Mowat to Laurier, December 26 and 31, 1891.

the union seemed to me a much higher and more honorable position than being a dependency for another country
in which we could not exercise national powers.

Gregory mentioned that the Continental Union Association,
as the Canadian annexationist organization was called, was
started in the autumn of 1892 with Goldwin Smith as its
principal source of financial support.[14]

Meanwhile, interest in political union had also taken more
organized form in the United States. Goldwin Smith had
vaguely expressed the hope that this would be the case in a
letter to Andrew Carnegie in September 1891. In January
1893, Erastus Wiman wrote to Laurier about the recently
organized Continental Union League, telling of the League's
apparent success, and warning of its "having for its purpose a
motive . . . [which] may defeat your purposes." "As I understand it, the Liberal Party are earnestly desirous of the
closest trade relations with the United States without political
union. That was possible at the last General Election and
since but now I believe that the powerful influences of a desire
for acquisition of country will stand in the way of closer trade
relations." "The effort of the Continental Union League,"
he explained, "so far as it is at present controlled wd. certainly be against any change in the tariff as far as Canada is
concerned." Rather than entice Canada with tariff favors,
the League was advocating that Canada be coerced into
political union by retention of the present high tariff on
Canadian goods. Wiman further explained that the League
had considerable financial backing, saying that Andrew Carnegie had pledged $10,000 to the cause.[15]

Charles A. Dana, publisher of the *New York Sun* aided the
League's efforts immeasurably. Not only did his paper spread

[14] Gregory Papers, MS autobiography, pp. 104 ff.

[15] New York Public Library, Carnegie Autograph Collection, Smith
to Carnegie, September 30, 1891; Laurier Papers, 7, Wiman to Laurier,
January 17, 1893.

the annexationist gospel, he also provided encouraging letters of introduction for Francis Wayland Glen, who solicited funds for the League, to such influential persons as Charles S. Fairchild, President Cleveland's Secretary of the Treasury. In November 1893, Carnegie and Dana cosigned an open letter appealing for funds for the League. "Continental Union is one of the most important questions before the American people," the letter read, "and we commend it to your kind consideration. Its consummation will deliver the Continent from any possible complications and add enormously to the power, influence and prestige of North America. It would securely dedicate the continent to peaceful industry and progress." Among the subscribers were listed: Andrew Carnegie, $600; R. P. Flower, $500; Charles A. Dana, $460; John Jacob Astor, $200; W. C. Whitney, $100; and Elihu Root, $25.[16]

Among other activities the League drew up a resolution which it was proposed would be introduced into the House of Representatives by the influential New York Democratic Congressman, W. Bourke Cochran. The resolution invited "the Canadian people to cast in their lot with their continent and [we] assure them that they shall have all the continent can give them. We will respect their freedom of action, and welcome them when they desire it, into an equal and honorable union." This resolution was not introduced, apparently

[16] New York Historical Society, C. S. Fairchild Papers, Dana to Fairchild, May 11, 1893; Denison Papers, 5, copy of letter by Carnegie and Dana, November 6, 1893. This document, and other information cited from this collection, is a copy of evidence obtained for David Creighton, and thence Sir John Thompson and Clarke Wallace, by a "spy" within the Continental Union League in New York. The "spy," "Marcus R.," as Creighton referred to him, was for a time given $30 a week for his efforts out of funds of the Canadian Customs Department. See Denison Papers, 5, explanatory note by Creighton accompanying the evidence; 6, Denison to Salisbury, July 27, 1895; Thompson Papers, 196, Creighton to Thompson, January 11, 1894; 203, Creighton to Thompson, March 19 and 20, 1894.

REJECTION OF CONTINENTALISM

at the insistence of John Jacob Astor, though Goldwin Smith continued to urge its introduction to Bourke Cochran throughout the year 1894. The Continental Union League, or National Continental Union League as it came to be called, continued in existence (though its activities were apparently very limited) for many years after any meaningful annexation sentiment had passed from the Canadian scene. Its moving spirit was Francis Wayland Glen, one-time member of the Canadian House of Commons, and a persistent though—to say the least—erratic advocate of annexation. As late as July 1900, with the son of Charles Dana, Paul Dana, as President, Glen as Secretary and General Manager, and Bourke Cochran among the many Vice Presidents, the National Continental Union League was advocating annexation. On 26 July Glen sent to hundreds of newspapers throughout the United States a copy of the declaration of purpose of the League and invited press comments on the League's aims. In a covering letter Glen claimed that "we shall organize in every state and territory in the Union and in every province and territory of the Dominion of Canada." [17]

Throughout 1893 a series of meetings was held in New York City between Canadians and Americans interested in political union. Smith and John Morison, President of the Canadian association, met Carnegie and Dana in May. Gregory recalled another meeting a short while after at which he and Farrer from Ontario and Mercier, Robidoux, Tarte, J. X. Perrault, and Papineau discussed annexation again with Carnegie and Dana. In August Mercier appealed to Dana for help. "Allow me to bring to your attention," he wrote, "my state of poverty & ask you if our New York friends could not come to my rescue, in order that I might continue the work." Mercier apparently did receive money from R. P. Flower of

[17] Denison Papers, 5, copy of resolution drafted by the Continental Union League; Goldwin Smith Papers, letter by Francis Wayland Glen, July 26, 1900.

New York in return for assistance in getting the French Canadians in the city to vote the Democratic ticket.[18]

At another meeting at Carnegie's home on the evening of 1 December 1893, Carnegie, Dana, and Goldwin Smith discussed the giving of financial aid to certain Canadians. Glen later reported the result of the meeting to Farrer:

It was agreed . . . between Professor Smith, Mr. Carnegie and Mr. Dana not to contribute one dollar to aid Mr. Laurier at the next general election, but to support Mr. Mercier in obtaining control of the Quebec Legislature upon the platform of independence as a prelude to continental union. The next morning I called upon Mr. Carnegie and he instructed me to draft a letter to Mr. Mercier telling him of the decision arrived at. . . . I was simply candid, sincere and honest with Mr. Mercier; this gave offence to Mr. Morrison [sic] who had led Messrs. Mercier, Tarte, Pelletier and Robidoux to believe that funds would be supplied to assist the Liberal Party the

[18] Carnegie Autograph Collection, Dana to Carnegie, May 15, 1893; Denison Papers, 5, Copy, Mercier to Dana, August 9, 1893, enclosure in Dana to Morison, August 12, 1893; Gregory Papers, MS autobiography, pp. 110-11; Warner, *The Idea of Continental Union,* pp. 236-37. Mercier's "work" was his independence campaign in eastern Canada of which Warner writes it was "the easiest avenue to political union!" I think this is misleading. Americans might have so regarded it but it is doubtful that French Canadians equated independence with annexation. Tarte commented that "nous aurions toujours pu prendre l'argent pour faire des élections. Cela ne nous obligeait pas à livrer le pays ensuite." Many French Canadian nationalists were ardent advocates of independence. "Hommes, femmes et enfants, à vous de choisir," Mercier told his audience at Le parc Schmer on 4 April 1893, "vous pouvez rester esclaves dans l'état de colonie, ou devenir indépendants et libres, au milieu des autre peuples qui vous convient au banquet des nations." Robert Rumilly, *Histoire De La Province De Quebec,* Montreal, n.d., VII, pp. 101-4, 133-35. See also C. Langelier, *Souvenirs Politiques, 1890 à 1896,* Quebec, 1912, p. 209-12; Rumilly, *Henri Bourassa,* Montreal, 1953, pp. 19-20.

evening before. He was not candid enough to tell them of the decision which was arrived at after consulting with Prof. Smith, while I was. . . . Mr. Carnegie heartily approved of Prof. Smith's suggestion. . . . Mr. Morison may rest assured that the Liberal Party with its present platform dictated by Sir Oliver Mowat will not get any financial support from the friends of continental union in this country.

Glen added that on 23 February 1894, John Charlton had visited Dana seeking financial aid for the Liberal party but that, in line with the decision taken in December, Dana had refused.[19]

Even before these latest meetings between Canadian and American political unionists took place, annexation sentiment was withering away in Canada. To at least one observer the new Liberal platform, adopted at the Ottawa Convention in June 1893 appeared to be very important. "The annexation movement here," Denison cheerily wrote to Lord Salisbury in August, "is flatter than ever—the action of the Liberal Convention at Ottawa was most significant. Sir Oliver Mowat was pushed to the front, evidently on account of the strength of his position due to his loyalty. Mercier was kept out altogether. Cartwright was not obtrusive and the 'Unrestricted Reciprocity' fad was decently buried." "The death blow to the movement however," he added, "has been the financial distress in the States." After all, there was little prospect that Canadians would continue to support annexation when they saw the United States again slip into a disastrous depression while at home the Canadian economy was not only holding steady but, in fact, beginning to recover from the years of financial stress. And in the United States as well there appeared to be

[19] Thompson Papers, 202, Copy, Glen to Farrer, March 8, 1894. There is no other evidence to confirm or deny this report. It is, however, unlikely that Laurier was a knowing party to these appeals for financial aid from the American political unionists.

no prospect that the political unionists would receive any meaningful political support. All attention seemed to be on the depression and the cry for repeal of the Sherman Silver Purchase Act of 1890. In October Representative Hitt wrote to Goldwin Smith that "the absorption of all public interest in the struggle over the Silver Purchase Repeal has made it useless to even think of securing serious attention, or action, concerning affairs on the North." "How slowly this great movement proceeds," he wearily concluded.[20]

iii

The first indications that the Liberal party might be backing away from a whole-hearted endorsement of Unrestricted Reciprocity came from John Willison. The Tories had bound themselves tightly to the Empire; the annexationists, to the United States. He wondered if Laurier ought not "go pretty far in the way of Canadian Independence." "It is vital to our prosperity that we have large and liberal trade relations with the United States and . . . as an independent country we could make reasonable trade relations with the United States." Certainly something had to be done. The West Durham letter, the Conservative by-election successes, the apparent attraction of political union and Mowat's threat all had a shattering effect on political cohesion. Cartwright complained that "the work to be done here is, if possible, to re-establish our organization which thanks to the meanness of our well-to-do supporters has been allowed to go to pieces." [21]

An answer to the problem of organization and policy seemed to be found in Willison's suggestion, in July 1892, of a party convention. It would "give the party an enthusiasm and a sense of responsibility that are needed." Further, it was

[20] Denison Papers, 5, Denison to Salisbury, August 12, 1893; Goldwin Smith Papers, Hitt to Smith, October 18, 1893.
[21] Laurier Papers, 6, Willison to Laurier, November 26, 1892, Cartwright to Laurier, October 20, 1892.

now clear that Willison, like Blake and Mowat, was urging the Liberals to soft-pedal their trade policy. "I am convinced that little can be said about discrimination against Great Britain and that we must not admit the idea of a common tariff [with the United States]," he told Laurier. "We want Reciprocity if we can get an arrangement on terms that will not infringe upon our national integrity. . . . I do not see why a Reciprocity policy and a low tariff policy cannot be run together." [22]

The convention idea was certainly a good one, but a matter of timing was involved. "I doubt if any adequate good would come from holding a convention just now," Cartwright wrote in October 1892. Rather, he proposed to hold "a quiet meeting of our Ontario M.P.'s and chief office bearers for the purposes of organization." Louis Davies thought that "the Liberal party would gain much more by letting the people stew in their own juice than by any policy of active aggression." It was true that a convention would bolster organization of the party, but there had to be preliminary steps at organization even before the convention. Besides, since the United States would loom large in any policy decisions at the convention, Davies believed that "until the Presidential election is over it would be madness to hold a convention." [23]

Wisely, the convention was postponed until the following summer. In the meantime the Liberals went about the business of organization, watched the election of Grover Cleveland for a second term as President of the United States and viewed the hardening of opinion against annexation in Canada. In the meantime, too, Laurier began to move away from the uncompromising attitude he had taken with Blake in the argument over trade policy. The reasons for his retreat from Unrestricted Reciprocity are not entirely clear. It is quite proba-

[22] *ibid.,* Willison to Laurier, August 4, 1892.
[23] *ibid.,* Cartwright to Laurier, October 20, 1892, Davies to Laurier, October 14, 1892.

ble that what Cartwright called the "meanness of our well-to-do supporters" had a great deal to do with the gradual change of front. Canadian businessmen who might otherwise have supported the Liberals without question viewed Unrestricted Reciprocity with suspicion. It was not simply a matter of facing unbridled American competition should Unrestricted Reciprocity be achieved. More important, it was a matter of what Willison had called "our national integrity." F. T. Frost, a prominent Smith Falls, Ontario, Liberal and successful farm implement manufacturer, wrote to Laurier in November 1892 that:

> my faith in Unrestricted Reciprocity has not been lost because of any dread of American competition in my business, should it ever become a 'fait accompli,' but rather because it looks to me like an un-British policy and I can see no hope for our Liberal party as long as it is a prominent plank in our platform. Since the election I have been studying this question a good deal, much more than I did before it, and the more it is investigated the more apparent it becomes to me to be only a step on the way to political union.[24]

John Crerar, an influential Hamilton Liberal, told Laurier that "in dealing with the trade question in this city, a public speaker would necessarily have to be absolutely orthodox in the Cobden school sense, to avoid criticism of a very pungent character." It was obvious that continental free trade with a McKinley barrier against the rest of the world was not Cobdenism. "I think the time is opportune," he said, "for you to reiterate your attachment to British institutions, and British policy, touching the freedom of the subject to buy and sell." Then, too, in January 1893 John Charlton saw President-elect Grover Cleveland in New York City to disabuse him of any ideas of a "formidable" annexation movement in Canada.

[24] *ibid.,* Frost to Laurier, November 18, 1892.

They talked about "reciprocity"—the term "Unrestricted Reciprocity" appears nowhere in this entry in Charlton's diary—and Cleveland said that "reciprocity was in the line of Democratic policy and that he was in favor of more intimate trade relations with contiguous states." Probably many factors, then, played a part in the Liberal decision to climb down from the Unrestricted Reciprocity fence. But even if the Liberals did draw back from Unrestricted Reciprocity in their forthcoming convention, it did not mean that they would be left without an aggressive policy that would inspire support. On the contrary. "One other thing I hope the Convention will speak in no uncertain manner on and that is the tariff," a correspondent told Laurier on 15 June 1893. "I believe that a bold policy is required. . . . The Liberal party cannot now go the length of Free Trade but it can satisfy these people if it nails to the mast a declaration that the system of Protection is a fraud and that taxation must be for revenue alone." [25]

Four days later, when Laurier arrived in Ottawa on the day before the first meeting of the Convention, the *Ottawa Free Press* gave a hint of the revised Liberal stand on the tariff. "Reformers," it said, "are ready to denounce protection as legalized robbery of the people for the benefit of monopolists, and to declare that the proper fiscal policy for the Dominion is the British policy of free trade, limited only by necessities of revenue." Significantly, Sir Oliver Mowat was chairman of the Convention and in a short address denounced annexation and called for tariff reform and "such a measure of reciprocity as can be obtained on fair and honest terms." On the evening of 20 June, before an audience reportedly 4,000 strong in Ottawa's gaily bedecked Rideau Rink, the Liberal leader said that "the ideal fiscal system was the British system of free trade (great applause), and it was the policy of the Liberal party to get as near that ideal policy as the requirements of

[25] *ibid.,* Crerar to Laurier, November 28, 1892; 7, Zanach to Laurier, June 15, 1893; Charlton Papers, Diary, January 12, 1893.

revenue would permit." "It was also necessary," he added, "that Canadians should obtain the best possible markets for their products. Reciprocity of trade with the United States was required. . . . *TARIFF REDUCTION AND RECIPROC-ITY* ought to form the two main planks in the platform of the party." [26]

When the tariff resolution was presented to the Convention the next afternoon the official acknowledgement was made that the Liberal party of Canada had receded from Unrestricted Reciprocity. As if to assure the "well-to-do supporters" of Canadian Liberalism, the resolution affirmed that Canada should adopt "a sound fiscal policy" which would "not do injustice to any class." In contrast to the former policy the Liberals urged with due ambiguity and safety that the tariff "should be adjusted as to make free, or bear as lightly as possible upon the necessaries of life, and should be so arranged as to promote freer trade with the whole world, more particularly with Great Britain and the United States." Louis Davies read the reciprocity resolution which called for a "broad and liberal trade intercourse" between Canada and the United States which should include "a well considered list of manufactured articles." In a rather obvious twist of the abused loyalty cry, the *Ottawa Free Press* cheerily greeted the new Liberal trade policy by exclaiming that "the Reformers stand for the British policy of no taxation except for revenue purposes; while the Conservatives are for the American policy of protection as exemplified in the McKinley bill." Although somewhat more independent in its views of the Liberal gathering, the *Manitoba Free Press* nevertheless saw fit to "congratulate" the Liberals "on the abandonment of unrestricted reciprocity." "This country could not afford to throw down all the customs barriers between it and the United States, while maintaining them

[26] *Ottawa Free Press,* June 19 and 21, 1893.

against Great Britain. It would be entirely too revolution-ary." [27]

Martin Griffin, Parliamentary Librarian, assured the Prime Minister, Sir John Thompson, that the flurry over the suc-cess of the Liberal convention "will not outlast the excitement of the next base-ball match." Liberals, however, did not agree. William Mulock wrote to Laurier from Toronto that "the convention has greatly impressed the public mind here. It is conceded that our platform is proof against the disloyalty cry whilst the moderate character of our trade policy fails, ap-parently, to create alarm in monetary circles. These are two most important considerations. If we adhere firmly to the convention platform . . . I have no doubt the Country will give us a majority at the next election." And perhaps even sooner than expected it appeared that the new policy was paying dividends. In December Joseph Martin, Liberal candi-date, won an important by-election in Winnipeg on the trade issue. "The protection theory is completely demolished up here," Martin reported to Laurier, "and unless the govern-ment give a very large measure of reform they are doomed in the west." [28]

iv

In the three years that elapsed between the Liberal Conven-tion and the general election on 23 June 1896, Laurier and his colleagues studiously concentrated on efforts to strengthen the Liberal party in Dominion politics.[29] Late in 1894 Willison

[27] *ibid.,* June 22, 1893; *Manitoba Free Press,* June 24, 1893.

[28] Thompson Papers, 182, Griffin to Thompson, June 24, 1893; Laurier Papers, 7, Mulock to Laurier, June 29, 1893, Martin to Laurier, December 6, 1893.

[29] Curiously enough, one of these efforts was apparently to effect an alliance with D'Alton McCarthy. It appears that the first approach was made by Cartwright and Edgar in February 1894. Late in that year, when Cartwright and Laurier were concerned about the chances of the Liberals in Ontario in a general election, the former proposed that the

enthusiastically reported that as far as Ontario was concerned, "Liberals were never more united and Conservatives never more divided and lacking in enthusiasm." The shift away from Unrestricted Reciprocity was paying off for the Liberals. Apparently the tariff resolution was a prime factor in the revitalization of the Liberal party for the weakest point in its organization had been the lack of support from Canadian business. And that support was vitally needed. As Willison said, "the next election, it seems to me, will be won by the party that can best command the confidence of the best elements of the country." In January 1895, Laurier gave a speech at Montreal which, reported A. T. Wood, Hamilton merchant, was well received. "It . . . will do an immense good all over the country, and particularly that part of it where you state that violent changes will not be made, but that a gradual reduction will be the way in which the desired end is to be reached. . . . Many of your warm admirers personally hesitate to cast in their lot with us simply on the ground that they are afraid of the ultra free traders insisting on radical changes immediately. The assurance of your Montreal speech on this point will quell their fears and bring many of them into line." [30]

Just a few days before the election of 1896 a letter by the Liberal party leader was published in the *Toronto Globe* in a further effort to assure the business community that their interests would not be in danger after a Liberal victory. Laurier's letter was published as a reply to a letter by

Liberals "co-operate quietly with McCarthy in the centre and the Patrons in the east." In December 1896, Laurier told McCarthy he was grateful for his "fair and honourable support" and that he "should be entitled to all the privileges which patronage can give you." See Laurier Papers, 8, Cartwright to Laurier, February 8, 1894, Edgar to Laurier, February 20, 1894, Cartwright to Laurier, October 22, 1894; 35, Laurier to McCarthy, December 31, 1896.

[30] Laurier Papers, 8, Willison to Laurier, November 29, 1894; 9, Wood to Laurier, January 25, 1895.

George H. Bertram of Toronto who seemed to question whether a Liberal Administration "would reform the present tariff . . . taking a practical business view of the whole question as to what was best for our own Dominion, without regard to theoretical opinions as to the merits of protection or free trade." Laurier replied that "the intention of the Liberal party is not and never was to establish absolute free trade in this country." Rather, the existing conditions of the country, its economic situation, and its "enormous financial obligations" all required a fiscal policy based on a revenue tariff. There would be "stability and permanency" which "are essential to the security and prosperity of manufacturing interests." Liberal trade policy, Laurier concluded, would be such that "the manufacturing class would find the security which it needs, and the consuming classes that relief which they must have." [31]

Even more important than placating the "well-to-do" with reassuring speeches and letters was a practical understanding between Laurier and the leaders of the Ontario financial community suggested by Alex Smith, secretary of the provincial Liberal Association. Smith told Laurier that George A. Cox, president of the Canadian Bank of Commerce, "is not only willing but anxious that you should meet the leading financial men in this Province." B. E. Walker, general manager of the Bank of Commerce "would be delighted to discuss the financial affairs of the country minutely" and Cox had told Smith that "I know all these men Grit and Tory alike and I will be only too glad to arrange that Mr. Laurier meet them." That an understanding was reached, at least with Cox, is certain. In April 1896, in an effort to induce Sir Oliver Mowat to take part in the forthcoming general election and become a member of the Government if the Liberals were successful, Laurier saw to it that Sir Oliver would have no financial

[31] *Toronto Globe,* June 3, 1896.

worries if he went to Ottawa. "A syndicate of capitalists, at the head of which are George Cox and A. H. Janes, two of the most wealthy men in Toronto," Laurier wrote, "is ready to guarantee him an annuity for the rest of his life." [32]

The Liberals, then, spent the years 1893 to 1896 building and mending their fences. They had abandoned the Unrestricted Reciprocity cry in favor of freer trade with Great Britain, the United States, and the world and had declared for a revenue tariff. They had solicited in every possible way the favor of their "well-to-do supporters." In short, by 1896 Laurier's party was ready to fight the Conservatives on the trade question. And probably they were entirely justified in believing that they had eradicated the "disloyalty" image. Colonel Denison crowed to Lord Salisbury: "even if Laurier came into power now, I think he and his party would be loyal and true to the Empire. There has been a great change." "The Liberals have seen the great mistake they made in 1890-91 and are now very careful not to squint towards the United States. In fact, they remind one of the Indian's tree that stood so upright that it leaned a little the other way." [33]

Unfortunately, ever since the election of 1891 the trade question had been losing its place as the great issue in Dominion politics. Replacing it was the Manitoba Schools Question

[32] Laurier Papers, 8, Smith to Laurier, December 8, 1894; 10, Laurier to Ewart, April 20, 1896. There is also a hint that the Liberals were not confining their drive to curry favor in financial and business circles to Toronto. Cartwright, commenting on the line the *Globe* should take on a report of Van Horne's resignation from the presidency of the C.P.R., wrote to Willison: "I would be disposed to be civil but not at all gushing over him. He and his road are in the market, politically speaking, now and always and it is significant that he does not even talk of retiring till a date by which the general elections will be over." Public Archives of Canada, Willison Papers, 14, Cartwright to Willison, December 10, 1895.

[33] Denison Papers, 7, Denison to Salisbury, January 20 and May 2, 1896.

which successive Conservative Governments had so badly bungled that it threatened to destroy traditional political alignments and replace them with parties based solely on religious or cultural principles, parties which would also, at best, destroy the essential duality of Canadian nationhood embodied in the British North America Act. "What I most dread and would most particularly deprecate," Laurier wrote to a friend, "would be to have all Catholics on one side and all Protestants on the other side, when the question comes to be tried in the House." Again and again Willison badgered Laurier in 1895 and 1896 about Protestant Ontario's point of view on the school question and again and again Laurier urged—as on 30 March 1895—"let us bring back public opinion to the tariff." Finally the Liberal leader's pleadings ceased and he resigned himself to fighting the election on the Manitoba Schools Question. But it was not without great misgivings. The Liberals were sound on the trade question. Neither Liberals nor Conservatives were sound on Manitoba Schools and the election was full of danger for everyone.[34]

Still, where possible, the Liberals campaigned on the trade issue. G. W. Ross, Sir Oliver Mowat's Ontario colleague, wrote to George Bertram, Toronto industrialist, about Laurier. "I hope when he comes to Ontario he will take pains, at every meeting, to show that the tariff the Liberals propose will not be destructive of our manufacturers nor injurious to our working men." In Quebec West the Liberals supported the candidature of R. R. Dobell, former protectionist Conservative. Dobell favored "tariff reform" and believed "protection as only wise and prudent to adopt for the purpose of fostering infant industries." He campaigned for "measures to have the freest possible trade with all our sister colonies and above all to bind strongly the link which unites us to the

[34] Laurier Papers, 9, Laurier to Anglin, April 2, 1895; Willison Papers, 109, Laurier to Willison, March 30, 1895.

Greatest Empire the world has ever known" and he supported "fair reciprocal trade with the United States." [35]

In spite of—or perhaps because of—the lack of a united Liberal stand on the Manitoba Schools Question, Laurier and his colleagues won 118 seats in the 1896 general election to the Conservatives' 88. In Ontario each party captured 43 seats and only some 20,000 votes more were registered by the Conservatives than the Liberals. Across the Dominion the Liberals obtained 11,000 fewer popular votes than their opponents and parliamentary majorities in only the Territories, Prince Edward Island, British Columbia, and Quebec. But it was Quebec, along with the Liberals' strong showing in Ontario, which gave Laurier his victory. His own Province gave his party 49 of its 65 seats. There may have been a grain of truth in Charles Hibbert Tupper's complaint to Lady Aberdeen that Laurier's majority of thirty seats was not united. "It is a great puzzle to me to say what his majority of representatives

[35] *ibid.,* 11, Ross to Bertram, May 13, 1896, Fitzpatrick to Laurier, May 28, 1896. Robert Rumilly wrote of this aspect of the election in Quebec: "Laurier, Cartwright et leurs amis, pour se concilier le monde industriel, tempéraient leurs principes, et se prononçaient pour une réduction, une mise au point du tarif plutôt que pour sa suppression. Trois principaux lieutenants travaillaient, en faveur de Laurier, l'opinion des Anglais riches de la province: Richard Reid Dobell à Québec; Sydney Fisher, le gentleman-farmer du comte de Brome, dans les cantons de l'Est; et Robert Mackay à Montréal. Dobell présidait le Board of Trade et siégeait dans les principaux conseils d'administration à Québec. Sydney Fisher annulait l'influence du ministre Ives. Robert Mackay, longtemps associé de ses oncles, avait figuré dans ce groupe d'importateurs écossais, libre-echangistes—au contraire des industriels—par intérêt primordial. La maison d'importation fermée, Robert Mackay s'était mêlé à beaucoup d'entreprises, en restant bon libéral. Il entraînait, par son exemple, quelques grosses sousscriptions. Candidat sans espoir à Montréal-Ouest, il affirmait secrètement à ses amis—et électeurs éventuels—que le tarif serait peu modifié. D'une manière aussi secrète, mais formelle, Tarte confirmait la promesse. . . ." *Histoire De La Province De Quebec,* VIII, p. 58.

are in favour of—on Remedial Legislation or on Trade." In any case, only one thing really mattered: for the first time in twenty-two years the Liberal party had won an election.[36]

Almost immediately Canadian businessmen and financiers began to have second thoughts about the preelection assurances of the Liberals to protect their interests. They realized that the two-decade-old Conservative-business alliance had been crushed. They began to fear that immediate and revolutionary changes in the tariff would be introduced in the second Parliamentary session of 1896. The Liberals, of course, were quick to dispel such fears. "It is not the intention of the Liberal Party in the session, which is to open on the 16th instant, to deal with the tariff at all or to attempt any legislation of any kind," Laurier wrote in answer to an anxious inquiry in July. "The only thing that we feel called upon to do now, is to have the budget voted for the present financial year; nothing else." Laurier told Willison that immediate action to reform the tariff was "absolutely impossible." "The tariff should not be reformed, in my estimation, except after ample discussion with the businessmen, and by consulting with them, as we must do and will do, we will do a good deal to avert the consequences, which you fear, of the uncertainty as to the future. If they are fully and amply consulted, the businessmen will feel reassured." [37]

But reassurance of the financial titans with words was apparently not enough. They demanded immediate action from Laurier to show that he fully appreciated their trust.

[36] J. G. Foley, ed., *Resume of General Elections*, Ottawa, 1916, p. 16; Public Archives of Canada, Aberdeen Papers, 5, C. H. Tupper to Lady Aberdeen, June 30, 1896. There is an admirable discussion of the election of 1896 in J. T. Saywell, ed. *The Canadian Journal of Lady Aberdeen 1893-1898*, Toronto, 1960, pp. lxix-lxxx. Professor Saywell's excellent analysis of the Manitoba Schools Question precedes and follows the pages mentioned.

[37] Laurier Papers, 13, Laurier to Blique, July 4, 1896; Willison Papers, 109, Laurier to Willison, June 29, 1896.

This demand took the form of insistence that Sir Richard Cartwright be sacked. Cartwright had been Mackenzie's Finance Minister and hence was associated with the disastrous depression of the 1870's. As the Liberal financial critic for two decades the "knight of the rueful countenance" had further estranged himself from Canadian businessmen by holding the position of the most hated and most feared enemy of the National Policy. And as the most forceful exponent of Unrestricted Reciprocity, Cartwright, unlike his colleagues, had never been able to cleanse himself of the taint of disloyalty. As early as February 1896 the *Canadian Manufacturer and Industrial World* had mentioned with some satisfaction "the sacrifice of Sir Richard" should the Liberals win the coming election. Willison wrote to Laurier two days after the election that "in view of the critical condition of many manufacturing establishments throughout the country, the general stagnation, the fear of the banks of trade disturbance, I fear that to put Sir Richard Cartwright into the government may precipitate a very serious scare with unfortunate consequences." [38]

Laurier replied that "it would be impossible not to take him into the Cabinet. This would be a personal affront, and I would rather lose everything than do such a thing." But Laurier was ready to capitulate to the demands of the businessmen on the main point and not give Cartwright the Finance portfolio. This was apparent in a letter he received from George Bertram who gave a Toronto businessman's view of the situation:

> The name of Premier Fielding which you mentioned to me, I have since learned is an exceptionally strong name. I trust you will secure him, if he is not available I am

[38] *Canadian Manufacturer and Industrial World,* February 21, 1896; Laurier Papers, 12, Willison to Laurier, June 25, 1896. See also Gibson to Laurier, June 29, 1896 where Gibson wrote: "it will never do to have him Minister of Finance."

sure you will easily get a new man who will command the confidence of all. I do not desire to utter one unkind word regarding Sir Richard Cartwright, but the interests of the country and the party are paramount to all others and I am sure that Liberals generally *do not on any account* desire to see Sir Richard back into his old position of Finance Minister. I am well aware that there is not much danger of this, but one never knows what might happen. . . . Revision and reform of the tariff would be more difficult, and create a want of confidence, if Sir Richard was at the head of that department, in fact I know of nothing that would upset business calculations so much as the appointment of Sir Richard.

W. S. Fielding of Nova Scotia was named Minister of Finance and the Blue Ruin Knight had to be satisfied with the Ministry of Trade and Commerce.[39]

In framing the tariff for which the manufacturers anxiously awaited, Laurier kept his promise to consult fully Canadian businessmen. A tariff commission, composed of Ministers Fielding, Cartwright, and Paterson traveled about Canada seeking advice from all interested parties. Of course the traditional allies of the Liberal party, the Canadian agricultural interest, had an opportunity to present their views. The Dennis County, Manitoba Liberal Association urged upon the Government "the present necessity of a rearrangement of the Tariff in order to relieve to as great an extent as possible the burdens now pressing so heavily upon the Farming community of Manitoba." And the East Northumberland Patrons

[39] Willison Papers, 109, Laurier to Willison, June 29, 1896; Laurier Papers, 12, Bertram to Laurier, June 27, 1896. Cartwright's daughter recorded in her diary: "People were surprised that my Father did not accept the position of Finance Minister. He told Mother to-day that he had his reasons for not doing so and he has just as much power as if he had." Toronto Public Library, E. W. Banting Collection, Mollie Cartwright Diary, September 1896.

of Industry requested of the Tariff Commission that "luxuries be taxed to the fullest revenue producing extent in the interest of the toiling masses of Canada and that the following necessities be placed upon the free list, namely, cottons, woollens, tweeds, working men's tools, farm implements, fence wire, binder twine, coal oil, iron and corn." But Canadian farmers, unfortunately, simply were not organized to present effectively their views to the Tariff Commission. Furthermore, the interests of eastern Canadian and prairie agriculture were often varied, sometimes even contradictory. In contrast, in both organization and interest, Canadian businessmen deluged the Tariff Commission with a united and powerful appeal for their welfare.[40]

While the Tariff Commission solicited Canadian opinion, the Liberals also sounded the American Government on the possibilities of making a reciprocal trade agreement. Sydney Fisher, Laurier's Minister of Agriculture, visited Washington in December 1896 to discuss the cattle quarantine problem. Richard Olney, Secretary of State in the recently defeated Cleveland Administration, "expressed regret that the present administration would not be long enough in power to meet us & said that he thought had we Liberals been in power four years ago a Reciprocity treaty could have been made." John Charlton visited the President-elect, William McKinley, on a business trip to Cleveland, Ohio, and received a "very cordial" welcome. On a second trip south of the border, Charlton apparently traveled under false pretenses and earned a sharp rebuke from his chief. It was reported in the newspapers that he had gone to Washington on "an official mission." Laurier ordered him to "contradict this report." "I wish you would be careful to let it be known that you came simply

[40] Laurier Papers, 32, Dennis County Liberal Association to Laurier, January, 1897; 38, Patrons of Industry Convention, East Northumberland to Tariff Commission, February 27, 1897; McDiarmid, *Commercial Policy in the Canadian Economy*, p. 206.

as a citizen of Canada, and in no other capacity. I wish also that you would utilize your stay there to obtain information and for nothing else. A good many of our friends are nervous about your actions," Laurier told Charlton. Laurier, in fact, was quite skeptical about the possibilities of obtaining a reciprocity treaty. The new Republican Administration was headed by the author of the McKinley tariff, the new Chairman of the House Ways and Means Committee was going to be the archprotectionist Nelson Dingley, and it was quite clear that McKinley's victory had been made possible in large part because of the support of midwestern agricultural interests who had been promised substantial protection. Laurier told Charlton that "we must hold our hands free to deal in any direction which the interests of Canada may demand, and whilst, for my part, I am strongly impressed with the view that our relations with our neighbours should be friendly, at the same time I am equally strong in the opinion that we may have to take the American tariff—if conceived in hostility to Canada—& make it the Canadian tariff." [41]

Skeptical though he was, Laurier did send an official mission to Washington early in February. Louis Davies, Minister of Marine and Fisheries, reported on the general good feel-

[41] *ibid.*, 29, Fisher to Laurier, December 10, 1896; 28, Charlton to Laurier, December 3, 1896; 30, Charlton to Laurier, December 23, 1896; 33, Laurier to Charlton, January 18, 1897. Gilbert C. Fite writes that "McKinley also stressed the advantage of increasing domestic markets for farm produce by raising tariff rates to protect both farmers and manufacturers" in the 1896 campaign. He concludes that "if he had received an overwhelming farm vote between the Ohio and the Missouri Rivers, Bryan would have won the presidency. Failing to accomplish this, he lost the election. Hundreds of thousands of farmers were distrustful of Bryan and Democratic policies, and they trooped to the polls to vote loyally for McKinley whose party over the years and during the campaign had effectively sold itself to them." G. C. Fite, "Republican Strategy and the Farm Vote in the Presidential Campaign of 1896," *American Historical Review*, LXV, 1960, pp. 787-806.

ing in Washington shown to the Canadians. Robert Hitt, as might have been expected, was strongly "in favour of broader and freer trade relations" as was Senator Aldrich of Rhode Island. Davies urged the Americans to appoint members to a Canadian-American commission which "after discussing the whole affair, would report to their respective Governments." Nelson Dingley "seems in full sympathy with the desire for a reciprocity treaty." He had told Davies that his tariff bill, which would increase duties even beyond those in the McKinley tariff, was not being introduced to provide "further protection, but as a revenue producer." Dingley did not think that his tariff bill would interfere with reciprocity plans. "He, however, intimated that Mr. McKinley's whole mind was engrossed at present with the idea of making ends meet, and until the tariff bill effecting that object is passed, and in operation . . . no steps would probably be taken by Mr. McKinley." Nothing, then, could be done about Canadian reciprocity plans for some time. Meanwhile, despite what the intentions of the American Government were, the Dingley tariff would be closely watched in Canada and judged as a further step toward closing off Canadian-American trade. As such it could hardly be calculated to be viewed as other than a hostile measure by most Canadians. Nonetheless, Davies enthusiastically told Laurier that he felt assured "our mission will be productive of much good and I *think* we have good grounds for believing that we will accomplish much, very much more than most of our colleagues contemplated." [42]

Other correspondents were not nearly as optimistic. One told Laurier that "the general tone of feeling" in the United States "is contrary to the granting of concessions or of catering at all towards meeting the idea which [is] called 'Canadian.'" Some Canadians, not appreciating the overly subtle distinction between "revenue" needs and "protection" in reports of the Dingley Bill, were frankly advocating a "get

[42] *ibid.*, 791a, Davies to Laurier, February 7, 9, and 11, 1897.

tough" tariff policy toward the United States. If there could not be a reciprocity treaty, wrote one correspondent, "it seems to me that we ought to retaliate by increasing our duties." Another said that a Canadian tariff which discriminated against the United States "in favour of British imports . . . will meet with very general favour. . . ." Alex Smith noted that "the feeling with reference to the action of the United States on the tariff is growing stronger and the people of this province appear to be very anxious to develop trade with Great Britain. They are desirous that it should be done without any display of animosity towards the States though I am constrained to say that the emotional feeling has been to discriminate boldly and 'give it to the Yankees.' " [43]

As opinion against the Dingley Bill hardened, the twin proposals of discrimination in favor of Great Britain and retention of a large measure of protection for Canadian interests became more frequent. Clifford Sifton, who in 1893 had advised the Liberal party to "strike at the root of the evil and propose a radical and thorough measure of tariff reform," now wrote to a friend that "to so construct the tariff as to wantonly destroy the industries that have been built up under it would be utterly unjustifiable from any possible standpoint of reason." As Minister of the Interior he told Laurier: "I hope the free trade theory, which has been already shattered, will not be permitted to stand in the way when it is plainly not in our business interests." John Willison advised that "the press of the country, both Liberal and Conservative, seems to be almost unanimous in favor of a pro-British tariff. . . ." [44]

[43] ibid., 38, Mills to Laurier, February 25, 1897; 35, Coveney to Laurier, February, 1897; 41, Frost to Laurier, March 23, 1897, Smith to Laurier, March 28, 1897.

[44] Public Archives of Canada, Sifton Papers, 291, Sifton to Laurier, February 2, 1893, Sifton to Fleming, March 13, 1897, Sifton to Laurier, April 29 [19?], 1897; Laurier Papers, 42, Willison to Laurier, April 2, 1897.

Laurier sought counsel outside the circle of his Cabinet colleagues. He suggested to George Bertram the desirability of giving goods from the Mother Country a preferred position in the new tariff. The problem was how to do this while at the same time protecting vital Canadian interests and not overtly offending the United States by outright discrimination against American products. Bertram replied that the Dingley tariff increased "the necessity for preserving our own against the Americans and extending our trade in other directions." He suggested that the way to accomplish all the objects Laurier desired was to copy the two level French tariff,

> giving all countries the benefit of our Minimum Tariff, who will admit a limited schedule of our natural products free of duty, such as lumber, fish, wheat, barley, hay, etc. This would mean that all importation from Britain would be admitted under the minimum tariff as she imposes no duty on our products, and so long as the American Government exclude our lumber, fish, &c. so long American importations would be subject to our general Tariff. This is not discrimination any more than the American Tariff does not discriminate.

A general and minimum tariff policy would protect Canadian industries, increase foreign markets for Canada's natural products and "build up the St. Lawrence route. . . . Such a Canadian policy," Bertram assured Laurier, "would sweep the country." [45]

When Finance Minister Fielding introduced the long awaited tariff to the House of Commons on 23 April 1897, he proudly proclaimed that the Liberals were going to "turn away" from the "mistaken policy" of the past, the National Policy. But he hastened to reassure his listeners that the Liberals were not going to adopt "a radical free trade tariff . . . at one step" and reminded them of the gradual progress

[45] Laurier Papers, 40, Bertram to Laurier, March 22, 1897.

toward free trade in the Mother Country. A few items, such as binder twine to conciliate the farmers, would go on the free list, but generally the reductions from the previous tariff were few. Fielding indicated that the Dingley Bill, "whatever the motive of it may have been . . . affects the trade relations between Canada and the United States to a very considerable degree." It would be foolish to lower the duties on American imports, "if our American friends are willing to negotiate, . . . in advance of such negotiations." He declared:

> This leads to the conclusion that we must be prepared to deal with this question from the point of view of having one tariff for the countries which are willing to trade with us and a different tariff for the countries which are not. . . . We propose, therefore, to have a general tariff, and that general tariff will be, to a large extent, the tariff of today . . . and then we propose to adopt a special tariff having reference to the countries which are desirous of trading with us; and, as a matter of course, not by the express words of resolution, but by the condition of affairs which exists, that preferential tariff gives preference above all others, to the products of Great Britain.

Fielding went on to explain that any country which consented to admit Canadian products on terms which matched the proposed Canadian minimum tariff terms, would be granted entry of its goods under the minimum Canadian tariff. The Canadian terms were simply a 12½ per cent reduction on the Canadian general tariff until July 1898 and thereafter a 25 per cent reduction on the Canadian general tariff. Obviously, Great Britain, with its free trade policy, would be granted the advantage of the minimum Canadian tariff immediately. In short, the Fielding tariff followed in principle Bertram's plan. Fielding concluded: "if our American friends wish to make a treaty with us, we are willing to meet them and treat on fair and equitable terms. If it shall not please them to do that, we shall in one way regret the fact, but shall nevertheless go on our way rejoicing, and find other markets to build up the prosperity of Canada independent of the American people." [46]

True to its independent-mindedness, the *Manitoba Free Press* quickly pointed out in its review of the Fielding tariff that "the National Policy is as much in evidence as at any time these past eighteen years," but it did hail the concession of free binder twine and the introduction of a British preference. Liberal papers, naturally, crowed with satisfaction. The *Halifax Morning Chronicle* noted that the Liberals had kept faith with the people by "lessening the restrictions imposed on trade by the national policy" and had kept faith with the manufacturers "by guarding against drastic reductions of duty." Emphasizing the effect of the new minimum tariff, the *St. John Daily Telegraph* said "this one act of the Liberal government will do more to strengthen the ties between Great Britain and Canada than all the cheap talk about loyalty that the Tories have been indulging in for the past twenty years." Both the *Regina Leader* and the *Edmonton Bulletin* agreed that the new tariff, which the former labelled "an extraordinarily bold endeavour," would benefit western agricultural interests.[47]

On the other hand, as was expected, Conservative journals found little to their liking in Fielding's work. "This reads very well, but . . . no amount of loyalty will make an impractical scheme workable," observed the *Victoria Daily Colonist*. At first the *Montreal Gazette* dismissed "the double tariff idea" as "not likely . . . to have any serious effect." But the next day, on reconsideration, the paper attacked the idea vigorously. The new tariff, the *Gazette* cried, "proposed an abrogation of parliamentary power by Parliament . . . the

[46] *Official Report of Debates,* April 22, 1897, pp. 1091-1134.
[47] *Manitoba Free Press,* April 24, 1897; *Halifax Morning Chronicle,* April 23, 1897; *St. John Daily Telegraph,* April 23, 1897; *Regina Leader,* April 29, 1897; *Edmonton Bulletin,* May 3, 1897.

astonishing proposal is made that the Government of the day shall have power, without consulting Parliament, to grant not to one or two countries, but to a dozen or a score, if it pleases, a preferential treatment in the matter of customs duties." Taking its cue from the remarks of Foster and Tupper in the House of Commons, the *Toronto Daily Mail and Empire* raised a more fundamental point. The paper observed that the onerous clauses in the Belgian and Zollverein treaties were still in effect. They, of course, stipulated that any preference given to British goods in the Colonial markets would also apply to Belgian and German goods. And, by virtue of the most-favored-nation clause, this preference would also extend to all those countries with which the Mother Country had most-favored-nation treaties. The *Globe* retorted with the emotional argument that "it would be a rather disagreeable feature of our colonial position if it turned out that we cannot give trade advantages to Great Britain without letting in the goods of nations to whom we have no particular desire to show favor." It claimed that the *Mail and Empire's* charge was not true; on the contrary, "by the new tariff Canada claims the supreme right of self-government." [48]

But newspaper rhetoric could not solve this very real problem and a long discussion ensued between the Canadian and British Governments. Fielding had foreseen the difficulty in his budget speech and claimed that if a direct preference to British goods had been given, then the Conservative point would be well taken. But, he said, this had not been done. The clauses in question had reference to a preference given British goods, but the minimum tariff gave a preference to the goods of *any* country which could meet its terms. He had stressed the point that the British preference was only incidental to the large scheme of a dual tariff. Great Britain

[48] *Victoria Daily Colonist*, April 30, 1897; *Montreal Gazette*, April 23 and 24, 1897; *Toronto Daily Mail and Empire*, April 24, 1897; *Toronto Globe*, April 24 and 26, 1897.

happened to apply automatically for the minimum tariff because of her free trade policy which put no restrictions on Canadian imports. As he said, "we make this offer not to Great Britain only, but to every nation which is prepared to accept it." And thus, since the British preference was only incidental, the clauses in the Belgian and Zollverein treaties did not apply. This was the crux of the Canadian argument in the discussions with the British Government. But it took, in the end, a united appeal from all the self-governing colonies to solve the problem. At the Colonial Conference of 1897 the Colonial Premiers unanimously resolved to "earnestly recommend the denunciation, at the earliest convenient time, of any treaties which now hamper the commercial relations between Great Britain and her Colonies." On 28 July 1897, the Belgian and Zollverein treaties were denounced by Lord Salisbury.[49]

All of this was important. But, politically speaking, the more important thing was the impression Fielding's tariff made on Canadians. Joseph Pope, with an appreciable bias, wrote in his diary that "the feeling is general that the Govt., though sacrificing every shred of consistency or principle in bringing down a protectionist tariff, with preferential arrgt. for England, have made a big hit, and completely taken the wind out of the Conservative sails." But the rejection of continentalism by the Liberals could also be seen as a vindication of the National Policy. Not a few Canadians agreed with ex-Prime Minister Mackenzie Bowell when he happily told his fellow Senators:[50]

When one reflects on the past, and what has taken place during the 17 or 18 years in which the protective policy

[49] *Official Report of Debates,* April 22, 1897, p. 1131; Ollivier, *Colonial and Imperial Conferences,* v. 1, pp. 139-40; Garvin, *Chamberlain,* v. 3, p. 194.
[50] Pope Papers, Diary, April 26, 1897; *Debates of the Senate of the Dominion of Canada,* March 30, 1897, p. 18.

of the government has been in force, and then reads the utterance of the leaders of the Liberal party of to-day, if one could only blot out the names of those who utter them and read them without knowing who gave expression to those views, one would say they came from the veriest Tories in the land. I congratulate my hon. friends upon their conversion.

CHAPTER IX
The Alaska Boundary

JUST before the turn of the century Canadian-American relations appeared to be suddenly complicated by a new question, the determination of the boundary line between the Dominion of Canada and the Territory of Alaska. In one sense it is quite true to say that this was a new question. The definition of the Alaskan boundary did not become a matter of immediate importance until rich deposits of gold were discovered in the Yukon area in 1896-1897 and, until that time, the matter had received little attention in the media of public communication. On the other hand, it would be wrong to conclude that the settlement of the Alaskan boundary had not been a longstanding unsolved problem in Canadian-American relations. Various attempts at solution had been made ever since "Seward's folly" had been acquired by the United States in 1867. The discovery of gold in or near disputed territory only gave a sense of urgency to the question and made an immediate solution imperative. But long before 1896 the Canadian and United States Governments had taken very decided opinions on the manner in which the disputed boundary should be defined and the lines of dispute were clearly drawn.

When the American Government acquired the vast territory of Alaska, it clearly did not intend that it should immediately receive an influx of settlers from the general westward movement of population. For nearly two decades the civil organization of the territory was practically nonexistent: some five hundred troops were put in charge of administering the territory under a military governor. In 1868 the customs laws of the United States were extended to the territory, and the district courts of California, Oregon, and Washington were given jurisdiction over offenses committed in Alaska. But no provision was made for the arrest of criminals or their transportation from Alaska to the courts. When the troops were withdrawn in 1877, the sole remaining United States official with authority in the territory was the Collector of Customs at Sitka. No more sophisticated form of government was provided until President Grover Cleveland signed "An Act for The Civil Government of Alaska" on 17 May 1884. This Act, commonly known as the "Organic Act," made the territory a civil and judicial district of the United States. Still the government provided was minimal, provision being made only for a governor, a judge, a district attorney, clerk of the court, marshall, and United States Commissioners at Sitka, Wrangell, Juneau, and Unalaska. The mining, but not the land laws of the United States, were made operative in the district. Otherwise, the laws of the State of Oregon were extended to Alaska insofar as they were applicable and not *ultra vires* of the laws of the United States. The Territory of Alaska was governed under the "Organic Act" until the large influx of gold seekers made a more complete system of government necessary in 1898.[1] In fact, the United States Government paid scant attention to this potentially rich territory before gold discoveries were made in 1896.

Scarcely more attention was given to the matter of the boundary line between Alaska and the Dominion of Canada by the Canadian Government. Late in the 1860's gold discoveries were made in the Cassiar region of British Columbia. The only easy route of access to the region was by the Stikine River but somewhere along that route lay the boundary between the Province and the southeastern panhandle of Alaska. In September 1872, at the request of the British Columbia Government, the Canadian Government proposed that a Canada-United States boundary commission be formed to delimit the boundary. In December President Grant, in his annual message to Congress, recommended the formation of

[1] F. W. Gibson, "The Alaskan Boundary Dispute," M.A. Thesis, Queen's University, 1944, v. 1, pp. 71-91.

the commission, but Congress refused to grant the necessary funds. In 1876 in the Choquette and Peter Martin cases, the matter of the boundary line at the Stikine River was again brought to the attention of the Canadian and American Governments. When the United States Government would not act, the Canadian Government decided to conduct an independent provisional survey of the boundary in the Stikine River region. In June 1877, Joseph Hunter submitted a report to the Mackenzie Government stating where the boundary line should be fixed on the Stikine River. In February 1878, the United States Government accepted Hunter's determination as the provisional boundary line on the Stikine.[2]

Though the refusal of the United States Congress to appropriate funds for a survey appeared to be the obstacle blocking a settlement of the boundary question, in reality it was one of the least of the difficulties involved in the matter. Much more important was the confusion surrounding the question of how the boundary would be fixed. At first sight this seemed to be a relatively simple problem, for the method of determining the boundary was set forth in some detail in the Anglo-Russian Treaty of 1825. Articles Three and Four of that Treaty gave instructions as to where the boundary lay between Russian and British territory and it appeared that all that had to be done was to have surveyors follow the terms of these articles.[3] Starting from the Arctic Ocean, the main

[2] *ibid.*, pp. 73-77; Tansill, *Canadian-American Relations,* pp. 131-37.
[3] The articles specified that:

III   La ligne de démarcation entre les possessions des Hautes Parties Contractantes sur la côte du Continent et les Iles de l'Amérique Nord-Ouest, sera tracée ainsi qu'il suit:—
A partir du point le plus méridional de l'île dite Prince of Wales, lequel point se trouve sous le parallèle du 54°40′ de latitude nord, et entre le 131e et le 133e degré de longitude ouest (méridien de Greenwich), la dite ligne remontera au nord le long de la passe dite Portland Chanel, jusqu'au point de la terre ferme où elle atteint le 56e degré de latitude nord; de ce dernier point de ligne de démarcation suivra la

portion of the Alaska-Canada boundary was precisely defined; it followed the 141st meridian south to Mount St. Elias. From Mount St. Elias to the southernmost tip of Prince of Wales Island, however, it was quite another matter. Using Vancouver's maps as a guide, the Russian and British negotiators stipulated in Article Three that the line of demarcation on the Alaska panhandle should follow the crests of the chain of mountains "situées parallèlement à la côte." Unfortunately, when the boundary question was discussed half a century later, most people—though not the Canadians—agreed that no such clearly discernible chain of mountains existed, that Vancouver's marking were merely conventional markings to indicate the presence of mountains along the coast, and that there was in fact a "sea of mountains" none of which would indicate a chain or range at the coast line. That being the case, presumably the surveyors could move on to the more explicit provisions of Article Four of the Treaty of 1825. If no such

---

crête des montagnes situées parallèlement à la côte, jusqu'au point d'intersection du 141e degré de longitude ouest (même méridien): et, finalement, du dit point d'intersection, la même ligne méridienne du 141e degré formera, dans son prolongement jusqu' à la Mer Glaciale, la limite entre les possessions Russes et Britanniques sur la Continent de l'Amérique Nord-Ouest.

IV Il est entendu, par rapport à la ligne de démarcation déterminée dans l'article précédent:

1. Que l'île dite Prince of Wales appartiendra tout entière à la Russie.

2. Que partout où la crête des montagnes qui s'étendent dans une direction parallèle à la côte depuis le 56e degré de latitude nord au point d'intersection du 141e degré de longitude ouest, se trouverait à la distance de plus de 10 lieues marines de l'ocean, la limite entre les possessions britanniques et la lisière de côte mentionnée ci-dessus comme devant appartenir à la Russie, sera formée par une ligne parallèle aux sinuosités de la côte, et qui ne pourra jamais en être éloignée que de 10 lieues marines. Details of the Treaty of 1825 may be found in Tansill, *Canadian-American Relations,* pp. 121-27; J. S. Galbraith, *The Hudson's Bay Company As An Imperial Factor,* Berkeley, 1957, pp. 118-32; Memorandum by John Anderson, March 4, 1898: CO42/756.

chain existed, the line "sera formée par une ligne parallèle aux sinuosités de la côte, et qui ne pourra jamais en être éloignée que de 10 lieues marines."

Yet this posed a further problem. The Alaskan panhandle is deeply indented with fiords or inlets, such as the Lynn Canal which is approximately one hundred miles long. In determining the lisière would the surveyors measure the ten marine league distance from the heads of such inlets or across their mouths? The question was, of course, of immense importance. If the line were measured from the heads of the inlets the United States would have an unbroken lisière along the length of the panhandle. But if the line were measured across the mouths of the inlets (few of which were more than six miles wide and hence could be considered "territorial waters") then the heads of some important inlets such as Lynn Canal would be in Canadian territory and give the Canadians egress to the sea from the Yukon territory. Correspondingly, the American-owned Alaska panhandle would be a series of discontinuous promontories on the edge of the coast.

The extreme southern limit of the boundary was also believed to be open to argument. Here, from the southern tip of Prince of Wales Island, "la dite ligne remontera au nord le long de la passe dite Portland Chanel, jusqu'au point de la terre ferme où elle atteint le 56e degré de latitude nord." Portland Channel, however, was almost directly east of the southern tip of Prince of Wales Island and the line could not, then, immediately ascend to the north but must travel easterly and then travel in a northeasterly direction up the Portland Channel until it struck land. From there it presumably continued in a northeasterly direction until it touched the 56th parallel. But, if the words "Portland Chanel" were omitted from the stipulations of Article Three, it could be argued that the line would immediately ascend to the north through the Duke of Clarence Strait and touch at the 56th parallel. This argument, sanctioned by the British Columbia Government, was presented by Judge J. H. Gray to the Canadian Government in 1884. Gray based the argument on what he believed to be an "interpolation" in later editions of the Treaty of the words "Portland Chanel." He contended that these words, which did indeed appear to conflict with "la dite ligne remontera au nord," were not in the original document. Unfortunately for Gray, the basis of his argument was absolutely without foundation for the words "Portland Chanel" were, in fact, in the original Treaty. Oddly enough, however, this did not stop the Canadian Government from adopting Gray's untenable argument at a later date.

Greater knowledge of the topography of the Alaska panhandle, further exploration of the Alaskan seacoast, and increasing interest in possession of land along the Northwest coast of the North American continent all contributed to the confusion which surrounded the supposedly simple instructions for the demarcation of the Alaskan Boundary as set down in Articles Three and Four of the Treaty of 1825. By the 1880's it was becoming increasingly clear to both Canadians and Americans that the Treaty of 1825 was not, in itself, an adequate instrument for determining the boundary. It was also quite clear that the longer delimitation was postponed, the more difficult it would be to reach any agreement. With these thoughts in mind, Doctor W. H. Dall of the United States Coast and Geodetic Survey, sought to renew discussion of the Alaskan Boundary question in 1884.

ii

Dall wrote to Doctor G. M. Dawson, the director of the Geological Survey of Canada, suggesting that the boundary question "be stirred up. . . . The language of the Treaty of 1825 is so indefinite that were the region included for any cause to become of evident value, or if any serious international question to arise regarding jurisdiction, there would be no means of settling it by the Treaty." He referred to the lack of a natural boundary and the absence of a chain of mountains parallel to the coast. That being the case, the United States would undoubtedly wish to "fall back on the 'line parallel to the windings of the coast and which shall never exceed the distance of ten marine leagues therefrom'" as set forth in Article Four. Dall was firmly convinced that it would be "impracticable to trace any such winding line over that 'sea of mountains.'" He therefore recommended that a Canadian-American committee of geographers be established, that a survey of the disputed territory be made, and a new treaty "stating determinable boundaries" be drawn. The letter was referred to Sir John Macdonald by the Minister of the Interior, Sir David Macpherson. Macdonald, in turn, passed the letter on to Tupper in London with instructions that the High Commissioner should collect all the relevant documents on the problem. But there the matter lay dormant and Dall never did receive a reply to his letter.[4]

Apparently, however, the Cleveland Administration was anxious to find a solution to the boundary question. The President called for an immediate settlement of the boundary in his first message to Congress on 8 December 1885. A few days before, Secretary of State Bayard had written to Minister Phelps in London about the "urgent necessity" of a settlement and of the "uncertain if not impossible location" of the line under the terms of the Treaty of 1825. Bayard said the time had come to fix "some boundary line capable of survey at a reasonable cost, yet so precisely and practically described that in case of need any given point thereon may be readily determined." After preliminary inquiries Phelps proposed to Lord Salisbury a joint high commission to determine the boundary. If this could not be done, the commission might report to the respective Governments on the "facts, data, and recommendations" concerning the matter. The proposal was

[4] Dall to Dawson, April 24, 1884, enclosure in High Commissioner to Colonial Office, February 3, 1886: CO42/786.

passed on to Lord Lansdowne for the consideration of the Canadian Government.[5]

Macdonald and Lansdowne studied the American proposal carefully. Lansdowne doubted "the expediency of allowing such a commission to actually determine the international frontier" and suggested that its functions be limited to exploration and the recommendation of a new line. The commission should ascertain "the extent of which the terms of the treaty [of 1825] are applicable" to the boundary line and, where the configuration of the country made this impossible, it should determine "the best means of carrying out the spirit and intention of the treaty." On 9 March, the Governor-General wired home that Canada "agrees in principle to preliminary survey by Commission." A week later, after further discussion with the Prime Minister, Lansdowne wrote a despatch to the Colonial Office explaining Canada's view of the Phelps' proposal. The Canadian Government could not accept the American Minister's proposal outright. Rather, Canada desired "a preliminary reconnaissance conducted on the spot," preferably by a mixed Canadian-American party, to discover "that precise information as to the geographical configuration of the country which is now wanting." A formal commission, without such information, would simply be "an inviation . . . to dispute over every inch of ground." Finally, if the United States should accept the Canadian proposal, the main object of the preliminary study should be to find "a frontier according with the spirit, if not with the letter, of the Convention of 1825." [6]

Three days later the Prime Minister explained the reasons

[5] Cited, Tansill, *Canadian-American Relations,* Bayard to Phelps, November 20, 1885, pp. 141-42; Macdonald Papers, 1, Lansdowne to Macdonald, February 23, 1886.

[6] Macdonald Papers, 1, Lansdowne to Macdonald, February 23 and 26, 1886; 526, Macdonald to Lansdowne, March 9, 1886; Governor-General to Colonial Office, March 16, 1886: CO42/784.

for the Canadian stand in a letter to Sir Charles Tupper. Macdonald was frankly skeptical of the whole proposal. Sir Lionel Sackville West, British Minister in Washington, said "the Americans are not sincere at all in the matter and that most likely it will end in a fizzle as it did once before." Therefore, Canada having shown her readiness to join a preliminary commission, "our policy . . . is to lie upon our oars" until Congress responds by sanctioning a commission and appropriating expenses for it. Macdonald reminded Tupper that this was not simply a question that could be settled by a topographical survey. The interpretation of the clauses of the Treaty of 1825 was certainly open to question. And the Americans were pressing for a conventional line "which would have the effect of our surrendering a country believed to be valuable for minerals to which we have a fair right." Then, too, as he had told Lansdowne, "I should like to try to secure an ocean port for Canada along that coast." All in all "British America has suffered so much in all negotiations with the United States that we must take great care not to be cheated again." In the end, the proposal of a joint preliminary reconnaissance was not agreed upon. Bayard was quite convinced that the preliminary studies could be done independently, though "some form of joint determination" would have to be applied to the final settlement of the boundary.[7]

The Canadian Government did not, however, entirely rest upon its oars. In cooperation with the British Government, Colonel D. R. Cameron, who had been associated with the boundary question since 1873, was asked to study the problem. In April Cameron submitted a preliminary report on his work to the Colonial Office. His report stressed that the heart of the boundary problem lay in the interpretation of the Treaty of 1825. From his study he drew a number of im-

[7] *ibid.*, 526, Macdonald to Tupper, March 19, 1886; Lansdowne Papers, Macdonald to Lansdowne, March 15, 1886; Tansill, *Canadian-American Relations*, p. 146.

portant conclusions. While dismissing Judge Gray's argument about Portland Channel, Cameron did note that there was a dispute about Portland Channel and concluded that "Portland Chanel" of the Treaty of 1825 referred to the main northerly channel of the Portland Canal and not, as the United States contended, to the southern channel called Observatory Inlet. He also believed that the negotiators of the Treaty of 1825 did not have "any belief that a continuous mountain ridge generally parallel to the coast would be found." This, of course, meant that the boundary would have to be determined by a ten marine league line from the windings of the coast. On this point he contended that the deep narrow inlets could not be considered as part of the "windings of the coast" because these inlets were less than six miles wide and hence territorial waters and not part of the ocean or coast from which the line was to be measured. Cameron thus believed that the heads of inlets more than ten marine leagues deep, such as Lynn Canal, were within Canadian territory.[8]

All the same, when Cameron submitted his final report to the Colonial Office in October 1886, he clearly recognized the difficulty and expense of determining the disputed boundary between Portland Channel and Mount St. Elias. Further, Cameron firmly believed that it was necessary that all of Portland Canal, i.e. Observatory Inlet and the main northern channel, should belong to Canada. "The inlet," he said, "is nearer to Japan and China than the present railway terminus, and . . . at no distant date one may reasonably expect this remarkable waterway to become the channel of a very large volume of trade." And because of the dispute over the boundary, Cameron recommended that the whole matter be settled simply by having the United States cede the coastal strip to Canada in return for a money payment. He argued

[8] Tupper Papers, 6, Cameron to Colonial Office, October 3, 1887; Gibson, "The Alaskan Boundary Dispute," pp. 100-102.

that each Government would have to spend £250,000 for fixing the boundary. If the British Government offered the
United States £100,000 for the panhandle, then the Americans
would have a gain of £350,000 and the boundary problem
would be solved. Sir Robert Herbert considered this suggestion "a very sensible and reasonable one" but "with the
present feeling of exasperation against Canada in regard to
the Fisheries, we can hardly expect the U.S. to be reasonable—
much less liberal." [9]

By 1887 the Alaskan boundary had been relegated by both
the Canadian and American Governments to a position of
minor consideration among the many problems facing the
Joint High Commission of 1887-1888. Yet there was general
agreement that the problem should be considered by the
Commission. Chamberlain wrote to Bayard on 17 December
1887 that "any demarcation of the boundary in accordance
with the terms of the old treaty will be a very difficult and
expensive business, and I sincerely hope that we may agree on
some easier and more reasonable method." Chamberlain told
Lord Salisbury that Bayard "admitted the practical impossi-
bility of having a line to follow the sinuosities of the coast
and the crests of mountains and he received with some approval a suggestion that we should consider a conventional
Line—on the give and take principle—which might lease to
Canada the whole or some part of the strip of Coast facing
British Columbia in return for a corresponding extent of
territory left to the United States by advancing their boundary
to the East. Sir John Macdonald views this suggestion with
approval and I trust something may come of it." [10]

[9] Macdonald Papers, 1, Cameron to Colonial Office, October 29,
1886; Minute by Herbert on Foreign Office to Colonial Office, January
11, 1887: CO42/793.
[10] Cited, Tansill, *Canadian-American Relations,* Chamberlain to
Bayard, December 17, 1887, p. 150; Chamberlain Papers, Chamberlain
to Salisbury, December 22, 1887. See also Chamberlain to Salisbury,

At the meeting of the Joint High Commission on 9 January 1888, Chamberlain brought up the subject of the boundary and suggested that meetings between Doctors Dall and Dawson be held so that the two experts might decide on some recommendations to put before the Commission. Chamberlain again raised the question at the meeting of 23 January and Bayard replied that "it did seem desirable that the details should be considered by experts." He stipulated only that any final agreement on the boundary question by the Joint High Commission would have to be the subject of a separate treaty from the North Atlantic Fisheries agreement. One week later Macdonald wrote to Tupper that Dawson had left for Washington. The Prime Minister was pleased to note that the Alaska boundary question would not be included in the Fisheries Treaty with which there was "trouble enough" already. Further, Macdonald thought that British Columbia should be represented at the boundary talks as "that Province is principally and vitally interested in the Question" and "geographically speaking, there is a good deal to be said for the B.C. contention" that the boundary runs north from Prince of Wales Island along the Duke of Clarence Strait rather than east to Portland Channel.[11]

Dawson arrived in Washington prepared for his task. For more than a month he had been advising General Cameron on the Alaska boundary problem. Apparently the latter had been having private discussions with Dall whom, Dawson warned, "you may expect to find . . . extremely patriotic from a U.S. point of view. . . . With others in the U.S. he seems rather to consider it a piece of impudence on our part

January 5, 1888; Macdonald Papers, 87, Lansdowne to Macdonald, December 23, 1887 enclosing Chamberlain's memo of his conversations with Bayard. Salisbury "noted with satisfaction the proposals for dealing with the Alaska Boundary question."

[11] Macdonald Papers, 178, Commission Proceedings, January 9 and 23, 1888; 527, Macdonald to Tupper, January 30, 1888.

to possess any coast line on the Pacific." He further warned of the "unfortunate delimitation of the boundary of the Alaska Coast strip on both English and Canadian official maps" which generally supported the American contentions regarding the heads of inlets and the position of the boundary at Portland Channel. Regarding the latter, Dawson found on his arrival in Washington that he did not agree with some of his political colleagues. Tupper reported to Macdonald that at a meeting with Thompson, Foster, Cameron, and himself, Dawson contended that the line should run northerly from Prince of Wales Island through the Duke of Clarence Strait to the 56th parallel rather than easterly and through Portland Channel. Dawson was not alone in this opinion for Foster thought this position, stubbornly held by the British Columbia Government, was arguable and might bring advantageous results. And a few days later Macdonald wrote from Ottawa warning that "great care must be taken by you at Washington not to create a feeling in B.C. that you have sacrificed them for the sake of making things pleasant with the U. States." "Looking only at the language of the Treaty itself and the maps," he said, "it seems to me that were it not for the words 'called the Portland Channel,' B.C. makes out a strong case." But at the meeting on 2 February, Thompson's view, shared by Tupper, that the British Columbia position was "untenable" prevailed.[12]

When Dawson found that he could make even less headway with Dall, the experts' meetings broke up without furnishing substantial recommendations to the Joint High Commission. Dawson held that the only line of mountains consistent with the Treaty of 1825 in the Alaska panhandle was that of "the summits of mountains [which] are as a matter of fact found to be everywhere visible from the coast, & are probably at an

[12] Tupper Papers, 9, Dawson to Cameron, January 8 and 17, 1888; Macdonald Papers, 527, Macdonald to Tupper, February 6, 1888; 177, Tupper to Macdonald, February 2, 1888.

average distance of considerably less than five miles from it."
Dall and Dawson had both used Vancouver's Atlas for reference, but in contrast to the Canadian, Dall believed the Atlas
did not contain "any continuous line of mountains represented as arising everywhere immediately from the coast and
which borders on the sea. The sea-shore forms the edge of
an area conventionally indicated as mountainous, which is a
different thing." In addition, Dall disagreed with Dawson's
stand that the ten marine league line "has to be drawn without
reference to inlets." Dawson believed that "all the waters
within the mouths of the inlets are as much territorial waters,
according to a universally admitted international law, as
those of a fresh water lake or stream would be under analo-
gous circumstances." Ironically, the only point the two experts could agree upon was the necessity of an immediate
settlement of the boundary dispute. And with this in mind,
at the Joint High Commission meeting of 8 February, Secretary of State Bayard proposed that each Government should
make topographical surveys of the land in dispute "before
acting by way of Convention or otherwise." Two years of
serious consideration of the Alaska Boundary question had
left the Canadian and American Governments exactly where
they started. Bayard's proposal of February 1888 was identical
to the Macdonald-Lansdowne proposal of March 1886.[13]

iii

Between the conclusion of the meetings of the Joint High
Commission of 1887-1888 and the 1891 election the Canadian
Government took no practical action toward a solution of the
Alaska boundary problem. In October 1888, when it was
learned that the United States was going to start preliminary
surveys in the area around Portland Channel, Lord Stanley

[13] *ibid.*, Dawson to Tupper, February 7, 1888; Macdonald Papers,
178, Commission Proceedings, February 8, 1888; Gibson, "The Alaskan
Boundary Dispute," p. 111.

urged that "the Foreign Office be moved to remonstrate with the United States Government against its being supposed that the action of such Government in making the survey in question may be considered as a taking of possession or of fixing of boundaries between the two countries." On 6 December Edward Phelps requested of Lord Salisbury that "a surveying party may be sent out . . . to join that of the U.S. Govt. & to participate with it in the examination & survey, in such a manner as to reach, if possible, a joint & concurrent conclusion in respect to the facts material to be determined." Though the Colonial Office immediately sent this proposal to the Canadian Government, the latter did not respond until two years later in December 1890. Again, in July 1889, Macdonald asked Thompson's opinion about the efficacy of approaching the United States Government with a view to settling outstanding questions in Canadian-American relations. Thompson replied in the affirmative: "All the questions which affect our relations with the United States" ought to be discussed. Significantly, there was no mention of the Alaska boundary as one of "all the questions." Later, in December 1890, when under the pressure of the Bond-Blaine negotiations the Canadian Government proposed a joint high commission to settle all outstanding disputes, the Alaska boundary was given last place among those problems which the Canadian Government deemed necessary of solution.[14]

Finally, after four years of inactivity, the Canadians again turned their attention to the Alaska boundary question in the

[14] Stanley to Knutsford, October 8, 1888: CO42/796; Phelps to Salisbury, in Foreign Office to Colonial Office, December 13, 1888: CO42/799; Minute by Anderson on Foreign Office to Colonial Office, February 18, 1890: CO42/805; Stanley to Knutsford, December 13, 1890: CO42/803; Thompson Papers, 89, Macdonald to Thompson, July 4, 1889; 239, Thompson to Macdonald, July 11, 1889; Macdonald Papers, 90, Stanley to Knutsford, December 13, 1890.

spring of 1892. The occasion was the conversations between Secretary of State Blaine and Canadian Ministers Thompson, Foster, and Bowell. Though the talks were intended to and did revolve around the topic of reciprocity, the boundary question was prominent among the other matters discussed. At the first meeting, on 10 February, Sir John Thompson reminded Blaine of the various points of dispute regarding both the interpretation of the Treaty of 1825 and the method to be used in delimiting the boundary. The Secretary of State replied that "there seemed to be no reason why a commission should not at once be appointed to dispose of these questions" and asked the Canadians to hand in a proposal.[15]

Certainly the boundary question was in need of quick settlement. In fact, it appeared that Canadian interests might be heavily sacrificed by any further delay. Doctor Dawson, who had accompanied the Canadian Ministers to Washington and who had had conversations there with Professor Mendenhall, Superintendent of the United States Coast and Geodetic Survey, informed Thompson that "the U.S. has been proceeding with an alleged survey of the boundary of the Coast Strip. This survey is to be pushed next summer by several increased parties." Dawson said that the American surveyors were working up each river valley and planting a monument at a distance of thirty miles from tide water. Because they believed that no coastal chain of mountains existed, they were working on the assumption that the thirty-mile limiting clause was the only operative one in the Treaty of 1825. The danger was clear: "This method assures the greatest *possible* extension of the width of the U.S. Coast Strip to our proportionate loss, & though such surveys cannot be considered as in any way binding, they are evidently intended to be

[15] Thompson Papers, 254, Papers relating to Washington Conference, 1892 . . . precis of discussions and proposals made and agreed to, pp. 431½-89. See also, Canada, Parliament, *Sessional Papers,* 1893, no. 52.

advanced as a sort of prescriptive claim to territory which, it will probably be stated, we never gave any attention to." [16]

On 12 February, Thompson put before Blaine "quite informally" a two-fold proposal. He suggested "a reference to some impartial authority" who should decide on the "true boundary," due regard being paid to treaties relating to it and to arguments and testimony which either government may produce. Secondly a commission of four experts should be appointed to report "as to the best and most convenient mode of delimiting the boundary as established by the award." Alternatively the experts might recommend "the adoption of a conventional boundary" if this were more convenient and did not prejudice the interests of either country. [17]

There is no detailed record of Blaine's reaction to this proposal. Thompson recorded only that after the Canadians had made it, "the various contentions relating to the boundary were then explained." But it is clear that the Secretary of State thought the Canadian plan too elaborate and the "existing difference of views was not of such a character as to call for more than a joint survey and report which would enable the two Governments to agree upon the fixation of the boundary." Blaine therefore proposed that a joint survey be established to

[16] *ibid.*, 148, memorandum by Dr. Dawson, February 12, 1892. It should be remembered that the American surveys from "tide water" were particularly dangerous to Canadian interests. In the case of Lynn Canal, for example, it would mean that the Americans would fix the boundary at least thirty miles inland from the head of the canal and not from the point where the canal met the ocean. The difference, of course, would be some 80 to 100 miles between what the Canadians and the Americans considered the proper boundary and, also, the American survey would deprive the Canadians of access to or control of the head waters of the Canal and hence of an outlet to the sea via the Lynn Canal.

[17] *ibid.*, 254, Papers relating to the Washington Conference, 1892. See also Abbott Papers, 3, Thompson to Abbott, February 10, 1892, draft reply to Thompson to Abbott of February 10, 1892, Abbott to Thompson, February 11, 1892.

spend two years preparing a report of the terrain in question. When that report was received then the Governments might "permanently establish the boundary line in question . . . in accordance with the spirit and intent of the existing treaties in regard to it." As Thompson recorded, "after some explanation and discussion," the American counterproposal was accepted.[18]

It could be argued that the Canadian Government had put forward its proposal to submit the boundary question to arbitration, particularly on the interpretation of the Treaty of 1825, only to drop it within three days. But, in fact, submission of the question of interpretation of the Treaty to an impartial authority became a fixed part of Canada's policy on the boundary question. When the survey agreed to in 1892 was completed, Canada again quickly pressed for the matter being brought to arbitration. The difference was one of approach, not of policy. The Abbott Government asked for arbitration before the joint survey in order to guide the survey in its work. Later, the Laurier Government wished to use the findings of the joint survey as a guide to arbitration. In either case, the Canadian Government clearly recognized that the key to settlement of the dispute lay in the interpretation of the Treaty of 1825 and that only some impartial authority could be entrusted with the problem of deciding the correct interpretation of the Treaty.

In any case, the treaty ratifications on the joint survey agreement were exchanged in August 1892 and in September the United States appointed its commissioner, Professor Mendenhall. In March 1893, W. F. King was appointed as Canadian commissioner and the first serious cooperative attempt to settle the boundary problem began. The task of gathering the pertinent facts on the topography in the region of the Alaska boundary was completed in 1895 and on 31 Decem-

[18] *ibid.*, cited, Tansill, *Canadian-American Relations*, p. 159.

ber the Canadian and American commissioners presented a joint report embodying their findings. This report was tabled in the Canadian House of Commons early in the session of 1898. Meanwhile, the circumstances surrounding the boundary question had been radically changed.

iv

By 1896 abundant nature and inquisitive man had conspired to complicate the Alaskan boundary question and force upon the Canadian and American Governments the necessity of a rapid solution. Vast quantities of gold were discovered in or near the disputed territory and resulted in the influx of huge numbers of miners in the second great North American gold rush. In November 1896, Inspector Constantine reported that 17,647 ounces of gold worth some $300,000 had been taken out of the Yukon District of the Dominion during the year. This was only "a slight increase on last year." On the other hand a rich discovery of coarse gold had been made on Bonanza Creek in August and "new creeks are being found daily, all prospecting well." In these circumstances the two Governments turned to the complication to the boundary dispute first and temporarily ignored the dispute itself.[19]

In July 1897, Laurier, who was in London attending the Colonial Conference, was notified by his colleague, Secretary of State R. W. Scott, of "the fabulous quantities of gold that are being found . . . $50 worth of the pure yellow metal to a pan has not been an uncommon take. . . . There is, as you can already understand, a tremendous rush going into that country, and it becomes necessary to take prompt action to protect Canadian interests." Scott had reported earlier that it was thought that "Americans have taken out of the creeks flowing into the Yukon, probably a million dollars, Canada

[19] Laurier Papers, 26, Report by Inspector Constantine, November 20, 1896.

receiving no benefit whatever." The Cabinet had therefore decided to restrict mining licenses to Canadian residents and to reserve a large royalty on all gold discoveries. But, as Scott said, "we will . . . have to double the police force in that region, if we are to get any benefit in either Customs or royalty from the great gold find." Accordingly, after discussing the matter with Paterson and Sifton, it was decided that "the Police force in the Yukon territory and its approaches must be increased to 100, that winter communication from the head of Lynn Inlet must be opened and maintained in order that we may get advices of what is transpiring in the interior." The police officers were sent with the cooperation of the United States Government, and in September 1897, the United States Government agreed "without prejudice to boundary or other claims of either country" to the construction of telegraph communication from the head of Lynn Canal into Canadian territory in the Yukon district. And on 24 July the *Victoria Daily Colonist* noted with pleasure that customs officers were to be sent to the White Pass and Chilkoot Pass above Lynn Canal. "Hereafter," said the *Colonist,* "there will be an end to the wholesale entry of goods from the United States into the Canadian Yukon without paying duty, and British Columbia will secure its share of the trade." [20]

This was all routine, the necessary activity of a Government responsible for newly opened territory. Not so routine, and of much greater interest to Canadians, was the matter of trade. Miners needed a considerable amount of supplies before they started their hazardous trip into the Yukon, and, once there, they needed even more to keep them alive. The dif-

[20] Public Archives of Canada, Scott Papers, 4, Scott to Laurier, July 23, 1897; Laurier Papers, 49, Scott to Laurier, July 20, 1897; Sifton Papers, 291, Sifton to Templeman, January 5, 1897 [1898]; Adam to Salisbury in Foreign Office to Colonial Office, September 16, 1897 and Aberdeen to Adam in Foreign Office to Colonial Office, August 26, 1897: CO42/853; *Victoria Daily Colonist,* July 24, 1897.

ficulty, as far as Canadians were concerned, was that Americans were capturing nearly all this valuable and growing trade. As early as January 1897, Clifford Sifton expressed his concern to a friend. "We suffer from one end of Canada to the other from the fact that our trade is drawn off through American channels and the bulk of the business goes to the people on the other side of the line instead of to our own people." Sifton did not favor "retaliatory legislation" but "I do favour a continued and persistent effort to stop these leaks and get the benefit of our own natural resources." In part, this problem could be solved by the sending of Customs officers to the border of the Yukon district. A British Columbia correspondent told Sir Richard Cartwright that nearly all the miners' supplies and outfits were being purchased in Seattle or Juneau and then taken into Canadian territory without paying any duty. "I need scarcely tell you that this constitutes a gross injustice to the Mercantile classes of our own coast cities, who, if the collection of duties at the passes . . . were enforced, would have the bulk of the trade in their own hands. Otherwise, they cannot successfully compete with the Americans." After the Customs Officers had been sent to the passes at the head of Lynn Canal, Sifton was able to write that "enormous purchases of goods are taking place in Canada at the present time." [21]

But securing the Yukon trade for Canadian interests also rested upon the sufferance of the American Government. Miners who purchased Canadian supplies and outfits and wished to take them into the Canadian Yukon had to pass their goods through American territory either at Dyea or Skagway on the Lynn Canal route or at St. Michaels on the Yukon River route. There, of course, the goods were subject to American customs duties. The miners could transport their

[21] Sifton Papers, 291, Sifton to Bodwell, January 5, 1897, Sifton to Templeman, January 5, 1898; Laurier Papers, 49, T. R. McInnes to Cartwright, July 21, 1897.

goods in bond through the American territory, but, if they did so, they had to pay unreasonably high inspection fees to the American Customs officers. It was only natural, then, that an intense anti-American reaction arose among the Canadian west-coast politicians and businessmen. But, as Sifton explained to William Templeman of Victoria, "the necessity of passing through American territory made it absolutely essential that we should preserve the most friendly possible relations with the United States." British Columbia interests were advising retaliation in kind by Canadian officials or even the closing off by Canadian Police of the White and Chilkoot Passes as routes into the Yukon. Sifton could not agree. In another letter to Templeman he pointed out that "the remedy which suggests itself as the most obvious is not always the most effective." "More than that," he wisely added, "I think it would imperil the whole business which it is desired to secure; if it were given out to the world that strained relations existed between the United States and Canada on the borders of the Yukon District, and that a conflict might break out at any moment, the general movement to the Yukon District during the coming season would in all human probability be very greatly checked, if not altogether destroyed. It would mean the loss of millions of dollars to the Canadian people." [22]

But Sifton's caution did not mean inactivity on his part. In the last week of December 1897, the Minister of the Interior unofficially traveled to Washington to protest against the restrictive practices of American Customs officials at Dyea and Skagway. He told Secretary of the Treasury Gage that "Canadians crossing the strip of territory at Dyea or Skagway have their choice of paying the duty or paying inspector's fees and expenses which latter fees and expenses generally amount to more than the duty would be upon a small outfit. It had, in fact, been found impracticable in such cases to do anything

[22] Sifton Papers, Sifton to Templeman, January 5 and 26, 1898.

except pay the duty, and the bonding privilege was, therefore, valueless." The Americans apparently accepted the Canadian representations in a cooperative spirit and it was agreed that the inspection fees would be reduced or abolished so that the transport of Canadian miners' supplies in bond across American territory would become practical. But the Treasury Department delayed, much to Sifton's annoyance, in issuing appropriate instructions to the Customs officials in Alaska. And by February 1898, the question of the bonding privilege had been complicated by the monopoly railway clause in the Canadian Yukon Bill. The Bill provided for the building of an "all-Canadian" railway from the Stikine River to Teslin Lake in the Canadian Yukon. In the contract with the railway builders, for which the Bill sought approval, was a monopoly clause by which the Canadian Government agreed not to allow other railways to be built into the Canadian Yukon for a period of five years.[23]

The American Government, which was as interested in railway communication with the Yukon through Lynn Canal as was Canada via the Stikine River, had its own Alaska Railway Bill (Public Bill No. 95) pending in the United States Senate. In order to get a railway from Lynn Canal into the American Yukon, the line would have to pass through the Canadian Yukon District. The Americans thus considered the monopoly clause in the Canadian Yukon Bill as a distinctly retaliatory measure because it obviously negated any American attempt to build a railway. Clause 13 of the

[23] *ibid.,* Sifton to Lyman J. Gage, January 27, 1898. Clause 4 of the Canadian Yukon Bill read: "For five years from the first of September, 1898, no line of railway shall be authorized by Parliament to be constructed from Lynn Canal or thereabouts or from any point at or near the international boundary between Canada and Alaska into the Yukon District, and for five years from said date no aid in land or money shall be granted to any person or company other than the contractors and the contractors' company to assist in building any such railway." *Official Report of Debates,* February 15, 1898, p. 647.

American Bill therefore became loaded with various provisions which sought to deny the Canadian bonding privileges in American territory at the Lynn Canal and elsewhere. At various points in the formation of the American Bill, the Canadians were to be denied bonding privileges unless they granted 1,000 pounds of outfit duty-free admittance to each American citizen going into the Canadian Yukon, unless the "unequal restrictions as to the issuance of miner's licences" be removed, and unless (Senator William Frye's pet provision) Canada grant the privilege of free bonding of American-caught fish across Canadian territory on the North Atlantic Coast.[24]

When Sir Julian Pauncefote, on instructions from Lord Salisbury, confidentially protested against these coercive tactics to Senator Hansborough, chairman of the committee in charge of the Bill, the Senator replied that "all that Congress really requires is that Canada should abandon policy of railway monopoly, and to secure liberty to connect Canadian territory with Alaskan Railways." When the Canadian Senate killed the Canadian Yukon Bill on 30 March 1898, Edward Wingfield noted on a despatch from Aberdeen to Chamberlain that the Canadian Senate's action "may make the U.S. Senate disposed to modify the Alaska Railway Bill." That was, in fact, what happened. When the American Bill was approved on 14 May 1898, clause 13 provided for reciprocal Canadian and American mining rights by their respective citizens in the territory of the other and clause 14 provided for reciprocal bonding and transshipment privileges.[25]

[24] Laurier Papers, 68, Farrer to Boudreau, March 8, 9, and 10, 1898; 69, Van Horne to Sifton, March 18, 1898; 71, Farrer to Boudreau, March 26, 1898; 75, copy of U.S. Public Bill #95 approved May 14, 1898.

[25] Chamberlain to Aberdeen in Foreign Office to Colonial Office, April 1, 1898: CO42/862; Minute by Wingfield on Aberdeen to Chamberlain, April 10, 1898: CO42/857; Laurier Papers, 75, copy of U.S. Public Bill #95 approved May 14, 1898.

The discussion about securing equitable bonding privileges for Canadian goods to pass over American territory pointed to the heart of the problem of securing for Canada a share of the Yukon trade. The simple fact was that the United States controlled all the access routes to and from the Yukon, as well as all the transport facilities using these routes. Scott told Laurier in July 1897, that "heretofore the American boats have monopolized the traffic and the goods have been bought in American ports." This, more than the lack of Canadian Customs officials at the White and Chilkoot Passes, and more than the bonding difficulties, accounted for the fact that in early 1898 some 90 per cent of all the Yukon trade was in American hands. By July 1897, the Pacific Navigation Company of Victoria had started to put Canadian transportation into competition with American steamers. But, as the boats had to land at Dyea or Skagway, thus encountering the bonding difficulties, this was not an adequate solution of the problem.[26]

Certainly more ambitious measures were needed. In the summer of 1897 great pressure was being put on the Canadian Government by the Toronto and Montreal press to build a wagon road into the Yukon district. In Cabinet discussions Sifton urged the building of a railway, probably via the Lynn Canal, while A. G. Blair, Minister of Railways and Canals, urged the immediate construction of a wagon road from the head of the Lynn Canal. But there was an obvious flaw in both plans, just as there was in the efforts of the Pacific Navigation Company. Either the railway or wagon road would begin at Dyea or Skagway which, Sifton later conceded in the House of Commons, "the United States have had undisputed possession of . . . for some time past." At the time the Minister of the Interior told Hewitt Bostock, British Columbia M.P., that "the fact which we have to con-

[26] Scott Papers, 4, Scott to Laurier, July 23, 1897; C. S. Campbell, *Anglo-American Understanding, 1898-1903*, Baltimore, 1957, p. 71.

sider is that the head of Lynn Canal has been in the possession of the Americans for many years and while we do not admit that they are entitled to it, it is contrary to the well-known rule in cases of dispute to attempt to enforce an entrance. That would mean a declaration of war & exclusion from the Yukon." On the other hand, of what use would be a Canadian wagon road or railway based in American-held territory and subject to American control? Bostock replied that "the best solution . . . is to open up other routes in our own territory as quickly as possible. There will I think be found to be several good overland routes into the Yukon which will be much better for Canada than going through American territory." In November 1897, Sifton went to the Yukon with a number of technicians in order to find such a route.[27]

Late in January Sifton wrote that "a contract has been made for the opening up of a road by way of the Stikine River, and the construction of a railway from the river to Teslin Lake in sufficient time to make next Winter's provision supply secure, thus furnishing a Canadian route where the embarrassments which have taken place at Dyea and Skagway will be unknown." Indeed, the prospects looked bright for the "Canadian route." The passes at the head of Lynn Canal were so difficult to cross with supplies that Sifton believed a "well directed effort will result in the whole trade going up the Stikine River." He expected the Americans would "harrass our people on the Stikine as well, but there we have the right of free navigation and stand on firm ground." Mackenzie and Mann were to be the builders of the railway and they had promised to build a wagon road within six weeks and to open the 150-mile railway by 1

[27] Sifton Papers, 21, Greenshields to Sifton, July 23, 1897; 12, Blair to Sifton, July 24 and August 2, 1897; 221, Sifton to Bostock, August 3, 1897; 13, Bostock to Sifton, August 12, 1897; *Official Report of Debates*, February 11, 1898, p. 407.

September 1898. The contractors had deposited $250,000 with the Government as a guarantee. They received no cash subsidy but a land grant—alternate three- by six-mile sections—along the railway. Sifton related that he was "having a tremendous amount of troubles with Customs officials in Alaska, but when all the trade switches on the Canadian route Canadians will have the inside track." [28]

When Mr. A. G. Blair, Minister of Railways and Canals, introduced the Canadian Yukon Bill to give Parliamentary approval of the Mackenzie-Mann contract, he said that "an imperative reason for immediate action" was that Canadian trade in the Yukon depended upon the acceptance of the railway bill. "The importance of securing that trade and preserving it to Canada becomes a national question of the greatest interest." The Yukon trade "is ours, it is within our own borders and of right belongs to us, if, by any legitimate or proper means we can secure it for the people of our own country." Blair explained that there were five possible routes into the Yukon: from Skagway through White Pass to the Hootalingua River; from Lynn Canal through Chilkat Pass to Fort Selkirk; from Lynn Canal through Chilkat Pass to Teslin Lake; from Taku Inlet to Teslin Lake; and from Glenora, on the Stikine River, to Teslin Lake. The Canadian

[28] Sifton Papers, 291, Sifton to Templeman, January 26, 1898, Sifton to Walsh, January 26, 1898. The Rothschilds, represented by H. Maitland Kersey, had also been interested in the Stikine-Teslin Lake Railway as they were already building a sleigh road along that route and apparently had boats working on the Stikine. But on 23 January, Kersey informed Laurier that "my Syndicate cannot see their way to make an offer." Laurier Papers, 63, Kersey to Laurier, January 23, 1898. A Toronto business lawyer and agent for Mackenzie, Mr. C. E. L. Porteous, noted that Sir William Van Horne, among others, had a financial interest in the Mackenzie and Mann scheme. He recorded in his Journal that "Mackenzie agreed that he would give Mr. Ross enough Tl Stk Ry stock to give me 150 shares at 30 and G. W. Ross 100. Adjusted Van Horne's & Angus holdings." Public Archives of Canada, Porteous Papers, Journal, January 28, 1898.

Government had rejected the first four routes, principally because "in respect of them all it was necessary that they should cross a portion of territory from the sea which was claimed, or at all events, was in possession of a foreign government." George Foster quickly pointed out that in order to navigate the fifth route, the United States Customs port at Fort Wrangell, at the mouth of the Stikine, would have to be used. Blair, basing his argument on the privilege of free navigation of the Yukon, Porcupine and Stikine Rivers granted to Canada in Article 26 of the Treaty of Washington of 1871, replied that "the Stikine River, whose waters we propose to use, is a river that, under treaty with that country, we are entitled to use without being subject to any conditions." [29]

Unfortunately, Blair was not the man to present the Bill to a House of Commons full of wily Conservatives skilled in the handling of railway contracts. He found himself totally unprepared for the barrage of Opposition criticism. He did not know why public tenders were not let for the contract; he did not know the cost of the project; and he admitted that the Government had not even consulted its own law officers—much less the United States Government—on the vital question of whether transshipment at Fort Wrangell was considered part of the free navigation of the Stikine granted in the Treaty of Washington. Charles Porteous, Mackenzie's agent in Toronto, referred to the incident as "Blair's treachery . . . it never recovered from his introduction in the Commons." [30]

The blame for Blair's obviously ill-prepared presentation of the Canadian Yukon Bill had to be shared by his colleagues. Despite the fact of immediacy which Blair and other Government spokesmen emphasized over and over again, the Liberals had not presented a well-considered Bill to the House of Commons. It was not until 9 February, the day after Blair

[29] *Official Report of Debates,* February 8, 1898, pp. 191-92.

[30] *ibid.,* pp. 192-98; Porteous Papers, letterbook, 1898, Porteous to J. Ross, April 1, 1898.

introduced the Bill, that Aberdeen hurriedly wired Pauncefote to inquire of the United States Government what the regulations were for the navigation of the Stikine River. The next day Pauncefote sent back the disappointing reply that the "Treasury Department are not prepared to state that the Regulations respecting the navigation of the Porcupine and Yukon Rivers shall apply to the Stikine. The case of the Stikine was reserved in framing the Regulations, especially with reference to bonding privileges granted under them, which are considered very liberal." On 11 February Aberdeen asked Chamberlain to have Pauncefote press for an early decision regarding the bonding regulations on the Stikine. Again, it was not until 27 February that the Minister of Justice, David Mills, officially informed Laurier that in his opinion Article 26 of the Treaty of Washington allowed Canadians to transship goods from ocean to river steamers at Fort Wrangell as an "incidental" right to the free navigation of the Stikine River. Nor did the Law Officers Department inform the Foreign Office that they agreed with Mills' opinion until 23 April. Chamberlain apprised Aberdeen of this comforting fact on 13 May 1898, a month and a half after the Bill had been killed in the Senate and more than three months after its introduction in the House of Commons.[31]

Meanwhile, of course, the ever alert American Senate had used the monopoly clause in the Mackenzie-Mann contract as a reason for refusing any bonding or transshipment privileges at Fort Wrangell or elsewhere unless unreasonable concessions were given by Canada in turn. This twisting of the screw by the American Senate while the debate raged in the Canadian House of Commons made a mockery of the Liberal

[31] Laurier Papers, 65, Pauncefote to Aberdeen, February 10, 1898; Aberdeen to Chamberlain, February 11, 1898, Mills to Laurier in Aberdeen to Chamberlain, March 1, 1898: CO42/856; Law Officers to Foreign Office and Chamberlain to Aberdeen in Foreign Office to Colonial Office, May 5, 1898: CO42/862.

boasts of an "all-Canadian" route and caused further embarrassment to the harassed Government forces. The Liberals might reply, as they did, that a minor clause in the contract did provide for the future extension of the Stikine-Teslin Lake Railway southward from Glenora to Alice Inlet (an extension of Observatory Inlet) thus giving a true all-Canadian route. But the simple fact was that the extension was part of a possible future plan. The present contract called only for a railway between Glenora and Teslin Lake and was wholly dependent upon the good will of the Americans at Fort Wrangell.

As early as 17 February Porteous reported "the indications were that the Stikine Teslin Ry scheme would fail. . . . Public opinion is coming to see how much better the Edmonton route would be for the country." Laurier received resolutions from the Hamilton, Montreal and Quebec City Boards of Trade favoring an all-Canadian route via Edmonton. Laurier managed to push the Bill through the House of Commons with a reduced majority but it was thrown out by the Conservative dominated Senate on 30 March. Joseph Pope recorded in his diary that some Conservatives had told him that "if the bill passed the contractors would have given the Liberal machine such a huge rake-off as to have assured them power for 20 years. That may be so." The Canadian Yukon policy had suffered a severe—perhaps a fatal—reverse.[32]

It appeared that the Government would not back down under fire from the Senate. "I do not intend," wrote Sifton, "to give up the idea of having the railway built this summer." Support came from the Vancouver and Montreal Boards of Trade who urged the Government to build a railway from Port Simpson on Observatory Inlet to Glenora simultaneously with a railway from Glenora to Teslin Lake.

[32] Porteous Papers, letterbook, 1898, Porteous to Ross, February 17, 1898; Laurier Papers, 65, #20743, #20772; 66, #20801; Pope Papers, 116, Diary, March 30, 1898.

On 12 April J. C. McLagan of Vancouver told Laurier that the British Columbia Government was considering giving $4,000 per mile to Mackenzie and Mann to build the railway to Teslin Lake if the Dominion Government would further supplement the plan to insure an immediate start. A few days later the British Columbia M.P.'s told Laurier that they had received "strong and urgent representations from our respective constituencies as to the absolute necessity for im-

ADDING INSULT TO INJURY

THE SENATE—Now then, Mr. Taxpayer, don't stand idly leaning against that post; hustle around and find some other means of saving your Yukon trade that we cannot bring to nought!

311

mediate action being taken on the part of the Government to afford facilities for transportation to the Yukon gold fields." [33]

By late April, under this pressure, the Government was said to be considering a new railway contract with Mackenzie and Mann for a line from a Canadian port to Teslin Lake. Early in May Dobell wrote to Sifton about the new plan. Apparently there had been some disagreement in Cabinet whether the Government should submit to caucus the proposal for a railway or only a proposal for a wagon road over the same route. "I feel strongly that we ought not to abandon the railroad," Dobell told Sifton. "It can be constructed almost as quickly as a waggon road and it will be ten times as useful." By the middle of the month the details of the new plan were near completion. Mackenzie and Mann were to build a 450 mile railway from Observatory Inlet to Teslin Lake. In return, the contractors would receive either $10,000 a mile for the first 200 miles, $4,000 a mile for the last 250 miles and 10,000 acres of land per mile along the route, or $4,000 a mile for the length of the route, 6,000 acres per mile, and $80,000 a year for twenty years. Then, within a matter of days the whole project was once again dashed. On 27 May Porteous wrote:

Mackenzie left here fully convinced that the Yukon scheme as re-arranged would go through, and to make his financial arrangements therefore. On the 25th the Government backed down completely, and refused to go on. I hear the Council stood equally divided for and against, the decision remaining with Laurier, who funked. The Ontario Ministers were united against it. It has been a shockingly bungled affair. . . .

[33] Sifton Papers, 291, Sifton to Walsh, March 26, 1898; Laurier Papers, 68, Resolution, Vancouver Board of Trade, March 4, 1898; 71, Resolution, Montreal Board of Trade, March 25, 1898; 72, McLagan to Laurier, April 12, 1898; 73, British Columbia M.P.'s to Laurier, April 25, 1898.

In his secret despatch of 20 June, Aberdeen informed Chamberlain that as far as he knew nothing more would be done by the Government concerning the Yukon railway project.[34]

Nevertheless, the Glenora-Teslin Railway was the key to the successful application of the National Policy in the Yukon. Had it been completed the Canadian Yukon would have been economically tied to central Canada in the same way that the Canadian Pacific Railway a decade earlier had linked the St. Lawrence valley with the prairies and British Columbia. Trade goods manufactured in Hamilton, Toronto, and Montreal might have been shipped over the Canadian Pacific to the west coast, transported by water to Glenora and thence by another Canadian railway to market. The "all-Canadian route" envisaged by Sifton as a counter to the American trade monopoly was not simply a Canadian railway into the Yukon but rather the last link in a Canadian trade route that originated in central Canada and terminated in the wilds of the gold rush district.

Sifton and his colleagues chose the route for two reasons. First, they thought, rather naïvely, that they could rely upon the privileges granted them in the Treaty of Washington and upon the good will of the United States—despite the fact that their avowed object was to destroy the American Yukon trade. Second, and much more important in their minds, was the factor of time. The Glenora-Teslin Lake route was short and the work could be completed in one summer. A truly all-Canadian route from Edmonton or by extension from Glenora to Fort Simpson on Observatory Inlet was much longer and, considering the short northern summer, would take years to build. In the meantime the Americans would probably become so firmly entrenched in the Yukon on both sides of the undefined border that they could never be dislodged. But,

[34] Porteous Papers, letterbook, 1898, Porteous to Ross, April 29 and May 17 and 27, 1898; Sifton Papers, 42, Dobell to Sifton, May 2, 1898; Aberdeen to Chamberlain, June 20, 1898: CO42/857.

ironically, the factor of time which was so important for the accomplishment of Canada's purpose in the end proved the reason for the failure of Canada's policy.

Meanwhile, the problem of the boundary itself remained to be solved. There were a few hopeful signs of a settlement. As early as 1895 some discoveries of gold along the Yukon River near the boundary at the 141st meridian had led the Canadian Government to send some North West Mounted Policemen into the area to maintain law and order and to collect customs duties. In June the Canadian Government also asked Mr. Ogilvie to go to the area and fix the boundary along the 141st meridian. The Bowell Government "proposed to do this by themselves provided the U.S. will provisionally and without prejudice accept the line so fixed, or they offer to bear half the expense of a joint expedition to fix the line." In September the United States requested that the survey be delayed so that an appropriation might be made when Congress convened but Ogilvie had already gone to the Yukon to survey the line.[35]

In March 1896 Secretary of State Olney informed Ambassador Pauncefote that he was "not at all satisfied" that a new joint survey along the 141st meridian was necessary because "so far as the recent and existing surveys on either side have progressed, they exhibit a close coincidence of results." He therefore proposed that a new convention be drawn up under which the Canadian and United States Governments would agree on fixing certain points along the 141st meridian midway between those fixed by Ogilvie and those fixed by the United States Coast and Geodetic Survey. The fixing of these midway points would be done by "convenient joint surveys as occasion may require until the entire line shall in time be established." In October the Canadian Government decided to accept Olney's proposal and asked that the joint survey

[35] Foreign Office to Colonial Office, July 19, 1895: CO42/834; Foreign Office to Colonial Office, September 12, 1895: CO42/835.

of the midpoints start in the spring of 1897. In January 1897 the Canadian Government approved a draft convention embodying the Olney proposal and Sir Julian Pauncefote signed the convention on 31 January 1897.[36]

This pleasingly cooperative spirit was, however, not in evidence when the Canadian and United States Governments came to consider the boundary south of Mount St. Elias. Here the public statements of the Laurier Government in the spring of 1898 were, to say the least, confusing. On 11 February, in answer to a question by Sir Charles Hibbert Tupper, Sifton said "I believe one contention is that Skagway and Dyea are really in Canadian territory, but as the United States have had undisputed possession of them for some time past, we are precluded from attempting to take possession of that territory." Sifton explained to the House of Commons that the "unfortunate" fact was that none of the records of the Canadian Government showed that Canada had ever protested against possession of Dyea and Skagway by the United States. He continued that "we have taken the position that the claim of Canada to occupy the territory inside of the summit from the boundary at White Pass and Chilkat Pass is not deniable, and we cannot admit it as debatable." He finally added that this position was taken "without making any admission as to the right of the United States to the territory on the seaward side [of the summit]." [37]

When a similar point was raised by Mr. Prior on 16 February, Prime Minister Laurier also said no protest had "ever been raised by any Government against the occupation of Dyea and Skagway by the United States. . . . Although this

[36] Olney to Pauncefote in Aberdeen to Chamberlain, March 25, 1896: CO42/838; Deputy Governor Strong to Chamberlain, October 19, 1896: CO42/840; Aberdeen to Chamberlain, January 7, 12 and 23, 1897: CO42/846; Foreign Office to Colonial Office, January 28 and February 1, 1897: CO42/851.

[37] *Official Report of Debates,* February 11, 1898, pp. 407-8.

is disputed territory, it has been in the possession of the United States ever since they acquired this country from the Russian Government in 1867." And yet Laurier and Sifton both argued that the head of Lynn Canal was "disputed territory." Contemporary observers rightly viewed the two Canadian assertions as contradictory. They could not be reconciled. Or could they? Laurier thought so and informed the House of Commons that

> if the treaty [of 1825] is correctly interpreted, [Dyea] is in Canadian territory. It ought to be; but the fact is, . . . that possession is nine points of the law; and even though by the letter of the treaty, Dyea is in Canadian territory, the fact remains that from time immemorial Dyea was in possession of the Russians, and in 1867 it passed into the hands of the Americans, and it has been in their hands ever since. . . . At this moment we cannot dispute their possession, and . . . before their possession can be disputed, the question must be determined by a settlement of the questions involved in the treaty. . . .

Thus, although the Americans had possession of the Lynn Canal, the Canadians believed that if the Treaty of 1825 were correctly interpreted and the boundary drawn according to that interpretation, the head of Lynn Canal would become Canadian territory. Since January 1898, they had been pressing this point on the Colonial Office.[38]

Late in January Sifton sent a memorandum to Lord Aberdeen regarding the boundary at the head of Lynn Canal. The question was important, Sifton said, because the only access routes to the Yukon were through Dyea and Skagway. "Though asserted to be in Canadian territory," they were nevertheless held by the Americans. That being the case, the Minister of Interior believed that the summits at the White and Chilkat Passes were "the farthest inland limit which

[38] *ibid.*, February 16, 1898, pp. 619-20, March 7, 1898, p. 1277.

the United States could possibly establish. Instructions have been sent to our police and Customs officers to establish posts at these summits and collect duties there." "We learn this morning," Sifton wrote, "that American officials have lately received instructions to claim jurisdiction down to Lakes Lindeman and Bennett, and disputes have already occurred. Above instructions to our officer have now been repeated." This information, Laurier told Aberdeen, makes it "painfully true that we are going to have some serious trouble with our neighbours, about the boundaries of Canada & Alaska. Already they are in possession of territory which we are of opinion, belongs to us, & they are claiming additional territory which by no possible interpretation, can be held to belong to them." [39]

Aberdeen wired Sifton's memorandum to Chamberlain so that the Colonial Office might have prior information if trouble broke out at the head of Lynn Canal. Minuting the telegram, John Anderson noted that he did not think that "any person who knows anything about the boundary question has asserted that Canada has a good claim to the Lynn Canal. It has certainly never been put forward either by the Dominion Govt. or H.M.G. hitherto." [40] Anderson went on to suggest that it was time that the boundary south of Mount

[39] Aberdeen Papers, 1, memorandum, Sifton to Aberdeen, January 28, 1898; 3, Laurier to Aberdeen, January 29, 1898.

[40] In the strictest sense this was true because, as Laurier and Sifton admitted, no protest had been made *officially* against the possession of the head of the Lynn Canal by the United States. But, as Anderson soon realized, if the boundary was drawn according to the terms of the Treaty of 1825, the Canadians did have good grounds for claiming the head of Lynn Canal. And, while no official protest had been filed against possession by the United States, persons who did "know anything of the boundary question" did, in fact, believe the Canadian claim was just. Both General Cameron, in his study in 1886, and Doctor Dawson, in his talks with Doctor Dall in Washington in 1888, advocated a boundary that would have given Canada possession of the head of Lynn Canal.

St. Elias be fixed. On 2 February Chamberlain suggested to the Governor-General: "Your Ministers shd. consider whether the time has not now arrived when the U.S. Govt. shd. be approached with a view to bringing the question of the boundary south of Mt. Elias to a definite settlement." [41]

Chamberlain's telegram was welcomed by the Canadian Government. The Colonial Secretary's initiative had given them the opportunity they desired to suggest the mode of settlement they thought most equitable to both sides. "My Govt. suggest," Aberdeen replied, "subject of course to modification, appt. of three Commissioners of recognized legal standing, to be named one by U.S., one by Gt. Britain, & third by independent power—France wd. be satisfactory to Canada." John Anderson spoke for the whole Colonial Office when he noted that "this is very satisfactory." In fact, the Colonial Office believed that arbitration was the only way to approach a settlement. "It appears to Mr. Chamberlain," read a note to the Foreign Office on 18 February, "That in the present circumstances it would be hopeless to expect that an agreement on the question could be reached by discussion, and he is of opinion that its reference to such a tribunal as that proposed is the most likely to insure an early decision which wd. be accepted by both parties." To emphasize the point to the Foreign Office, another note was sent three days later. After reviewing the various Canadian and American contentions, Chamberlain again said it was "hopeless" to expect a settlement "diplomatically" and he urged that Paunce-fote suggest the proposed arbitration commission to the United States.[42]

Though the Colonial Office agreed with Canada on the way to approach a settlement, it did not agree with the Canadian

[41] Chamberlain to Aberdeen, February 2, 1898 and minute by Anderson in Aberdeen to Chamberlain, January 30, 1898: CO42/856.

[42] Minute by Anderson on Aberdeen to Chamberlain, February 16, 1898; Wingfield to Villiers, February 21, 1898: CO42/856.

contentions as to where the boundary should be drawn in accordance with the Treaty of 1825. The Canadians, foreseeing that their case might come before an arbitral board, took the most favorable interpretation possible as their stand. Sifton prepared a memorandum which even began by accepting Judge Gray's argument though it had been dismissed out-of-hand by General Cameron in 1886. "The line," Sifton wrote, "is to be drawn . . . beginning at Cape Chacon, thence up the middle of Clarence Strait to the entrance to Ernest Sound and of Seward Passage which divides Deer Island from the mainland, reaching the 56th parallel in this Passage." From there the line was to follow the summits of the mountains "situated parallel to the coast" until it struck the 141st meridian. "The framers of the Convention," Sifton argued, "assume that there are mountains nearer the coast than ten marine leagues—an assumption in accordance with the facts—and these mountains the line is to follow. If there is a break or a recession in the mountains, the line is to cross this break, keeping its general direction parallel to the coast. It makes no difference what causes the break, whether the recession of the mountains, a river, valley, or arm of the sea not wide enough to be considered part of the ocean, for, by Article IV, the coast is defined as synonymous with the limit of the ocean." [43]

It will be remembered that John Anderson, minuting Aberdeen's despatch about the movements of Canadian and American forces at the summits of White and Chilkat Passes, believed that the Canadians had no just claim to the head of Lynn Canal. This view was held by the Colonial Office throughout the month of February. On the 21st, when the second note was sent to the Foreign Office urging the appointment of an arbitration commission to determine the boundary, it was stated as Chamberlain's belief that such a

[43] Memorandum by Sifton in Aberdeen to Chamberlain, March 4, 1898: CO42/856.

commission "could at once proceed to define the frontier *at the head of Lynn Canal*"—not across the Lynn Canal as the Canadians suggested. The note read in conclusion that Pauncefote should seek the approval of the United States Government to a commission "to fix the frontier *at the head of the inlets* through which the traffic for the Yukon valley enters." [44] On 4 March, Anderson himself wrote a memorandum dealing with the various Canadian contentions. He dismissed the contention that the boundary line should go through Duke of Clarence Strait rather than Portland Channel as "untenable." He noted that "the chain of mountains which the negotiators of the Treaty had in view . . . does not exist in that form." On the other hand, "there are mountains more or less continuous along the coast . . . and generally within the ten league limit, and it is along these that the boundary must in the first instance no doubt be sought." When the line came to the inlets, it could not simply be drawn across to the mountain nearest the coast on the other side as Sifton argued. Rather, the line, according to the treaty, had to follow the parallelism of the coast, and never be more than ten marine leagues from it. And, since the mouths of the inlets were less than six miles wide, they were territorial waters, and the coast line was drawn from headland to headland. Therefore, the parallelism of the coast included the line from headland to headland. It was from there, and not at the heads of the inlets, that the ten-league line was drawn, and, in the case of Lynn Canal, the head of the inlet would still be Canadian. A boundary line so measured, Anderson believed, "will give the United States a good deal more perhaps than the Canadians propose, but still only a fraction of what they claim, and will, at all events, leave the heads of all the main inlets in possession of Canada, which from the point of view of access to the interior is of the first impor-

[44] Wingfield to Villiers in Aberdeen to Chamberlain, February 16, 1898: CO42/856.

tance." Thus, while the Colonial Office and the Canadian Government did not agree on the exact position of the boundary line, they did agree that, if the Treaty of 1825 were correctly interpreted, the head of Lynn Canal belonged to Canada. This was clear from a note from the Colonial Office to the Foreign Office on 7 April. "Mr. Chamberlain considers," it read, "that even the summits of the passes referred to [White Pass and Chilkat Pass] are far beyond the boundary, which can never be more than ten leagues from the Ocean." [45]

By April the difficulties at the head of Lynn Canal had been stirred up once again. The commanding officer of the United States forces at Dyea had written to the Canadian Police Officers requesting them to cease the exercise of jurisdiction at the summits of Chilkat and White Passes. In January, an American military force had been gathered at Portland and prepared to go to Skagway, Sifton explained to Walsh, "and in another ten days they would have been in possession of the territory down to Lake Bennett and it would have taken twenty years of negotiating to get them out." It was for this reason that the Canadian police at the passes had been reinforced. "If we had not taken the course which we did take," Sifton explained in another letter,

> we would have lost the territory; the Americans would have been in command of the land route from Skagway to Dyea to the navigable waters of Lake Bennett and we would have had nothing whatever to say about what routes should be opened up to the Yukon. They would have had the power to charter their railroads and build them as they saw fit to navigable waters. We required at any cost to prevent them from taking possession of that territory. . . .

In the light of this new and unorthodox demand by the officer commanding at Dyea, which in essence was a claim to ter-

[45] Memorandum by Anderson, March 4, 1898; Colonial Office to Foreign Office in Chamberlain to Aberdeen, March 31, 1898: CO42/856.

ritory by a military officer, the Canadians proposed that a temporary boundary for administrative purposes be fixed at the "watershed at the first summit North of Dyea." In making the proposal, Aberdeen reminded Chamberlain, "Canada's claim that Skagway and Dyea are in Canadian territory is in no way thereby waived or prejudiced." On the 9th of May the United States Government consented to a marking of the temporary line without prejudice to American claims. But the formal agreement for marking a line was delayed. Eventually, the temporary line at the head of Lynn Canal, as well as the larger topic of the settlement of the Alaska boundary itself, was turned over to the consideration of the Joint High Commission of 1898-1899. Perhaps in the Joint High Commission an answer could be found to the boundary problem which had defied solution for more than two decades.[46]

[46] Sifton Papers, 291, Sifton to Walsh, April 1 and 4, 1898; Aberdeen to Chamberlain, March 31, 1898: CO42/856; Pauncefote to Day and Day to Pauncefote in Aberdeen to Chamberlain, May 5, 1898: CO42/858.

CHAPTER X
Reconciliation

NONE of the problems in Canadian-American relations, nor any combination of them, was of such a nature as to carry a serious threat of full-scale recourse to arms if no other solution could be found. Rather, despite flamboyant pronouncements by the press and politicians, they were the tiresome problems of diplomacy that exasperate the friendly intercourse of nations. Generally—as in the case of the North Atlantic fisheries dispute after 1888—it was easier to let the problems rest quietly in a state of semi-solution than it was to precipitate another Anglo-American crisis in an attempt to find a final resolution. But in the late 1890's a larger problem in Anglo-American relations did much to pave the way for an attempted settlement of Canadian-American disputes. Spurred on by American imperialistic ferver, the Spanish-American War gave vent to a righteous sense of mission and lure of exploitation through conquest. Unfortunately, however, the "splendid little war" nearly left the United States without a friend in the world.

Most of the major European powers were shocked by the unreasonable demands made on the Spanish Government by the United States and even more shocked when the Americans went to war after their demands had largely been met. Great Britain alone of the European powers came to the side of the United States in a spirit of "friendly neutrality." Chiefly through the efforts of the British Government and its Ambassador in Washington, Sir Julian Pauncefote, the other European powers were kept from rallying to Spain's side. Of course, there were many reasons for British friendliness during the Spanish-American War, not the least of which was Great Britain's own need of an ally, or at least a cooperative friend, in world counsels.[1] But not untypical of the British reaction was the comment of Charles Freeman Murray to Colonel Denison: "We would not have countenanced a Cuba —say off the shores of Canada—for half the time the Yankees put up with it. We hope we should have set about its amelioration or liberation in a more dignified manner and given Spain every chance to make graceful concession instead of making it impossible for her to do so by bluster and abuse. On the other hand, it would be difficult to put a limit to the indignation which would have swept over this country if one of our men-of-war had been blown up like the Maine." [2]

Illustrative, perhaps, of the British Government's interpretation of friendly neutrality was a suggestion from the Colonial Office. Since 1894 the Admiralty, ably seconded by the Colonial Office, had complained about the necessity of sending British warships to Behring Sea to police the seal fisheries during the pelagic sealing season. In July 1898 the Admiralty notified the Colonial Office that the *Icarus* and the *Pheasant* had started out on patrol duty. Minuting this letter, John Anderson noted that the United States usually sent six patrol ships and Great Britain two. But the Foreign Office had learned from Pauncefote that because of the war the United States was unable to send any ships to Behring Sea during the current season. "It would be politic for us to send another," Anderson concluded. Chamberlain warmly approved of his subordinate's suggestion and added "instruct H.M.

[1] The best description of the rise of Anglo-American friendship during the Spanish-American War is in C. S. Campbell, *Anglo-American Understanding, 1895-1903*, Baltimore, 1957, ch. 2. See also Gelber, *Rise of Anglo-American Friendship, passim*. Joseph Chamberlain, commenting on the Spanish-American War, told a Birmingham audience on May 13, 1898 that "terrible as war may be, even war itself would be cheaply purchased if, in a great and noble cause, the Stars and Stripes and the Union Jack should wave together over an Anglo-Saxon alliance." Cited, Gelber, p. 24.

[2] Denison Papers, 8, Murray to Denison, June 15, 1898.

ON THE EVE OF WAR

JACK CANUCK—We have our own little border squabbles, Sam, and will attend to them in due course; but when it comes to fighting foreigners in a righteous cause you know where my heart is!

Ambassador at Washington to inform the U.S. Govt. of the action taken by H.M. Govt. and of the friendly intention which has inspired it." [3]

Naturally, such "friendly intentions" were warmly appreciated by the Americans, even to the point that Canadians were receiving unaccustomed pats on the back in Washington.

[3] Minutes by Anderson and Chamberlain on Admiralty to Colonial Office, July 6, 1898, Colonial Office to Foreign Office, July 8, 1898: CO42/859.

"Just back from Washington," Sir William Van Horne confided to Clifford Sifton, adding, "nothing but brotherly love there now." Canadians were pleased with this display of friendship on the part of their neighbors. Generally they talked about the bright prospects of an Anglo-American alliance, which, Laurier approvingly told Whitelaw Reid, "must be the most potent factor that has yet taken place in history in the advancement of civilization." One Canadian summed up his joy at the new turn in Anglo-American relations and, hence, in Canadian-American relations, in "the latest war song":

> God guide our Cousins—o're the Border!
>   Rescue Cuba—in the fight,
> Trust in God, He'll help you conquer:
>   Drive the Spaniards out of sight
>
> Johnney Bull is slow to anger,
>   And may not in—this war—engage:
> But if the powers should break their treaty;
>   The Grand Old Lion, will leave its Cage.

"Anglo-American Unity," Colonel Denison told Lord Salisbury, "is a good thing to talk about just now, and following the English lead, our papers almost universally, as well as our public men in public utterances, are friendly to the States." [4]

Still, thoughtful people asked, how much of this Anglo-American friendship from which Canadians benefited was genuine and lasting? How much of it was not simply another manifestation of the war hysteria which had swept over the United States? Speaking of the loud professions of Anglo-American friendship that emanated over the border, Charles Mair said, "I, for one, mistrust so remarkably sudden a con-

[4] Sifton Papers, 54, Van Horne to Sifton, July 1, 1898; Laurier Papers, 79, Laurier to Whitelaw Reid, June 24, 1898; 77, #23994; Denison Papers, 8, Denison to Salisbury, June 12, 1898.

version." "The present wave of enthusiasm that is reported to be passing over the American people in favour of England," commented Lord Salisbury, "is not an emotion on whose stability we can very safely count." Certainly Salisbury hoped that the Spanish-American war crisis would leave England with more friends in the United States. But he doubted the permanence of Anglo-American friendship in a "democratic community largely tinged with Irish blood." But equally, every opportunity should be taken to settle the outstanding problems between Canada and the United States before the war was over. With the Joint High Commission scheduled to hold its first meeting in Quebec City before the end of the month, Martin Griffin, Canadian Parliamentary Librarian, regretfully told Laurier early in August that "the prospects of Peace are a sad blow to us at present." [5]

Nevertheless, despite this warning note of caution, certain facts could not be denied. The Joint High Commission of 1887-1888 had grown out of a hot dispute over the North Atlantic fisheries. When Macdonald had requested a joint high commission in December 1890, Secretary of State Blaine had replied with a brusque negative answer. Though all Canadian-American problems had been discussed with Blaine by Foster and Thompson in the Spring of 1892, an agreement to survey the boundary line between Canada and Alaska had been the only signficant result. And, as shall be seen, when the negotiations over Behring Sea regulations that ultimately led to a joint high commission began in 1897, the chief American negotiator, John W. Foster, was distinctly uncompromising. Yet in March 1898, with the Cuban crisis coming to a head, President McKinley told Sir Julian Pauncefote that he warmly approved a preliminary Canadian-American discussion to decide on the subjects to be put before

[5] Denison Papers, 8, Mair to Denison, May 5, 1898, Salisbury to Denison, June 25, 1898; Laurier Papers, 83, Griffin to Laurier, August 3, 1898.

a joint high commission. The comparison with previous attempts to settle all outstanding Canadian-American problems was striking. To that extent, at least, as Charles Mair put it, "the war I should think ought to benefit Canada." [6]

ii

The agreement to establish a joint high commission to settle problems between Canada and the United States grew directly out of negotiations over the revision of the regulations for the Behring Sea Seal Fishery laid down by the Paris Tribunal of 1893. The American Government had pressed for revision since 1893. In February 1897 the Foreign Office was "very anxious to make some show of concession to the U.S. in this matter." Probably this friendly spirit was prompted as much by pressures within the British Government as it was by a desire to show a conciliatory attitude to the United States. For, as Chamberlain reminded Aberdeen, "the naval force on the Pacific Station is small, and the complete withdrawal from it of three ships for patrol purposes during a large portion of the year is very objectionable, and has been the subject of frequent complaint by the Admiralty." But, even if the Foreign Office desired to accommodate reasonable requests by the United States, it would refuse to surrender the rights of British subjects to pelagic sealing in the face of uncompromising demands from the American Government.[7]

This more strident attitude on the part of the Americans was due to the influence the North American Commercial Company had with the Republican Administration. Two of

[6] G21, 93, No. 192A, Memorandum as to Behring Sea Regulations Discussion and Preliminary Discussion as to Questions in Dispute between Canada and the United States by Aberdeen, May 4, 1898; Denison Papers, 8, Mair to Denison, May 5, 1898.

[7] Minute by Anderson and Chamberlain to Aberdeen in Foreign Office to Colonial Office, February 10, 1897: CO42/851.

the company's shareholders were D. O. Mills (father-in-law of the editor of the powerful *New York Tribune,* Whitelaw Reid) and Senator Elkins, who had been Secretary of War in the Harrison Administration. It was rumored that John W. Foster, former Secretary of State, was the company's legal adviser. The company itself was in serious financial difficulty because the outgoing Cleveland Administration had sued it for more than a million dollars in back taxes. Obviously, the company's main competition came from the British pelagic sealers and it strongly desired the total abolition of pelagic sealing. The American Government quickly adopted the view of the North American Commercial Company, and John W. Foster and C. S. Hamblin (who soon resigned from his post) were appointed special commissioners to deal with the fur seal negotiations.[8]

Early in April 1897 Secretary of State Sherman informed both Ambassador Hay and Sir Julian Pauncefote of President McKinley's great anxiety over the "depleted condition and the prospective early extinction of the Alaskan seal herd" and of his conviction that immediate steps should be taken to stop "indiscriminate slaughter through pelagic sealing." Sherman therefore proposed a *modus vivendi* to "suspend all killing for the season of 1897" and a joint conference of interested powers to fix new measures to preserve the fur seals. John Anderson of the Colonial Office noted that according to British information there was "absolutely no ground for supposing that the extinction of the herd is imminent" and thus there was no reason to advance the time set for revision of the regulations from August 1898, the date set by the Paris Tribunal. On the other hand, Chamberlain observed that "the question is a very sore one with the Americans who are quite unreasonable on the subject. I should desire to take every possible opening for an amicable settlement before the

[8] Campbell, *Anglo-American Understanding,* pp. 82-83; Salisbury Papers, Pauncefote to Salisbury, April 16, 1897.

matter is further embittered." Nevertheless, the Colonial Office informed the Foreign Office that H.M.G. should "firmly decline" the proposal, adding that, though Canada would be informed of it, Chamberlain was "fully confident that they will strongly oppose" it. When the belated answer came from Canada, it was noted that the Dominion "could not at the present moment entertain any views on this proposal for a modus vivendi" without "an entire reversal of her position." [9]

Meanwhile, Lord Salisbury had rejected the American offer and John W. Foster had written a distinctly insulting reply saying "the British Government has from the beginning and continuously failed to respect the real intent and spirit of the Tribunal or the obligations imposed by it." Officially Great Britain remained silent about Foster's accusations. But when Foster's note was published in Whitelaw Reid's *New York Tribune* in July, Ambassador Hay told McKinley that the British lion began "standing on his head and lashing his tail all around the lot." Chamberlain told Foster, who had gone to London, that American diplomacy was "peculiar," adding that "you will carry it too far someday and get hurt." The American position was most uncompromising. In September an English friend wrote to Lady Aberdeen about a conversation he had had with Lyman J. Gage, McKinley's Secretary of the Treasury. Gage had told him that although the United States recognized that Canada's right to pelagic sealing "was unassailable from the point of view of international law" the Americans were equally convinced that pelagic sealing had to be stopped. His own view was that the Canadians should be given $500,000 to put an end to pelagic sealing forever and that "the Canadians would be very ill advised if they refused such an offer." If no solution could be found to the problem, the Americans would brand all the

[9] Tansill, *Canadian-American Relations,* p. 353; Foreign Office to Colonial Office, April 12, 1897: CO42/851; P.C. Report of May 20, 1897 in Foreign Office to Colonial Office, July 1, 1897: CO42/853.

seals on the Pribilof Islands, rendering their skins worthless, and, if that did not stop pelagic sealing, then the Americans would "reluctantly order the extermination of the whole herd at once." [10]

Fortunately, such extreme measures were not necessary. Secretary of State Sherman requested a conference of the interested powers, including Russia and Japan, to settle on protective measures. A British counter proposal that a conference of British and American experts be convened was accepted by the United States. Actually, both conferences met in Washington in the fall of 1897, and, ironically, they produced contradictory results. On 6 November, the Japanese, Russian, and American Governments signed a treaty providing for the suspension of all sealing operations for one year if Great Britain would adhere to the treaty. A few days later, Professor Thompson, the British expert at the other conference, reported that it had been decided that "pelagic sealing has in past years been in excess of natural increase but shews tendency to equilibrium: actual extermination of species is not involved or threatened." [11]

The prospect of breaking through this stalemate of contradictions was afforded by still another informal meeting also in progress in Washington. Sir Louis Davies, on the pretext of going to oversee the experts' conference, and Sir Wilfrid Laurier traveled to the American capital for private talks with John W. Foster. Davies and Laurier strongly urged appointment of a joint commission to consider all Canadian-American problems. At a meeting on 16 November Foster submitted a twofold proposal. First, the British and American Governments should agree to an immediate suspension

[10] Tansill, *Canadian-American Relations,* pp. 355, 357; Aberdeen Papers, 2, W. T. Stead to Lady Aberdeen, September 24, 1897.

[11] Aberdeen to Chamberlain, September 21, 1897: CO42/848; Foreign Office to Colonial Office, October 15 and November 17, 1897: CO42/854.

of killing of seals both on land and at sea for one year. Second, Canadian, British, and United States representatives should convene "with as little delay as possible" to settle all questions in dispute between Canada and the United States. After returning to Ottawa, Laurier replied to Foster on 24 November that his Government could not accept Foster's first proposal. The British Columbia sealers were already preparing to go to sea and "the prohibition of pelagic sealing for a year would practically destroy the business for several years because the masters, mates and the white crews, for the larger part belonging to other parts of Canada, would leave British Columbia!" Further it would be impossible to ask Parliament to compensate the sealers, and the experts' conference had decided that the seal herd was not in danger of extinction from pelagic sealing. On the other hand, Laurier urged the immediate convening of a joint commission. Such a commission could quickly solve the Behring Sea problem and all others and "so attain the object you have in view." But Foster stood his ground. "We seem to have failed to impress upon the Canadian Government, past or present," he argued, "our view that pelagic sealing ought to be voluntarily given up because it is unneighborly in that it is destroying a valuable industry of our Government, and inhumane because it is exterminating a noble race of animals useful to the world." "Notwithstanding the President," he concluded, "has consented that all these questions should be embraced in one series of negotiations, if meanwhile a *modus vivendi* could be agreed upon which would save the seals from destruction while the negotiations were in progress." [12]

There the matter rested over the Christmas holidays. In January Foster paid a private and informal call on Sir Julian

[12] Laurier Papers, 57, #18441, memorandum dated November 16, 1897, Laurier to Foster, November 24, 1897, Laurier to Pauncefote, November 26, 1897; 58, Foster to Laurier, December 2, 1897; Aberdeen to Chamberlain, November 26, 1897: CO42/848.

Pauncefote. He told the British Ambassador that the mood of Congress was "so bitter as to preclude the idea of any money being voted by way of compensation to Canadian fishermen." If an agreement were not quickly reached, "the desire was to pass every possible measure which could harass pelagic sealers and injure the British [seal skin processing] industry." Foster proposed that Dr. Jordan, the American scientific expert, and Professor Thompson, the British expert, meet at once, select an umpire, and then agree that the two Governments should accept for the 1898 season whatever amendments to the present regulations the three men might suggest. If this proposal were acceptable to the British Government, the United States would then consent to a mixed commission to settle Canadian-American differences. "The Yankee Spider is again inviting the British fly into his pretty parlour," commented John Anderson. Foster wanted a "compulsory settlement" of the sealing question "while all the others are to be left to the mercy of a negotiation which will end in smoke." The Canadian Government informed the Colonial Office that it would accept the proposal on two conditions; that the experts' recommendations be unanimous and that those recommendations also be submitted to the mixed commission for approval. The Canadian conditions were refused and the stalemate continued.[18]

Early in March Sir Julian Pauncefote, on a visit to the White House, spoke to President McKinley about the great desirability of appointing a commission to settle Canadian-American problems. He complained that such a commission "would be sitting now had not General Foster insisted on an impracticable condition, namely, the immediate suspension of pelagic sealing." "The President," Pauncefote told Salisbury, "expressed the most earnest desire to facilitate the settlement

[18] Foreign Office to Colonial Office, February 4, 1898: CO42/861. See also Foreign Office to Colonial Office, February 25 and 28, 1898: CO42/861; Aberdeen to Chamberlain, February 16, 1898: CO42/856.

of all those questions, and especially those which related to the development of the gold mining industry of the Valley of the Yukon." But McKinley thought it "useless" to appoint a commission until a "preliminary investigation" had taken place to decide on the basis of discussion of a commission. McKinley suggested that Pauncefote undertake such a preliminary investigation with Mr. Kasson, United States Reciprocity Commissioner, and Assistant Secretary of State Day. Happily Pauncefote wrote that "the effect of that arrangement would be to transfer the negotiation from the Fur-Seal Commissioner [Foster] to the Reciprocity Commissioner, and to let the fur-seal question rest until revived by the Mixed Commission." [14]

At last a breakthrough had been made. Quickly the Canadian Government agreed to send a delegate, Sir Louis Davies, to join Pauncefote in the talks with the United States. It was decided that two sets of talks would be held. "The Honourable J. W. Foster," Pauncefote informed Salisbury, "is designated to conduct, on the part of the United States, the discussion respecting the revision of the Behring Sea Regulations, and the Honourable John A. Kasson to conduct that respecting the other questions between Canada and the United States, it being agreed that both discussions shall proceed *pari passu.*" On 24 May, Sir Louis Davies arrived in Washington. The next day he reported to Laurier that "all our interviews were satisfactory. The President was exceedingly cordial and evidently felt the sympathy extended to the U.S. by the British people. He seemed anxious that we should successfully conclude our preliminary consultations with Messrs. Kasson & Foster." Apparently, in time of war the

[14] Pauncefote to Salisbury, March 10, 1898; Pope Papers, 23, Correspondence Respecting the Proceedings of the Joint High Commission, Foreign Office Confidential Print 7135, p. 1; hereafter referred to as Confidential Print 7135.

United States Government felt that the anti-British influence of the North American Commercial Company was a luxury it could not afford.[15]

iii

The Canadian Government had been considering the list of subjects to be placed before the mixed commission for many months before Sir Louis Davies went to Washington. Early in December 1897 the Governor-General informed Chamberlain that in addition to the Behring Sea question, the Canadian Government desired settlement of the bonding system on a "better basis," mutual abolition of the alien labor laws, joint regulations for protection of the inshore fisheries, settlement of the North Atlantic and Pacific Coast fisheries problems, location of the Alaska boundary (with reference of disputed points to "an independent tribunal"), and reciprocity in "wood, lumber, fish, coal, pulp, and possibly a few other products, but no interference with preference to Great Britain." By May 1898 three other problems had been added to the list. The first, submitted by the United States, was a suggested revision of the 1817 agreement regarding naval vessels on the Great Lakes and was a direct outgrowth of that country's experience of the inadequacies of the existing agreement during the Spanish-American War. Secondly, it was thought desirable that the rights of miners of one country in the territory of the other ought to be discussed. And, again, arrangements should be made for the clearer marking or more complete definition of the Canadian-American border at points where the line was not sufficiently well defined.[16]

[15] Aberdeen to Chamberlain, March 22, 1898 (two telegrams): CO42/856; Pauncefote to Salisbury, April 1, 1898, Confidential Print 7135, p. 2; Laurier Papers, 791B, Davies to Laurier, May 25, 1898.

[16] Aberdeen to Chamberlain, December 2, 1897: CO42/848; Laurier Papers, 791B, Davies to Laurier, May 25, 1898.

In the meetings between Davies, Pauncefote, Kasson, and Foster, two of the Canadian proposals were amended. Though Laurier continued to press for settlement of the Alaska boundary by a "tribunal of legal experts," it was decided that the boundary question would be referred to "legal and scientific experts, if the Commission shall so decide, or otherwise." Davies explained to his chief that the Commissioners would first have to examine the facts and difficulties of the case, adding "neither would it seem right in this preliminary basis to suggest the exact method by which the Commission should deal with it." Kasson and Foster also objected to reference to specific products that might be treated in a reciprocity agreement. It was agreed that the Commission should discuss "such readjustment and concessions as may be deemed mutually advantageous of customs duties applicable in each country." Finally, reciprocity in wrecking and salvage on sea coasts, the conveyance of prisoners through the other country, and "any other question remaining unsettled between Canada and the United States" were added to the bases of reference for the Commission.[17]

Reviewing the results of the meeting, John Anderson observed that "this is so far satisfactory. There are none of the questions on which, if there is a real wish for a settlement on both sides, an agreement should be impossible." He noted that each side was to present to the other a memorandum of its views on the questions to be discussed before the Commission met and said it was imperative that the Imperial Government see the Canadian paper before it was presented to the Americans. "The Canadians hold or pretend to hold views on the Boundary question at all events which we could not support," he explained, and "we don't want untenable

[17] Protocol of the Conferences at Washington in May 1898, enclosure in Pauncefote to Salisbury, May 31, 1898: Confidential Print 7135, pp. 5-8; Laurier Papers, 791B, [Laurier] to Davies, May 27, 1898, Davies to Laurier, May 27, 1898; 76, Davies to Laurier, May 28, 1898.

propositions put forward at the outset." [18] Chamberlain agreed but cautioned that there should be "no unnecessary delay. The present is a fruitful time and when the war is over they [the United States] may be less anxious [?] for a settlement." [19]

Actually the British Government made very few changes in the memorandum when it was received from Canada.[20] Canada, recognizing the "undoubted fact" that even under the 1893 regulations both land and pelagic sealing had become "less and less remunerative," was willing to consider abolition of pelagic sealing if "adequate compensation" was given to the Canadian sealers and "some fair equivalent be given to Great Britain for the remuneration by her of the exercise of an undoubted right." Salisbury's final instructions to the Commissioners were less generous. They might consider foregoing *"for a time* the exercise of her right of pelagic sealing." The Canadians believed that the Treaty of 1888 was a fair basis of settlement for the North Atlantic fisheries dispute "with the exception, however, of the provisions . . . which treated land-locked bays having an entrance of more than 10 miles wide as part of the open sea." Salisbury simply wrote that "some of the provisions of that Treaty will require reconsideration."

[18] This refers specifically to the Canadian contention to run the line up the Duke of Clarence Strait rather than through Portland Channel and to the extreme Canadian view on where the boundary line should cross the inlets.

[19] Minutes by Anderson and Chamberlain on Foreign Office to Colonial Office, June 11, 1898: CO42/862.

[20] In some cases such as the citation of the Behring Sea Regulations and the provisions of the Treaty of 1825 regarding the Alaska boundary, Salisbury's instructions are more detailed and explicit than Laurier's memorandum. Otherwise, most of the changes were in phrasing to take out the rough spots in Laurier's wording. The Laurier memorandum is found in Confidential Print 7135, pp. 33-37. Salisbury's instructions are found in Confidential Print 7135, pp. 24-30.

Turning to the Alaska boundary, Laurier said that the "object of the Commissioners should be strictly to organize a Tribunal of legal experts to determine the exact location of that boundary, and, in the meantime, to agree upon a conventional line embracing the concession to Canada of one of the ports on the shores of Lynn Inlet." But the Prime Minister did not rule out the possibility of a permanent diplomatic settlement by the Joint High Commission: "A proposition may be made to fix and determine the boundary by agreement. . . . This aspect of the question ought to be left entirely to the judgment and discretion of the Commissioners." Salisbury told the Commissioners that Her Majesty's Government sought the earliest possible agreement with the United States "as to the intention of the Parties to the Treaty of 1825 as to how the boundary line along the strip from Portland Canal to Mount St. Elias should be drawn." It was up to the "discretion and judgment of the Commissioners to devise some machinery for this purpose." Meanwhile, a provisional arrangement should be made regarding the inlets and rivers crossing the strip "pending a final settlement." He added that "the boundary-line must, in the first instance, be sought in the mountains which border the coast and in no case should it exceed 10 marine leagues from the ocean."

Sir Wilfrid Laurier observed that the Liberal party had always believed that "the relative position of the United States and Canada made a large measure of free trade most desirable." The high tariffs of both countries, however, made mutual concessions difficult. Furthermore, "Canada . . . has in recent years, by the judicious subsidizing of freight steamships, and the introduction of the cold-storage system, succeeded in finding a profitable market for a large portion of her surplus natural products in Great Britain; . . . this market is capable of indefinite expansion, and . . . in consequence the desirability of obtaining access to the markets of the United States has been appreciably minimized." Nevertheless, "the proposition is still maintained that negotiations on and for a wide list of natural products and a carefully selected list of manufactured products are still desirable and possible, though, it is important to remark, concessions to be made by Canada should in no wise conflict with the preferential Tariff given to Great Britain by the legislation of 1897." Lord Salisbury's instructions only added that Canada could not grant tariff concessions to the United States unless they were given to all other nations having most-favored-nation treatment in Canada.[21]

In the case of each of these important matters, the views of the United States Government as expressed in the memorandum given to its Commissioners were more brief. The United States hoped that a "reasonable and equitable basis" could be found for "the total abolition of pelagic sealing." It claimed that "the two Governments, in dealing with the Convention of 1818, should take into consideration the subsequent development between the United States and Canada, by a series of reciprocal legislative and executive acts, of a system of liberal and friendly intercourse with which the restrictions of that ancient instrument are incompatible, and that American fishing-vessels should be admitted to the same privileges in Canadian ports as are extended to other American vessels, and as are extended in American ports to Canadian vessels without distinction." The United States desired that the clause of the Alaskan boundary convention of 1892 calling for the permanent establishment of the boundary line be implemented by

[21] One student of Canadian-American reciprocity problems has argued that the phrase "a carefully selected list of manufactured products" is omitted from Salisbury's instructions. This is incorrect. See Joan M. V. Foster, "Reciprocity in Canadian Politics from the Commercial Union Movement to 1910," Ph.D. Thesis, Bryn Mawr, 1937, p. 264; Foster, "Reciprocity and the Joint High Commission of 1898-1899," *Canadian Historical Association Annual Report,* 1939, p. 89.

the Joint High Commission, that the boundary be fixed "upon proper maps" and provision be made for marking the boundary in Alaska "by a Joint Commission to be hereafter appointed." Regarding reciprocity, the United States was content to have its Commissioners simply be guided by "the basis indicated in this paragraph of the Protocol" of the May 1898 talks between Davies and Pauncefote and Foster and Kasson.[22]

iv

The matter of greatest importance to the Canadian Government was what subjects would be referred to the Joint High Commission. But also of importance was the question of who would represent the British side of the Commission and how these members would be chosen. There were, of course, various precedents from which to choose. In 1854 Lord Elgin alone had "floated" the famous Treaty which bore his name through the American Senate. In 1871 Sir John Macdonald was the first Canadian politician to participate directly in negotiations dealing with Canadian-American problems. Though appointed as an Imperial High Commissioner, it is clear that the Canadian Prime Minister really regarded himself as the Canadian negotiator. Likewise, in 1887-1888, Sir Charles Tupper was one of the three High Commissioners on the Commission which negotiated the Treaty of 1888. Certainly the 1854 precedent was useless. No one considered that the Governor-General should be the spokesman of Canadian interests in 1898. As in 1871 and 1887, Canadian representation was imperative. But there were two vastly important differences which reflected the growth of Canadian national stature. In 1871 Sir John Macdonald had four British colleagues. In 1898 Lord Herschell had four Canadian

[22] Confidential Print 7135, pp. 45-47.

colleagues. Again, in 1871 the British side of the Joint High Commission took its instructions from Downing Street. In 1898, at the suggestion of the British Government, the British Commissioners were guided by the wishes of the Laurier Government in Ottawa on all points of substance in the negotiations.

As with the subjects to be discussed by the Commission, the British and Canadian Governments gave early considera- tion to the matter of personnel. "What are the views of your Ministers as to personnel?" Chamberlain asked Aberdeen on 26 November 1897. The Governor-General replied that "Cana- dian representative to act with British Ambassador or other representative shd. in the opinion of my Ministers be named by Great Britain." The Laurier Government having thus taken no decision on the matter, the Colonial Secretary next consulted Lord Salisbury. He replied that though an agree- ment might be reached to form a Commission, he

has, however, some doubts as to whether . . . it would be desirable to follow altogether the precedent of 1887 when Plenipotentiaries were appointed to take part in a Conference on the North Atlantic Fisheries question. In the present instance several of the questions included in the list furnished by the Canadian Government for dis- cussions are of a purely local character, about which this Department [the Foreign Office] at least, is without in- formation on which any instructions to the British Rep- resentatives on the Commission could usefully be framed.

In these circumstances it appears to Lord Salisbury that the direct representation of Her Majesty's Govern- ment on the Commission might be confined to Her Maj- esty's Ambassador at Washington while [the Canadian Representatives] being appointed by Royal Commission should take their instructions from the Dominion Govern- ment.

Chamberlain thoroughly agreed with Lord Salisbury's suggestions.[23]

With these fundamental decisions made, nothing more could be done about the personnel problem until the preliminary talks with the United States began. Apparently the Canadians, through Sir Louis Davies, had suggested a six-man Commission to Kasson and Foster. But Davies reported that the Americans wanted more than three men from each side. Sir Julian Pauncefote told Lord Salisbury that "the President is most anxious that the Commission should be composed of five members on each side, as he deems it necessary, in order to facilitate the adoption of its conclusions by Congress, that the influential members of the Senate and House of Representatives should be included. . . . I have objected to so large a number." But the Colonial Office thought that "President McKinley is right in wishing to rope a considerable number of Senators and prominent politicians into this commission, and I think Sir J. Pauncefote when he objects underestimates the magnitude of the task he has to face. The questions to be dealt with are numerous and many of them are difficult & wide so that it will be necessary for the Commission to deal with them by subcommittees, and five commissioners on each side will greatly facilitate this." Pauncefote was accordingly instructed that Her Majesty's Government saw "no objection" to five men on each side of the Commission.[24]

The Colonial Office recommended that "some prominent man from this country . . . be sent over as a member of the Commission. As an unprejudiced person he would have the

[23] Chamberlain to Aberdeen in Aberdeen to Chamberlain, November 26, 1897, Aberdeen to Chamberlain, December 2, 1897: CO42/848; Foreign Office to Colonial Office, December 10, 1897: CO42/854.

[24] Pauncefote to Salisbury, May 27, 1898, Salisbury to Pauncefote, June 2, 1898: Confidential Print 7135, pp. 4-5; Minute by Anderson on Foreign Office to Colonial Office, May 28, 1898: CO42/862.

greatest influence in abating extreme pretensions on either side, and would improve the prospect of a permanent settlement." Both Lord Dufferin who had served as Governor-General of Canada two decades before and Lord Jersey who had represented the British Government at the Intercolonial Conference in 1894 were considered. But in the end Chamberlain wired Aberdeen that "if work can be completed so as not to interfere with Venezuelan Arbitration, expected to begin in May, Lord Herschell has agreed to represent this country." Speaking of Lord Herschell, Laurier explained to Senator Boulton of Manitoba that "the British Government have thought that in a matter of this kind, it was more fitting to appoint a man well versed in the International Law. Their selection ends the possible controversy as to who, among the many men that would have been available, should have been chosen." [25]

Thus, as suggested by Salisbury in December, the Imperial Government would appoint only one man to the Commission. The Canadians, thanks to McKinley's insistence on five men to a side, would have four representatives. But who would they be? The Laurier Government had originally suggested that Canadian representation be chosen by Her Majesty's Government. But on 10 June, Chamberlain handed the problem back to the Canadians. "We propose that Yr. Ministers shd. nominate 4 members of British Commission for submission to H.M.," he wired to Aberdeen, "one member being nominated by us." Nine days later the Governor-General replied that Sir Wilfrid Laurier, Sir Richard Cartwright, Sir Louis Davies, and Mr. John Charlton, M.P., had been nominated by the Canadian Government. His Ministers, Aber-

[25] Colonial Office minutes on Foreign Office to Colonial Office, May 28 and June 1, 1898: CO42/862; Chamberlain to Aberdeen, June 17, 1898, Confidential Print 7135, p. 10; Laurier Papers, 82, Laurier to Boulton, August 2, 1898.

deen concluded, "desire to express appreciation of proposal that there shall be 4 Canadians among the 5 British representatives." [26]

But the discussions over representation on the Joint High Commission were not over. Throughout the various Anglo-Canadian exchanges an essential consideration had been ignored. At no time had the interests of Newfoundland been discussed. No doubt, following the 1871 precedent, the Canadian and British Governments believed they could complete their work with the United States and hand the island Colony a treaty to sign or reject at her peril. But such was not the case. Both had apparently forgotten that in 1887-1888 Sir James Winter, though not a High Commissioner, had been at Washington to protect his Colony's interests and that the Newfoundland Government was still anxious to renew the abortive Bond-Blaine treaty of 1890. As early as the fall of 1897 the Canadian Government had been informed that Sir William Whiteway's Government was anxious to resume commercial negotiations with the United States. The despatch reminded the Canadians that the negotiations had been suspended at the insistence of Canada, much to the Island's displeasure. "H.M.G.," it read, "feel some difficulty in refusing to resume the negotiations for an arrangement which the people of Newfoundland believe would be of great benefit to them, especially in the present depressed condition of its staple industry [fishing]." Nothing was done about the matter pending a general election in Newfoundland in which Whiteway's Government was subsequently defeated and Sir James Winter assumed the Premiership. "The new Govt.," Anderson noted on 9 November, "will be much more disposed to cast in their lot with Canada in negotiations with

[26] Chamberlain to Aberdeen in Foreign Office to Colonial Office, June 3, 1898: CO42/862; Aberdeen to Chamberlain, June 19, 1898: CO42/857.

the U.S. or at any rate to consider the Canadian difficulties and susceptibilities in the matter." [27]

When the matter was again brought to the attention of the Colonial Office in July 1898, Anderson's prediction seemed to be far off the point. Winter and A. B. Morine, who were in London, wrote a strongly argumentative letter to Chamberlain protesting against the composition of the Joint High Commission. It was with "great surprise" that Newfoundland learned of the impending Joint High Commission and considered it to be a breach of the "principles contended for by the Canadian Government in 1890." According to those principles, it would be "manifestly unjust to permit Canada to make a separate arrangement with the United States, or any arrangement without the concurrence of Newfoundland." Winter and Morine admitted that if only the material interests of Newfoundland were considered, they would be "best served by a separate arrangement" with the United States. But "we recognize the desirability of unity of action and interest between the Colonies in such matters," and "upon this basis, the rights and interests of the Colony cannot be adequately secured by any course short of a representation of the Colony upon the present Commission." The Newfoundlanders rightly pointed out that the Joint High Commission could not deal with the North Atlantic Fisheries question conclusively without their representation. For all these reasons, Newfoundland desired either representation or the privilege of separate negotiations.[28]

Newfoundland's interests could not be ignored. If Newfoundland would not cooperate, any arrangement on the North Atlantic Fisheries question would go up in smoke and might even destroy the efforts of all the work of the

[27] Laurier Papers, 52, Colonial Office to Governor-General, September 15, 1897; Minute by Anderson on Foreign Office to Colonial Office, November 8, 1897: CO42/854.

[28] *ibid.,* 80, Winter and Morine to Chamberlain, July 2, 1898.

Commission. The island Colony did have a very strong bargaining card and its interests should have been considered long before July 1898 when the arrangements for the Joint High Commission were virtually completed.

Chamberlain's first reaction was that "the best course would be to allow a separate negotiation on behalf of Newfoundland." He reasoned that the Commission was already large enough and that Newfoundland was only interested in two of the dozen questions to be submitted to it, the North Atlantic Fisheries and reciprocity. He did, however, ask the Canadian Government whether they favored representation or separate negotiations. Quite naturally, the Canadians chose the former. From their point of view, just as in 1890, separate negotiations for Newfoundland carried the threat of isolating Canada. Laurier did insist on one thing, however. He wired to London to "see that Premier of Newfoundland and no one else for that Colony is on [the Commission]." In a further telegram he explained that Newfoundland's "proposal is not unreasonable, but before we decide it would be convenient to know exactly what is the intention of Newfoundland as to her representation. If assured that Newfoundland would be represented by Her Premier alone we would be satisfied. We might have objections to some others. See Chamberlain, convey this view to him confidentially. . . ." [29]

On 17 July Pauncefote was instructed to ask the United States if it would agree to the addition of a Newfoundland representative to the Commission. Two days later Pauncefote replied in the affirmative and Chamberlain informed Aberdeen and Governor Murray of Newfoundland that Sir James Win-

[29] Colonial Office to Foreign Office, July 7, 1898: Confidential Print 7135, p. 19; G21, 93, Chamberlain to Aberdeen, July 11, 1898; Laurier Papers, 82, Laurier to ?, July 31, 1898, Laurier to ?, n.d., #25486. Probably these were sent to Lord Strathcona, the High Commissioner. But they might well have been sent to any of the three Ministers in London, Mulock, Blair or Dobell.

ter had been appointed to the Commission. On all points not affecting Newfoundland Winter would be instructed to support Canadian views. Mr. Jefferson Coolidge, former American Minister in Paris, was added to the American side of the Commission which consisted of Senator C. S. Fairbanks (Indiana), Senator George Gray (Delaware), Representative Nelson Dingley (Maine), John W. Foster, and John A. Kasson. At least one member of Laurier's Government was happy about the addition to the Commission. Richard Dobell wrote to Sir Wilfrid that he "was pleased to learn that you had fallen in with the views of Newfoundland." "This will pave the way," he added hopefully, "for their admission into the Dominion and complete our area." [30]

iv

In the late 1880's and early 1890's a very large number of Canadians cast envious eyes toward the United States. Many left their homes in Canada to take up residence on what seemed to be the greener side of the fence. In certain parts of Canada a significant number of people looked favorably upon the project for Commercial Union. Many many more, across the Dominion, heartily supported the Liberal proposal of Unrestricted Reciprocity. Even the Conservatives, who for years had made much more of reciprocity in tariffs than of reciprocity in natural products, were forced by the attraction of the American market to suggest, just before the 1891 election, that they were going to go to Washington once again to seek freer trade relations with the United States. Gradually, over the years after the 1891 election, Canadian sentiment began to harden against the attractions of the Republic to the south. The last gasp of Commercial Union, under its truer colors of political union, received but passing extremist sup-

[30] Foreign Office to Colonial Office, July 19, 1898: CO42/863; Chamberlain to Murray and Aberdeen, July 19, 1898, Confidential Print 7135, pp. 37-38; Laurier Papers, 82, Dobell to Laurier, July 24, 1898.

port in Canada. Publicly, the Liberal party made its biggest step of redirection in its policy at the great convention of 1893, when it declared for "freer trade" with all the world and especially—the order of placement is significant—with Great Britain and the United States. Happily the Conservatives discovered that their suppositions about the validity of an east-west trade axis were correct in spite of the McKinley Tariff. The Liberals climaxed this realignment of Canadian thinking in 1897 by stealing old Tory thunder and implementing a British preference in the Canadian tariff.

One of the most significant results of this change in Canadian sentiment was the realization on the part of all Canadians that Canada could and would survive on the North American Continent as an independent entity. Certainly the Conservatives had always considered this to be possible; this assumption was the foundation-stone of the whole National Policy. But the possibility had been very seriously questioned by the hard economic times of the late 1880's and 1890's. Never before and never afterward did such a thorough examination of the National Policy take place as in those years. By the mid-1890's the possibility of an independent existence on the Continent seemed largely to have become a reality; so much a reality that when the Liberals took over the Government of the country they also took over the National Policy. And this belief in a permanent division of North America into two entities naturally colored the thinking of all Canadians as they speculated on the prospects of the Joint High Commission of 1898-1899.

In part this assurance was reflected in the willingness of Canadians to concede certain points to their neighbors. In earlier years, when their existence was in question, as Joseph Chamberlain so correctly observed, Canadians had been totally "irreconcilable" in their dealings with the United States. But now there was evident a desire to meet the United States half way on some of the points in dispute between the two countries. "No one denies," admitted the *Queen's Quarterly* in January 1898, "that the regulations instituted by the Paris award for the protection of the seals are inadequate, and that these can be revised with more light on the subject than was attainable four years ago. The industry now is not very profitable for either the Alaska company or the Canadian sealers." "The Behring Sea question sounds big," James Edgar told Laurier, "but I do not believe that 99 percent of the people of Canada care what you do about it." Writing from New Glascow, Nova Scotia, D. C. Fraser told Laurier that "I find a prejudice existing among our inshore fishermen against the right of Americans to fish inside the three mile limit." But, he said, "every other right our people have they would willingly grant the Americans, provided always they had their free markets, including transshipment of their fish. It would be a great boon to our people in this county to be able to trade with the American fishermen, selling them everything they want. . . . If the Americans insist on the inshore fisheries, and you will lose the chance of making a good treaty by not yielding, let them have it." [31]

On the other hand, this new assurance of identity was also reflected in a less compromising attitude toward the United States in trade relations. In the years of economic distress, all Canadians wished to extend freer trade relations with the United States. The difference between the Liberals and the Conservatives was really one of degree rather than kind. By 1898 this attitude had changed. Laurier voiced the mind of the Canadian Government when he told Erastus Wiman, in January 1898 that "we are not making much progress in the way of reciprocity, and, to tell you the truth, I am not particularly anxious for it, with the exception of a few articles which, unless adjusted, will lead to trouble. The feeling in Canada on the subject of reciprocity is very far from what it

[31] *Queen's Quarterly,* January 1898; Laurier Papers, 86, Edgar to Laurier, September 23, 1898; 84, Fraser to Laurier, August 29, 1898.

was some few years ago. Since our American neighbours will not trade with us, we have come to the conclusion that we will have to do without it, and I think we can do without it very successfully." [32]

Laurier was echoing the sentiment of a large number of Canadians. "I am astonished at the letters I receive even from old Commercial Union Liberals against concessions to Washington," wrote Willison. Sifton informed his chief that "the people generally will not feel very badly if a reciprocity arrangement does not materialize." Even John Charlton appeared to have moderated his strong desires for reciprocity. In an article entitled "Canadian Trade Relations with the United States" in *Canada, An Encyclopaedia,* in 1898, he wrote that "the parting of the way is just before us; we have a preference as to which road we shall take; but if access [to the American market] is denied us, we will enter upon the other with high resolve to make it the road to victory over all the obstacles that may confront us." "If we cannot increase our exports to the United States," Charlton threatened, "it will not be unnatural to seek to reduce the balance of trade against us by the reduction of American imports." [33]

The reasons for this attitude were cogently presented in a letter from the Ontario Minister of Education, George W. Ross, to Laurier:

Now that you have committed yourself to a system of cold storage, quick and direct transportation and a preferential tariff towards Great Britain, any Reciprocity treaty that you may negotiate must divert public attention as well as public trade from the new channels which you have so successfully established, and you will there-

[32] Laurier Papers, 62, Laurier to Wiman, January 21, 1898.

[33] *ibid.,* 59, Willison to Laurier, December 27, 1897; Sifton Papers, 291, Sifton to Laurier, August 24, 1898; J. Charlton, "Canadian Trade Relations with the United States," J. C. Hopkins, ed. *Canada, An Encyclopaedia of the Country,* Toronto, 1898, v. 1, p. 378.

fore be, to a certain extent, neutralizing the advantages which the country has the right to expect from its expenditures on a fast ocean service and from the introduction of the Intercolonial into Montreal. Besides I may say that I am by no means confident that any reciprocity at all would be in the long run a boon to Canada. Just at the time our trade has established new channels with the United States, some infatuated President may recommend the repeal of this treaty, and disturb the commerce of the whole country. At its best it is uncertain in duration, and is a weapon in the hands of the Americans to terrorize Canadians in dealing with their own affairs. That position would be intolerable. In fact our expectations since 1866 in the direction of a Reciprocity with the United States, to my mind, have seriously interfered with the development of the industries of the country. Now that we are free from the Americans let us remain so.

Ross, of course, like other Canadians, did not believe that Canada would be better off without the Joint High Commission. Canadians, as well as Americans, were anxious to settle outstanding Canadian-American problems. But Laurier was aware that his fellow countrymen were concerned that the Joint High Commission should not make such large concessions to the United States that Canada's freedom to develop in her own way was bound by "entangling alliances." "I wish you earnestly every success," wrote Colonel Denison, "but cannot fail to feel anxious that any treaty must be more or less a compromise based on the principle of give and take." For once, perhaps, the Colonel spoke for most Canadians when he added that "Canada will be one of the greatest countries in the world before long—and we must all do our best that no bonds or shackles shall be allowed to check her progress." [34]

[34] *ibid.*, 56, Ross to Laurier, November 13, 1897; Denison Papers, 8, Denison to Laurier, August 6, 1898.

CHAPTER XI

Self-Confidence Triumphs over International Amity

HEN the members of the Joint High Commission gathered in Quebec City in August 1898, the friendly disposition of the members seemed to point to an eventual successful conclusion of the meetings. "No work has been done yet," noted Joseph Pope who advised the British Commissioners on the North Atlantic Fisheries question, "but I hear the Yankees are in a proper frame of mind." After two meetings of the Commission, Lord Herschell reported to Salisbury that "our relations with the United States' Commissioners are very cordial, and, so far as I can judge, they are animated by a sincere desire to arrive at a fair settlement of all the points of difference." In general there was little disagreement between the British and American Commissioners on the minor subjects before the Joint High Commission. For the most part these were the result of misunderstanding or lack of communication between the Canadian and American Governments. Realistically, any one of them could just as well have been settled at almost any time without the impressive formality of a Joint High Commission. A case in point was the Canadian-American boundary west of Lake Superior. The Canadian Government contended that the maps attached to the Webster-Ashburton Treaty gave Canada a more favorable boundary line than the existing one. When Sir Richard Cartwright and John Kasson, who formed a subcommittee to study the problem, reviewed the evidence the Canadian contention was proved correct and a draft article of agreement was drawn up to remark the boundary line.[1] Other problems

---

[1] Pope Papers, 116, Diary, August 25, 1898; Herschell to Salisbury, August 29 and October 10, 1898: Confidential Print 7135, pp. 59, 94; W. C. Cartwright Memorandum A, March 25, 1899: Confidential

were also found to have quick acceptable solutions. On 11 October Lord Herschell told Salisbury that the Commission had reached agreements on the alien labor laws, the conveyance of prisoners, wreckage and salvage of ships, the control of the inland and Pacific fisheries, and cattle branding. He reported that he believed a solution would be found to the problem of reciprocal mining regulations. "On all the minor questions," he said, "the prospect of a satisfactory arrangement is all that can be desired." [2]

Two minor problems, however, did cause the Commission some concern. The Commission's labors to revise the 1817 Convention regulating the use of naval vessels on the Great Lakes were accompanied by howls of protest from influential Canadian citizens. And the Canadian Pacific Railway and members of Laurier's Cabinet (chiefly Clifford Sifton and J. Isreal Tarte) objected strongly to the efforts of the Joint High Commission to put the regulation of transportation of goods in bond between or across the two countries into the form of a treaty.

The Canadian and British Governments were not at all satisfied that the Convention of 1817 should be revised. But the United States Government considered the agreement "obso-

---

Print 7135, pp. 208-09. W. C. Cartwright, the British Secretary at the Joint High Commission, submitted two memoranda to the Foreign Office after the adjournment of the Commission and Herschell's death on the state of negotiations at the time of adjournment. Memorandum A of March 25, 1899 (Confidential Print 7135, pp. 208-14) was a general summary and was sent to Canada. Memorandum B of March 27, 1899 (Confidential Print 7135, pp. 214-17) was limited to observations on (a) Naval vessels on the Great Lakes, (b) Behring Sea Seal Fisheries, and (c) the Alaska Boundary dispute. Memorandum B was confidential and for the use of the Imperial Government alone, or, as John Anderson put it, "only for home consumption." See Foreign Office to Colonial Office, April 20, 1899: CO42/871.

[2] Herschell to Salisbury, October 11, 1898: Confidential Print 7135, p. 98.

lete" and admitted that it was a "serious grievance" to the ship builders of the Great Lakes who were precluded from competition with the ship builders of the Atlantic seaboard in constructing naval vessels. The danger existed that the United States Government could at any time abrogate the Rush-Bagot Agreement on six months' notice and thus leave Canada faced with the problem of no regulations concerning the building or maintenance of naval vessels on the Great Lakes. Lord Herschell observed that the result of such action might be a prolonged naval race on the Great Lakes with "great evils, both financial and political" for both Canada and the United States. Herschell was therefore of the opinion that the Rush-Bagot Agreement should be modified. He said that "if the Agreement of 1817 were modified by continuing a restriction on the number of vessels of war to be maintained on the lakes, the evils to which I have adverted would be prevented, and I cannot see that our position would be at all prejudiced." He recommended that the United States be allowed to build naval vessels on the Great Lakes but not arm them until after they had passed through the Canadian canals and out the St. Lawrence River to the eastern seaboard. Herschell added that his Canadian colleagues "take the same view as myself of the situation and of the course which it would be well to pursue." [3]

The Canadian public did not, of course, know the details of the Commission's negotiations. But they did know that a revision of the Agreement was being discussed and further that the Great Lakes ship builders wanted to construct naval vessels and send them through the Canadian canals (the only exit from the lakes) to the sea. A particularly vocal group in Tory Toronto protested vehemently against granting "the treaty right of sailing these war vessels down our canals past the wharves of our great cities practically behind our fortifica-

[3] Herschell to Salisbury, August 22, 1898: Confidential Print 7135, pp. 50-52.

tions and through the heart of our country." "A treaty with such a clause," they warned, "could never pass either the Commons or the Senate, and the people of Canada would make very short work of any Government that attempted to father it." This group constantly badgered Laurier with protests from August until the end of 1898. As might have been expected, Colonel Denison led the protestors. "He, Principal Grant and others," wrote Willison, "are resolutely determined to fight any proposal to have American war vessels permitted to pass through Canadian canals. I have reason to believe that both Denison and Grant and all that school would take the stump against the Government if such a clause were put into the treaty. At the same time all of these men are more than friendly towards the Government." [4]

In December 1898 Laurier answered the harsh cries of his critics with a reply of plain common sense. "You seem to forget that there are two sides and two parties to the question, and you treat it as if there were only one party and one side," he told Willison.

> You seem to treat the question as if we were masters of the situation and quite at liberty to grant or not to grant the power to the Americans of building war vessels on the lakes. There is one thing we have the power to do. We can refuse them the use of our canals to take their warships to the Ocean. The question is whether we should allow them that privilege, or refuse it and let them fill the lakes with as many war vessels as they see fit.

Laurier realized that the United States, victorious in the Spanish-American War and the owner of an overseas empire, was going to build naval vessels whether Canada liked it or not. As far as he was concerned, the revision of the Rush-Bagot Agreement was not a question of benefit to Canada; rather, it was the question of a greater or lesser danger to

[4] Denison Papers, 8, Denison to Salisbury, September 17, 1898; Laurier Papers, 87, Willison to Laurier, September 28, 1898.

Canada. "Which is the better course," he asked Denison, "to allow the Convention of 1817 to come to an end with the consequence of strong armaments on the lakes, or to revise the convention so as to admit naval construction on the lakes & to make provision for the prompt pulling out to the ocean of all war craft so built?" [5]

Actually, by December a draft agreement had been reached with the Americans and approved by the Colonial Defence Committee. Neither Government would maintain any vessels of war on the Great Lakes. Each Government might keep two unarmored training vessels and six revenue cutters on the lakes. Both Governments might build naval vessels on the lakes but they could not be armed or equipped for war until they had passed out of the lakes and only one vessel was to be completed at a time. John Anderson concluded that the agreement was a "gift horse" that should not have been given to the Americans. Colonial Secretary Chamberlain agreed that the proposal was "not satisfactory." But, he added in summing up the question, "it is the best we can get." Besides, Chamberlain believed that Canada was becoming stronger and "must take care of herself. She will have to avoid causes of offences to her great neighbour, but it is impossible to foresee and provide for all the contingencies of the future in North America." [6]

The second minor problem which caused considerable comment was the transport in bond of goods of one country across the territory of another. The question was discussed by the Commission late in August. In stating the American case

[5] Willison Papers, 109, Laurier to Willison, December 12, 1898; Laurier Papers, 95, Laurier to A. W. Thomas, December 23, 1898; Denison Papers, 8, Laurier to Denison, December 13, 1898.

[6] Herschell to Salisbury, December 2, 1898: Confidential Print 7135, p. 120; Foreign Office to Colonial Office, September 12, 1898: CO42/863; Minutes by Anderson and Chamberlain on Foreign Office to Colonial Office, December 16, 1898: CO42/864.

Senator Fairbanks concentrated upon the grievances of the American railways against the Canadian Pacific Railway. The Canadian Pacific Railway on its American lines was not bound by the Interstate Commerce law of the United States and carried on alleged unfair competition with American trunk lines by cutting rates, granting rebates to shippers, and the like. Senator Fairbanks added that the Grand Trunk and other Canadian railways did abide by the provisions of the Interstate Commerce law. Lord Herschell later reported to Salisbury that the Canadian Pacific had agreed to abide by the conditions of the Interstate Commerce Law on its American lines. This action by the Canadian Pacific undoubtedly helped to clear the atmosphere for a discussion of transit in bond. But it clearly did nothing to solve the basic problem. As far as Laurier was concerned there was "a very urgent reason" for settling it "with some degree of satisfaction to both countries." "At present," he told Clifford Sifton, "intransit of American merchandise into the United States over Canadian territory by Canadian railways and vice versa exists only by sufferance; it is not regulated by treaty and can be impaired and even stopped at any moment. This is not a healthy condition of things." The Prime Minister desired that the bonding privilege be "made secure by treaty." "Some tribunal," he added, "must be provided to settle conflicts or difficulties between rival roads." The American railways were under the jurisdiction of the Interstate Commerce Commission. Though the Canadian railways might abide by the Interstate Commerce law, it certainly could not be expected that they, too, should come under the Commission's jurisdiction. "That proposition is out of the question and cannot be entertained." Rather, Laurier favored "an International Court of Arbitration" to settle bonding disputes.[7]

[7] Herschell to Salisbury, September 20, 1898: Confidential Print 7135, pp. 74-75; Sifton Papers, 46, Laurier to Sifton, November 22, 1898.

The Canadian Pacific Railway was opposed even to this suggestion and the Railway was heartily backed by Sifton and J. Isreal Tarte. Sifton also reported that "Mulock and Paterson agree that it would be impossible to make a treaty providing for mutual bonding privileges which would be satisfactory to Canada."

I do not believe that any international tribunal can be constituted which will be satisfactory, and I regard with very great fear the constitution of such a body where the United States would constantly appear for the purpose of driving us into a corner and compelling concessions on an unfair and strained construction of the Treaty. Moreover, such a Treaty would give the United States to some extent territorial rights in Canada with the privilege of asserting the right of the stronger power to insist upon what they would claim to be the fair interpretation of the Treaty. It would be the thin edge of the wedge, which would ultimately result in seriously injuring us. Moreover, the American Railway Companies are desperately anxious to have this matter taken up. It is quite clear that they see the advantage would be to them, consequently it would be very likely to be a disadvantage to us. I do not think myself that there is any danger of the bonding privileges being abrogated.

This was a classic expression of National Policy thinking, and, as such, was quite at variance with the desire to cooperate to find solutions to common problems which was evident at the Joint High Commission. Sifton worked from the assumption of competition, not cooperation. He failed to see that there were two sides to the transit question. If the United States would gain some sort of "territorial rights" in Canada by the establishment of an international tribunal to regulate transit in bond, then surely Canada would gain some sort of "territorial rights" in the United States because while the Canadian Pacific crossed American territory, American trunk lines crossed Canadian territory, particularly in the Western Ontario Peninsula. The "thin edge of the wedge" worked both ways. Again, was it valid to assume that Canadian railways would be at a disadvantage simply because American railways would find the international tribunal advantageous? Was it not possible that both Canadian and American railways might benefit from an international tribunal? Indeed, there seemed to be a clear contradiction in Sifton's thinking. He, and Tarte, Mulock, Paterson and the Canadian Pacific Railway would not cooperate with the United States in the desire to settle the bonding question by a treaty agreement. This they distrusted as the "thin edge of the wedge." But by believing that the bonding privileges would not be revoked, they placed all their trust in the sufferance or good will of the United States to maintain the bonding privileges.[8]

In any case, the British and Canadian Commissioners did not heed Sifton's advice. They firmly believed that the bonding privileges had to be established in treaty form. Late in December, in a correspondence between Lord Herschell and Senator Fairbanks, the Canadian and American proposals were exchanged. The Americans asked that the Canadian Railways be under the jurisdiction of the Interstate Commerce Commission when carrying American merchandise on the American portions of their lines. The Canadians rejected this and proposed that the two countries either set up an international tribunal or agree to regulate the bonding problem by reciprocal legislation.[9]

In the end no agreement was reached by the Joint High

[8] Laurier Papers, 93, Sifton to Laurier, November 29, 1898, Laurier to Tarte, December 5, 1898.

[9] *ibid.*, 94, Laurier to Van Horne, December 14, 1898; 95, Laurier to Schaughnessy, December 28, 1898; Fairbanks to Herschell, December 24, 1898, Herschell to Fairbanks, December 31, 1898 in Cartwright to Salisbury, March 3, 1899: Confidential Print 7135, pp. 187-97.

Commission. Ironically, both sides agreed in principle. It was only the means of implementing the principle where they disagreed. Lord Herschell told Senator Fairbanks that "I fully agree that Canadian transportation Companies carrying between two points in the United States ought, in respect to such traffic, to obey the laws of the United States which apply thereto when conveyed by United States Companies, and that this obedience should be capable of being effectually enforced. My criticisms . . . have reference not to the end in view, but to the means proposed to be employed." Herschell eventually found solace in Sifton's belief that the United States would not abolish the bonding privileges. He concluded, wrote W. C. Cartwright, that "no Treaty stipulation could be devised which would be entirely satisfactory, and he considered that the existing state of things might be allowed to continue without risk of serious complications. There seemed to him to be little danger of the bonding privileges on both sides being abolished." [10]

On two minor questions before the Joint High Commission considerable pressure was put on the Canadian Commissioners by Canadians not to conclude any agreement with the United States. In both cases the Canadian Commissioners ignored this advice. A draft agreement was reached on the amendment of the Convention of 1817 and an agreement was sought on the bonding problem. But this pressure by Canadian politicians and politically influential Canadian citizens did point out one thing: they considered themselves to be the masters of their own house and they wished to preserve the *status quo* however dangerous that was. The "thin edge of the wedge" of American dominance, whether in the form of American warships passing through Canadian canals or by American representation on an international tribunal to

[10] Herschell to Fairbanks, December 31, 1898: Confidential Print 7135, p. 195; Memorandum A by W. C. Cartwright, March 25, 1899: Confidential Print 7135, p. 209.

regulate transportation in bond, was not desired and would not be tolerated. This same hard line of assertion of self-interest over common interest was present in the negotiations on the major problems before the Joint High Commission.

ii

The North Atlantic Fisheries question was discussed early in the Commission's negotiations. From the first it appeared to be the most difficult problem to solve. As Lord Herschell told Salisbury on 11 October, "the subject appears likely to present the greatest obstacles in the way of a satisfactory settlement." The Canadians desired a settlement based on the agreement made in the abortive Treaty of 1888, i.e. the exchange of commercial privileges to American fishing vessels in Canadian ports for the free entry of Canadian fresh fish into American markets. This the Americans stoutly refused to give. They claimed that the American fishing vessels already had the right to the use of commercial facilities in Canadian ports. Up until 1830, so the argument ran, all American vessels had been excluded from British and Canadian ports. The only exception was American fishing vessels which, under the Convention of 1818, could enter Canadian ports for wood, water, shelter, and repairs. This, the Americans claimed, was not a *restriction* on the rights of American fishing vessels as Canada argued, but rather a generous *concession* to American fishing vessels. Then, in 1830, with President Jackson's Proclamation and reciprocal British concessions in the Navigation Laws, the commercial facilities of ports in British North America were opened to *all* American trading vessels. All American registered vessels, including fishing vessels, had trading rights under American law and it was argued that American fishing vessels were no different from other American commercial vessels. Therefore American fishing vessels were entitled to the same commercial privileges in Canadian ports possessed by other American vessels. This argument, the American Commissioners claimed, had been the main reason why the Senate had rejected the Treaty of 1888 embodying the opposite view that American fishing vessels were precluded from commercial privileges in Canadian ports under the restrictive clause 1 of the Convention of 1818. Certainly the American Commissioners could not be expected to admit what the Senate had so firmly denied a decade before. Thus, the Canadian proposal of an exchange of commercial privileges for free fish could not be entertained by the United States.[11]

If the Americans were going to reject the Canadian offer, thought Lord Herschell, then it was up to them to present a counterproposal. The Americans stubbornly refused to do so and Herschell, believing that this was "the question upon which the difference between us appeared most acute," decided to take it up privately with Senator Fairbanks. Herschell suggested that the majority report of the Senate Foreign Relations Committee in 1888 rejecting the Bayard-Chamberlain Treaty showed conclusively that Canada and the United States held very different interpretations of their respective rights under the Convention of 1818. In recent years Canada

[11] Herschell to Salisbury, October 11, 1898: Confidential Print 7135, p. 100. The Americans also frankly admitted that political pressure from New England fishing interests made the concession of free fish impossible. Senator Hoar, who had led the fight against the Treaty in the Senate in 1888 with success and considered it one of the great triumphs of his career, was adamant against the granting of free fish. Senator Henry Cabot Lodge's stand against free fish was derived from a combination of political self-interest (like Hoar) and a sense of the relation of the fishing fleet to the navy in the United States' new imperial mission. It was, he told Lord Herschell, "utterly out of the question that we should give Canada free fish. That notion may as well be abandoned first as last. It is not a question of the value of the Gloucester fisheries, although the value is considerable and the industry large. It is the fact that they are a nursery of seamen. . . . In the late war, Gloucester alone sent over 400 men, first-class seamen, into the regular navy of the United States." Cited, Tansill, *Canadian-American Relations*, p. 91.

had been especially lenient in the assertion of her rights under the *modus vivendi* of 1888 and that if no agreement was reached, "it would be impossible for the Government [of Canada] to avoid enforcing those rights, and if the United States adhered to the position which they maintained in 1888, a situation of acute controversy would immediately arise." It was, therefore, "essential" that the respective rights of Canada and the United States under the Convention of 1818 "be conclusively determined by agreement or arbitration, which (except war, which might be dismissed from consideration) were the only ways of ending the controversy." A settlement by negotiation of the Joint High Commission was certainly most desirable for both parties, Herschell said. It was clear, as he had earlier told Salisbury, "my Canadian colleagues would certainly find it difficult to agree to . . . an arbitration." On the other hand, if no diplomatic solution could be found, arbitration was the "only solution." Should that be the case, the British Commissioners would insist on a new *modus vivendi* until the arbitral award was announced, preferably the admission of Canadian fish free of duty into the United States. Fairbanks continued to maintain silence. He neither assented to nor rejected Herschell's suggestions but only asked that the fisheries problem "should not be pressed forward for the present." [12]

[12] Herschell to Salisbury, October 11 and November 25, 1898: Confidential Print 7135, pp. 101, 115-16. Chamberlain was very pleased about settling the fisheries dispute by arbitration: "I am convinced that the 'rights' are not worth fighting for and I should be quite ready to agree to an Arbitration on the subject if the Canadians could be brought to accept it & possibly go further & say that if they refused a tribunal we could not support their contention further. Both sides in this matter are the slaves of petty vested interests, and there is really no great national object at stake. It would be of immense advantage to get rid of the question even if the award was against us." Minute by Chamberlain on Foreign Office to Colonial Office, October 27, 1898: CO42/864.

On 21 December Lord Herschell again urged Senator Fairbanks to give some reply to the British proposals regarding the North Atlantic Fisheries. Fairbanks passed over the opportunity to make a diplomatic settlement and answered that the United States would accept arbitration. Pending the award, the American Government would pay Canada the license fees required for fishing vessels under the *modus vivendi* of 1888. Herschell answered that this was a new and very different proposal. Originally the American Commissioners agreed only to pay an annual lump sum based on the average number of vessels requiring licenses over a period of years. This new proposal meant that "a much larger number of vessels might take advantage of the arrangement than have hitherto taken out licences, with the result that a much smaller sum per vessel might be received for the licences than at present." He countered by suggesting that the *modus vivendi* of 1888 should be continued pending arbitration and there the matter rested for some weeks.[13]

In contrast to some of the other problems, the North Atlantic Fisheries question stirred few Canadians to send advice to their Commissioners. Only one Maritime correspondent urged the Prime Minister to take a "hard line" with the Americans. "The three mile limit is too much for our Yankee neighbours," he wrote, "while a sixty mile zone is not sufficient for them around the Pribyloff Islands. I think, Sir, that it is your especial duty as the Premier of the Dominion and head of the Canadian Commission to maintain the rights of Canada." David Mills was anxious that the problem be settled diplomatically. And, he told Laurier, Canada could afford to concede a good deal to get a settlement. Canada might consent to the transshipment of fish in bond by the United States. "This has always appeared to me by far the weakest point in

13 Herschell to Fairbanks, December 21 and 31, 1898, Fairbanks to Herschell, December 24, 1898: Confidential Print 7135, pp. 128, 188, 193.

our position." Again, if American fishing vessels "were admitted to our ports for the purpose of buying the supplies which they may need, other than bait, it certainly would be to the advantage of the people of the Maritime Provinces." A diplomatic settlement would not give the United States the opportunity to question Canadian rights under the Convention of 1818. That question, in Mills' opinion, "ought to be avoided." But Mills' distrust of arbitration did not carry over to the question of which bays were Canadian territorial waters. A diplomatic settlement in which certain bays were enumerated as belonging to Canada was unsatisfactory. "If this matter must be dealt with," he advised, "it would be far better that it should go before a tribunal of arbitration for the purpose of having decided the larger question:—what bays and waters connected with the open sea may a State lawfully claim under the law of nations? If the matter is to be settled, let us have an ascertained rule that will apply to our neighbours as well as ourselves." [14]

Davies and Fielding, however, distrusted any arbitration at all. "I do not like the proposal to refer the question to arbitration," Davies wrote to Sifton. He preferred a diplomatic settlement which would allow American fishing vessels to enter Canadian harbors for provisions, supplies and transshipment of cargo "but not *to obtain bait or ship men.*" Such an arrangement would be admirable for Canada; selling supplies would benefit Canadians and still, "while we hold the *bait and shipping of men* in our hands, we hold the key of the position." This position was ultimately adopted by the British Commissioners in preference to settlement by arbitration. And they decided that if the bays question could be settled diplomatically they would abandon their right to exclude American fishing vessels from commercial privileges in Canadian harbors. They would reserve to Canada, however, "full

[14] Laurier Papers, 89, W. Doyle to Laurier, October 20, 1898; 98, Mills to Laurier, January 25, 1899.

power, if it were deemed advisable, to prohibit the sale or exportation of bait and the shipping of crews, or to impose conditions or restrictions upon them." A prospect of settlement of the bays question seemed likely. W. C. Cartwright told the British Government that "the question of bays (or headlands) would [not] cause much difficulty. The American Commissioners expressed their willingness to accept the exclusion of American fishing-vessels from such bays as might be thought worth protecting, without being too particular as to the width of the entrances."[15]

There was, however, one other very important condition to the Canadian proposal which Lord Herschell explained to Salisbury. Though the Commissioners readily admitted that the Canadian "rights of exclusion" could be given up "not only without detriment but with advantage to Canada," the fishermen of the Maritime provinces have "always been taught to look upon them as of great value, and their abandonment would unquestionably raise a great outcry." Because of this both Sir Louis Davies and Sir James Winter were demanding tariff concessions in agricultural and mineral products by the United States. In short, for domestic political considerations, the settlement of the North Atlantic fisheries question finally rested on the success or failure of the reciprocity negotiations.[16]

iii

The British Government and its representative on the Joint High Commission played the role of observer rather than participant in the reciprocity negotiations. Lord Herschell was not a member of the subcommittee composed of Fairbanks,

[15] Sifton Papers, 60, Davies to Sifton, January 23, 1899; Herschell to Salisbury, February 7, 1899, Memorandum A, W. C. Cartwright, March 25, 1899: Confidential Print 7135, pp. 154, 210.

[16] Herschell to Salisbury, February 7, 1899: Confidential Print 7135, p. 155.

Dingley, Kasson, Cartwright, Davies, and Charlton. "Although he followed its proceedings with interest," W. C. Cartwright reported in March 1899, Lord Herschell "used to say that the matter was one for negotiations between the United States and Canada, and that it did not affect the home Government. He was further of opinion that these Tariff questions should be dealt with separately, and he did not approve of their having been mixed up with the political differences with which the Commission had to deal." [17]

Sir Wilfrid Laurier first brought the subject before the Commission on 2 September 1898. His approach was cautious. He asked for a "pretty full free list of reductions of Tariff on raw materials," principally lumber, mining products, sea products, and agricultural goods, adding that a list of manufactured goods would be submitted at a later date. Two members of the Commission, however, were anxious to go much further in proposals for reciprocity. One of these was Sir Richard Cartwright who noted the great benefits that would accrue from the abolition of the customs barrier between the United States and Canada and believed that "the nearer the Canadian Provinces could be assimilated to the general system of interstate commerce, the more quickly trade would develop on both sides of the frontier." The other member of the Commission with advanced views on reciprocity was the American representative, Nelson Dingley, Chairman of the House Ways and Means Committee. W. C. Cartwright, British Secretary to the Commission, told a Foreign Office friend that Dingley "has actually suggested to Laurier to make a complete Zollverein between the U.S. & Canada and has guaranteed to carry such a measure through Congress." [18]

[17] Memorandum A, W. C. Cartwright, March 25, 1899: Confidential Print 7135, p. 210.

[18] Herschell to Salisbury, September 20, 1898: Confidential Print 7135, p. 75; Cartwright to Campbell, October 10, 1898, cited, Campbell, *Anglo-American Understanding*, p. 101.

In fact, no such ambitious plans were ever seriously considered. According to the account of the negotiations in the subcommittee which John Charlton recorded in his diary, the subcommittee did not even seriously consider a list of manufactured goods. The Canadians stood firm for a select list of natural products and met with equally stubborn American resistance. "The Americans will grant tariff concessions very grudgingly," wrote Charlton with despair. The fact of the matter was that in both countries the protective tariff had nurtured vested interests of such power that neither Government could afford to let down its tariff barrier to any significant degree. Lord Herschell commented on this to Lord Salisbury when he reported on the progress of negotiations in October. "The truth is," he said, "that where two countries have each pursued a policy of protection, there are almost insuperable difficulties in the way of a reciprocity Treaty of any considerable extent." Whenever it was rumored that the slightest modification of the tariff was being discussed both the Canadian and American governments were deluged with protests from vested interests. Herschell believed "the utmost to be hoped for is . . . that some small step may be taken towards a freer interchange of commodities, and that the way may be paved for further progress in that direction in the future." [19]

There were, of course, many who sincerely desired a large reciprocity treaty. The Cleveland, Ohio Chamber of Commerce transmitted a resolution to the Joint High Commission begging a reciprocal trade arrangement and both Senator Fairbanks and President McKinley told Lord Herschell that they agreed with its sentiments. McKinley even told

[19] Charlton Papers, Diary, October 7, 1898; Herschell to Salisbury, October 11, 1898: Confidential Print 7135, p. 100. See also Joan M. V. Foster, "Reciprocity and the Joint High Commission of 1898-99," *Canadian Historical Association Annual Report,* 1939, pp. 91-93, and Tansill, *Canadian-American Relations,* p. 450-52.

Herschell that "the time had come to reconsider the question of the Tariff." The President said that while no one appreciated the benefits of protection more than he did, "at the same time, he thought that the circumstances had changed, and rendered freer trade relations with countries outside the States expedient." The same generosity was apparently exhibited by the Canadian Commissioners but not by their compatriots in Ottawa. Looking back on six months of practically fruitless reciprocity negotiations, Herschell told Salisbury in February 1899 that "the members of the Canadian Government who are my colleagues on the Commission have exhibited a very reasonable disposition, but from what I have heard from themselves, as well as from conversations I have had with other members of the Dominion Government, it is evident to me that all the members of that Government are not actuated by an equally reasonable spirit." [20]

Sir Wilfrid Laurier was painfully aware of the vast forces in Canada working against reciprocity. James Edgar wondered how a treaty could be arranged that would not injure the British preference. A cotton goods manufacturer in Montreal wrote that a reduction in the duty on cotton goods would ruin the Canadian industry and make Canada a slaughter market for American products. The Toronto Board of Trade resolved that it would be "no calamity . . . if no reciprocal trade relations were established with the United States" and added that "no treaty should be entered into which shall be out of harmony with, or in any way disturb the present preferential trade relations which have been established with Great Britain." The Fort William Board of Trade went even further. It not only protested against reciprocity but also "insists that any change should be made in the other direction by raising the tariff of Canada, as regards the United

[20] Herschell to Salisbury, November 25, 1898, February 7, 1899: Confidential Print 7135, pp. 116-17, 154-56.

States, to a level with that which the latter has raised against Canada and other countries." [21]

It was this sort of pressure which led to the differences in the Canadian Cabinet over reciprocity. The difficulty was that of reconciling reciprocity with practical politics in Canada. J. Isreal Tarte wrote to Sifton that he would "consent to reciprocity on coal and flour. It would be rather popular in the Province of Quebec. But we certainly can do without it and if it was going to injure you and our friends in Ontario, we should not have it. This is, in two words, my position." In fact, the Canadians had a choice between freer trade relations with the United States and maintaining the Liberal Government in power in Canada. They could not have both, and practical politicians like Sifton and Fielding (and eventually Laurier) chose the Canadian vote in preference to reconciliation with the Americans.[22]

As Tarte said, flour was a case in point. On 11 November the Canadian Commissioners had expressed a desire for free flour. A few days later Laurier told Sifton that he was convinced only the large milling companies such as the Ogilvies and the Lake of the Woods Company might possibly be hurt by free flour and asked if they could not be compensated in some other way. Sifton replied that the political effect of free flour would be disastrous: "the large millers would be rendered determinedly hostile to us, and the small millers would never be heard in our defence. . . . As a matter of fact the large millers always control the small millers so that the political influence is all in favour of retaining the duty." When, on 7 December, the American Commissioners included flour in a list of goods proposed to be made free of duty, Charlton

[21] Laurier Papers, 93, Edgar to Laurier, November 22 and 27, 1898; 92, F. W. Thomas to Laurier, November 18, 1898; 87, Resolution of Toronto Board of Trade, October 3, 1898; 96, Resolution of Fort William Board of Trade, January [5?], 1899.

[22] Sifton Papers, 73, Tarte to Sifton, January 26, 1899.

recorded that "we asserted that these concessions would do us little or no good." [23]

On some products there was agreement. Senator Fairbanks was quite correct in reminding Lord Herschell on 24 December that "the pending negotiation has . . . established the fact that we can safely agree upon a larger measure of reciprocity than has been possible at any time except in 1854." Agreement was reached on a free list of mineral products that would benefit Newfoundland and hence ease the problem there of presenting the Fisheries question to an arbitral tribunal. But a similar agreement on agricultural products and lumber that would benefit the Maritime Provinces and soften opinion on the Fisheries problem there could not be reached. Under the Dingley Tariff Canadian lumber paid a duty of two dollars per thousand feet when imported into the United States. In 1898 the Ontario Government had retaliated by passing a law forbidding the export of logs to the United States. The lumber interests in both countries were so vociferous in their criticism of reciprocity in lumber that neither the United States nor the Ontario Government (backed by the Dominion Government) could recede from its extreme position. On this rock foundered not only the hopes of a wide measure of reciprocal free trade but also any settlement of the North Atlantic Fisheries question by arbitration.[24]

By the time the Joint High Commission adjourned for the Christmas holidays it was clear that, for the present at least, there was little hope of agreement on reciprocity. Pauncefote dismally confided to Salisbury that "Lord Herschell is driven nearly wild by the American Commissioners whose notions of right & justice & reciprocity are so distorted." He made the

[23] Charlton Papers, Diary, November 11 and December 7, 1898; Sifton Papers, 46, Laurier to Sifton, November 22, 1898; 291, Sifton to Laurier, November 29, 1898.
[24] Fairbanks to Herschell, December 24, 1898: Confidential Print 7135, p. 189.

interesting suggestion that the reciprocity negotiations be postponed and the Commission be made permanent. "It is a convenient Tribunal to which minor Canadian questions (which are always cropping up) can be referred, & if for no other purpose I should be glad to see it made permanent, the members being changed from time to time, according to the nature of the questions in difference." Gradually the idea of postponing the reciprocity negotiations took hold of the Canadian Commissioners and their colleagues in Ottawa. This was especially true when the subcommittee was forced in January to abandon its discussions due to the illness and subsequent death of Nelson Dingley. Both Dobell and Scott advised Laurier of the advantages of postponement. And Fielding told Laurier that if postponement was suggested "we could accept such a result with much advantage . . . the whole trend of events in the States just now is towards a better condition. Probably if we had to conclude a Treaty next fall, instead of at this moment, the result would be more satisfactory." [25]

Thus when the Joint High Commission adjourned in mid-February, it was not correct to say that negotiations for a reciprocity agreement had failed. Some measure of agreement had been reached and, as W. C. Cartwright noted in his memo to the British Government, "the reciprocity negotiations would have a better prospect of success if resumed at a later date, and Lord Herschell was in favour of putting them aside for the moment." Meanwhile, more encouraging results were being achieved in the Behring Sea negotiations.[26]

[25] Salisbury Papers, Pauncefote to Salisbury, December 23, 1898; Laurier Papers, 63, Dobell to Laurier, January 30, [1899]; 101, Scott to Laurier, February 14, 1899; 97, Fielding to Laurier, January 7, 1899.

[26] Memorandum A, W. C. Cartwright, March 25, 1899: Confidential Print 7135, p. 211.

iv

At the first meeting of the Joint High Commission at which the Behring Sea dispute was discussed Lord Herschell indicated to the Commission that an agreement in principle to a solution was within easy reach. The American Commissioners believed that the only possible solution of the problem was the total abolition of pelagic sealing. Lord Herschell agreed that the retention of pelagic sealing, even under strict regulations, "was in several respects unsatisfactory." The regulations gave rise to complaints on the part of the sealers and were a constant source of friction in Canadian-American relations. The necessity of policing the regulated zone was both expensive and inconvenient. Therefore, Herschell said that "Her Majesty's Government were willing to negotiate for the suspension of pelagic sealing for a lengthened period on condition that the sealers were compensated, and that some concession were granted by the United States in return for such suspension." Sir Louis Davies added that "the surrender of the national right would, he hoped, be met by a relaxation of trade regulations in the United States as affecting Canada." Having made this concession to the United States, the question was referred to a subcommittee consisting of Senator Fairbanks, General Foster, Sir Louis Davies, and Lord Herschell.[27]

Granting that negotiations should proceed on the basis of a cessation of pelagic sealing was a drastic reversal of policy for the British and especially the Canadian Governments. For years they had argued that the problem should be solved on the basis of improvement of the Paris Regulations of 1893. At no time had they conceded the validity of the American claim that pelagic sealing was causing the rapid extermination of

[27] Herschell to Salisbury, September 2, 1898: Confidential Print 7135, pp. 63-64.

373

the fur seal herd. After all, only a year earlier in 1897, the British and American fur seal experts, Professor Thompson and Dr. David Starr Jordan, had issued a joint report which concluded that while pelagic sealing had, in fact, diminished the number of fur seals, the herd was in no danger of immediate extermination. Why, then, did the British Commissioners reverse their position? In part it must be assumed that they were making a large concession to Anglo-American and Canadian-American amity. If adequate compensation could be gotten from the Americans a very troublesome problem would be solved. Again, the British Government, at least, was most anxious to be relieved of the expensive necessity of tying up part of the Pacific Squadron of the Royal Navy in patrol duty. Then, too, Senator Fairbanks was entirely correct in pointing out the unprofitableness of pelagic sealing in a letter to Lord Herschell on 24 December 1898. "As you are aware," he wrote, "fully 40 per cent of the fleet [of British sealers] has been out of commission during several years past. Why? Obviously because there was, and is, no reasonable or profitable demand for it. With a continued diminution of the seal herd, is it not fair to presume, not only that the vessels not in commission will continue inactive, but that the number in commission will diminish?" [28]

Sir Wilfrid Laurier admitted the validity of Fairbanks' argument when he expressed the opinion of the British Commissioners in a letter to David Mills on 28 January 1899. Mills had written to say that "in respect to Pelagic sealing, I have found the view generally prevailing among our best informed people that we ought not to abandon a sovereign right; that it is unworthy of us to do so" and that better regulations, including regulations for land sealing on the Pribilof Islands, would be the best solution of the problem. "I have just writ-

[28] Fairbanks to Herschell, December 24, 1898: Confidential Print 7135, p. 189.

ten Sifton on this subject," Laurier replied, "I cannot do better than to quote it here."

We have an opportunity of making an honourable settlement of this question, giving to our sealers a legitimate compensation, and obtaining for us an honourable and profitable recognition of our rights. If, in addition to it, we obtain free fish on the Pacific, as I think we will, we will have made, I am sure, not only a fair settlement but a wise thing. You know as well as I do that if pelagic sealing is allowed to continue for two or three years more, it will then come to an end by the gradual destruction of the herds. Then the sealers would be left without any compensation, but with a fleet on their hands, and there would be much discontent in the country against us for having failed to do what we should do now.

Laurier thus admitted that the American claim was correct; pelagic sealing was in fact destroying the seal herd. Was it not better, then, to seek compensation for the sealing fleet while it still had some semblance of usefulness? And was it not better to negotiate a sovereign right while the exercise of that right still had some meaning? It was for these reasons that the British and Canadian members of the Joint High Commission decided to seek a settlement on the basis of cessation of pelagic sealing.[29]

As in the earlier fur seal negotiations, General Foster proved to be more the fomenter of argument than the conciliatory diplomat. In truth, Foster knew the intricacies of the fur seal problem as neither Fairbanks nor Davies and Herschell did. Early in the proceedings of the subcommittee he so embarrassed the British members on the question of compensation to the sealers that they asked for an adjournment so that they

[29] Laurier Papers, 98, Mills to Laurier, January 25, 1899, Laurier to Sifton, January 28, 1899; 60, Laurier to Mills, January 28, n.d. [1899]. In his letter to Sifton Laurier added that "it is the true part of statesmanship to act with some courage and in prevision of future events."

might send their experts to Victoria to inform themselves of the facts in question. In his letter to Salisbury of 11 October, Lord Herschell complained of General Foster's attitude. Foster, he said, "has put the case of the United States in the most aggressive and uncompromising fashion, in spite of occasional statements that he was desirous of dealing with the question in a friendly and conciliatory spirit." He hastened to add that "Senator Fairbanks volunteered the statement in confidence that General Foster was only representing himself, and was certainly not representing either Senator Fairbanks or the President." But despite Foster's intransigence, the Behring Sea negotiations continued with some success. Herschell reported the United States Commissioners admitted that Canada and Great Britain were entitled to some compensation for giving up their right to pelagic sealing in addition to the compensation to be paid to the sealers. The Americans did not indicate, however, what that compensation might be. Certainly it was not going to be in the form of the large trade concessions to Canada which Davies requested.[30]

The British members of the Commission asked for $750,000 as the compensation to be paid to the sealers. This the Americans claimed to be much too high a price to pay to buy out a dying industry. But Herschell pointed out to Fairbanks on 21 December that the whole American case was based on the assumption that pelagic sealing was killing the industry. If pelagic sealing were abolished, the industry, according to the American case, was no longer in danger. "It is surely much more difficult for us to defend taking a smaller sum than we think reasonably necessary for the compensation of those whose calling is to be violently put an end to by the abandonment of a national right than for you to justify a somewhat larger sum than you may think adequate when the abandon-

[30] Campbell, *Anglo-American Understanding,* p. 91; Herschell to Salisbury, October 11, 1898: Confidential Print 7135, pp. 98-99.

ment of that right will, according to the views insisted upon by the United States for many years, not only prevent an asset of the United States from ceasing to have any value, but make it a very valuable one," wrote Herschell. On 7 February Herschell told Salisbury that the United States would offer no more than $500,000 compensation. This was a "great advance," he said, on any previous proposal and "did not substantially differ" from the modified British proposal of $600,000. In addition, although the British proposal included the cession of the sealing vessels, the Americans were willing to leave the vessels in the possession of the sealers. Thus the difference between the two sides of the Commission was negligible and it was clear that an agreement could be reached on compensation to the sealers.[31]

Despite hard bargaining, agreement as to the general terms of compensation for giving up the right to pelagic sealing was also reached. The Americans accepted the British suggestion of compensation by way of payment of a percentage of the receipts from land sealing and suggested $7\frac{1}{2}$ per cent. The British countered with a figure of 10 per cent of the receipts. When this was refused the British Commissioners suggested a graduated scheme of percentages starting with 5 per cent on the first 50,000 skins and ending with 25 per cent on all skins above the first 100,000. This, too, was refused and the British Commissioners made a further "modified" proposal. "Taking 20,000 roughly as the number of seals which might be obtained on the islands even if pelagic sealing continued," Herschell reported to Salisbury in February 1899, the British Commissioners proposed that the percentage of receipts apply only to the excess over 20,000 seals taken annually. They added that a graduated scheme of percentages be used, the amount growing proportionately with the growth

[31] Herschell to Fairbanks, December 21, 1898, Herschell to Salisbury, February 7, 1898: Confidential Print 7135, pp. 129, 155.

of the catch. The Americans accepted this proposal in principle.[32]

The Behring Sea negotiations had reached this point when the Joint High Commission adjourned its sittings in mid-February. Although the talks had been interspersed with acrimonious argument, it was clear that both sides wanted to settle this vexatious problem. As far as Canada was concerned, two things must be said. First, by her reversal of policy and willingness to negotiate on the basis of a cessation of pelagic sealing, Canada was making a large concession to the United States. In this sense, her position was one of strength. But it is equally true that her position was also one of weakness. As Sir Wilfrid Laurier so clearly pointed out, this might be the last chance Canada would have to negotiate at all. Once pelagic sealing had destroyed the fur seal herd (and both sides now admitted that this was inevitable if pelagic sealing continued) Canada would have nothing to negotiate about. Secondly, the agreement nearly reached in 1898-1899 provided the framework for the final settlement of the problem in 1911. On the whole, both sides approached the Behring Sea negotiations with a reasonable and conciliatory attitude. Unfortunately, this could not be said of either side when the Commissioners turned to the Alaska boundary question.

v

The subcommittee which discussed the Alaska boundary question was composed of Sir Wilfrid Laurier, Lord Herschell, Senator Fairbanks and General Foster. By far the largest part of the negotiations were conducted between Herschell and Fairbanks, though the British Commissioners justly assumed that Fairbanks was really being guided by his more knowl-

[32] W. C. Cartwright to Campbell in Foreign Office to Colonial Office, January 5, 1899: CO42/870; Herschell to Salisbury, February 7, 1899: Confidential Print 7135, p. 156.

edgeable colleague, Foster. As in the Behring Sea negotiations, Foster's tenacious arguments and uncompromising attitude made discussion of the problem most difficult. At the critical stage of the talks, in mid-February 1899, General Foster was taken ill and had to leave the Commission meetings. Rather wistfully, Herschell told Lord Salisbury that "it may be hoped that, in his absence, matters will proceed more smoothly, if we take into account the strong disinclination which he has always shown to submitting the Alaska boundary question to arbitration." [33]

Herschell believed that he received no such expert help from the Canadians as Fairbanks did from Foster. "I found that [the question] had not been thoroughly studied or thought out by any Canadian official," he wrote to Salisbury. W. C. Cartwright complained that the only Canadian attached to the Commission who had a complete knowledge of the question was W. F. King who was "addicted to whiskey and has no power of speech." Nevertheless, Herschell was convinced that the Canadians, generally, had a strong case. "When I had carefully investigated it, and got together all the materials available," he wrote, "I came to the conclusion that the British claim so to draw the boundary line as to leave the greater part of Lynn Canal, or at least the upper part of it, within the British possessions was much stronger than it at first appeared." [34]

The weak point in the Canadian argument was their case for drawing the southernmost part of the boundary line from the southern point of Prince of Wales Island through the Clarence Strait rather than to Portland Channel. When Herschell first presented the Canadian case to the Commission on 30 August 1898, he advocated the Canadian point of

[33] Herschell to Salisbury, February 17, 1899: Confidential Print 7135, p. 164.
[34] Herschell to Salisbury, October 11, 1898: Confidential Print 7135, p. 100; cited, Campbell, *Anglo-American Understanding,* p. 106.

view. "But," he told Lord Salisbury, "I may as well observe that I regard the contention as hopelessly untenable." Having voiced their opinion, the Canadians were willing to agree with Lord Herschell. "Of course we must concede that the line runs from the southern point of P. of W. Island through Portland Canal," Sir Louis Davies wrote to Sifton.[35]

Lord Herschell's first impression was that the Alaska boundary question could be settled with relative ease. It will be recalled that on 11 October he thought the North Atlantic Fisheries question presented the "greatest obstacles" to settlement. And, in fact, at only one point along the boundary, Lynn Canal, did serious difficulties arise. "As regards the rest of the boundary line," Herschell wrote to Salisbury in February 1899, "we have been able to adjust almost every part of it, conditionally on a satisfactory settlement being arrived at with reference to the harbour on Lynn Canal." At Lynn Canal the Americans frankly admitted they could not give up their essential interests and even to compromise them would be extremely difficult. W. C. Cartwright recalled in his secret memorandum to the British Government that "the Americans have been in possession of the whole canal for

[35] Herschell to Salisbury, September 2, 1898: Confidential Print 7135, p. 64; Sifton Papers, 60, Davies to Sifton, January 23, 1899. "But," Davies added, "we have *proved conclusively* that it must run up the narrow canal north of Pearse and Wales Islands & so up the Portland Canal. The evidence that this was called Portland Canal & the larger opening to the south of these islands Observatory Inlet by Vancouver is simply irresistable and that these two channels were known in 1825 at the time of the treaty respectively by these two names by the British and Russian negotiators is to my mind beyond any doubt. The value of this conclusion if agreed to lies in the fact that it throws both Pearse and Wales Islands to us also the exclusive possession of the great entrance to Observatory Inlet." At the Alaska Boundary Tribunal in 1903 Lord Alverstone suddenly changed his mind and decided that the line ran *south* of Pearse and Wales Islands, thus giving them to the United States. It was this decision which so infuriated the Canadians about the Alaska Boundary Tribunal.

some few years, and that two towns, Dyea and Skagway, have sprung up under American auspices, and are now under American Administration. Lord Herschell recognized that it is practically impossible to oust the Americans from those places." Laurier also recognized the strength of the American case. "I think myself that we have the letter of the treaty on our side & that we should have the line drawn at the entrance of Lynn Canal," he told Lord Minto, "but on the other hand the Americans are in possession of it, & as you know: possession is nine points of the law." [36]

The arguments presented on either side regarding possession of Lynn Canal were what might have been expected. Lord Herschell contended that "the line should follow the mountains, crossing all narrow waters which were of such width as to be within territorial jurisdiction." Lynn Canal, he conceded, was "not at its mouth within this category." But, he held, it "soon became so, and for 70 or 80 miles this channel extended as a narrow inlet to the interior of the country." The line should therefore be drawn across the Lynn Canal at that point where it did become narrow enough to be part of the territorial waters. Herschell buttressed his argument by maintaining that "it could not be considered as part of the 'ocean' within the meaning of that part of the Treaty which prescribed that the 10 marine leagues should be measured therefrom. I pointed out, as a notable fact, that the word 'ocean' had been expressly inserted in the place of 'mer,' which was in the original project, and which might be held to apply to salt water generally." In contrast, the Americans believed that "the eastern boundary line of the strip of territory, or 'lisiere,' on the mainland or continent follows the crest of the mountains (but never more than 10 marine

[36] Herschell to Salisbury, February 7, 1899, W. C. Cartwright, Memorandum B, March 27, 1899: Confidential Print 7135, pp. 155, 215; Public Archives of Canada, Minto Papers, 7, Laurier to Minto, February 13, 1899.

leagues from the coast), along the sinuosities of the coast, and always on the mainland, till it reaches the 141° of longitude, in the vicinity of Mount St. Elias." This, of course, meant that the line went around the head of rather than crossed Lynn Canal.[37]

The first substantial offer in the negotiations came from the United States in mid-December. The Americans suggested that British ships have the right of ingress and egress from Lynn Canal and the same harbor and port privileges on Lynn Canal that obtained to American ships. They also offered transshipment privileges from Dyea and Skagway across American territory to the Yukon territory of the Dominion. The British and Canadian Commissioners could not accept this proposal which "decides the entire question there at issue in favour of the United States" and Lord Herschell made two alternative suggestions. The first was that "the United States should have the whole of the land bordering on the Lynn Canal except Pyramid Harbor and a strip of land from that harbor to the boundary line, such as to secure access thereto by the Dalton trail. This would give almost the whole of the disputed territory in that region to the United States." The second proposal was to submit the boundary to delimitation by "legal and scientific experts" with the proviso that whatever their decision might be, Dyea and Skagway would be retained by the United States and Pyramid Harbor would be given to Canada.[38]

[37] Herschell to Salisbury, September 2 and 30, 1898: Confidential Print 7135, pp. 64-65, 84-85.

[38] Herschell to Salisbury, December 22, 1898: Confidential Print 7135, pp. 123-32. Herschell noted that President McKinley, "whilst not expressing directly his concurrence in this view, . . . did not intimate dissent" about Canada getting Pyramid Harbor. "You must have something you want," McKinley told Herschell. However, the British secretary to the Commission, W. C. Cartwright, argued that the American offer of commercial priviliges on Lynn Canal was of more value to Canadians than the cession of Pyramid Harbor. "It would not

The Americans viewed the first of Herschell's proposals with favor. It seemed to be a suitable compromise of a very difficult problem. They did, however, propose certain conditions on the grant of Pyramid Harbor. The area could not be fortified, the United States would have to retain nominal sovereignty although the territory would be exclusively administered by Canada and Canadian law would have exclusive jurisdiction, and, finally, the grant would be for a term of fifty years. The last condition, Laurier told Sifton, was "absolutely unacceptable." Rather than a stipulated time limit, the Canadian and British Commissioners proposed that "the occupation should last so long as Canada kept there a Custom house and a Police post, but that if Canada failed to keep there a Custom house and a Police post, then the territory would revert to the United States." There was also some protest within Laurier's Cabinet against the retention of sovereignty of Pyramid Harbor by the United States. David Mills noted that "it would be little short of a calamity to accept a mere easement, which would give us admission to a harbour on the Lynn Inlet. A concession which falls short of sovereignty is not worth taking." In general, however, the proposal of a cession of Pyramid Harbor to Canada, with retention of U.S. sovereignty and the length of time based on maintenance of a Canadian Customs house and Police post,

---

be difficult to construct a competing railway from Pyramid Harbour by the Dalton Trail," he wrote. "But it is not likely that this would be done. A good deal of British capital is invested in the railway now in the course of construction, and there would be much opposition on the part of British subjects, as well as from Americans, to any other railway scheme. It is far more probable that, after incurring considerable expense in forming settlement and in organizing an Administration at Pyramid Harbour, the Canadian Government would find it impossible to divert trade from Dyea and Skagway, and Pyramid Harbour would become a useless possession—in fact, a white elephant." Memorandum B, W. C. Cartwright, March 27, 1899: Confidential Print 7135, p. 216.

met with approval. Sifton believed that "a treaty upon these lines will be quite satisfactory. Of course it is capable of being attacked, you cannot hope to make a treaty which is not capable of being attacked, but this treaty is one which when properly placed before them will commend itself to the common sense and good judgment of the people." He only cautioned that "it must be clear . . . that we can charter a railroad and provide for its expropriation and all matter of that kind, and that we can transport troops and munitions of war, and that the harbour will be a Canadian harbour." [39]

At long last, it appeared that a peaceful and equitable diplomatic settlement of the Alaska boundary problem was going to be made by the Joint High Commission. Then, suddenly, the news of the Lynn Canal compromise leaked out.[40] Almost instantly a great flurry of protest arose on the West Coast of the United States. The Legislature of the State of Washington adopted a memorial against the "surrender" of American property and rights. President McKinley received telegrams of protest threatening the secession of the three West Coast States. Added to these were appeals from West Coast shipping interests which warned that giving Canada a harbor on Lynn Canal would be "highly detrimental" to their interests. Perhaps not entirely by coincidence, the American Commissioners discovered that they had made a grievous mistake. The proposed grant of Pyramid Harbor to Canada would involve a contravention of American navigation laws. Since sovereignty was retained by the United States, it would allow British ships to carry goods between two American

[39] Herschell to Salisbury, February 7, 1899: Confidential Print 7135, p. 155; Laurier Papers, 98, Laurier to Sifton, January 28, 1899, Mills to Laurier, January 25, 1899, Sifton to Laurier, January 21, 1899.

[40] Sir Joseph Pope recorded that the Americans blamed the Canadians for letting out the news of the Lynn Canal compromise. They said that "Sir Richard is the culprit, he wrote it so the story goes to his son." Pope Papers, 116, Diary, February 11, 1899.

ports i.e. between other American ports and Pyramid Harbor. But American ships could be precluded from carrying goods from Canadian ports to Pyramid Harbor. The American Commissioners therefore insisted that Pyramid Harbor, for the purpose of the navigation laws, be treated as a United States harbor. The Canadians, naturally, refused: there was no point in having a Canadian port which, for practical purposes, was an American port subject to American law. Rather, they suggested—reverting to the American proposal of mid-December—that all the ports on the Lynn Canal be used on the same terms by the vessels of both nations. The Americans would not accept this and accordingly the offer of a Canadian port at Pyramid Harbor finally had to be withdrawn by the United States.[41]

Suspecting the worst possible consequences of this turn of events, Herschell telegraphed to Salisbury on 12 February, requesting if necessary, permission to break off the negotiations of the Joint High Commission. Herschell said that he had "repeatedly pointed out that if we leave unsettled the question which is most likely to give rise to conflict and which, moreover, is capable of adjustment by methods well recognized among friendly Powers, it seems useless to remove the smaller causes of difference. . . . If it is impossible to agree on arbitration, my present impression is that we shall have to break off the negotiations." Salisbury informed Herschell that the Cabinet had decided to leave it to the discretion of the British and Canadian Commissioners to break off negotiations if they wished.[42]

When the Pyramid Harbor negotiations broke down, the only alternative solution to the Alaska boundary problem seemed to be to resort to arbitration. Actually, this alternative

[41] Herschell to Salisbury, February 7, 1899: Confidential Print 7135, p. 155.
[42] Herschell to Salisbury, February 12, 1899, Salisbury to Herschell, February 14, 1899: Confidential Print 7135, pp. 152-53.

had constantly been before the Commission. But both the Canadians and Americans were anxious to avoid arbitration. The American attitude was entirely understandable. "The American Commissioners fear that they would run the risk of being dislodged from Dyea and Skagway if the question were submitted to a foreign umpire," Pauncefote told Salisbury. Equally realistic was the reluctance of the Canadians to resort to the arbitration they had insisted on for so long. As early as October 1898, Sifton told Laurier that "we will never get any more from the commission than we have at the present time. I think in all probability that the result of such a commission would be that we would be confirmed in what we have at the present time, and the Americans would be confirmed in what they have . . . I would insist as a provision antecedent to the reference of the Boundary question to a commission that whatever the decision of the commission might be respecting the territory at the head of Lynn Canal, we should have undisputed ownership of a port and territory leading to a port upon the canal." If a diplomatic settlement on equitable terms could be made, it was by far the best answer to the problem. Resort to arbitration would mean further negotiation, and, more important, further prolongation of a potentially dangerous Canadian-American quarrel. Both Canadians and Americans agreed with Lord Herschell when he told Senator Fairbanks that "it would, I think, be a lamentable conclusion to be obliged on this question also to have recourse to arbitration." [43]

Nevertheless, arbitration seemed the only answer when a diplomatic settlement proved fruitless. During the last days of the meetings of the Joint High Commission numerous proposals were put forth by both sides. At first the Americans

[43] Pauncefote to Salisbury in Foreign Office to Colonial Office, February 10, 1899: CO42/870; Laurier Papers, 87, Sifton to Laurier, October 3, 1898; Herschell to Fairbanks, December 21, 1898: Confidential Print 7135, p. 130.

would only agree to an arbitration which already decided the boundary question at Lynn Canal in their favor. Eventually they conceded that the whole boundary line south of Mount St. Elias should go to arbitration. But, still, the British and American proposals were at wide variance and neither side was willing to give way. The discussion came to a climax in the two meetings of the Joint High Commission on 18 February 1899. The British proposed a three-man tribunal, one jurist each from the United States and Great Britain or Canada and the third from a European country. Under the rules of the British proposal, provision was implicitly made for the reservation of Dyea and Skagway to the United States no matter what the decision of the tribunal might be regarding the head of Lynn Canal. The Americans proposed that the tribunal be composed of six jurists, three nominated by each side. In amendment of the rules of the British proposal they insisted that "all towns or settlements on tidewater, settled under the authority of the United States and under the jurisdiction of the United States at the date of this Treaty, shall remain within the territory and jurisdiction of the United States." The American proposal was curtly rejected. As far as Lord Herschell and his colleagues were concerned, an even-numbered tribunal offered no solution at all; it merely prolonged the dispute. Herschell told the American Commissioners, "we might be no nearer to the solution of our differences or to the delimitation of the boundary than at present, and . . . although some boundary disputes might be left undetermined even for a long period without danger, the speedy delimitation of this boundary was, under existing circumstances, of urgent importance." [44]

The American Commissioners were in a difficult position. The British proposal followed the lines of the Venezuelan tribunal which the United States had forced on the British

[44] Herschell to Salisbury, February 12 and 24, 1899: Confidential Print 7135, pp. 152, 178, 180-83.

Government less than three years previously. In this sense, to refuse the British arbitration proposal was highly embarrassing. On the other hand, they could not agree to an arbitration which might entail the loss of American interests on Lynn Canal. The howl of protest about the Pyramid Harbor proposal had proved that fact. As Representative Payne (who had replaced the deceased Nelson Dingley) told the British and Canadian Commissioners, the Alaska boundary question "was vital, and could not be compromised." Momentarily, at the second meeting on the 18th the Americans sought a compromise. If they accepted a three-man tribunal, they asked, would the British consider a Latin American jurist as the third member? The reply was a decisive "No." The British Commissioners "thought it most objectionable, in view of the policy long maintained and recently reasserted by the Government of the United States towards the other countries on the said continent. The selection of an Umpire by any such nation would not, in their opinion, offer the guarantee of impartiality, which is the first qualification requisite for the discharge of the duties intrusted to him." With this refusal the Americans reverted to their proposal for a six-man tribunal.[45]

Further discussion of the Alaska boundary question, both sides agreed, was hopeless. The American Commissioners, however, wanted to proceed with the other questions before the Commission. "Several subjects," they said, "were so far advanced as to assure the probability of a settlement." "The British Commissioners do not consider it practicable to adopt that course," was the reply. "The manner in which they would be prepared to adjust some of the other important matters under consideration must depend in their view upon whether it is possible to arrive at a settlement of all the questions which might at any time occasion acute controversy, and even conflict. Of these the Alaska boundary question, in

[45] Protocol No. 63 and Notes of Proceedings at the Second Meeting of February 18, 1899: Confidential Print 7135, pp. 184, 186.

their opinion, stands in the forefront." And thus, two days later the Joint High Commission issued a statement saying that its meetings had been adjourned until August 1899. In part, the Canadian stand on the Alaska boundary question and, in part, an unfortunate accident combined to upset the stated plan.[46]

vi

The adjournment of the Joint High Commission was not desired by any of the Commissioners. Laurier spoke with deep sincerity when he told Lord Minto that "it would be lamentable . . . to depart without settling some of the most dangerous questions." Yet with negotiations deadlocked on the most pressing issues there was little point in going on and the Prime Minister believed that it was high time he returned to Ottawa. "I feel that there are duties awaiting me there," he told the Governor-General, "which I cannot neglect much longer." In addition, more subjective considerations arising out of the Alaska boundary negotiations helped Laurier to make up his mind. "We may separate," he told Premier Hardy of Ontario. "There is a question of dignity involved which must make it incumbent upon us to refuse to negotiate on anything else, and this we will unless they give way." "The Americans are certainly in the wrong," he wrote to Willison, and "I am not to be either bulldozed or bamboozled by them." [47]

Whether from a sense of outraged dignity or because of pressing business in Ottawa, the Canadians went home. But none of them, nor any of the American Commissioners considered that the months of negotiation had ended in failure.

[46] Herschell to Salisbury, February 24, 1899: Confidential Print 7135, p. 178.

[47] Minto Papers, 7, Laurier to Minto, February 7 and 13, 1899; Laurier Papers, 100, Laurier to Hardy, February 16, 1899; Willison Papers, 109, Laurier to Willison, February 15, 1899.

It was partially true that the adjournment of the Joint High Commission until August was, as Joseph Pope recorded, "only to let [the Americans] down easy . . . the Commission is dead and will never meet again." Certainly the difficulty of negotiating in a formal Commission, under the glare of intense publicity and public scrutiny, was momentarily abandoned. But, unknown to the public, negotiations were not abandoned with the adjournment of the Commission. In fact, the plan was quite the reverse. Lord Herschell, just a few days before the adjournment, had fallen and injured himself. His injury was serious enough that he expected to be detained in Washington for some time and he proposed to put his time to good use. "Our American colleagues were most anxious that the negotiations should not be broken off but merely adjourned," Herschell wrote to Salisbury. "I think they hope that a solution of [the Alaska] difficulty may be found by means of diplomatic negotiations, and the other matters may, not improbably, be adjusted without serious difficulty after that has been done." He suggested that personal negotiations by himself would meet with the approval of the United States Government and Salisbury concurred in the plan. Thus, Herschell would attempt to break through the Alaska boundary deadlock and pave the way for a settlement of all the outstanding problems, probably when the Commission reassembled in August. Unfortunately, within a matter of days Herschell was dead, and with his death vanished the main hope for successfully concluding the meetings of the Joint High Commission. It is hard to escape Professor Campbell's conclusion that "the long delay that ensued before the Canadian questions were finally adjusted, in some instances not until over a decade later, was perhaps due not so much to their intrinsic difficulties, great as they were, as to Lord Herschell's tragic accident one wintry day in Washington." Still, the "intrinsic difficulties," especially those of the Alaska boundary question, could not be denied and, after Herschell's death, they proved to be an insuperable obstacle to reassembling the Joint High Commission.[48]

As the months passed, the hope of a settlement rapidly faded away. Generally, the reason for this was that the Canadians abandoned any active part in the negotiations and preferred to act merely as critics of the more active role played by the British and American Governments. It was true that the Canadian Government was occupied with the meeting of Parliament which had been delayed until after the adjournment of the Commission and during the Parliamentary session less time could be devoted to Canadian-American problems. More important, however, was the attitude of the Canadian Government. Sir Wilfrid Laurier told William Van Horne that it certainly was not up to Canada to make the first move in the question.[49]

It seems to me that the first overtures should come from the American side. We have not been able to agree upon a compromise. There is nothing left but an arbitration. We have proposed to follow identically the precedent of the Venezuela case. Our position is so strong that it is not for us to depart from it in any way.

The British Government did not agree. "We should . . . warn the Canadians that the consequences of delay in a settlement appear to be more serious for them than for the U.S. who are in possession," wrote John Anderson. "I am afraid," Chamberlain wrote to Minto, "that our position is not a very strong one owing in part to the neglect of Canada in past years." In July Chamberlain issued his most blunt statement to Lord Minto. "We desire to impress upon your Ministers," the Colonial Secretary wrote, "that whatever arguments may be based on letter of Treaty of 1825, careful examination of

[48] Pope Papers, 116, Diary, February 20, 1899; Herschell to Salisbury, February 21, 1899: Confidential Print 7135, pp. 162-63; Campbell, *Anglo-American Understanding*, p. 119.

[49] Laurier Papers, 105, Laurier to Van Horne, March 24, 1899.

United States' case for possession of shore of [Lynn] Canal based on continuous uncontested jurisdiction since date of Treaty, and admissions of Hudson Bay Company, Imperial and Dominion Governments, shews that it is unassailable." Isreal Tarte reported that Chamberlain had told him, "notre opinion ici . . . est que votre cause est faible." The British Government was not going to abandon Canada on the Alaska boundary question. But the warning was very clear; it was not going to back up Canadian intransigence if a reasonable solution could be found for the Alaska boundary problem.[50]

Despite this warning, between May and September 1899, the Canadian Government refused to consider three different proposals for settling the problem. The first was a suggestion by President McKinley that negotiations should proceed on all the other questions before the Joint High Commission, leaving the Alaska boundary for subsequent diplomatic talks. This proposal was simply out of the question; it left the most pressing matter unsettled, and the Canadians replied that "the moment arbitration has been agreed upon, they will be ready to proceed with all other questions." A second suggestion by the British Government was based on discussions held between Sir Julian Pauncefote (who was home on leave) and Joseph Choate, the United States Ambassador to the Court of St. James's. In substance, the proposal was to arbitrate the boundary dispute on the lines of the Venezuela Treaty with two modifications: that there should be seven arbitrators rather than five, the seventh chosen by the other six who were appointed by the two Governments, and that Dyea and Skagway should remain the property of the United States whatever might be the decision of the arbitrators.

[50] Minute by Anderson on Minto to Chamberlain, May 14, 1899: CO42/868; Minto Papers, 14, Chamberlain to Minto, May 8, 1899; Chamberlain to Minto, in Minto to Chamberlain, July 19, 1899: CO42/869; Laurier Papers, 118, Tarte to Laurier, July 11, 1899.

Based on the evidence, Chamberlain warned Minto, "we feel certain that what we suggest is the utmost that can be got. If this is refused we fear that the Commission will not meet again & that no settlement is possible." Nevertheless, after less than a day's consideration of the proposal, it was rejected by the Canadians. They would not agree to the reservation of Dyea and Skagway unless a similar reservation of Pyramid Harbor was made to Canada. Unless this was acceptable to the United States, Minto replied, "My Ministers urge that United States can offer no valuable reasons against arbitration on terms of Venezuela precedent" with no reservations of territory to either party.[51]

This simply was not so. The Americans had always claimed the head of Lynn Canal, and moreover, had established settlements at Dyea and Skagway. In contrast, the Canadians had never either set foot upon nor laid claim to Pyramid Harbor. In fact, before the meeting of the Joint High Commission, they had never *officially* claimed the head of Lynn Canal. Despite Canadian denials, the most they had ever *officially* made known to the Americans before 1898-1899 was that they considered the whole of the boundary line south of Mount St. Elias as in dispute. This was a very strong point, and, coupled with the Canadian interpretation of the Treaty of 1825, it gave the Canadians a good case. But if Canada had a good argument for arbitrating the whole boundary, that did not mean that she was in an equally strong position when she suddenly made an implicit claim of territorial rights at Pyramid Harbor. Clearly recognizing this, Secretary of State Hay informed Mr. Tower, the British Chargé d'affaires at Washington, that the reservation of Pyramid Harbor to Canada "so completely changed the terms recently suggested [by Choate and Pauncefote] as to render

[51] G21, 93, No. 192A, Chamberlain to Minto, May 4 and 10, 1899 with enclosures; Laurier Papers, 751, Minto to Chamberlain, May 5 and 13, 1899, Chamberlain to Minto, May 12, 1899.

the entire proposition unacceptable." "We must try to persuade the Canadian Ministers that they would not be wise to press claims which will preclude a settlement of a question which it is more important for Canada than for the U.S. to get settled," Edward Wingfield observed with dismay.[52]

In July Isreal Tarte had a series of conversations in London with Chamberlain which led to the second British proposal. On the 18th Lord Salisbury told Joseph Choate that "I have reason to believe the Canadian Government would be prepared to accept [a proposal] that Canada should have a perpetual lease of territory to the extent of half a square mile at a suitable spot on the Lynn Canal, on similar conditions to those on which territory is held by Her Majesty's Government at the Chinde mouth of the Zambesi River, with liberty to construct a railway from there to the Yukon territory." The basic terms of the Chinde lease were its ninty-nine year duration and the fact that, aside from commercial privileges, jurisdiction of the leased territory remained under the Portuguese Code. This proposal struck Secretary of State Hay as most attractive, especially since it maintained American sovereignty, and it momentarily appeared that it would be accepted by the United States. Though claiming the contrary, the Canadian Government rejected the proposal by demanding what both London and Washington agreed was an impossible condition. Minto told Chamberlain on 19 July that "unless such an offer included harbour in which Canada would have jurisdiction, it would not be acceptable." "Delay in settlement highly prejudicial to Canadian interests," the Colonial Secretary angrily replied,[53]

[52] Foreign Office to Colonial Office, May 18 and 22, 1899: CO42/871; Minutes by Wingfield on Minto to Chamberlain, May 14, 1899: CO42/868.

[53] P.C. Report 1525K of August 19, 1899 in Minto to Chamberlain, August 24, 1899; Minto to Chamberlain, July 19, 1899, Chamberlain to Minto, July 21, 1899: CO42/869.

and we cannot but think that your Ministers will not wish to sacrifice only chance of obtaining an all British route to Yukon, and will acquiesce in action of Her Majesty's Government which was only taken after discussion with Mr. Tarte in full belief that it would be acceptable to Dominion Government. It is doubtful whether U.S. Government will accept in any case but we think it worth pressing.

Twice then, the British Government was placed in the extremely embarrassing position of making offers to the United States only to withdraw them because Canada considered their terms inadequate. The root of the difficulty was a lack of sufficient communication and consultation between the two Governments. There is no evidence to suggest that there was any prior consultation with Canada before the Choate-Pauncefote agreement was officially presented to Washington. And regarding the lease, it is clear that the reason for the embarrassment was a misunderstanding between London and Ottawa. In large part the blame rested on Chamberlain's shoulders. Tarte reported to Laurier that he had told Chamberlain:

"Si au moins les Etats-Unis nous offraient un terrain neutre sur le canal Lynn, à Pyramid Harbour, par exemple, et un droit de passage sur la lisière de terrain qu'ils réclament, nous verrions en une pareille offre de la bonne volonté."

M. Chamberlain a de suite observé:

"C'est de cette manière que nous avons réglé nos difficultés avec la France en Afrique. Nous avons donné aux français une zone, sur laquelle nous gardons notre suzeraineté, mais dans les limites de laquelle ils sont absolument maitres d'agir comme ils l'entendent, au point de vue des douanes, du commerce, etc. Si vous obteniez de semblables concessions des Etats-Unis, votre gouvernement serait-il satisfait?"

Je lui ai repondu que je le croyais, mais que naturellement je n'avais pas mission d'engager le gouvernement. Chamberlain, anxious to work out a settlement, seized on Tarte's statement without taking the precaution of consulting Ottawa, and, to this extent, he was at fault in going ahead with the second British proposal. On the other hand, Tarte had wired to Laurier on the 10th and the 12th asking if such a proposal would be acceptable to Canada. On the latter date, six days before Salisbury put the proposal to Choate, Laurier wired Tarte: "No. Leave matter altogether to us here." There is no evidence to suggest that Tarte ever communicated Laurier's telegram to Chamberlain. If he had done so, the second British proposal probably would not have been made.[54]

Eventually, a provisional boundary line at Lynn Canal, based on the previous provisional line at the summits of the White and Chilkoot passes and extended to the Chilkat pass in back of Pyramid Harbor, was agreed to by the Canadian and American Governments. The proposal had first been made by Secretary of State Hay in March 1899 and the agreement was signed on 20 October 1899. This line proved to be a suitable *modus vivendi* until a settlement was reached with the award of the Arbitration Tribunal four years later. In the meantime, by October 1899 the Alaska boundary question was overridden by the South African War as the matter of prime consideration for the Canadian and British Governments.

vii

Canadian stubbornness regarding negotiations for the resumption of the Joint High Commission, or more immediately, concerning the Alaska boundary, was not really surprising. Rather, it was the logical result of paying heed to a sentiment that was evident in Canada long before the adjourn-

[54] Laurier Papers, 117, Tarte to Laurier, July 10, 12 and 13, 1899, Laurier to Tarte, July 12, 1899; 118, Tarte to Laurier, July 11, 1899.

ment of the Joint High Commission. "The best for us all and for the continuance of friendly feelings between the two countries would be a quiet withdrawal without any treaty," Colonel Denison told Lord Salisbury in December 1898. This feeling was not confined to extremists like Denison whose anti-Americanism was probably unsurpassed in the Dominion. There was much truth in Denison's remark to Laurier that "your friends are the most anxious to see the negotiations broken off. The others think they can kill the Treaty anyway." G. W. Ross said that "nothing would please our people more than to be able to say that Sir Wilfrid Laurier and his colleagues contended with the Americans for four or five months for a fair treaty with Canada, and being unable to make such a treaty, they were content to trust the future of Canada to the self-reliance of its own people." Even Lord Minto appeared to be among those opposed to a treaty. Noting the prevalence of the sentiment in Canada, the Governor-General said "possibly such a course might be the most dignified, and there seems to me something to be said for it." [55]

Most important, of course, were the feelings of Laurier's political colleagues in Ottawa. The continual testing of the political weather gave a fairly accurate picture of what the Government could and could not do in its negotiations with the United States, and this picture was reflected in their letters to Sir Wilfrid Laurier. As early as November 1898, Sifton wrote that he was "convinced that the Americans will not make a treaty unless it is altogether jug-handled in their favour." He added that:

> I think it would be a serious blow to your popularity in
> the country and to the great confidence with which the
> people look to your control of the affairs of Govern-
> ment if any weakness were shown in this matter, and I

[55] Denison Papers, 8, Denison to Salisbury, December 24, 1898; Laurier Papers, 95, Denison to Laurier, December 28, 1898, Ross to Laurier, December 27, 1898; 100, Minto to Laurier, February 10, 1899.

think that most of your strong friends who are giving the matter attention and who take the trouble to look beneath the surface and find out what is going on in the business community and what the sentiments of the people are, would a thousand times rather that you came back from Washington without any treaty than that you brought back a treaty which could be successfully attacked.

Coming from Laurier's most astute political lieutenant, these were thoughts worthy of weighty consideration. And, as this sentiment increased, other Cabinet colleagues added their voices to the chorus. In February Scott informed Laurier that *"any* treaty now made will be subject to severe criticism. The independent spirit of the people has been aroused by the selfish and grasping policy shown by the Americans." [56]

When the Commission adjourned, the Liberal press in Canada hailed the returning Prime Minister for "having been firm and maintained the rights of the Dominion intact." The Conservative press responded by doing its best to discredit the work of the Canadians on the Joint High Commission. Taking a cue from the intemperate statements of the leader of the Opposition, Sir Charles Tupper, it pronounced the Joint High Commission an absolute failure, accused Sir Wilfrid Laurier and his colleagues of "grovelling" for favors at Washington, called the American stand on the Alaska boundary question an outright "insult," and demanded immediate retaliation against the United States. Naturally, the Liberal press responded with denials of failure and laid stress on the not unusual feature of adjournment in international negotiations. More significant than the political bickering, however, was the evident agreement on fundamentals. Liberals and Conservatives argued whether Sir Wilfrid and his colleagues had taken a strong stand, but both stressed the importance

[56] Sifton Papers, 291, Sifton to Laurier, November 29, 1898; Laurier Papers, 101, Scott to Laurier, February 14, 1899 (stress original).

of maintaining Canadian rights and interests. "There is no alternative for Canada but to pursue [a] self-reliant and independent course," said the *Montreal Gazette,* "let us have done with negotiations where the concessions are all on one side." "We seek no favors, no coddling, no consideration," the *Toronto Globe* proclaimed. The *Regina Leader* argued that "Canada is capable of holding her place and privileges in relation to the United States with dignified consciousness of a desire to maintain international friendliness and in confident knowledge at the same time that United States friendliness towards us is by no means essential to our well-being, whatever reasons may exist for courting it from an Imperial point of view." [57]

The rising economic prosperity of Canada that happily coincided with the assumption of office by the Liberal party infused in Canadians a greater feeling of self-reliance and self-confidence than they had experienced since the early years of the National Policy. Added to this was a seemingly inherent distrust of the United States which was an ever-present element of Canadian sentiment. Clearly, this feeling of distrust was shared by Liberals as well as Conservatives. Lord Minto commented on the phenomenon in a letter to his brother a few days after the adjournment of the Joint High Commission. "There certainly was no love lost between this country and the States before the Commission met," Minto wrote,[58]

and recent events have not encouraged the growth of any affection. In fact, there is a general dislike of the Yankees here and I do not wonder at it. It's all very well for people

[57] *St. John Daily Telegraph,* February 28, 1899; *Montreal Gazette,* February 23 and 25, 1899; *Toronto Mail and Empire,* February 22, 23, 24 and March 4, 1899; *Toronto Globe,* February 21, 1899; *Regina Leader,* March 2, 1899.

[58] Minto Papers, 36, Minto to Arthur Elliott, M.P., February 26, 1899.

in England to romance about the sentimental love of his Anglo-Saxon Race on either side of the Atlantic but mercifully England has an ocean between him and his love. Here there is nothing of the sort. What the Canadian sees and hears is constant Yankee bluff, and swagger & that eventually he means to possess Canada for himself. And he reads with wonder of the so-called rapproachement of the old country with a people with which he, the Canadian, has no sympathy and whom he thoroughly distrusts. There is a certain wish perhaps amongst leading men here to encourage friendly relations as much as possible, but I believe it goes against the grain even with them to do so.

Certainly the best hope for making a success out of the efforts of the Joint High Commission rested on the planned private negotiations between Lord Herschell and Secretary of State Hay. After Herschell's unfortunate death, the fate of the Joint High Commission could be determined only by the success or failure of negotiations on the Alaska boundary conducted through the regular and complicated diplomatic channels. At this point the sentimental factors of Canadian self-confidence and distrust of the Americans came into play. The Canadian Government realized that it was politically impossible to back down from its stand on the Alaska boundary question. Sir Louis Davies, in October 1899, bluntly informed Colonial Secretary Chamberlain of this elemental fact in Canadian political life. "I then stated," Davies reported to Laurier, "that I was satisfied public opinion in Canada, believing we had a right to the territory at the head of Lynn Canal, would never sanction the voluntary surrender by us of Dyea and Skagway to the United States . . . unless we had a reciprocal and distinct concession to Canada of the only remaining harbour in Lynn Canal [Pyramid Harbor]; and I went further and said that it was not a matter of the present Government's existence, but of the existence of any government." Canadian opinion on the attempted reconciliation in Canadian-American relations was, perhaps, best summed up in a few words by the *Toronto Globe*. Reviewing the stand taken by the Canadian members on the Joint High Commission, the *Globe* confidently proclaimed that "we believe our commissioners will stand justified in the face of the world." [59]

[59] Laurier Papers, 791C, Davies to Laurier, October 12, 1899; *Toronto Globe*, February 21, 1899.

CHAPTER XII

An Expression of Canadian
National Sentiment

THE problem of sharing the North American continent
forced the Canadian Government to make a number of
critical decisions concerning Canadian-American relations in the latter part of the nineteenth century. As the years
passed and as the problem increased in magnitude and intensity it is apparent that these Canadian decisions were not hasty
opinions to serve a momentary purpose, but rather, segments
of an evolving Canadian policy in Canadian-American relations. Surprisingly, for a nation so inexperienced and immature
in foreign relations, for a nation which remained a "colonial
nation" both in fact and in law, and for a nation torn by
domestic quarrels between English- and French-speaking
Canadians, this policy appeared to be carefully thought out
and rooted in the principle of national survival in the future
as well as in the present. And, interestingly enough, though
there were some exceptions, most Canadians unquestioningly
accepted this principle. Where they differed was on how best
to maintain their national character, not on whether their
national character was worth maintaining. This was true
even in the long debate within the Liberal party over Unrestricted Reciprocity. Edward Blake believed that the Liberal
trade policy threatened the emerging Canadian identity;
Laurier, Cartwright and Davies thought that the National
Policy threatened that identity and that their policy would
preserve it.

Gradually both the United States and Great Britain came
to accept the fact of a Canadian nation on the North American continent. Secretary of State Bayard told Sir Charles
Tupper in 1887 that "the confederation of Canada and the construction of the Canadian Pacific Railway have brought us

face to face with a nation, and we may as well discuss public questions from that point of view." Joseph Chamberlain recognized the same point when he noted in December 1898 that "Canada is becoming stronger & must take care of herself." And this recognition of growing Canadian stature was evident in both form and substance. Herein lay the significance of the difference of the Canadian role in the Joint High Commissions of 1871 and 1898. In the former year Sir John Macdonald was the lone Canadian appointment taking his instructions from London. In the latter the four Canadians took their instructions from Ottawa.

With the abrogation of the fishery clauses of the Treaty of Washington, 1871, the Canadian Government adopted a policy of protection for their inshore fisheries. There were three main parts to the policy, the revision of the Fisheries Act of 1868, the equipping of a force of marine police, and the active cooperation of the Royal Navy in the enforcement of the policy. The first two parts were accomplished, though with the reluctant assent of the Imperial Government, and the third would have been brought to bear against the Americans had not agreement been reached to settle the problem at the Joint High Commission of 1887-1888. In essence, the Canadian Government believed that only through a strict enforcement of a policy of protection could they preserve a valuable national asset. At the same time, the Government recognized that only flagrant encroachments by Americans should be punished and that it was less dangerous to ignore the minor or questionable violations in the inshore waters than it was to risk war with the United States.

The persistent desire to settle the fisheries dispute by treaty was based on two readily apparent facts. First, while some Canadian fishermen might benefit by exclusive use of the inshore fishery in the short run, over a longer period of time the commercial, transportation, and fishing industries of the Maritime Provinces would receive greater benefit from a shared fishery. Denial of commercial privileges and facilities to American fishermen was sound policy to take to the diplomatic table as a bargaining point, but it was not sound economic policy for Maritime commerce. This was implicit in the *modus vivendi* which had been negotiated as a substitute for the abortive Treaty of Washington, 1888, and remained as the settlement of the fisheries dispute throughout the nineteenth century. Secondly, the inshore fisheries were clearly regarded as a Canadian national asset. Their primary benefit would always go to the Maritime Provinces. But because the Americans did desire entrance into them and use of them, they could be turned to the benefit of the whole of Canada. It was for this reason that the Canadians always sought trade concessions in natural products in their fishery negotiations with the United States. In short, Canadian fishery policy was not to surrender their national asset but rather to use it to the best advantage at least of the Maritime Provinces and, if possible, of all of Canada.

In the Behring Sea dispute the Canadian Government had less opportunity to develop an independent policy. In contrast with the North Atlantic Fisheries problem, it could not revise an existing law or pass a new one which would protect the sealers. It could not send Canadian cruisers to Behring Sea as escorts for the sealing vessels. And even the Canadians, with the exception of Sir Charles Tupper and a few British Columbians, saw the danger of actively engaging the Royal Navy in support of their cause. Fundamentally, the dispute centered around the question of freedom of the seas. It was more an Imperial than a Canadian question and the Dominion Government was obliged to rely on the Colonial and Foreign Offices for decisions as to how and when negotiations would be conducted. All the same, the pelagic sealing industry was primarily a Canadian industry, developed by and maintained by Canadians. And, in recognition of this fact, Canadians—particularly Sir Charles Hibbert Tupper and Sir Louis

Davies—exercised a substantial influence on the formulation of Imperial policy. As a result of Canada's role in this segment of Imperial diplomacy, friction developed between the Imperial and the Canadian Governments. But even the disagreements between Canada and Great Britain had a twofold benefit for the Dominion. The divergence of opinion made both the Canadian Government and the Canadian people aware of the fact that in Canada's foreign as well as in her domestic policy, there were times when the national interests of the Dominion might be quite different from the collective interests of the British Empire. Also, the Imperial Government soon realized that Canada would and could take a stand of its own in foreign relations.

On both of these maritime problems the Canadian public expressed its outrage at the willful violation of Canadian or British rights. More than that, the Canadian public was determined not to allow its Government to surrender these rights under pressure from the United States. It is true that the Liberal party when in Opposition accused the Conservatives of surrender on both the Washington Treaty of 1888 and the Paris Arbitration Tribunal Award of 1893. Regarding the latter, Sir Richard Cartwright said "Canada gets the shells and the United States gets the oyster." But the remark was calculated solely to boost the fortunes of the Liberals in the House of Commons and the Press Gallery. Moreover, its content revealed that Cartwright was just as concerned as was the Government about the protection of Canadian national interests.

At first glance Cartwright's concern over the protection of Canadian interests in the Behring Sea dispute seems at variance with his ardent advocacy of Unrestricted Reciprocity. Apparently much more consistent was the goal Edward Blake, the leading Liberal critic of Unrestricted Reciprocity, envisaged for Canada. Blake admitted that joining the American union would be "no ignoble lot." But, he added,

I cling to the hope of a higher though more arduous destiny for the great Dominion. I look for the regeneration of my own country. I cling to the hope that—sooner or later, and rather soon than late—there may be born into the world an independent Canadian Commonwealth, nerving itself to solve, after its own fashion, the many racial and religious, moral and political, economic and material problems which confront us; united by enduring links of kinship and sympathy, hope and aspiration with three of the leading nations of the world; advancing . . . together with the fullest freedom of trade and the widest measure of intercourse compatible with the provision of our revenue and the preservation of our autonomy. May these things be! [1]

It was, perhaps, inevitable that Canadians should question Canada's destiny during the depression years of the late 1880's. The Dominion was young, still in its testing time; its validity as an economic and political entity had not been proved. For most Canadians loyalty remained focused on the provinces or sections of the country in which they lived. The Ottawa Government was regarded as a great experiment, not as the foundation-stone of a Canadian national structure. Continentalism was an attractive alternative to the National Policy and appeared to have the support of influential Americans as well as Canadians. Yet the attractiveness of the proposal rested in its generality and lack of definition. Attempts at definition led to the recognition that Commercial Union, in both political and economic terms, presented a clear choice between continentalism and nationalism, despite what most Canadian Commercial Unionists said to the contrary.

It must be emphasized that the Liberal party did not view Unrestricted Reciprocity as leading to the destruction of Canadian nationality; that role they had already consigned to the

[1] Blake Papers, Blake to Mills, April 12, 1892.

National Policy, as the "Blue Ruin Knight" stressed over and over again in his criticisms of Conservative budgets. Rather, they believed that their trade policy would preserve Canadian identity. After all, Unrestricted Reciprocity was a compromise with Commercial Union designed for that very purpose. Its main point was tariff autonomy rather than tariff unity against the outside world. And the Liberals believed—though I think naïvely—that Unrestricted Reciprocity would assure Canada's economic future without endangering her political future. But more important than any of these considerations was the principal motive for adopting Unrestricted Reciprocity as the trade policy, indeed, *the* policy of the Liberal party. Sir Richard Cartwright gave the fundamental reason for the Liberals' flirtation with continentalism. "As a political organisation we simply had no alternative," he said. "We had to adopt this project or go to pieces."

For the Conservatives Unrestricted Reciprocity was a direct threat to their National Policy. It was also a challenge to the separate Canadian entity on the North American continent and to the Imperial connection upon which that entity depended for political and military support. Hence, the Conservatives went to the country in March 1891, on the double-barreled issue of loyalty to country and to Empire. Emerging victorious from the electoral battle, the Government then went ahead with its plans for the consolidation and expansion of the power of the Dominion. The expansion of trade with Great Britain and the creation of the Department of Trade and Commerce were seemingly unrelated to Canada's problems with the United States. But Canadians of the time did not take such a narrow view of their efforts. The fact was that they were an essential part of the economic and political defense of Canada against ultimate absorption into the American Republic.

The Liberal party chieftains believed that their party would "go to pieces" without Unrestricted Reciprocity. In the end, the Liberal party nearly went to pieces with Unrestricted Reciprocity. The attack by their political opponents was expected, though the victory of Sir John A. Macdonald in 1891 was a serious blow to Liberal party hopes. And when the Canadian agriculturalists did not meet with calamity at the hands of William McKinley as the Liberals predicted, but rather, found a ready market for their surplus crops in Great Britain, the Liberals were further disillusioned with their trade policy. The party suffered even more from the internal criticism of Blake, Mowat, and Mackenzie and from the abandonment of its pseudo-allies in Canada and the United States when the Commercial Unionists became advocates of political union. But the critical factor in the decision to abandon Unrestricted Reciprocity was the same as that which led to its adoption, political necessity. Interestingly enough, it was the same Sir Richard Cartwright, who had complained about the party's going to pieces in 1887, who complained about the "meanness of our well-to-do supporters" in 1893. With the adoption of a platform of "freer trade" with all the world by the Liberal Convention in 1893, the well-to-do supporters once again moved back into the ranks of Canadian Liberalism, but not without demanding their pound of flesh. From the Liberal victory in 1896 they asked and received the rejection of Cartwright as Minister of Finance and the virtual adoption of the National Policy by its former critics.

Not the least important of the objects of the National Policy was to bring under Canadian control all of the trading and commercial activities affecting the Dominion. With the discovery of gold in the Yukon this aspect of the National Policy became the primary consideration of the Canadian Government in the Alaska boundary dispute. Though most of the gold was being mined within Canadian territory, it found its way into American rather than Canadian hands. Even more important was the fact that American commercial interests were attempting to control an ever expanding market for trade goods in the Yukon territory. It was this "imperative reason for immediate action" which led to the introduction of the Yukon Bill in the House of Commons in 1897. The Alaska boundary problem had become "a national question of the greatest interest," Railways Minister Blair explained. The Yukon trade, he said, "is ours, it is within our borders and of right belongs to us." And when the attempt to secure an "all Canadian" route to the Yukon was thwarted by the Conservative Senators, this same objective led the Dominion Government to adopt an uncompromising attitude to the settlement of the Alaska boundary dispute. In this sense, then, the Canadian Government was anxious to settle the boundary problem, but only if an agreement could be reached which would guarantee them a Canadian access route to the Yukon through Lynn Canal. On the other hand, the American Government was equally determined to protect the vested trading interests of its citizens in Alaska. As Representative Payne told his colleagues on the Joint High Commission of 1898-1899, the Alaska boundary question "was vital, and could not be compromised." On that point the attempt at reconciliation in Canadian-American relations faltered and then, with the death of Lord Herschell, collapsed.

The failure of the Joint High Commission of 1898-1899 was not a disaster for Canada. In fact, many Canadians firmly believed there were positive benefits in the unsuccessful conclusion of the Commission's meetings. A. G. Blair told Laurier there would be "a certain amount of kudos" for the Liberal government if it firmly stood out against terms which "we had not considered sufficiently favourable." Certainly all Canadians agreed that Canadian-American problems had to be settled. But they also agreed that the settlement should be on equitable terms and not, as Clifford Sifton put it, "altogether jug-handled in their favour." Canada existed as a separate nation on the North American continent and expected to be treated as a separate nation. By 1900, then, Canadians had renewed their faith in the achievement of 1867 and in the National Policy. An old Toronto Liberal, George W. Ross, spoke for his countrymen when he said "they were content to trust the future of Canada to the self-reliance of its own people."

BIBLIOGRAPHY

PRIMARY SOURCES

Manuscripts: Personal

PUBLIC ARCHIVES OF CANADA

J. J. C. Abbott

Lord Aberdeen

Mackenzie Bowell

G. T. Denison

A. T. Galt

G. M. Grant

Lord Granville

Wilfrid Laurier

John A. Macdonald

D'Alton McCarthy

Lord Minto

Joseph Pope

C. E. L. Porteous

R. W. Scott

Clifford Sifton

J. S. D. Thompson

Charles Tupper

Charles Hibbert Tupper

J. S. Willison

PUBLIC ARCHIVES OF ONTARIO

Edward Blake

Alexander Campbell

Richard Cartwright

J. D. Edgar

William Kirby

NEW YORK PUBLIC LIBRARY

Andrew Carnegie Autograph Collection

William Bourke Cockran

Miscellaneous Collection. There are a few items concerning Erastus Wiman in this collection.

NEW YORK HISTORICAL SOCIETY, C. S. Fairchild

MANN LIBRARY, CORNELL UNIVERSITY, Goldwin Smith

UNIVERSITY OF TORONTO LIBRARY, John Charlton

DOUGLAS LIBRARY, QUEEN'S UNIVERSITY, W. D. Gregory

TORONTO PUBLIC LIBRARY, E. W. Banting Collection, Mollie Cartwright Diary

UNIVERSITY OF BIRMINGHAM LIBRARY, Joseph Chamberlain

BOWOOD, WILTS, The Fifth Marquis of Lansdowne

CHRIST CHURCH LIBRARY, OXFORD UNIVERSITY, The Third Marquis of Salisbury

Manuscripts: Official

PUBLIC ARCHIVES OF CANADA
Colonial Office Papers: CO42 (microfilm) 1880-1900; CO807 (microfilm) 1880-1900.
Records of the Governor-General's Office: G21 1880-1900.
Records of the Privy Council of Canada 1880-1900.
Records of the Department of Trade and Commerce 1880-1900.
LIBRARY OF CONGRESS, WASHINGTON, D.C., U.S.A.
Foreign Office Papers: FO115 (microfilm) 1880-1885.

Printed Documents

CANADA
Papers in Reference to Various Questions Affecting Newfoundland and Canada. Ottawa, 1893.
Report of the Royal Commission on Dominion-Provincial Relations. Book 1. Ottawa, 1954.
Department of Agriculture. *The Statistical Yearbook of Canada, 1900.* Ottawa, 1901.
Foley, J. G., ed. *Resume of General Elections.* Ottawa, 1916.
Parliament. *Sessional Papers.*
House of Commons. *Official Report of Debates.*
Senate. *Debates of The Senate of the Dominion of Canada.*
UNITED STATES OF AMERICA
Papers Relating to The Foreign Relations of the United States, 1880-1900. Washington, 1881-1901.
Fur Seal Arbitration. Proceedings of the Tribunal of Arbitration Convened at Paris. 16 vols. Washington, 1895.
Alaskan Boundary Tribunal. Proceedings of the Alaskan Boundary Tribunal, Convened at London. 7 vols. Washington, 1904.
GREAT BRITAIN
Behring Sea Arbitration. Report of the Behring Sea Commission, and Report of British Commissioners of June 21, 1892. London, 1893.
Behring Sea Arbitration. Case Presented on the Part of the Government of Her Britannic Majesty to the Tribunal of Arbitration Constituted Under Article 1 of the Treaty Concluded at

Washington on the 29th February, 1892, Between Her Britannic Majesty and the United States of America. London, 1893.

Behring Sea Arbitration. Counter-Case Presented on the Part of Her Britannic Majesty to the Tribunal of Arbitration Constituted Under Article 1 of the Treaty Concluded at Washington on the 29th February, 1892, Between Her Britannic Majesty and the United States of America. London, 1893.

Printed Collections

Haultain, A., ed. *A Selection from Goldwin Smith's Correspondence, 1846-1910.* Toronto, n.d.

Keith, Sir, A. B., ed. *Speeches and Documents on the British Dominions, 1918-1931.* London, 1932.

Lodge, H. C., ed. *Selections from the Correspondence of Theodore Roosevelt and Henry Cabot Lodge, 1884-1918.* 2 vols. New York, 1925.

The Collected Papers of John Bassett Moore. New Haven, 1944.

Ollivier, M., ed. *The Colonial and Imperial Conferences from 1887 to 1937.* 3 vols. Ottawa, 1954.

Pope, Sir Joseph, ed. *Correspondence of Sir John Macdonald.* Garden City, 1921.

Volwiler, A. T., ed. *The Correspondence between Benjamin J. Harrison and James G. Blaine, 1882-1893.* Philadelphia, 1940.

Newspapers and Journals

Canadian Manufacturer and Industrial World
Edmonton Bulletin
Halifax Morning Chronicle
Manitoba Free Press
Montreal Gazette
Montreal Herald
Ottawa Free Press
Queen's Quarterly
Regina Leader
St. John Daily Telegraph
Toronto Daily Mail and Empire
Toronto Empire
Toronto Globe
Victoria British Weekly Colonist
Victoria Daily Times
The Week

Pamphlets and Pamphlet Collections

Barker, Wharton. *Memorandum to Hon. Justin S. Morill, Chairman Finance Committee, United States Senate.* Philadelphia, 1887.

Butterworth, B. *Commercial Union between Canada and the United States.* . . . New York, 1887.

Commercial Union Club of Toronto. *Handbook of Commercial Union.* Toronto, 1888.

Commercial Union Pamphlets. A collection bound by the University of Toronto Library.

Sherman, Senator J. *Relations with Canada—Annexation.* Washington, 1888.

Smith, Goldwin. *The Political Relations of Canada to Great Britain and the United States.* Toronto, 1890.

Teller, Senator H. M. *The Fisheries Treaty.* Washington, 1888.

Wishart, A. *The Behring Sea Question.* Edinburgh, 1893.

SECONDARY MATERIAL

Books

Allen, H. C. *The Anglo-American Relationship Since 1783.* London, 1959.

Annett, D. R. *British Preference in Canadian Commercial Policy.* Toronto, 1948.

Beale, H. K. *Theodore Roosevelt and the Rise of America to World Power.* Baltimore, 1956.

Blum, J. M. *The Republican Roosevelt.* Cambridge, 1954.

Bodelsen, C. A. *Studies in Mid-Victorian Imperialism.* Reprint. London, 1960.

Brebner, J. B. *North Atlantic Triangle, The Interplay of Canada, The United States and Great Britain.* New Haven, 1945.

Callahan, J. M. *American Foreign Policy in Canadian Relations.* New York, 1937.

Campbell, A. E. *Great Britain and the United States, 1895-1903.* London, 1960.

Campbell, C. S. *Anglo-American Understanding, 1898-1903.* Baltimore, 1957.

Cartwright, Sir Richard. *Reminiscences*. Toronto, 1912.

Corbett, P. E. *The Settlement of Canadian-American Disputes.* New Haven, 1937.

Creighton, Donald G. *The Empire of the St. Lawrence*. Toronto, 1956.

———. *John A. Macdonald, The Young Politician*. Toronto, 1952.

———. *John A. Macdonald, The Old Chieftain*. Toronto, 1955.

Dafoe, J. W. *Laurier: A Study in Canadian Politics*. Toronto, 1922.

Denison, G. T. *The Struggle for Imperial Unity*. London, 1909.

Dewey, A. G. *The Dominions and Diplomacy: The Canadian Contribution*. 2 vols. London, 1929.

Dulles, Foster Rhea. *America's Rise to World Power, 1898-1954.* The New American Nation Series. New York, 1954.

Easterbrook, W. T. and H. G. J. Aitken. *Canadian Economic History*. Toronto, 1956.

Ensor, R. C. K. *England, 1870-1914*. Oxford History of England. Oxford, 1960.

Farr, D. M. L. *The Colonial Office and Canada, 1867-1887.* Toronto, 1955.

Faulkner, Harold U. *Politics, Reform and Expansion, 1890-1900.* The New American Nation Series. New York, 1959.

Flenley, R., ed. *Essays in Canadian History*. Toronto, 1939.

Galbraith, J. S. *The Hudson's Bay Company as an Imperial Factor*. Berkeley, 1957.

Garraty, J. A. *Henry Cabot Lodge, A Biography*. New York, 1953.

Garvin, J. L. and J. Amery. *The Life of Joseph Chamberlain*. 4 vols. London, 1932-1951.

Gelber, L. M. *The Rise of Anglo-American Friendship. A Study in World Politics, 1898-1906*. London, 1938.

Glazebrook, G. P. de T. *A History of Canadian External Relations*. London, 1950.

Goldman, Eric F. *Rendezvous with Destiny, A History of Modern American Reform*. New York, 1956.

Goodwin, C. D. W. *Canadian Economic Thought, The Political Economy of a Developing Nation, 1814-1914*. Duke University Commonwealth-Studies Center Publications. Durham, 1961.

Hayes, C. J. H. *Nationalism: A Religion*. New York, 1960.

Hays, S. P. *The Response to Industrialism, 1885-1914*. The Chicago History of American Civilization. Chicago, 1957.

Hodgins, T. *British and American Diplomacy Affecting Canada, 1782-1899*. Toronto, 1900.

Hofstadter, Richard. *The American Political Tradition and the Men Who Made It*. New York, 1957.

———. *The Age of Reform, from Bryan to F.D.R.* New York, 1955.

Hopkins, J. C., ed. *Canada, An Encyclopedia of the Country*. Toronto, 1898.

Innis, H. A. *The Cod Fisheries, The History of an International Economy*. Rev. edn. Toronto, 1954.

Jebb, R. *Studies in Colonial Nationalism*. London, 1905.

———. *The Imperial Conference: A History and Study*. 2 vols. London, 1911.

Jessup, Philip C. *The Law of Territorial Waters and Maritime Jurisdiction*. New York, 1927.

Johnson, A., ed. *Dictionary of American Biography*. 20 vols. New York, 1928-1936.

Keenleyside, H. L. and James Eayrs *et al. The Growth of Canadian Policies in External Affairs*. Duke University Commonwealth-Studies Center Publications. Durham, 1960.

Keith, A. B. *Responsible Government in the Dominions*. 2 vols. Oxford, 1928.

———. *The Sovereignty of the British Dominions*. London, 1929.

Kennedy, A. L. *Salisbury, 1830-1903, Portrait of a Statesman*. London, 1953.

Kohn, Hans. *American Nationalism, An Interpretive Essay*. New York, 1957.

Langelier, C. *Souvenirs Politiques, 1890 à 1896*. Quebec, 1912.

Leech, M. *In the Days of McKinley*. New York, 1959.

Lower, A. R. M. *Canada, Nation and Neighbor*. Toronto, 1952.

———. *Canadians in the Making, A Social History of Canada*. Toronto, 1958.

——— and F. R. Scott *et al. Evolving Canadian Federalism*. Duke University Commonwealth-Studies Center Publications. Durham, 1958.

McDiarmid, O. J. *Commercial Policy in the Canadian Economy.* Cambridge, 1946.

MacKay, R. A., ed. *Newfoundland, Economic, Diplomatic and Strategic Studies.* Toronto, 1946.

Mackenzie, A. *The Life and Speeches of Hon. George Brown.* Toronto, 1882.

Magnus, Sir P. M. *Gladstone, A Biography.* London, 1954.

Maycock, Sir W. *With Mr. Chamberlain in the United States and Canada, 1887-88.* Toronto, 1914.

Morley, J. *The Life of William Ewart Gladstone.* 2 vols. London, 1908.

Morton, W. L. *Manitoba, A History.* Toronto, 1957.

——. *The Canadian Identity.* Madison, 1961.

Neuendorff, G. *Studies in the Evolution of Dominion Status.* London, 1942.

Nevins, Allan. *Grover Cleveland, A Study in Courage.* New York, 1932.

Ormsby, M. A. *British Columbia: A History.* Toronto, 1958.

Perkins, Dexter. *The Monroe Doctrine, 1867-1907.* Baltimore, 1937.

Pope, Maurice, ed. *Public Servant, The Memoirs of Sir Joseph Pope.* Toronto, 1960.

Pope, Sir Joseph. *Memoirs of the Right Honourable Sir John Alexander Macdonald, G.C.B.* 2nd edn. Toronto, 1930.

Porritt, E. *Sixty Years of Protection in Canada, 1846-1912.* Winnipeg, 1913.

Pratt, J. W. *A History of United States Foreign Policy.* Englewood Cliffs, 1955.

Pringle, H. F. *Theodore Roosevelt.* New York, 1931.

Rumilly, R. *Histoire De La Province De Quebec.* Vols. VII, VIII. Montreal, n.d.

——. *Henri Bourassa.* Montreal, 1953.

Saunders, E. M., ed. *The Life and Letters of the Rt. Hon. Sir Charles Tupper, Bart., K.C.M.G.* 2 vols. London, 1916.

Saywell, J. T. *The Office of Lieutenant-Governor.* Toronto, 1957.

——. ed. *The Canadian Journal of Lady Aberdeen, 1893-1898.* Toronto, 1960.

Shippee, L. B. *Canadian-American Relations, 1849-1874*. New Haven, 1939.

Skelton, O. D. *Life and Letters of Sir Wilfrid Laurier*. 2 vols. New York, 1922.

———. *The Life and Times of Sir Alexander Tilloch Galt*. Toronto, 1920.

Smith, Goldwin. *Canada and the Canadian Question*. Toronto, 1892.

Smith, Goldwin. *The Treaty of Washington, 1871*. Ithaca, 1941.

Stovel, J. A. *Canada in the World Economy*. Cambridge, 1959.

Strauss, W. L. *Joseph Chamberlain and the Theory of Imperialism*. New York, 1942.

Tansill, C. C. *Canadian-American Relations, 1875-1911*. New Haven, 1943.

———. *The Foreign Policy of Thomas F. Bayard, 1885-1897*. New York, 1942.

Thayer, W. R. *The Life and Letters of John Hay*. 2 vols. Boston, 1915.

Thompson, F. F. *The French Shore Problem in Newfoundland, An Imperial Study*. Canadian Studies in History and Government. Toronto, 1961.

Thompson, D. C. *Alexander Mackenzie, Clear Grit*. Toronto, 1960.

Thornton, A. P. *The Imperial Idea and Its Enemies*. London, 1959.

Tomasevich, Jozo. *International Agreements on the Conservation of Marine Resources*. Stanford, 1943.

Tupper, Sir Charles. *Recollections of Sixty Years in Canada*. London, 1914.

Tyler, J. E. *The Struggle for Imperial Unity, 1868-95*. London, 1938.

Underhill, F. H. *In Search of Canadian Liberalism*. Toronto, 1960.

Van Alstyne, R. W. *The Rising American Empire*. New York, 1960.

Wade, Mason. *The French Canadians, 1760-1945*. New York, 1955.

Wallace, E. *Goldwin Smith, Victorian Liberal*. Toronto, 1957.

418

Warner, D. F. *The Idea of Continental Union*. Lexington, 1960.

Willison, J. S. *Sir Wilfrid Laurier and the Liberal Party, A Political History*. Toronto, 1903.

Willson, B. *Friendly Relations: A Narrative of Britain's Ministers and Ambassadors to America, 1791-1930*. Boston, 1934.

Articles

Bailey, T. A. "Theodore Roosevelt and the Alaska Boundary Settlement," *Canadian Historical Review*, XVIII (1937), 123-130.

Banks, M. A. "Edward Blake's Relations with Canada during His Irish Career, 1892-1907," *Canadian Historical Review*, XXXV (1954), 22-43.

———. "The Change in the Liberal Party Leadership, 1887," *Canadian Historical Review*, XXXVIII (1957), 109-128.

Bemis, S. F. "American Foreign Policy and the Blessings of Liberty," *American Historical Review*, LXVII (1962), 291-305.

Brebner, J. B. "Relations of Canada and the United States, Persistent Problems," *Canadian Historical Review*, XXIV (1943), 117-126.

Brown, R. C. "Canadian Nationalism in Western Newspapers," *Alberta Historical Review*, 10 (1962), 1-7.

———. "Goldwin Smith and Anti-Imperialism," *Canadian Historical Review*, XLIII (1962), 93-105.

Burke, Sister Teresa Avila. "Mackenzie and His Cabinet, 1873-1878," *Canadian Historical Review*, XLI (1960), 128-148.

Burt, A. L. "Peter Mitchell on John A. Macdonald," *Canadian Historical Review*, XLII (1961), 209-227.

Campbell, C. S. "The Anglo-American Crisis in the Behring Sea, 1890-1891," *Mississippi Valley Historical Review*, XLVIII (1961), 393-414.

Careless, J. M. S. "Canadian Nationalism—Immature or Obsolete?" *Canadian Historical Association Annual Report*, 1954, pp. 12-19.

Creighton, D. G. "The Victorians and the Empire," *Canadian Historical Review*, XIX (1938), 138-153.

———. "Canada in the English-Speaking World," *Canadian Historical Review*, XXVI (1945), 119-128.

Creighton, D. G. "The United States and Canadian Confederation," *Canadian Historical Review*, XXXIX (1958), 209-222.

———. "Economic Nationalism and Confederation," *Canadian Historical Association Annual Report*, 1942, pp. 44-51.

Dean, E. P. "How Canada Has Voted, 1867-1945," *Canadian Historical Review*, XXX (1949), 227-248.

Fite, G. C. "Republican Strategy and the Farm Vote in the Presidential Campaign of 1896," *American Historical Review*, LXV (1960), 787-806.

Foster, J. M. V. "Reciprocity and the Joint High Commission of 1898-99," *Canadian Historical Association Annual Report*, 1939, pp. 87-98.

Fraser, B. "The Political Career of Sir Hector Louis Langevin," *Canadian Historical Review*, XLII (1961), 93-132.

Gibson, F. W. "The Alaskan Boundary Dispute," *Canadian Historical Association Annual Report*, 1945, pp. 25-41.

Graham, W. R. "Liberal Nationalism in the Eighteen-seventies," *Canadian Historical Association Annual Report*, 1946, pp. 101-119.

———. "Sir Richard Cartwright, Wilfrid Laurier, and Liberal Party Trade Policy, 1887," *Canadian Historical Review*, XXXIII (1952), 1-18.

Gundy, H. P. "Sir Wilfrid Laurier and Lord Minto," *Canadian Historical Association Annual Report*, 1952, pp. 28-38.

Lafeber, W. "The Background of Cleveland's Venezuelan Policy: A Reinterpretation," *American Historical Review*, LXVI (1961), 947-967.

Landon, F. "D'Alton McCarthy and the Politics of the Later Eighties," *Canadian Historical Association Annual Report*, 1932, pp. 43-50.

Longley, R. S. "Peter Mitchell, Guardian of the North Atlantic Fisheries, 1867-1871," *Canadian Historical Review*, XXII (1941), 389-402.

Mitchell, H. "Canada's Negotiations with Newfoundland, 1887-1895," *Canadian Historical Review*, XL (1959), 277-293.

Naamani, I. T. "The Anglo-Saxon Idea and British Public Opinion," *Canadian Historical Review*, XXXII (1951), 43-60.

Neatby, H. B. "Laurier and Imperialism," *Canadian Historical Association Annual Report*, 1955, pp. 24-32.

—— and J. T. Saywell. "Chapleau and the Conservative Party in Quebec," *Canadian Historical Review*, xxxvii (1956), 1-23.

Robson, M. M. "The *Alabama* Claims and the Anglo-American Reconciliation, 1865-71," *Canadian Historical Review*, xlii (1961), 1-22.

Rothstein, M. "America in the International Rivalry for the British Wheat Market, 1860-1914," *Mississippi Valley Historical Review*, xlvii (1960), 401-418.

Savage, R. L. "American Concern over Canadian Railway Competition in the North-West, 1885-1890," *Canadian Historical Association Annual Report*, 1942, pp. 82-93.

Scott, F. "Political Nationalism and Confederation," *Canadian Journal of Economics and Political Science*, 8 (1942), 386-415.

Stacey, C. P. "Canada and the Nile Expedition of 1884-85," *Canadian Historical Review*, xxxiii (1952), 319-340.

Stanley, G. F. G. "Further Documents Relating to the Union of Newfoundland and Canada, 1886-1895," *Canadian Historical Review*, xxix (1948), 370-386.

Tansill, C. C. "The Fur Seal Fisheries and the Doctrine of the Freedom of the Seas," *Canadian Historical Association Annual Report*, 1942, pp. 71-81.

Trotter, R. G. "Relations of Canada and the United States, Reciprocity in Attitudes," *Canadian Historical Review*, xxiv (1943), 126-134.

Underhill, F. H. "Edward Blake, The Liberal Party, and Unrestricted Reciprocity," *Canadian Historical Association Annual Report*, 1939, pp. 133-141.

——. "Laurier and Blake, 1882-1891," *Canadian Historical Review*, xx (1939), 392-408.

——. "Lord Minto on His Governor Generalship," *Canadian Historical Review*, xl (1959), 121-131.

——. "Laurier and Blake, 1891-92," *Canadian Historical Review*, xxiv (1943), 135-156.

de Varigny, C. "La Doctrine Monroe et le Canada," *Revue des Deux Mondes*, 3rd Period, xxxii (1879), 628-657.

Vevier, C. "American Continentalism: An Idea of Expansion, 1845-1910," *American Historical Review,* LXV (1960), 323-335.

Wade, Mason. "Some Aspects of the Relations of French Canada with the United States," *Canadian Historical Association Annual Report,* 1944, pp. 16-39.

Watt, F. W. "The National Policy, the Workingman, and Proletarian Ideas in Victorian Canada," *Canadian Historical Review,* XL (1959), 1-26.

White, J. "Henry Cabot Lodge and the Alaska Boundary Award," *Canadian Historical Review,* VI (1925), 332-347.

Unpublished Theses

Colvin, J. A. Sir Wilfrid Laurier and the Imperial Problem, Ph.D. Thesis, University of London, 1955.

Curnoe, L. J. John Charlton and Canadian-American Relations, M.A. Thesis, University of Toronto, 1939.

Delworth, W. T. Canada's Commercial Relations with Great Britain and Europe, 1878-1895, M.A. Thesis, University of Toronto, 1956.

Foster, J. M. V. Reciprocity in Canadian Politics from the Commercial Union Movement to 1910, Ph.D. Thesis, Bryn Mawr, 1937.

Fraser, B. J. The Political Career of Sir Hector Langevin, M.A. Thesis, University of Toronto, 1959.

Gibson, F. W. The Alaskan Boundary Dispute, 2 vols. M.A. Thesis, Queen's University, 1944.

Graham, W. R. The Alexander Mackenzie Administration, 1873-1878: A Study of Liberal Tenets and Tactics, M.A. Thesis, University of Toronto, 1944.

———. Sir Richard Cartwright and the Liberal Party, 1863-1896, Ph.D. Thesis, University of Toronto, 1950.

Heisler, J. P. Sir John Thompson, 1844-1894, Ph.D. Thesis, University of Toronto, 1955.

Hodson, I. A. Commercial Union, Unrestricted Reciprocity and the Background to the Election of 1891, M.A. Thesis, University of Western Ontario, 1952.

MacIntosh, A. W. The Career of Sir Charles Tupper in Canada, 1864-1900, Ph.D. Thesis, University of Toronto, 1959.

MacLean, G. R. The Imperial Federation Movement in Canada, 1884-1902, Ph.D. Thesis, Duke University, 1958.

Morgan, H. Wayne. The Congressional Career of William McKinley. Ph.D. Thesis, University of California at Los Angeles, 1960.

Neatby, H. B. Laurier and a Liberal Quebec, A Study in Political Management, Ph.D. Thesis, University of Toronto, 1956.

Parizeau, Jacques. The Terms of Trade of Canada, 1869-1952, Ph.D. Thesis, University of London, 1955.

INDEX

Abbott, Sir John, 206; on trade negotiations with U.S., 234, 235

Adams, John Quincy, 4

Alaska, 6, 42, ch. IX; U.S. administration of, 281-82

Alaska boundary dispute, 10-11, ch. IX, 338; survey agreement (1892), 298-99; effect of gold rush upon, 299; agreement of 1896-97, 314-15; *modus vivendi* of 1898, 322. *See also* Joint High Commission of 1898-99

Alaska Commercial Company, 7, 42, 45, 49, 91

Alaska Railway Bill (U.S.), 303-4

Alfred Adams, seized (1887), 53

Anderson, John, on Bayard-Tupper correspondence (1887), 60; on Behring Sea dispute, 93, 98, 100; on Alaska boundary, 320-21, 336

Angell, James B., 61

Arthur, Chester, annual message to Congress (1883), 15

Baker, Charles S., 204; correspondence with Blaine, 205

Barker, Wharton, 130

Bayard, Thomas F., 17, 21, 50, 54, 61, 66, 239; protests against Bill No. 136, 24-26; protests seizure of David J. Adams, 30; Tupper correspondence (1887), 58-60; on reciprocity, 67-68; on Behring Sea dispute, 92; urges settlement Alaska boundary (1885), 287

Behring Sea Arbitration Treaty, 117

Behring Sea Arbitration Tribunal, 118-24; membership of, 118-19; questions before, 120-21; award, 122-23

Behring Sea dispute, 6-8, 42-54, 60, ch. IV; Joint High Commission of 1887-88, 92; Chamberlain on, 92; Bayard on, 92; negotiations (1890), 105-14; *modus vivendi* (1891), 116-17; negotiations (1897), 328-35. *See also Corwin;* Joint High Commission of 1898-99

Behring Sea as *mare clausum,* 8, 43, 45, 46, 97-98; Canadian Government on (1886), 49-50; Bayard on (1886), 50, 51-52; Blaine on (1890), 106

Benjamin, Charles F., on Behring Sea negotiations (1890), 114

Bennett, H. Ogilvie, 224

Bertram, George, on Cartwright, 269-70; on Fielding, 269-70; on tariff (1897), 275

Bill No. 136 (1886), 23-29, 37; Lansdowne's attitude to, 25-27; reservation of, 27; royal assent to, 27

Blaine, James G., 31, 37, 97, 192n; on seizure of *Black Diamond,* 101; Behring Sea negotiations (1890), 105-14; interview with Sir Louis Davies, 185-86; agreement with Bond (1890), 196-99; on Canadian proposal joint commission (1890), 201; correspondence with Baker, 205; trade negotiations with Canada, 233, 234-36; Alaska boundary negotiations (1892), 296-99

Blair, A. G., on Yukon Bill, 307-8

Blake, Edward, 33, 147, 161, 212; on Commercial Union, 163-64; on Unrestricted Reciprocity, 179-80; West Durham letter, 245-47; on Liberal trade policy (1892), 247-49; on Canada's future, 405-6

Board of Trade, Fort William, on reciprocity (1898), 369-70

Board of Trade, St. John's Newfoundland, 19

425

433

42491